Eama,
Love to you!
David & Barbie

Every Day With God

Pathway
PRESS & RESOURCES

Every Day With God

DAVID & BARBIE COOPER

Unless otherwise indicated, Scripture quotations are taken from *The Holy Bible, New International Version*®. NIV®. Copyright © 1973, 1978, 1984, 2011 by International Bible Society. Used by permission of Zondervan Publishing House. All rights reserved.

Scripture quotations marked *Amp.* are taken from *The Amplified Bible*. Old Testament copyright © 1965, 1987 by the Zondervan Corporation. *The Amplified New Testament* copyright © 1958, 1987 by the Lockman Foundation. Used by permission. All rights reserved.

Scripture quotations marked *KJV* are taken from the King James Version of the Bible.

Scripture quotations marked *NASB* are taken from the *New American Standard Bible*®. Copyright © The Lockman Foundation 1960, 1962, 1963, 1968, 1971, 1972, 1973, 1975, 1977, 1995. Used by permission. All rights reserved.

Scripture quotations marked *NKJV* are taken from the *New King James Version*. Copyright © 1979, 1980, 1982, 1990, 1995, Thomas Nelson, Inc., Publishers.

Scripture quotations marked *NLT* are taken from the *Holy Bible, New Living Translation*, copyright © 1996, 2004, 2007, 2012. Used by permission of Tyndale House Publishers, Inc., Wheaton, Illinois 60189. All rights reserved.

Scripture quotations marked Ph. (or *Phillips*) are taken from *The New Testament in Modern English Revised Edition*. Copyright © 1958, 1959, 1960, 1972 by J. B. Phillips. Reprinted with permission of Macmillan Publishing Company. All rights reserved.

Director of Publications: David W. Ray
Managing Editor of Publications: Lance Colkmire
Editorial Assistant: Tammy Hatfield
Copy Editor: Esther Metaxas
Graphic and Layout Design: Michael McDonald

ISBN: 978-1-64288-129-5

Pathway
PRESS & RESOURCES

Copyright © 2020 by Pathway Press
1080 Montgomery Avenue
Cleveland, Tennessee 37311

All rights reserved. No part of this publication may be reproduced or transmitted in any form or by any means, electronic or mechanical, including photocopying, recording, or otherwise, or by any information storage or retrieval system, without the permission in writing from the publisher. Please direct inquiries to Pathway Press, 1080 Montgomery Avenue, Cleveland, TN 37311.

Visit *www.pathwaypress.org* for more information.

DEDICATION

This book is dedicated to the Mount Paran Church family, who gives me the privilege of preaching and teaching the Word of God. I am grateful for their partnership in ministry to fulfill our vision to give the world hope in Christ.

I commend every member, partner, and supporter for their "work produced by faith, your labor prompted by love, and your endurance inspired by hope in our Lord Jesus Christ" (1 Thessalonians 1:3).

CONTENTS

DAY 1 **HELP!**		11
DAY 2 **FACE OR FEET?**		12
DAY 3 **PROGRESS, NOT PERFECTION**		13
DAY 4 **STORM WATCH**		14
DAY 5 **RIGHT FOR THE PART**		15
DAY 6 **FIND YOUR PURPOSE**		16
DAY 7 **SWAYED**		17
DAY 8 **CHILDLIKE FAITH**		18
DAY 9 **NEW START**		19
DAY 10 **MASTER PLAN**		20
DAY 11 **_E_ FOR EFFORT**		21
DAY 12 **THE ANSWER**		22
DAY 13 **UNDER GREAT PRESSURE**		23
DAY 14 **WHO NEEDS HUMILITY?**		24
DAY 15 **WHERE IS YOUR FAITH?**		25
DAY 16 **DARWIN OR DIVINITY?**		26
DAY 17 **IMITATORS**		27
DAY 18 **COVERED**		28
DAY 19 **FREE AT LAST!**		29
DAY 20 **STOP WORRYING**		30
DAY 21 **ANTIQUE BUSINESS**		31
DAY 22 **DESERT TIMES**		32
DAY 23 **FINISH IT**		33
DAY 24 **FRAME IT**		34
DAY 25 **CHOSEN**		35
DAY 26 **JOY AHEAD**		36
DAY 27 **PRE-DESTINY**		37
DAY 28 **FREE, NOT CHEAP**		38
DAY 29 **HE GAVE HIMSELF**		39
DAY 30 **STAY OUT OF IT**		40
DAY 31 **SEAL THE DEAL**		41
DAY 32 **HEART CHECK**		43
DAY 33 **MILESTONE OR MILLSTONE?**		44
DAY 34 **TRANSITIONS**		45
DAY 35 **A NEW THING**		46
DAY 36 **AFTER THEY PRAYED**		46
DAY 37 **KEEP IT UP**		48
DAY 38 **WRESTLING**		49
DAY 39 **STRUGGLING FOR IT**		50
DAY 40 **UNHINDERED PRAYER**		52
DAY 41 **YOU CAN HELP**		53
DAY 42 **PRAYER MATTERS**		54
DAY 43 **MAKE A CHOICE**		55
DAY 44 **SEE IT**		56
DAY 45 **GREAT THINGS**		57
DAY 46 **PUSH BACK**		59
DAY 47 **AT ODDS WITH THE WORLD**		60
DAY 48 **CHRIST IS ALL!**		61
DAY 49 **TRUST HIM**		62
DAY 50 **YET WILL I TRUST**		63
DAY 51 **YOUR OPINION MATTERS**		64
DAY 52 **UNFAILING LOVE**		66
DAY 53 **WORK, NOT WORKS**		67
DAY 54 **GET THROUGH IT**		69
DAY 55 **BUILD TRUST**		70
DAY 56 **KEEP ON STANDING**		71
DAY 57 **FIGHT BACK**		72
DAY 58 **SATISFIED**		74

v

DAY 59 **WHAT REALLY MATTERS** 75	DAY 91 **WHEN DARKNESS COMES** 114
DAY 60 **FADED GLORY** 76	DAY 92 **JOY TO THE WORLD** 115
DAY 61 **COST VERSUS DIVIDENDS** 77	DAY 93 **UNCERTAINTY** 116
DAY 62 **UNWORTHY SERVANT** 78	DAY 94 **STARS** 117
DAY 63 **HOLD ON TO HOPE** 80	DAY 95 **SYNERGY** 118
DAY 64 **GRATEFUL FOR GRACE** 81	DAY 96 **COME TOGETHER** 119
DAY 65 **PURSUE HAPPINESS** 82	DAY 97 **WHAT IS YOUR LIFE?** 120
DAY 66 **THE POTTER'S HAND** 83	DAY 98 **BUILD A BRIDGE** 121
DAY 67 **GO FORWARD** 85	DAY 99 **PEACEMAKER** 122
DAY 68 **GOD'S WILL** 86	DAY 100 **ONE STEP AT A TIME** 123
DAY 69 **OVERWHELMED** 87	DAY 101 **PAY FOR IT** 124
DAY 70 **GIVE IT UP** 89	DAY 102 **RUN TO THE BATTLE** 125
DAY 71 **YES!** 90	DAY 103 **OUTWARD AND INWARD** 126
DAY 72 **SET YOUR FOOT** 91	DAY 104 **IMPOSSIBLE POSSIBILITY** 127
DAY 73 **FAITH WALK** 92	DAY 105 **LIVING LETTERS** 128
DAY 74 **NOT BY SIGHT** 94	DAY 106 **TURN RIGHT** 129
DAY 75 **CAN YOU SEE?** 95	DAY 107 **FREELY GIVE** 130
DAY 76 **CONFIDENCE CODE** 96	DAY 108 **LOOKING FOR GOD'S WILL** 131
DAY 77 **FIRST STEPS** 97	DAY 109 **A DROP OF WATER** 132
DAY 78 **HEALTHY HEARTS** 99	DAY 110 **PLANS AND PURPOSE** 133
DAY 79 **COME TO YOUR SENSES** 100	DAY 111 **GET PAST IT** 134
DAY 80 **SOW IT, REAP IT** 101	DAY 112 **GET SOME REST** 135
DAY 81 ***IF*** 102	DAY 113 **TREMBLE OR TRUST** 136
DAY 82 **THE MIRACLE OF PROVISION** 103	DAY 114 **HEALING TIPS** 137
DAY 83 **LOOK UP** 104	DAY 115 **LOVE TO THE END** 138
DAY 84 **ROLL WITH IT** 105	DAY 116 **MEASURE IT** 139
DAY 85 **VOCABULARY** 106	DAY 117 **TWO ROADS** 140
DAY 86 **NOT A CHANCE** 107	DAY 118 **NOAH'S ARK AND YOU** 141
DAY 87 **LITTLE BY LITTLE** 108	DAY 119 **STONE CUTTERS** 142
DAY 88 **PROUD OF IT** 110	DAY 120 **LEFTOVERS** 143
DAY 89 **FORGET NOT** 111	DAY 121 **VALIDATED!** 144
DAY 90 **LIVE THE MOMENT** 112	DAY 122 **COMMON DENOMINATOR** 145

DAY 123	WHAT'S THE THEME?		146
DAY 124	THE FEAR THAT CURES ALL FEARS		146
DAY 125	RUSTED OUT		148
DAY 126	KEEP MOVING		149
DAY 127	LISTEN UP		150
DAY 128	TAKE THE FIRST STEP		151
DAY 129	PACE YOURSELF		152
DAY 130	GOLD RING IN A PIG'S SNOUT		153
DAY 131	KEEP A SECRET		154
DAY 132	PLEASANT WORDS		155
DAY 133	HE KNOWS THE WAY I TAKE		156
DAY 134	WITHDRAW		157
DAY 135	KEEP IT TOGETHER		158
DAY 136	LISTEN TO YOUR HEART		159
DAY 137	BLAME OR BLESS?		160
DAY 138	WHICH WAY SHOULD I GO?		161
DAY 139	JUST HIT "DELETE"		162
DAY 140	THE RIGHT WORD		163
DAY 141	YOU GOTTA SEE IT		164
DAY 142	THE REAL YOU		165
DAY 143	PRIDE WATCH		166
DAY 144	A GOOD NAME		167
DAY 145	SERVE, DON'T LEAD		168
DAY 146	IT'S HOW YOU LOOK AT IT		169
DAY 147	DESTINY DISCOVERED		171
DAY 148	WHY ARE YOU HERE?		172
DAY 149	GET STARTED		173
DAY 150	OPEN DOORS		174
DAY 151	PRODUCTIVE LIVING		175
DAY 152	IF THE LORD IS WITH US		176
DAY 153	USE IT		177
DAY 154	MAKE IT HAPPEN!		178
DAY 155	BEHIND THE SCENE		179
DAY 156	DO WHAT YOU CAN		180
DAY 157	WHO CAN YOU HELP?		181
DAY 158	GOD, PUMPKINS, AND YOU		182
DAY 159	GOD SO LOVED		184
DAY 160	HE GAVE IT		185
DAY 161	SET YOUR FOOT		186
DAY 162	BREAK OUT!		187
DAY 163	ABOVE US AND AROUND US		188
DAY 164	TOMORROW		189
DAY 165	HIT "REFRESH"		189
DAY 166	REBUILD THE RUINS		190
DAY 167	CAN I HELP?		191
DAY 168	FOCUS		192
DAY 169	FEELING FAITH		193
DAY 170	TRIPPED UP		195
DAY 171	TURN IT OFF!		196
DAY 172	WORSHIP YOUR WAY TO HEALTH		197
DAY 173	COMPARING GOD		198
DAY 174	PATIENT PROMISES		199
DAY 175	SEEING JESUS		199
DAY 176	SPRING CLEANING		201
DAY 177	NOT TALK BUT POWER		201
DAY 178	WHEN GOD WONDERS		202
DAY 179	SPIRITUAL GRAVITY		203
DAY 180	DOWN AND OUT		204
DAY 181	GONE ASTRAY		206
DAY 182	DON'T GET CAUGHT LOOKING		207
DAY 183	TIMES AND DATES		208
DAY 184	REPAY IT		209
DAY 185	GET WELL SOON		210
DAY 186	STAY ON TOP OF IT		211

DAY 187 DON'T LOOK AT THE OBSTACLES 212	DAY 219 STORMS 244
DAY 188 WE FOLLOW, HE MAKES 213	DAY 220 THINK INSIDE THE BOX 245
DAY 189 I DIDN'T RECOGNIZE HIM 214	DAY 221 STRONG TO THE END 247
DAY 190 SHOCK WAVES 215	DAY 222 SURVIVE THE STORM 248
DAY 191 FACT, NOT FANTASY 216	DAY 223 YOU RECEIVED IT 249
DAY 192 DO IT NOW! 217	DAY 224 RUN AWAY 250
DAY 193 LOOK FOR A PROMISE 218	DAY 225 STILL HOLDING ON 251
DAY 194 HIDE YOURSELF 220	DAY 226 SELFIES 252
DAY 195 VICTORY IN THE VALLEY 221	DAY 227 ATHEISTS IN HEAVEN 253
DAY 196 LIKE IT, DON'T LOVE IT 222	DAY 228 WONDERFUL 254
DAY 197 UNASHAMED 223	DAY 229 CAUGHT BY SURPRISE 255
DAY 198 ADMIRED 224	DAY 230 START OVER 256
DAY 199 DON'T GO THRU IT; GROW THRU IT 225	DAY 231 GREAT EXPECTATIONS 257
DAY 200 WITHOUT A SWORD 226	DAY 232 THE BEST IN YOU 258
DAY 201 NO RECORD 227	DAY 233 LOST IN SPACE 260
DAY 202 LEARNED OBEDIENCE 228	DAY 234 DIFFERENT IS GOOD 261
DAY 203 ANCHORED 229	DAY 235 PROVEN TRUE 261
DAY 204 MAKE AN IMPACT 230	DAY 236 MY TIMES ARE IN YOUR HANDS 262
DAY 205 COST OR CONVENIENCE? 231	DAY 237 BIOGRAPHY 263
DAY 206 FIVE SMOOTH STONES 232	DAY 238 BRING BACK THE KING 264
DAY 207 CHOOSE WHAT'S BETTER 233	DAY 239 STAND STRONG 265
DAY 208 ERASE RACISM 234	DAY 240 TAKE TIME TO BE HOLY 266
DAY 209 STORED UP 235	DAY 241 PUT A LID ON IT 267
DAY 210 I AM 235	DAY 242 GIVE THE GIFT 268
DAY 211 GAINS AND LOSSES 236	DAY 243 SENT 269
DAY 212 WALK WITH GOD 237	DAY 244 ACT OF KINDNESS................. 270
DAY 213 COME HOME 238	DAY 245 BIRTHRIGHT 271
DAY 214 70 X 7 239	DAY 246 LOL 272
DAY 215 PASS THE SALT 240	DAY 247 WALK IN THE LIGHT 273
DAY 216 SOUND MIND 241	DAY 248 BOUNDARIES 274
DAY 217 ONE THING 242	DAY 249 WHAT DO YOU SEE? 275
DAY 218 DON'T THROW YOUR BRAIN AWAY 243	DAY 250 SING AND MAKE MUSIC 276

viii

DAY 251 SERVE GOD'S PURPOSE	277
DAY 252 GOT VISION?	278
DAY 253 THE GREATEST COMPLIMENT	279
DAY 254 INSIDE OUT	280
DAY 255 HEAVEN ON MY MIND	281
DAY 256 AFTER AN UPROAR	282
DAY 257 UP TO MY NECK	283
DAY 258 FEAR NO EVIL	284
DAY 259 WHAT IF?	285
DAY 260 CONVENIENT	286
DAY 261 GO ON!	287
DAY 262 LET NOTHING MOVE YOU	288
DAY 263 RAINY DAYS	289
DAY 264 DON'T GRAB A DOG BY ITS EARS!	290
DAY 265 KEEP DOWN THE DRAMA	291
DAY 266 ARM YOURSELF	291
DAY 267 MORNING HAS BROKEN	292
DAY 268 BLINDED BY THE LIGHT	293
DAY 269 THE POSSIBILITY OF CHANGE	294
DAY 270 IF YOU KNEW	295
DAY 271 SECRET STRENGTH	296
DAY 272 ABOVE ALL	297
DAY 273 MENTAL FLOSS	298
DAY 274 STILL CONFIDENT	299
DAY 275 GO TO THE DESERT	300
DAY 276 KING BY FORCE	301
DAY 277 CURE FOR SKEPTICS	302
DAY 278 SNATCHED	302
DAY 279 DON'T LEAVE HOME WITHOUT IT	303
DAY 280 SOME SAID IT THUNDERED	304
DAY 281 THE 10% MYTH	305
DAY 282 SIGNS AND SYMBOLS	306

DAY 283 JILTING JEALOUSY	307
DAY 284 HIDDEN	308
DAY 285 DAILY LIFE	309
DAY 286 #HATE IT	310
DAY 287 DRINK IN THE RAIN	311
DAY 288 GET SOME REST	312
DAY 289 MORE GRACE	312
DAY 290 VERBAL ARSON	313
DAY 291 STRIKE THE ROCK	314
DAY 292 TAKE POSSESSION OF IT	315
DAY 293 USE IT OR LOSE IT	316
DAY 294 IF YOU SUFFER	317
DAY 295 WIN WITHOUT WORDS	318
DAY 296 IF YOU OBEY	319
DAY 297 IMMOVABLE	319
DAY 298 ASK FOR RAIN	320
DAY 299 LEAVE IT	321
DAY 300 RADIANT	322
DAY 301 FORGOTTEN FAITH	323
DAY 302 MUTUAL INTEREST	324
DAY 303 KEEP IT REAL	325
DAY 304 IT IS WELL	326
DAY 305 SOW THE WORD	327
DAY 306 DONE AND TAUGHT	328
DAY 307 GROW BIGGER	328
DAY 308 SPIRITUAL INSIGHT	329
DAY 309 RESTORATION PROJECT	330
DAY 310 PICK UP THE PACE	331
DAY 311 GO WHERE YOU LOOK	332
DAY 312 SHARE IT	333
DAY 313 FIGHTING SPIRIT	334
DAY 314 DON'T LEAVE YET	335

DAY 315 **LAST CHANCE** 336	DAY 347 **GET YOUR OWN DIRT** 362
DAY 316 **RANSOMED** 337	DAY 348 **BLUEPRINT** 363
DAY 317 **FOR-*GIVE*-NESS** 337	DAY 349 **NEVER DIE** 364
DAY 318 **TAKE ADVICE** 338	DAY 350 **TRUTH HURTS** 365
DAY 319 **NO FEAR** 339	DAY 351 **PRIORITIES** 365
DAY 320 **DO WHAT YOU CAN** 339	DAY 352 **IT'S OK TO BRAG** 366
DAY 321 **BEND TOWARD JUSTICE** 340	DAY 353 **STAY IN ORBIT** 367
DAY 322 **FREEDOM FIGHTERS** 341	DAY 354 **GIVE THE GLORY** 368
DAY 323 **OVERFLOWING** 342	DAY 355 **GRAVITY** 369
DAY 324 **I AM NOT INFERIOR** 343	DAY 356 **WHAT'S GOING ON?** 370
DAY 325 **UNCHANGING** 344	DAY 357 **CONTRADICTIONS** 371
DAY 326 **POWERLESS** 344	DAY 358 **EXCEL** 372
DAY 327 **STRANGE ADVICE** 345	DAY 359 **CHURCH MATTERS** 373
DAY 328 **JUSTIFIED** 346	DAY 360 **SILENCE** 373
DAY 329 **BURIED TREASURE** 347	DAY 361 **SEE THE BEAUTY** 374
DAY 330 **FRUSTRATED** 348	DAY 362 **PURSUE GOD** 375
DAY 331 **OUT OF PLACE** 349	DAY 363 **FIRE AND RAIN** 376
DAY 332 **GOOD TIMES** 350	DAY 364 **OVERLOAD** 377
DAY 333 **THINK OF YOURSELF** 351	DAY 365 **RUN THE RACE** 378
DAY 334 **HEART OF A KING** 351	
DAY 335 **AUTHORITY** 352	
DAY 336 **OVERCOMERS** 353	
DAY 337 **DIFFERENCE-MAKERS** 354	
DAY 338 **HAPPY NEW YOU!** 355	
DAY 339 **BEHIND THE SCENES** 355	
DAY 340 **KINDLE THE FIRE** 356	
DAY 341 **END IT** 357	
DAY 342 **EXPIRATION DATE** 358	
DAY 343 **REGENERATE** 359	
DAY 344 **SPEAK** 359	
DAY 345 **CHANGE CLOTHES** 360	
DAY 346 **WAIT YOUR TURN** 361	

Every Day With God

Day 1

HELP!

Everyone needs help from time to time. Success is often based on the ability to ask for help. "I will lift my eyes to the mountains—where does my help come from? My help comes from the Lord, the Maker of heaven and earth" (Psalm 121:1). The psalmist looked to God for help. Where are we looking for help for our lives?

The fifteen "psalms of ascent" (120—134) were written over a diverse period of time (some by King David). They were arranged in their order after the Babylonian Exile (about 450 years before the birth of Jesus). They were sung during the festivals of Passover, Pentecost, and Tabernacles. The ascent described the upward journey out of Babylon back to Jerusalem. The city of Jerusalem and its Temple are always described in Scripture as being "up." In the rabbinical writings, the rabbis say the fifteen psalms correlate with the fifteen steps that led up to the Temple (although this is not mentioned in Scripture).

Life with God is always an ascent. God wants us to ascend in life, not descend. The fact that life is an ascent reminds us the walk of faith is a journey, not a destination. The purpose of the arrangement for these fifteen psalms is not certain. However, they do begin with the pilgrim in exile and surrounded by his enemies (Psalm 120:5-6) in the land of Meshech, located in central Asia Minor and Kedar, in Arabia. His journey back to Jerusalem then takes him to the house of the Lord (Psalm 122:1) and, finally, into the presence of the Lord himself where he declares, "Lift up your hands in the sanctuary and praise the Lord" (Psalm 134:2).

The "mountains" mentioned in 121:1 are Mount Zion, on which sat Jerusalem, and its surrounding mountains. The hills in its plural usage refer to the majesty of God revealed in Jerusalem (see Psalms 48:1-2; 125:2).

The Lord watches over Israel. The phrase "watches over" appears five times in Psalm 121. God is the guardian of His people and "the Maker of heaven and earth" (v. 2). Not only is He the Creator, He is the only true God in contrast to the idols of the ancient world (Psalm 124:8; 134:3).

What a description of real faith: "I will lift up my eyes!" Faith looks up, beyond the limitations of ourselves and the help we get from others, to the face of God himself in complete trust. Instead of looking out in fear, let us look up in faith!

Prayer for the Day: *Lord, I'm so glad I have You to help me through the situations and circumstances of life. Today I will lift up my eyes in faith as I wait on Your direction.*

Day 2
FACE OR FEET?

When Joshua's army was defeated at the battle of Ai, he prayed and asked God why they were defeated. God said to him, "Stand up! What are you doing down on your face?" (Joshua 7:10). Israel had sinned at Jericho by taking things from the city. God told Joshua to take action and remove those things from the camp of Israel. "Go, consecrate the people. . . . You cannot stand against your enemies until you remove [the forbidden items]" (Joshua 7:13). He had to take action and remove the things that kept them from success in battle.

We, too, pray and ask God why something is not working. God may be telling us to stop praying and take action. We too need to get off our faces, stand up on our feet, and get going. Success is based on what we do, not what we plan to do, or want to do, or think about doing, or get prepared to do.

Someone said, "The road to hell is paved with good intentions." Only what we do in life matters at the end of the day. Don't just dream it; do it. Don't just plan it; implement the plan. Don't wonder what will happen; make it happen.

We often don't take action because we are afraid of failure. The only people who never fail are those who never attempt anything. Procrastination comes from the fear of failure. James 2:17 says, "Faith by itself, if it is not accompanied by action, is dead." We need to move from planning and praying to take action if we expect to see results. There is a time to wait, and there is a time for action.

What projects have you been planning to do but still haven't gotten around to doing? House repairs? Writing a book? Composing a song? Volunteering in ministry? Getting an education? Looking for a new career? Making a financial investment? Writing a will? Saving for a house? Applying for a new job? Learning a new life skill?

Today is the best day to get started. Now is the time for action.

Prayer for the Day: *Lord, I have prayed and planned long enough. Today, I'm taking action. With Your guidance, I know I will succeed.*

Day 3

PROGRESS, NOT PERFECTION

Life is not about perfection; It is about progression. God works patiently with us in His own time and at our pace. We are the ones who put so much pressure on ourselves to be perfect.

There are three kinds of people: (1) Those who think they are perfect; they are self-deceived. (2) Those who know they are not perfect but always focus on their imperfections, so they live discouraged. (3) Those who know they are not perfect but know they don't have to be because they depend on God's unconditional love. They are free to develop their full potential as God works in them to conform them to the image of Jesus.

We should set high goals for ourselves, even though we will fall short: "We all stumble in many ways" (James 3:2). When we fail, we need to get up, dust ourselves off, and keep pressing on toward the goal. Sometimes we take three steps forward and two steps back. But at least we are one step further than we were when we started.

Someone said to me through her tear-filled eyes, "I feel like the chief of sinners."

"So do I," I replied. "That's why we need grace."

Grace takes your eyes off yourself and puts them on Jesus. "You are complete in Him" (Colossians 2:10 NKJV). If you constantly look at your failures, you will live in discouragement. If you keep your eyes on Jesus, you will discover the secret of real joy. You and I must fix our eyes on "Jesus, the author and finisher of our faith" (Hebrews 12:2 NKJV).

Prayer for the Day: *Lord, thank You for reminding me that failure is a part of life. Getting past my failures and progressing in my faith should be my goal. I look to You, Lord, knowing You are always with me.*

Day 4

STORM WATCH

When a storm approaches, community leaders issue a storm watch. Just as we have natural storms like tornadoes, hurricanes, thunderstorms, and winter storms, we face storms in our lives. Family storms. Health storms. Financial storms. The best way to survive a storm is to stick together with your family and friends. You never want to face a storm by yourself.

A tornado came through Atlanta, tearing a path through the north part of the city. Our family was living in an apartment for about six months while our house was being built. We were on the second floor when the tornado came roaring over us. We all huddled in the bathroom, with the kids in the bathtub. The noise and the shaking were overwhelming. We thought we would be taken up in the fierce wind.

The next morning we got in the car and drove around to see what had happened. All around us was debris. Large steel billboard structures were twisted like thin wire. Buildings had vanished. We only had two sources of comfort when that storm was raging. We held each other tight as we huddled together. We had the peace of God's presence, knowing He was with us.

Jesus told a story of a wise builder who built his house on the rock instead of sand: "The rain came down, the streams rose, and the winds blew and beat against that house; yet it did not fall, because it had its foundation on the rock" (Matthew 7:25). Jesus Christ is the foundation of our faith. "For no one can lay any other foundation other than the one already laid, which is Jesus Christ" (1 Corinthians 3:11).

"On Christ, the solid Rock, I stand; all other ground is sinking sand." When we build our lives on our faith in Jesus Christ, we have a strong foundation of faith that can stand strong and survive any storm and come through it safe and secure.

Prayer for the Day: *Lord, the storms of life sometimes overwhelm me. But I am reminded that You are always there to calm them and me!*

Day 5
RIGHT FOR THE PART

Justice Oliver Wendell Holmes said, "Most people die with their music still in them." You have incredible, untapped potential. You are made in the image of God. God created you with the potential for greatness.

Unfortunately, we get caught in the Charlie Brown syndrome. One day Charlie Brown was talking with Linus about his feelings of inadequacy. "You see, Linus," Charlie moaned, "it goes all the way back to the beginning. The moment I was born and set foot on the stage of life, they took one look at me and said, 'Not right for the part.'"

The truth is that you are right for the part. God has given you a part to play in life. So, play it well. God is counting on you and so are we. Besides, God believes in you, or else He wouldn't have created you. It is time for you to start believing in yourself. Jesus took twelve of the most unlikely men, transformed them from fishermen, tax collectors and political zealots into an army of leaders who made the greatest spiritual impact in history.

How did Jesus do it? Simple—in the company of sinners He dreamed of saints. He convinced them that they were capable of achieving more with their lives than they ever dreamed possible. And they did! They not only believed in Him—they believed in themselves.

In Jesus Christ, we are designed "for special purposes, made holy, useful to the Master" (2 Timothy 2:21).

Prayer for the Day: *Lord, thank You for the talent and gifts You have given me. Please show me where to develop and use them for Your glory.*

Day 6
FIND YOUR PURPOSE

People always ask, "Does God have a plan and purpose for my life?" The answer is yes! Our highest purpose is to live for "the praise of His glory" (Ephesians 1:12 NKJV). The word *praise* appears two hundred times in Scripture. *Praise* means to celebrate, to commend, to bless, to honor, and to glorify God as our Father, Jesus Christ as our Lord, and the Holy Spirit as our Comforter. We praise God first for who He is, then for what He has done, is doing, and will do!

Praise is our response of love to the love of God. "Love the Lord your God with all your heart, . . . [mind] and . . . strength" (Deuteronomy 6:5). "We love Him because He first loved us" (1 John 4:19 NKJV). Praise is living with reverence, humility, and gratitude to God. Praise is living life to glorify God so "whatever you do, do it all for the glory of God" (1 Corinthians 10:31).

How can we live for God's glory? Let's look at the great commandment to love the Lord with our hearts, minds, and strength. When we love the Lord with our hearts, then we honor Him with our goals, pursuits, and desires. When we love the Lord with our minds, then we honor Him with our thoughts, attitudes, and choices. When we love the Lord with our strength, then we honor Him with our actions (the way we relate to others). We also honor Him with our strength when we take care of our physical bodies, which are the "temples of the Holy Spirit" (1 Corinthians 6:19-20).

The highest purpose of our lives is not found in a career, business, education, or position but, rather, when we live "for the praise of His glory."

Prayer for the Day: *Lord, I have been searching for the purpose of my life for as long as I can remember. Now that You are in my life, I realize You are my purpose!*

Day 7

SWAYED

The word *integrity* refers to uprightness of character, honesty, the condition of being sound and whole, and the state of being complete and undivided. In math, an *integer* is a whole number. We need to live one life, not a double life.

The Pharisees told Jesus, "We know that you are a man of integrity" (Matthew 22:16). The Greek word translated "integrity" is *alethia*, meaning "truth." The King James Version reads, "We know that thou art true." *Character* is what you knew you would do if you knew you would never get caught. So being a person of integrity means to be honest, genuine, and truthful.

We often care too much about the opinions and judgments of others. We get into trouble trying to please others. Jesus was not swayed by the pressure to conform or by persecution. *Integrity* means to be true to your faith and values in the face of temptation to compromise. "No compromise," is the theme of a person of integrity.

The Pharisees said to Jesus, "You aren't swayed by others, because you pay no attention to who they are" (Matthew 22:16-17). Peter said in Acts, "I now realize how true it is that God does not show favoritism but accepts from every nation the one who fears him and does what is right" (Acts 10:34-35).

We tend to show favoritism based on how important people are on what we think they can do for us. God is without favoritism, and we are to follow His example. When we accept all people the same and treat everyone equally, we are well on our way to living with integrity in our relationships. Stop being swayed and stand strong on your principles as a follower of Jesus Christ.

Prayer for the Day: *Lord, it's such a temptation to go along with the crowd. It's easy, but not without pain. But, thanks to You, that isn't who I am anymore. I am a child of God, a person of character, growing stronger in my faith every day.*

Day 8

CHILDLIKE FAITH

One of the strongest needs we have is the need for significance. This is why *The Purpose Driven Life* was a best seller. Many people bought the book and never read it. The title itself resonated with people because we all have the need to love and to be loved. It is the greatest need we have and the greatest motivator of behavior.

We act in ways to be loved. We conform to group pressure to be loved. Now we call it by different names—attention, affirmation, encouragement, approval—but it's really *love*.

No one wants to be left out; to feel unimportant. No kid wants to be the last one picked for a team. But that need often makes us competitive and drives us to seek self-importance at the expense of others. It is a dog-eat-dog (even though dogs don't eat dogs) world out there. We fight and compete and have power struggles, because we want to be important. We get so full of ourselves that there is no room for others.

Jesus dealt with this need for love that goes awry in a pursuit of self-importance and self-promotion. One day the disciples asked Him, "Who, then, is the greatest in the kingdom of heaven?" (Matthew 18:1). Even in the kingdom of God, people strive for superiority wanting to be the greatest—to be number one, to be in first place.

Jesus had a little child stand in the midst of the group and said, "Truly I tell you, unless you change and become like little children, you will never enter the kingdom of heaven" (Matthew 18:3).

We want children to learn from us, but we also need to learn from them. He defines the greatness of a child by one virtue—*humility*. We have to humble ourselves if we want to be truly great in life. Jesus said, "Therefore whoever humbles himself as this little child is the greatest in the kingdom of heaven" (Matthew 18:4 NKJV).

The greatest act of humility is when we admit we are sinful and cannot save ourselves. Instead of trying to earn our way into the Kingdom by self-righteousness, we humble ourselves by trusting Christ alone as our

Savior. When we come to the end of ourselves, we come to the beginning of new life.

Prayer for the Day: *Lord, sometimes as adults we tend to overlook the simple humility, honesty, and wisdom of children. In their innocence, occasionally, they see what we cannot because of the hardness of our adult hearts. Help me, Lord, to see with the eyes of a child, that I may be more spiritually sensitive.*

Day 9

NEW START

Jesus said if we believe in Him, we will be "born again." Our culture now uses the term in many ways. Jesus first used this term in a conversation with Nicodemus, a Pharisee who came to Jesus one night in private looking for spiritual answers. It is easy to accept that others need to be born again, but not us when we feel like we have it all together. However, when Jesus said we must be born again to enter the kingdom of God, He meant everyone from the down-and-out and to the up-and-coming. To the rich and to the poor, to the religious and the unreligious, to the moral and the immoral, to the educated and to the uneducated, to the sophisticated and to the simple, Jesus says, "You must be born again" (John 3:7).

The term *born again* can also be translated "born from above." That means the new birth is God's work in us, not our work. The *new birth* means we are spiritually alive instead of spiritually dead (see Ephesians 2:1-5). We are a new creation in which old things are passing away and all things are becoming new (see 2 Corinthians 5:17). We now have a new nature of righteousness that desires to do what is right instead of what is wrong (see 2 Peter 1:4).

Nicodemus asked Jesus how a person could be born again. Their conversation began with spiritual ideas, then turned to personal experience. Knowledge cannot save us. The ancient philosophers sought wisdom. Buddha pursued enlightenment. We look for new technology. What we need is to experience the grace of God. It is in trusting Jesus as Savior, not trying, that we are born again.

An artist wanted to paint a portrait of the Prodigal Son at the low point of his rebellion when he was destitute and spent all his money. He walked the streets of the town and found a homeless man. He said, "I will pay you if I can paint your portrait." He told the man to meet him at his studio the next day. When the man arrived the next day at the studio, the artist did not recognize the man. He had a haircut, a clean shave, and was nicely dressed. The artist dismissed him and said, "I wanted you just like you were."

We come to Jesus just as we are, and He does the miraculous work of the new birth when we put our faith in Him.

Prayer for the Day: *Lord, the term "born again" seems foreign to a world of technology. We are born and we die—simple facts of life. While I have a physical life, accepting You as my Savior gives me a "spiritual life" that lasts forever. Please help me to live as a born-again Christian.*

Day 10
MASTER PLAN

When you build a house, you start with a master site plan and then work to complete the plan, making adjustments as you go. Can you imagine the chaos that would occur by trying to build a house without a set of blueprints?

Get a master plan for your life. Don't drift with the tide. Don't go with the flow. Decide where you want to go, set a course, and determine your destiny. Set concrete goals and develop a workable strategy to reach them.

Jesus talked about the need to sit down and count the cost before we start building to make sure we have what we need to finish (Luke 14:28-30). Without a master site plan for life, we react to one situation after another. Circumstances and emergencies plan our agenda instead of us setting our own agenda. We are the victims of what happens to us rather than being in charge of what happens.

When I went to college for my undergraduate degree, I saw this as the first step to my doctoral degree. Later, I earned my master's degree in counseling. While it brought me a great sense of accomplishment, I was still only two-thirds of the way to the finish line. When I graduated with my doctorate, my goal was reached.

Here are the two most important questions you need to ask to get a master plan for your life: Where do you want to go? How do you plan to get there? Ask these questions about every major decision you face, and you will find your way clearly to reach your goals.

Prayer for the Day: *Lord, I once heard someone say, "Our destiny depends on our destination." In other words, wherever we are headed is where we will end up. I'm grateful that where I was headed was interrupted by Your Spirit and You redirected my destiny.*

Day 11

E FOR EFFORT

Isaac D'Israeli said, "It is a wretched taste to be gratified with mediocrity when the excellent lies before us."

Excellence is the master key to success in life. *Excellence* means "the very best quality; superiority; first-rate; exceptionally good." Edwin Bliss once said, "The pursuit of excellence is gratifying and healthy. The pursuit of perfection is frustrating, neurotic, and a terrible waste of time."

Booker T. Washington said, "Excellence is to do a common thing in an uncommon way." There is no room for status quo and mediocrity in the kingdom of God. God created us for excellence. Jesus deserves our excellence. The Holy Spirit empowers us for excellence.

God has given us the potential for excellence. We are "fearfully and wonderfully made" by God (Psalm 139:14), and we are "crowned . . . with glory and honor" (Psalm 8:5).

Excellence requires us to mix hard work and diligence with the potential God has given us. Talent and ability are not enough. We must "make every effort" (2 Peter 1:5). Success does not come from simply making an effort but by making every effort. Let those three words become your standard for excellence—make every effort. Not some effort. Not an occasional effort. But every effort!

Here is God's standard of excellence for His people: "Whatever you do, work at it with all your heart, as working for the Lord, not for human masters" (Colossians 3:23).

Prayer for the Day: *Lord, all of us need a little motivation when it comes to doing our best. It is human nature to accept status quo. Today is my reminder to make every effort to make my life a journey of excellence, knowing You are the One I do it for.*

Day 12

THE ANSWER

A close friend told me about a family crisis he was facing. He had a dream and three times the Lord spoke these words to him: *Praise is the answer.* When he woke up, he prayed and asked God, *If praise is the answer, what is the question?* The answer came to him: *It doesn't matter the question, praise is always the answer.*

Life is lived on two levels—internal and external. Life consists of what goes on around us and what goes on within us. We cannot always control what goes on around us, but we can control what goes on within us. We can master our thoughts, attitudes, and the inclinations of our hearts, and that has more to do with our health and happiness than anything else. "As [a person] thinks in his heart, so is he" (Proverbs 23:7 NKJV).

We have the power by the grace of God to "take captive every thought to make it obedient to Christ" (2 Corinthians 10:5). Take your fearful and worried thoughts captive to God's promise to provide for you. Take your depressed thoughts captive to God's promise to always be with you. Take your defeated thoughts captive to God's promise to give you victory for every battle you face.

When we take time to praise the Lord for His blessings and grace, we receive fresh strength to handle any challenge of life. Praise gives us inner power to handle the pressures of life. This is what Paul the apostle meant when he said, "Outwardly we are wasting away, yet inwardly we are being renewed day by day" (2 Corinthians 4:16).

So, regardless of the questions you are struggling with or the problems you may be facing, praise is the answer. Take a power break right now and offer praise to the Lord for His abiding presence, His promise of faithfulness, and His power to provide for every need you are facing.

Prayer for the Day: *Lord, I've noticed that no matter what I'm struggling with and no matter how fearful I am, when I stop and praise You, the situation doesn't seem as bad. You have a way of calming my mind and bringing me into a place of peace. I put my trust in You and rely on You for the right answer.*

Day 13

UNDER GREAT PRESSURE

Mary C. Crowley, in *Be Somebody*, says, "Every evening I turn worries over to God. He's going to be up all night anyway." If I could choose one word to describe our times, it would be the word *pressure*. Pressure on the outside can create panic on the inside. *Panic* is a feeling of fear and anxiety.

God gives us the gift of prayer to handle life's pressures. The prophet Jeremiah felt pressure. His faithfulness to God got him thrown in jail by those who didn't want to hear his message. Jerusalem was on the verge of being attacked by Babylon. He warned the king and the leaders to turn to God, but they rejected his counsel. They threw him in prison the same way political prisoners are silenced in oppressive nations today.

While in the king's prison, God spoke to him: "Call to Me, and I will answer you, and show you great and mighty things, which you do not know" (Jeremiah 33:3 NKJV). Turn your pressure into peace by calling on the Lord in prayer.

My son David Paul got his first pair of glasses when he was three years old. An eye exam revealed he was extremely far-sighted. I will never forget the day we went to pick up his new glasses. Standing in the store, I put the glasses on him and he opened his eyes as big as saucers.

He jerked the glasses off and said, "Dad, everything is so big!"

"Put them back on, Son," I said. "For the first time in your life you're seeing the world the way it's supposed to look."

When you and I pray, God will show you great and mighty things of how He is going to work everything out as you trust Him.

Prayer for the Day: *Lord, when I feel the pressures of the world closing in and around me, and when I can't see for the distractions that blind me, I will pray that You reveal truth in a way that I can comprehend.*

Day 14
WHO NEEDS HUMILITY?

If "pride goes before destruction," as Proverbs 16:18 tells us, then humility goes before promotion. The kingdom of God functions by spiritual paradoxes. The way up is the way down. The way of leadership is the way of service. The way of promotion is the way of submission. The way of power is the way of weakness.

What is *humility*? Andrew Murray said, "Humility is perfect quietness of heart. It is to expect nothing, to wonder at nothing that is done to me, to feel nothing done against me. It is to be at rest when nobody praises me, and when I am blamed or despised. It is to have a blessed home in the Lord, where I can go in and shut the door, and kneel to my Father in secret, and am at peace as in a deep sea of calmness, when all around and above is trouble."

Jesus said, "Blessed are the poor in spirit for theirs is the kingdom of heaven" (Matthew 5:3). Paul testified, "When I am weak, then I am strong" (2 Corinthians 12:10). Peter taught us, "Humble yourselves, therefore, under God's mighty hand, that he may lift you up in due time" (1 Peter 5:6). Wisdom teaches us, "God opposes the proud but gives grace to the humble" (see Proverbs 3:34).

Humility means being honest with yourself, caring enough for others to serve them, and being fully dependent on God for everything in life. God promises to honor the humble person and to give us grace that is sufficient for every circumstance we face.

Prayer for the Day: *Lord, if humility means to be honest with myself, caring for others, and being dependent on You, then that is my desire. I will not seek promotion to prove myself to others; rather, I will depend on Your grace that is all-sufficient and wait on Your promotion.*

Day 15

WHERE IS YOUR FAITH?

Recently, I was struck by the impact of this question Jesus asked His disciples: "Do you still have no faith?" (Mark 4:40). True, it was early in their ministry. But they had so much evidence of who Jesus was and of His power that their faith should have been more developed at that point.

John the Baptist, whom they regarded as a true prophet, had announced Jesus as the Messiah and told His disciples to follow Jesus. They had heard Jesus' incredible teaching and had seen His miracles.

This particular night they were caught in a life-threatening storm on the Sea of Galilee. He was asleep from exhaustion and they woke Him up shouting, "Don't You care if we drown?" Jesus rebuked the wind and calmed the sea, declaring, "Peace, be still!" They were awe-struck and whispered among themselves, "Who is this that even the winds and the waves obey Him?" He then asked them, "Do you still have no faith?"

I wonder about people who are raised in Christian homes, yet they have not personally believed in Jesus. I consider the evidence of God we have in creation, our conscience, and our inner awareness of God and need of God, yet still have no faith. I wonder about scientists and physicians who study the intricacies of the world and of the marvel of the human body, yet dismiss it all as an evolutionary accident.

What about those strange unexplained "coincidences" we have all had of divine intervention that we dismiss as being lucky? How easy it is to be surrounded by the evidence of God and His grace every day, but be so wrapped in ourselves and our daily routines that we miss the wonders of His grace.

What more evidence do you need so that you truly believe in Him? After all you have heard of Jesus and seen with your own eyes and experienced in this life, do you still have no faith? Put your faith in God today and in Jesus as Lord, and you will never be disappointed in Him!

Prayer for the Day: *Lord, this is the question I ask to all my doubting family and friends, "Do you still have no faith?" So much historical evidence, yet they are still blind. Help me, Lord, to know how to pray for them so that their eyes are open to the truth of who You are: Jesus Christ, our Lord and Savior.*

Day 16
DARWIN OR DIVINITY?

The Bible begins by giving us the most important fact on which we build our faith: "In the beginning God created the heavens and the earth" (Genesis 1:1). Faith begins when we believe God exists and that He is our Creator. The height of His creating work was to make man and woman in His own likeness and image (Gen 1:26-28).

A healthy self-image is based on knowing we are made in God's image. We bear the likeness of God, our Creator. We are not an evolutionary accident but the masterpiece of God's creation. We are "fearfully and wonderfully made" (Psalm 139:14).

What does it mean to be made in the image of God? The word *create* is used three times in Genesis 1:27. Only God is said to create in the Bible. We are to partner with Him in managing the earth because He put us in charge to rule over everything in the world. Humanity is God's servants to care for the earth.

We bear the likeness of God in four ways. *First, we are made in God's mental image.* He endowed us with the capacity of intellect, emotion, and will. We do not live by instinct. We can think things through, create new thoughts, and make our own decisions.

Second, we are made in the moral image of God. God created us with a conscience that knows right and wrong. The law of God is written on our hearts. Some people try to ignore their conscience or pretend that something isn't wrong in God's eyes, but no one can escape the power of conscience that makes us feel guilt when we are in the wrong and also a sense of reward when we are in the right.

Third, we are made in the social image of God. We are created for relationships. When God created Adam, He said, "It is not good for the man to be alone." We develop and grow as a result of healthy relationships. Our greatest needs are to love and to be loved.

Fourth, we are created in God's spiritual image. Jesus said, "God is spirit, and his worshipers must worship in the Spirit and in truth" (John 4:24). Paul the apostle reminds us that God is at work to make us holy, "spirit, soul and body" (1 Thessalonians 5:23). We are spiritual beings made to worship God and to commune with Him. Augustine prayed: "Our hearts were made for You, O God, and they will not rest until they rest in You."

You are defined by the Divine, not by Darwin. You are made in God's image. You came from the hand of God, not from a lower life form. You are created; you did not evolve. You are intentional; you are not accidental. You are here because of God's purpose, not probability.

Prayer for the Day: *Lord, in high school we were pushed to accept the fact that we descended from apes. In college, we were pushed to believe the Big Bang theory over Creationism. I'm proud to say that no one has to push me to believe that I am made in Your image. It makes perfect sense! It also makes sense that You are the Creator of the universe and our earth.*

Day 17

IMITATORS

When you hear the word *disciple*, what comes to your mind? A disciple is a student of Jesus; more specifically, a follower, a learner, and an imitator of Jesus. A disciple aims to imitate Jesus in all areas of his or her life. Thomas à Kempis' classic, *The Imitation of Christ*, touches on the concept of discipleship as the imitation of Jesus.

Paul says, "Be imitators of God" (Ephesians 5:1 NKJV). Newborn babies imitate the facial expressions of their parents. Children learn by imitating what they hear their parents say and by what they see them do. Education is imitation. One of the best ways to master a skill is to imitate, or to mimic a teacher until that skill becomes second nature to us.

When we imitate Jesus, people see "Christ in [us], the hope of glory" (Colossians 1:27). Christians are called to reflect like mirrors "the Lord's glory" (2 Corinthians 3:18). We need to ask ourselves: *What would Jesus do in this situation? How would Jesus manage His money and time? How would Jesus respond to this crisis? What would Jesus do about this injustice? How would Jesus react to this challenge?*

Being a disciple boils down to the imitation of Jesus. Jesus said, "The student is not above [his] teacher, but everyone who is fully trained will be like their teacher" (Luke 6:40). Those three words are powerful—"like his teacher." That is the goal of learning about Jesus—to be like Him. We learn of Him so that we can be like Him, the Master Teacher.

A disciple of Jesus asks, "What is the Lord teaching me in this experience? What does He want me to learn?" When you approach life this way, then every situation of life becomes a chance to reflect like a mirror the glory of the Lord.

Prayer for the Day: *Lord, You are the One and only true God—the loving, kind, and patient God, a God of power and wisdom. I am Your disciple, and I delight in imitating You. Teach me to be more like You in every way, that I may lead others to You.*

Day 18

COVERED

The Christian life is one of both being forgiven and being forgiving. One of the meanings of *forgiveness* in the Hebrew language is "to cover." Psalm 78:38 says of God, "Yet he was merciful; he forgave [literally "covered"] their iniquities and did not destroy them." The same word in Hebrew is used in Genesis 6:14 when Noah covered the ark with pitch.

It is also the Hebrew word for *atonement*, which means "to cover." John the apostle tells us that Jesus is the "atoning sacrifice for our sins" (1 John 2:2). He is the covering for our guilt and our shame.

Let's go back to the Garden of Eden. When Adam and Eve sinned, God provided them coverings. He covered and clothed them when they felt ashamed for what they had done. In the same way, when we receive Jesus as our Savior, we are covered by the garment of the righteousness of Christ. When Jesus died on the cross, the soldiers gambled for His white seamless robe. Think about that—the only thing Jesus left us from the cross was His garment. He took our sins on Himself and left His covering of righteousness.

This is what the Scripture means: "God made him who had no sin to be sin [literally "a sin offering"] for us, so that in him we might become the righteousness of God" (2 Corinthians 5:21). Just as Adam and Eve were covered physically by the garments God provided them, we have been covered spiritually with the garment of the righteousness of Jesus.

No wonder the psalmist praised God, "You removed my sackcloth and clothed me with joy" (Psalm 30:11). He's got you covered!

Prayer for the Day: *Lord, what a great and amazing exchange, my sin for Your covering, forgiveness, and cleansing! I will remember what You did on the cross to make that possible, and I will forever praise You!*

Day 19

FREE AT LAST!

On August 28, 1963, Dr. Martin Luther King Jr. delivered his famous "I Have a Dream" speech that lasted sixteen minutes and is considered to be one of the most notable speeches in human history. In it, he called for ethnic equality and an end to discrimination. In that message, he thundered the now-famous declaration, "Free at last!"

Freedom is our most precious gift. The first words God spoke to Adam were, "You are free . . ." (Genesis 2:16). Yet, that freedom was lost when Adam disobeyed God and sinned against Him. Jesus Christ came to deliver us and set us from the penalty and the power of sin so that we might truly be free at last. Jesus said, "If the Son sets you free, you will be free indeed" (John 8:36).

Now that we are free, we need to guard our freedom by "say[ing] 'No' to ungodliness and worldly passions, and to live self-controlled, upright and godly lives in this present age" (Titus 2:12). Freedom can be lost by what we do or what we fail to do.

Freedom is anything but free. The high cost of freedom is personal responsibility to live up to the privileges of being free. "It is for freedom that Christ has set us free. Stand firm, then, and do not let yourselves be burdened again by a yoke of slavery" (Galatians 5:1).

Once we have been set free from any form of bondage, we need to live in such a way that we remain free and not allow ourselves to be enslaved to those things that once held us in bondage. Now that we are free, let us stand firm in that freedom.

Prayer for the Day: *Lord, I thank You for giving Your life that I may be free! Sin is bondage, and righteousness is freedom to be the person we were meant to be, and to accomplish what we were meant to accomplish.*

Day 20
STOP WORRYING

As a prisoner of Rome, the Apostle Paul found peace of mind by refusing to fret. "Do not be anxious about anything, but in every situation, by prayer and petition, with thanksgiving, present your requests to God. And the peace of God, which transcends all understanding, will guard your hearts and your minds in Christ Jesus" (Philippians 4:6-7).

Stop worrying and start trusting. Isaiah 26:3 tells us what God will do for us when we trust Him: "You will keep in perfect peace those whose minds are steadfast, because they trust in you."

Is your mind steadfast on the Lord? Do you trust Him in the tough times as much as you do in the good times? Can you say with conviction, "Yea, though I walk through the valley of the shadow of death, I will fear no evil: for thou art with me" (Psalm 23:4 KJV)? Or, do you only trust Him when you are on the mountain peak? Remember, not only is our God the God of the mountain, He is also the God of the valley.

Trust means, "Don't doubt in the dark what God has shown you in the light." It is easy for us to lose our faith when the darkness of adversity, suffering, or discouragement comes our way. But God is as faithful in the darkness as He is in the light.

Jesus said, "Do not worry about your life, what you will eat or drink; or . . . what you will wear" (Matthew 6:25). Instead, He tells us to make better use of our emotional energy. Worry is exhausting! Order your life by spiritual priorities. Take care of the things in your control and leave the rest to your heavenly Father. "Seek first his kingdom and his righteousness, and all these things will be given to you as well" (Matthew 6:33).

Prayer for the Day: *Lord, it is my nature to worry. Please remind me that You are God and if I will trust You with every detail of my life, You will give me supernatural peace of mind, knowing You are in control.*

Day 21
ANTIQUE BUSINESS

Antiques are popular. Many people are really into retro these days. We buy new clothes, furniture, and musical equipment that is made to look like it is aged. When it comes to religion, many people see God as an antique and the traditions of religion are locked in the past.

But God is not in the antique business! He is a God of the now. He is the Great I Am, not the Great I Was! He promises to do a new thing in us and for us as His people. God says to us, "Forget the former things; do not dwell on the past. See, I am doing a new thing! Now it springs up; do you not perceive it?" (Isaiah 43:18-19).

The key word here is "see." It is one thing for God to do a new work and another thing for us to see it. We can be so blinded by the past that we miss the new things God is doing. We can be so hurt by the past that we no longer expect to have anything new. Open your eyes today to new opportunities God will provide you, so you can move on from your past and get on with the business of living.

Prayer for the Day: *Lord, help me to keep my past in the past. Open my eyes today that I may see the new thing You are doing in my life.*

Day 22

DESERT TIMES

The desert is a dangerous place. A person can die quickly if he or she gets lost in a desert with no resources. We can dehydrate quickly in the heat of the desert. A desert is not defined by what happens there but, rather, by what does not happen—namely, *rain*. No rain means no water, vegetation, or growth. A desert is a barren and empty place. Sometimes our lives become deserts. We are more defined by what is not happening for us rather than what is happening.

In those desert times, God promises, "I am making a way in the wilderness and streams in the wasteland" (Isaiah 43:19). Turn to Him in your desert and He will give you a way through it. You will have to take the desert journey and the practical steps on the way He provides. He is not going to send an angel down to pick you and immediately transport you out of the desert. But follow the way He provides and you will get through it.

Maybe you are in a desert right now—a place that is barren, dry, and fruitless. God says He will make a way through that desert for you, and on the other side of the desert He will do something new in your life. Turn to Him in the desert and drink from the streams He will provide. Drink from the water of God's Word and let the promises of Scripture give you strength for the journey through the desert.

Water represents both the Word of God and the power of the Holy Spirit to give us strength. The Lord says, "I will pour water on the thirsty land, and streams on the dry ground; I will pour out my Spirit on your offspring, and my blessing on your descendants" (Isaiah 44:3).

Accept the Lord's offer: "Let anyone who is thirsty come. Let anyone who desires drink freely from the water of life" (Revelation 22:17 NLT).

Prayer for the Day: *Lord, I thank You that You are leading me out of this dry desert I have been living in. Just knowing that You are with me on this journey brings refreshment to my soul.*

Day 23

FINISH IT

Fred Lebow, cofounder of the New York City Marathon, said, "In running, it doesn't matter whether you come in first, in the middle of the pack, or last. You can say, 'I have finished.' There is a lot of satisfaction in that."

When we consider God's work in our lives and in the world around us, we can know that He finishes what He starts. "Being confident of this, that he who began a good work in you will carry it on to completion until the day of Christ Jesus" (Philippians 1:6).

We can be confident He will finish the good work He started in us. "Until the day of Christ Jesus" means until we meet Him in eternity. The word *finish* means to complete the process, to reach the goal. The good work of salvation is the good work He started in us, not that we started. We are saved by His grace and the free gift of salvation, not by religious deeds or self-righteousness. He is the One who started a good work in us, and He is the One who will finish it.

Even through the peaks and the valleys, the successes and failures, and the ups and downs, God never stops working on the masterpiece of our lives. The psalmist David expressed it this way: "The Lord will work out his plans for my life" (Psalm 138:8 NLT). You and I can rest in His promise today, that our God will never take His hand off our lives, but that He continues to mold us in is His image and guide us in His will as we trust Him.

Prayer for the Day: *Lord, I am blessed to know my life has purpose. I trust You with my salvation. I will trust You to complete what You have started in me.*

Day 24

FRAME IT

I had a construction job doing carpentry in my last year of college in Florida on the Island of Sanibel. I worked for six weeks on those houses and learned a lot from the foreman on the job. I enjoyed framing houses because you can work fast and see immediate results. When we framed a house, we used the biggest pieces of lumber and the biggest tools, and worked as fast as we could, which is the way I like to live. Once we finished framing the house and dried it in, we had to start the finishing work.

Then it all bogs down. Progress comes to a grinding halt. You go from warp speed to a snail's pace! I did not like finishing work—like putting up ceiling trim (sometimes in three layers), nailing baseboards, and painting and hanging cabinet doors—because it is slow, tedious, and must be flawless. You can hit a 16-penny nail as hard as you want with the biggest hammer you can swing when putting up studs in a wall, but you cannot do that when nailing up trim inside the house! You must use tiny nails and a smaller hammer.

Finishing work is slow and tedious. Yet, the finishing work is what people see. They don't see the studs inside the wall or the floor joists or the roof timbers. They see the finishing work.

When we are born again through faith in Jesus Christ, it is a dramatic work of God and it happens fast. We start growing spiritually, learning the Bible for the first time, making new discoveries, and experiencing big changes in our lives. Salvation is God framing our lives, and we see big changes fast.

However, as we continue to grow spiritually, the changes that God makes in us (and that we want to make) get smaller, more detailed, less noticeable to others, and are often more difficult to achieve. We move from God's framing work to His finishing work.

Just like construction, God's finishing work is time-consuming and intricate, yet He continues His work as He shapes us into the image of

Jesus Christ. It takes a lot more time and work to finish a house than it does to frame one. So, don't get discouraged when you struggle with issues trying to make changes in your life. The Lord is faithful to finish the good work He started in you when He saved you by His grace! "Fixing our eyes on Jesus, the pioneer and perfecter of faith!" (Hebrews 12:2).

Prayer for the Day: *Lord, today I looked in the mirror and realized that I am not the same person I was when we first met. You are shaping me into Your image, and it's even noticeable to me. Keep up the good work!*

Day 25

CHOSEN

On my way home from the airport one day, I decided to drive through the neighborhood I grew up in and stop by Parklane Elementary School, where I attended as a kid. A few people were working getting ready for the new school year, so I went in, introduced myself, and asked if I could walk around the school. Just about everything is the way it was when I attended. I went out back, up the same concrete steps to the ball field where we played kickball for recess. The field was just like it was when I attended there, so it brought back memories.

I remembered the feeling of two captains picking the teams. It was a great feeling when you got chosen early, but a terrible feeling to be the last one chosen. What an awkward feeling waiting to be chosen! Everyone has been overlooked or left out at one time or another. But in the kingdom of God, everyone is chosen!

Paul wrote, "For he [God] chose us in him [Jesus Christ] before the creation of the world to be holy and blameless in his sight" (Ephesians 1:4). You are no accident or afterthought; you were chosen by God for a life of purpose before the creation of the world. Jesus tells us, "You did not choose me, but I chose you and appointed you so that you might go and bear fruit—fruit that will last" (John 15:16). We are meant to be His "called, chosen and faithful followers" (Revelation 17:14). When you know you are chosen, you overcome feelings of insignificance, inadequacy, and insecurity. God did not choose you to be lost but to be saved; not to be judged but forgiven; not to fail but to succeed.

Prayer for the Day: *Lord, sometimes I feel so inadequate in this calling You have placed on my life. But knowing You have chosen me gives me the strength to move forward.*

Day 26

JOY AHEAD

Henry Wadsworth Longfellow said, "Great is the art of beginning, but greater is the art of ending."

Staying focused is one of the greatest challenges in life. We tend to get distracted, detoured, or discouraged. Instead of reaching our goals and fulfilling our dreams and keeping our commitments, we end up off track. Focus is one of the most important keys to living your life the way God wants you to live it.

Why did Jesus allow Himself to go to cross? He could have called ten thousand angels to rescue Him. The Bible tells us, "For the joy [that was] set before him he endured the cross" (Hebrews 12:2).

It is fascinating that the words *joy* and *cross* appear in the same sentence. The preposition *for* can be translated "in exchange for," in the sense of "to obtain" something important. The word *set* means "lying before." What was the joy that was set before Jesus, making Him endure the cross?

First, the joy of our eternal salvation that was accomplished by His sacrifice for our sins on the cross.

Second, He looked forward to returning to Heaven with the glory He had before He came into this world.

The same two things can give us joy, even though we are going through difficult times: the good we do for others, and God's promise of eternal life. Evangelist Dwight Moody said the greatest joy in life is making Jesus Christ known. So, look past whatever struggles or difficulties you may be facing today to the joy that lies ahead. Look beyond the pain to the promise!

Prayer for the Day: *Lord, sometimes I get bogged down in the mundane routines of life. I get so busy doing Your work that I forget to be thankful for all You did so that I can have joy in that work. Today I thank You for the joy that comes from loving and serving You!*

Day 27

PRE-DESTINY

When my mother had something important to say to me as a kid and wanted me to focus on what she was about to tell me, she would say, "David, put your thinking cap on." Today, I want you to put your thinking cap on as we talk about predestination. Perhaps no concept has caused more concern and confusion among Christians than *predestination*.

God is "not willing that any should perish but that all should come to repentance" (2 Peter 3:9 NKJV). To simply say we don't believe in predestination won't do, for Paul emphatically states, "In love He predestined us" (Ephesians 1:5). God is the One who predestined us. The word translated as "predestined" (*proorizo*) means "to decide beforehand." Simply add the prefix *pre*, meaning "before," to the word *destiny*. What is predestined? Who is predestined? Why are we predestined?

The motive is love: "In love He predestined us." It is out of love and through His love that we are predestined. This ought to erase once and for all the insidious notion that God arbitrarily chose some to be saved and others to be separated from Him. Predestination is about God's power and His plan of salvation. God marked out the plan of salvation before the world began. The Cross was predestined, for Jesus is called the Lamb "chosen before the creation of the world" (1 Peter 1:18-20). It is the plan, not individual people who are predestined. Predestination is associated with salvation, not judgment. Jesus said, "For God did not send his Son into the world to condemn the world, but to save the world through him" (John 3:17).

There remains our choice. *Predestination* and *free will* go hand in hand. We must believe in order to experience salvation (Ephesians 2:8-9). Love is always free to choose. God has chosen us in Christ. The question is, "Have we chosen Him?" As a father, I understand this. I have predestined a plan of provision and training for my children, but they had the freedom to follow my plan and counsel or not.

Where does free will come in? God has given us the power to respond to His predestined plan of salvation. I once heard it explained this way: "God votes for you. The devil votes against you. Your vote determines the election!"

Max Lucado said: "If there are a thousand steps between us and God, He will take all but one. He will leave the final one for us. The choice is ours."

Prayer for the Day: *Lord, I want to thank You for predestination: the plan of salvation You chose for humankind before the world began. In a world that loves conditionally, it is comforting to know that You made provision for our salvation before we ever sinned. You are a great God!*

Day 28
FREE, NOT CHEAP

Scientists are developing substitutes for blood that could be used everywhere from ambulances to battlefields. The oxygen-carrying resuscitative fluids are ideal for emergency scenarios. The substitutes have a longer shelf life than blood, can be stored at various temperatures, and may be given to anyone, regardless of blood type. The substitutes are made from chemically modified hemoglobin, and the fluids are nontoxic and disease-free. While science may find a substitute, there is no substitute for the blood of Jesus.

The word *blood* in Scripture means "life." "The life of a creature is in the blood" (Leviticus 17:11). When the Scripture speaks of the shed blood of Jesus, it means He gave His life for us. "Without the shedding of blood there is no forgiveness" (Hebrews 9:22). We are not our own; we are bought with a price, and that price is the precious blood of Jesus

(1 Corinthians 6:19; 1 Peter 1:18-19). When I think of the fact that I am redeemed by the blood of Jesus, it lets me know how valuable I am to God.

Grace is free, but it is not cheap. Salvation is free, but it is not cheap. Eternal life is a free gift, but it is not cheap. Heaven is free, but it is not cheap. Forgiveness is free, but it is not cheap. Today, let us remember the Lord Jesus who gave His life for us that we might live.

Prayer for the Day: *Lord, today all I hear from insurance companies vying for our attention is "Cheap-cheap, everywhere a cheap-cheap!" "It is a secure feeling to know that my life is in Your hands because You gave Your life for me. Priceless, but not cheap!*

Day 29
HE GAVE HIMSELF

A gathering of friends at an English estate nearly turned to tragedy when one of the children playing by the lake fell in. The groundskeeper heard the little boy cry for help, plunged in, and rescued him. The child was Winston Churchill. His grateful parents, who were very influential, asked the gardener what they could do to reward him. He hesitated, and then said, "I wish my son could go to college someday and become a doctor."

"We'll see to it," Churchill's parents promised.

Years later, while Winston Churchill was prime minister of England, he contracted pneumonia. The doctor who treated him was the best physician in England, Dr. Alexander Fleming, the man who discovered penicillin. He was also the son of the gardener who had saved young Winston from drowning. Later Churchill remarked, "Rarely has one man owed his life twice to the same person."

We owe our lives to One who did not risk His life for us, but who gave His life for us. "I live by faith in the Son of God, who loved me and gave himself for me" (Galatians 2:20). Jesus gave His life voluntarily on the cross to take the judgment of our sins. "God made him who had no sin to be sin for us, so that in him we might become the righteousness of God" (2 Corinthians 5:21). The word *sin* in this passage is literally translated "a sin offering." The writer of Hebrews tells us, Jesus "appeared once for all at the culmination of the ages to do away with sin by the sacrifice of himself" (Hebrews 9:26).

The Cross is the highest expression of the love of God. "This is how we know what love is: Jesus Christ laid down his life for us" (1 John 3:16). For "God demonstrates his own love for us in this: While we were still sinners, Christ died for us" (Romans 5:8).

What does that mean to us? When we realize Jesus gave Himself for us to save us from the penalty and power of sin, we know how valuable we are to God. You and I were worth the sacrifice of Jesus. The cost of something shows the value of that item. The cross of Christ is God's statement to us of how much we are worth to Him that He would not allow us to perish in our sins but would provide a way of eternal salvation.

Prayer for the Day: *Lord, there are people who can share stories about their physical lives being saved. But I am blown away when I realize that You, the Creator of the universe, gave Your life to save me from the eternal penalty and power of my sins! I am forever grateful!*

Day 30
STAY OUT OF IT

Have you ever been dragged into someone's problem and you wondered how you got tangled up in it? Sometimes the best thing we can do to help our friends and family is to simply stay out of it. That is what the proverb means: "Like one who grabs a stray dog by the ears is someone who rushes into a quarrel not their own" (Proverbs 26:17). That is a funny mental picture, grabbing a dog by his ears. Most dogs would not appreciate that and would let you know it by biting your hand. Well, people bite too!

It is so important to know when to be involved and when to stay out of it when it comes to other people's issues. We often want to help and do all we can, but sometimes people need to work things out by themselves. After all, that is how we all grow to independence and learn to stand on our own two feet. Too much help keeps people dependent and unable to cope with life on their own.

Paul the apostle gives us the same advice: "Make it your ambition to lead a quiet life: you should mind your own business and work with your hands" (1 Thessalonians 4:11). When Jesus was asked to sort out a family dispute about money, He told the man, "Who appointed me a judge or an arbiter between you?" (Luke 12:14). Jesus stayed out of their dispute and let them work things out for themselves. He had a higher purpose on His life as our Redeemer and to proclaim the goods news of the kingdom of God. We, too, need to stay out of people's personal and trivial matters and stay focused on our higher purpose as disciples of Jesus Christ.

After all, that is how we really help people—by teaching them the Word of God and what we have learned from trusting God, not by meddling in their personal disputes and problems. Encourage those you know to pray and then to work things out for themselves. They will then have the confidence they need to handle life and to know that if God is for them, who can be against them? (Romans 8:31). Remember, sometimes the best help is to simply stay out of it.

Prayer for the Day: *Ecclesiastes 3:7 says, "[There] is a time to be silent and a time to speak." Lord, please give me the wisdom to know the difference so that I don't stick my nose where it doesn't belong. Rather, teach me how to encourage and pray for those who need to work out their own problems.*

Day 31

SEAL THE DEAL

People today are looking for a guarantee—something they can count on . . . someone they can count on. We look for guarantees in business, in finance, and in our relationships. Jesus Christ has promised the guarantee of our salvation. The Bible says when we believe in Jesus Christ, we are "marked in him with a seal, the promised Holy Spirit, who is a deposit guaranteeing our inheritance" (Ephesians 1:13-14).

Historically, *seals* could mean ownership of property, allegiance (ancient soldiers used to brand themselves with the name of their commander), or a covenant or contract as documents were sealed. We use seals today. A notary public's seal verifies a document. The Presidential Seal represents the authority of the nation. Legal documents are kept "under seal" to protect the contents. A U.S. patent on a product or a copyright of a literary work secures it.

"The solid foundation of God stands, having this seal: 'The Lord knows those who are His'" (2 Timothy 2:19 NKJV). Early Christians considered water baptism to be a seal. Identity is big issue in our day. We must show our identity to drive, to board an airplane, and to withdraw funds from the bank. Meanwhile, we face the threat of identity theft. The devil has stolen many Christians' identity, and they don't know who they are anymore.

A little boy covered in dirt came into the house from playing and asked his mother, "Who am I?"

Ready to play the game she said, "I don't know! Who are you?"

"Wow!" he exclaimed. "Mrs. Johnson was right! She said I was so dirty that my own mother wouldn't recognize me!"

Paul wrote, "Do not grieve the Holy Spirit of God, with whom you were sealed for the day of redemption" (Ephesians 4:30). We use the phrase "seal the deal." Our salvation is a finished transaction! A signature on a letter verifies its authenticity, as do seals on important documents. The Holy Spirit is a seal guaranteeing that we belong to Christ.

Your everlasting salvation is guaranteed by the living God, who has placed His Spirit in your heart and set His seal of ownership on your life. You can know beyond a shadow of a doubt that you belong to Him.

At the end of His crucifixion, Jesus shouted in victory, "It is finished!" It is time we shouted by faith about our personal salvation, "It is finished!"

Prayer for the Day: *Lord, I have lived long enough to know there are no guarantees for anything in this life other than Your salvation. I am grateful for the seal of the Holy Spirit, which is my only guarantee for abundant life here and now, and eternal life hereafter.*

Day 32

HEART CHECK

Mark Twain said, "I can live two months on a single compliment." Personally, I cannot make it that long. We all need encouragement to help us achieve our best and to motivate us to reach our goals.

While we need encouragement, we need to be wary of flattery and false praise. There is a vast difference between encouragement and flattery. First, don't go fishing for a compliment. "Let someone else praise you, and not your own mouth; an outsider, and not your own lips" (Proverbs 27:2). The worst flattery is self-flattery. What a turn-off to see self-absorbed people who cannot stay out of the limelight and use every situation to promote themselves!

When people encourage us, they truly believe in us; but when people flatter us, they are manipulating us. They want something in return for their false praise. Jesus said, "I do not accept glory from human beings, but I know you. I know that you do not have the love of God in your hearts" (John 5:41-42). He knew when He was being manipulated, so He rejected such praise or flattery from people. Meanwhile, He did accept people's worship when they put their faith in Him as the Son of God.

Jesus asked, "How can you believe since you accept glory from one another but do not seek the glory that comes from the only God?" (John 5:44). When we know we have done a good job that honors God and that He praises us for the integrity of our work and effort, then we will be free from grand-standing, self-promotion, and from seeking the praise of others. We will also be able to encourage others without flattering them.

It is time for a heart check. Do we look for praise from others or commendation from the Lord? Do we seek to encourage others, or do we flatter them because we want something from them? Let us imitate our Lord, who said, "I seek not to please myself but him who sent me" (John 5:30).

Prayer for the Day: *Lord, sometimes I feel that no one notices the effort I put into all that I do. But I will continue to do my best, as working for You. And* should my work be praised, I will give You the glory for what You have done through me.

Day 33
MILESTONE OR MILLSTONE?

Samson had a great calling on his life, but he took his calling for granted. A man of great strength was reduced to weakness because of his sin and failure. The stories of his victories come to an end with the statement of his defeat: "But he did not know that the Lord had left him. Then the Philistines seized him, gouged out his eyes and took him down to Gaza. Binding him with bronze shackles, they set him to grinding in the prison" (Judges 16:20-21).

I picture Samson pushing the great millstone, crushing the wheat in the prison. Chained to a millstone! Sometimes we too get chained to the past, which is a millstone keeping us from being free. The sins and failures of the past can be a millstone to which we are chained. But, by the grace of God, we can turn the failures of the past from a millstone to a milestone!

That is what Samson did. "Then Samson prayed to the Lord" (Judges 16:28). While he prayed for one final victory over his enemies, I believe he had been praying while he was chained to that millstone in prison. I am convinced that he first prayed to repent of his sins and to get his life restored to God.

We too can turn the past from a millstone to a milestone and move forward to God's greater blessings in our lives if we pray to Him. You don't have to be chained to the past like a great millstone. "Forgetting what is behind and straining toward what is ahead, I press on toward the goal, to win the prize for which God has called me heavenward in Christ Jesus" (Philippians 3:13-14).

Prayer for the Day: *Lord, I too, have failures that weigh me down like a millstone. Although, I cannot forget the pain it has caused me, I can turn them into milestones that mark the place of forgiveness and cause me to move forward in my journey with You. I praise and thank You.*

Day 34

TRANSITIONS

Henry Wadsworth Longfellow said, "Great is the art of beginning, greater is the art of ending." Life consists of a series of beginnings and endings—transitions. A *transition* is defined as "the act of passing from one state or place to the next; a conversion; an event that results in a transformation; or a musical passage that moves from one key to another." Transitions include both a beginning and an end.

History had its beginning in the Garden of Eden. Then sin entered the picture, and it looked like the end. But God gave Adam and Eve a new beginning, and the human story continued. The great flood of Noah's time was an ending, but then came the sign of the rainbow. God gave a new beginning as the world continued after the Flood. When Jesus died on the cross, it was an end to the old covenant, but then came His resurrection and the beginning of the new covenant.

One day the world as we know it will end. The Bible describes the great and final war as "Armageddon." The heavens will part like a scroll, and Jesus Christ will return with power and great glory. History ends; yet, it begins again with "a new heaven and a new earth" (Revelation 21:1).

When you face an ending to something, don't get depressed or hopeless. The end can be a door into a new beginning. Move through life's transitions with a sense of faith, not futility. Embrace the change with expectation of "great and mighty things" that the Lord can do with you and for you as you enter a new season (Jeremiah 33:3 NKJV). Don't get stuck in the transition. Pass through it and enjoy a new season of life. In Christ, "old things pass away and all things become new!" (see 2 Corinthians 5:17).

Prayer for the Day: *Lord, I am in transition! Something precious to me has come to an end. Please help me to let it go and start expecting a new opportunity to present itself—a new season of life, a new beginning.*

Day 35

A NEW THING

One of the most powerful words in our language is the word *new*. We all like to get something new—a new car, a new house, a new job, a new opportunity, or a new relationship. The word *new* is used in different ways. Something can be new in existence. Or, it can be renewed or renovated. Something can also be given a new purpose and usefulness.

The first and last portrait of God found in the Bible is the God of new things. It starts with creation. God creates a brand-new world. The Bible ends with a new heaven and a new earth and God saying, "I am making everything new!" (Revelation 21:5).

What if we could hear God say that to us? "I am making everything new." Ask and believe God for new things in your life. It may be something new for you, in you, or with you that you need. Whatever the case, God is able to do it.

Here is His promise to you: "Forget the former things; do not dwell on the past. See, I am doing a new thing! Now it springs up; do you not perceive it? I am making a way in the wilderness and streams in the wasteland" (Isaiah 43:18-19).

It is up to you to let go of the old and make room in your life for the new work of God. Forget the past and stop dwelling on it. It is time to get your mind focused on the new.

Prayer for the Day: *Lord, I am ready for something new! I no longer want to dwell on the past, wishing I could have done things differently. I am looking for that new thing and moving forward as You direct me.*

Day 36

AFTER THEY PRAYED

John Wesley said, "God will do nothing apart from the prayers of His people." We know that God can do all things, but He committed to us the ministry of prayer. Prayer keeps us connected and dependent on God as our Father, Jesus as our Lord, and the Holy Spirit as our Helper.

The early church understood the power of prayer. When the apostles were first intimidated and told not to speak any more about Jesus, they went to the believers and gathered for prayer. "After they prayed, the place where they were meeting was shaken. And they were all filled with the Holy Spirit and spoke the word of God boldly" (Acts 4:31). Those three words are packed with power—"after they prayed!" The first thing they did was "they raised their voices together in prayer" (v. 24). Prayer is our first response, not our last resort! We are not ready to do anything in the kingdom of God until after we pray.

After you pray, start the new business. After you pray, select your college of choice. After you pray, start a new ministry. After you pray, run for public office. After you pray, take that missions trip. After you pray, share the gospel of Jesus with your friend. After you pray, take that new job offer. After you pray, get married. After you pray, buy that new house. After you pray, make that important decision.

You see, it is only after we pray that we know God's will about a matter. It is only after we pray that our minds are clear to make the best decision. It is in prayer where God does His great work in our minds and hearts. Sometimes He changes the agenda, modifies the plan, or gives us a sense that we are about to make the wrong choice. It is in the place of prayer where God gives us His peace about the decisions we are facing and the problems we are dealing with. You and I are not ready to take any important action or make an important decision until after we pray. Have you prayed about that situation, decision, or person you are concerned about? If not, stop now. Do not go any further until after you pray.

Prayer for the Day: *Lord, I have a decision to make, and I want to make sure I'm making the right one. Please give me wisdom and direction, but most of all, peace that comes from knowing You are leading me.*

Day 37

KEEP IT UP

Desperate for a child, a couple asked their priest to pray for them. "I'm going on sabbatical to Rome," he replied. "I'll light a prayer candle for you at Saint Peter's Basilica at the Vatican."

When the priest returned a year later, he found the wife pregnant and tending a set of twins. Elated, the priest asked to speak to her husband and congratulate him. "He's gone to Rome," she said, "to blow out that candle."

I have never doubted the power of prayer, but I often doubt my ability to pray effectively. Perhaps you are like me. Yet the Apostle Paul teaches us to "keep on praying" (Ephesians 6:18). He also tells us to "pray without ceasing" (1 Thessalonians 5:17 KJV).

We already have this discipline if you think about it. We text without ceasing, so we can also pray without ceasing. Barbie and I were at a movie the other day. The old advertisement for concessions has been replaced with a short cartoon designed to get people to stop texting during movies. I can tell you the ad is not working! If we could pray like we text, we would be getting somewhere.

Keep on praying because prayer works! God answers prayer. Prayer makes a difference. Prayer brings the grace of God to those for whom we pray. Prayer is a spiritual force that affects the natural world. We do not need to pray ritualistic prayers or habitual prayers but to allow the Holy Spirit to lead us in our prayers so that we pray according to the will of God. Jesus told us not to pray like the pagans who "think they will be heard because of their many words" (Matthew 6:7). Persevering in prayer doesn't mean to just keep saying meaningless words or phrases; it means to live every day in the presence of God and to bring every issue of our lives to Him.

What difference do you think it will make in our lives, our families, and our nation if we keep on praying? Let's take God at His Word and keep on praying, because He will answer us and do "exceedingly abundantly above all that we ask or [even] think [possible]" (Ephesians 3:20 NKJV).

Prayer for the Day: *Lord, sometimes I pray about a matter, then give up when I don't have an immediate answer. Thank You for reminding me that some prayers take time to answer.*

Day 38

WRESTLING

One of the most popular sports today is wrestling. I took wrestling in physical education in high school and hated it. I was one of the smallest guys, so I had to work extra hard. Since it was only a physical-education class and we had to wrestle outside our weight division, we were always mismatched. Wrestling is exhausting. You extend constant energy. Your opponent never lets up, and neither do you. I have known several professional wrestlers as well, so when I hear Paul compare prayer to wrestling, I get a picture of the struggle we go through in praying for other people.

Wrestling was a popular sport in Paul's day in the Roman games. What an interesting word picture for Paul to use to describe prayer—wrestling in prayer. He tells us about Epaphras, who was from the city of Colossae and may have been the pastor of this church. At the time of this writing Epaphras was visiting Paul, who was a prisoner in Rome. Sometimes prayer is a conversation. Sometimes it is simply experiencing the presence of God in worship. But sometimes prayer is wrestling and working until we get the results we desire.

Paul writes, "Epaphras, who is one of you and servant of Christ Jesus, sends greetings. He is always wrestling in prayer for you, that you may stand firm in all the will of God, mature and fully assured" (Colossians 4:12). Here we have insight into how to pray for others. We learn that prayer has a direct, definite, and dynamic spiritual effect on the people for whom we pray.

I once heard a message by Pastor Chuck Smith that made a

strong impression on me. He shared a message entitled "The Sin of Prayerlessness."

Samuel was the prophet and spiritual leader of Israel. He gathered the leaders together for his farewell address at the end of his ministry. They had admitted to him how wrong they had been in their attitude toward the Lord in asking for a king and were repentant. He reassured them to follow the Lord and that God would bless them and their king if they followed him. "For the sake of His great name the Lord will not reject His people. . . . As for me, far be it from me that I should sin against the Lord in ceasing to pray for you" (1 Samuel 12:22-23 NKJV).

Regardless of the struggle and waiting to see the results of our prayers in the lives of others, let us follow the footsteps of Epaphras and continue to wrestle in prayer for them because the bottom line is, prayer works!

Prayer for the Day: *Lord, please give me the strength to wrestle in prayer as I intercede for my loved ones. Sometimes I feel like I'm the only one fighting. But I know You are with me.*

Day 39
STRUGGLING FOR IT

Do you ever struggle in your faith? Do you struggle with the mysteries of life? Are you struggling with an issue in your life? The first Bible story of someone struggling with God is the story of Jacob, Abraham's grandson, who wrestled with the angel of the Lord (Genesis 32:22-32).

Here is what was going on: Jacob was going to meet his brother, Esau. Years before, he had deceived his father, Isaac, and manipulated him to give him the family blessing instead of his older twin brother, Esau. Then, to make matters worse, he caught Esau at a moment of weakness and got him to trade him his birthright for a meal!

It was not all Jacob's fault, since Esau is the one who gave him his birthright because he did not treasure it. He was more concerned with his immediate gratification. On top of this, his own mother helped him manipulate his father and his brother so that he could get the birthright and the blessing.

What a dysfunctional family! Esau hated him, and his father was disappointed in him, so he left and never returned. Esau swore to take revenge.

Over the years God blessed Jacob. Now he travels back home and is on a head-on collision to meet Esau! He is terrified. One night he sends his family ahead and crosses a river to a private place by himself. He needs God's help. That night, he wrestles with an angel sent from the Lord. Holding on to the angel, he says, "I will not let you go until you bless me" (Genesis 32:26).

Then comes the moment of truth: "What is your name?" the angel asks. Finally, he has to meet himself and admit his fault. "Jacob," he replies. The name *Jacob* means "manipulator" and "deceiver." To admit his name was to own up to his problem with manipulation. When he gets real with God, the Lord changes his name right there to *Israel*, meaning "you have struggled with God and with humans and have overcome" (Genesis 32:28). That is what the name *Israel* means.

Jacob names the place *Peniel* "because," he says, "I saw God face to face, and yet my life was spared" (Genesis 32:30). When he arises the next morning, he walks with a limp because the angel had knocked his hip out of joint. His limp is a sign of his new humility before God. From now on, he will trust God instead of manipulating for everything he wants in life.

The miracle is that when Esau sees him, he runs and hugs him and they are reconciled. God had worked on Esau's heart, and turning it from anger to forgiveness.

Whatever you are struggling for, don't give up the struggle until the blessing comes! Like Jacob, struggle with the issues of life in prayer until you overcome and see God face-to-face in your own life and experience His blessing.

Prayer for the Day: *Lord, life can be such a struggle. Even prayer feels that way at times. But I will continue to struggle in prayer as I wait for my answer from You, Lord.*

Day 40

UNHINDERED PRAYER

A news reporter in Jerusalem learned of a man who had been going to the Wailing Wall (the Western Wall) to pray twice a day, every day, for many years. She went to the Wailing Wall, and there he was.

"Sir," she asked, "how long have you been coming to the Wailing Wall and praying?"

He replied, "For fifty years."

"What do you pray for?"

He answered, "I pray for peace between the Jews and the Arabs, for our children to grow up in safety and friendship."

"How do you feel after fifty years of praying?"

He exclaimed, "I feel like I'm talking to a brick wall!"

Sometimes we feel our prayers are not getting anything done. Did you know there are things that can hinder our prayers? For example, the Apostle Peter writes, "Husbands, in the same way, be considerate as you live with your wives, and treat them with respect . . . so that nothing will hinder your prayers" (1 Peter 3:7). Our relationships are the most important part of our lives. Our greatest joy comes from our relationships, and so does our biggest stress. My relationship with God affects my relationships with others and vice versa. Peter teaches us to keep our relationships right so our prayers will be effective.

We need to connect the dots between our relationship to God and to others. Jesus connected the two great commands as one when He said, "Love the Lord your God and love your neighbor as yourself" (see Mark 12:28-31). The greatest law is love! When we are out of step with each other, we are also out of step with God. Jesus wouldn't allow others to talk about loving God without also talking about loving others. To be in a right relationship with God requires us to be in right relationship with others. When our relationships are broken, we need to make things right so that our relationship with God is right.

One morning Barbie and I had an argument (about what I don't remember). I left home to go to the office without resolving anything. On my way, I asked God to forgive me for my attitude. God said to me, *Why are you asking Me to forgive you? I wasn't the one you offended.* As soon as I got to my office, I called Barbie and apologized.

It is hard to pray with power when there is baggage in our relationships. We have to make things right with others so that nothing will hinder our prayers.

Prayer for the Day: *Lord, why are relationships so difficult? I have You and want to love others as You do, but it can be difficult. Please show me if there is anything in my life that could hinder my prayers so I can make it right.*

Day 41

YOU CAN HELP

Helping others is such an important part of life. Psychology has observed that when we live outside ourselves and put others first, this is the greatest sign that we have a healthy personality. Gordon Allport, in his study of human nature and the marks of maturity, called this quality "the extension of the self." On the other hand, self-centeredness is a sign of immaturity.

When we walk into a restaurant, a store, or a church, we expect someone to greet us and ask, "How may I help you?" The desire to help is a sign of a healthy business. A main reason companies go bankrupt is the lack of customer service.

As Christians, we are the light of Christ in the world. "You are the light of the world," He told us (Matthew 5:14). We are here to help others come to know Him as the Savior and Lord. Our attitude toward others needs to be, "How may I help you?"

One of the ways we can help others is by praying for them. Paul the apostle thanked the believers at Corinth for the way they helped him in prayer. He wrote:

> We were under great pressure, far beyond our ability to endure, so that we despaired of life itself. Indeed, we felt we had received the sentence of death. But this happened that we might not rely on ourselves but on

God, who raises the dead. He has delivered us from such a deadly peril, and he will deliver us again. On him we have set our hope that he will continue to deliver us, as you help us by your prayers. Then many will give thanks on our behalf for the gracious favor granted us in answer to the prayers of many (2 Corinthians 1:8-11).

Sometimes we feel powerless to help others in a tangible way, but we can always help them in prayer. I am struck with the significance of the phrase "as you help us by your prayers." Think of someone today who is in need of something beyond what you can provide—someone who is under great pressure, far beyond their ability to endure—and help them by your prayers. Pray for God's peace to flood their hearts, and for God's wisdom to come to their minds. Believe that as you pray for them, whatever they are going through will turn out for their deliverance.

Prayer for the Day: *Lord, I am unable to always be there physically to help my family and friends when they are in need, and Heaven knows my finances are limited. But it gives me great peace to know I can pray on their behalf, and You hear me and come to their aid.*

Day 42
PRAYER MATTERS

Our prayers are sacred to God. The Apostle John saw a vision of Heaven in the Book of Revelation. Around the throne of God, he saw twenty-four elders who had "golden bowls full of incense, which are the prayers of God's people" (Revelation 5:8). It is significant that the prayers of God's people are kept in a sacred place. Later, he saw another angel who had a golden censer "[filled] with the prayers of all God's people" (Revelation 8:3).

God honors our prayers so much that He keeps them. We keep things that are important to us. My father kept everything I ever drew or painted for him. He helped me make a notebook of trains for a school assignment when I was a little boy. He kept it because he valued it. My mother gave it to me after he passed.

My dad also kept a framed picture I drew of him on his nightstand until the day he died because he valued it. The actual photo of him from which I copied my drawing remained in a frame underneath the sketch I drew for him as a child. In the same way, God honors our prayers.

Your prayers matter. The people you pray for are blessed by your intercession. Our world is touched and changed spiritually as the result of our prayers. "The prayer of a righteous person is powerful and effective" (James 5:16). Prayer is a powerful form of ministry God has given us to bring spiritual blessings in the lives of others.

We must begin to understand and believe how powerful prayer really is. Hebrews 11:6 declares: "Without faith it is impossible to please God, because anyone who comes to him must believe that he exists and that he rewards those who earnestly seek him."

Prayer for the Day: *Lord, why do I try to solve my problems in my own power, when I know You are but a prayer away? Thank You for reminding me that prayer always matters.*

Day 43
MAKE A CHOICE

We all misplace things from time to time. When you do, someone asks, "Where did you put it?" We reply, "If I knew that, I wouldn't be looking for it!"

Where have you put your faith? The Bible says, "Even as Jesus spoke, many put their faith in him" (see John 8:30). However, others rejected Jesus, even though they heard Him speak the Word of God and saw Him perform miracles.

It is different to not believe in Jesus because you haven't heard about Him and to choose not to believe in Him once you learn of Him. We like to think that not believing in Jesus is a passive response, but it is as much an act of faith as believing in Him. Believing and unbelieving are conscious choices. We either put our faith in Jesus or we put it in something else.

Choosing not to believe in Jesus, once you have been introduced to Him, is believing in the wrong information about Him. Believing that Jesus is not the Son of God is as much an act of faith as believing He is God's Son. The people "put their faith in Him." I want to emphasize the word *put*. We have to *put* our faith in something or someone.

Every day you and I choose to put our faith somewhere. No one has the luxury of not believing. Everyone is a believer in *something*. The question is, Who do you trust? What do you believe?

Take Jesus' words to heart today: "Have faith in God!" (Mark 11:22).

Prayer for the Day: *Lord, I choose to put my faith and trust in You. You are the Son of God and Savior of my soul. In You is hope. In You is eternal life.*

Day 44

SEE IT

Albert Einstein said, "Imagination is greater than knowledge." Faith sees the end result and prays toward that end. We are often blinded by what we see naturally instead of visualizing the end result of our prayers and the completion of goals. If your business is struggling, see the business prosperous and pray toward that end. If you have a rebellious teenager, see her whole and complete honoring the Lord. If you are struggling with personal issues or battling an illness, see yourself healed and restored.

The Bible teaches us about the power of spiritual vision. In Proverbs 29:18 we read, "Where there is no vision, the people perish" (KJV). Without a vision of who we want to be, where we want to go, and what we want to achieve, we flounder in life. Vision pulls us upward and onward. The Apostle Paul challenges us, "Fix our eyes not on what is seen, but on what is unseen, since what is seen is temporary, but what is unseen is eternal" (2 Corinthians 4:18).

What, after all, is *faith*? "Faith shows the reality of what we hope for; it is the evidence of things we cannot see" (Hebrews 11:1 NLT). We are certain of what we do not see in the natural, but we can envision it spiritually.

Science has documented the power of visualization. In the 1980 Olympics, the Russians used this technique. They divided their athletes into four groups: Group A used 100 percent physical practice. Group B had 75 percent physical and 25 percent mental training. Group C had 50 percent physical and 50 percent mental training. Group D had 75 percent mental and 25 percent physical training. The mental training exercises included athletes seeing themselves on the field of competition and going through all the physical movements of their sport. They practiced in their minds. After the Moscow Olympics and the Lake Placid Olympics, these world-class athletes' scores were tallied. Those in Group D had won the most medals.

Another dramatic example of the power of mental vision is the story of Air Force Colonel George Hall during the Vietnam War. He was a POW locked in a dark box at a North Vietnamese prison for seven harsh years. Yet, every day Hall played 18 holes of golf in his mind. He imagined the golf course, the greens, the clubs, driving the ball, playing his short game, recovering from bad shots, and putting the ball. He practiced in his mind for seven years. One week after he was released from his POW camp, he entered the Greater New Orleans Open and shot a 76!

Prayer for the Day: *Lord, sometimes I wish I could see into the future. But, since my future is for Your eyes only, I will envision in my mind, my life whole and achieving what You have called me to do and be. The rest I trust to You.*

Day 45

GREAT THINGS

Have you ever asked the questions, "If God is omnipotent, omnipresent, and omniscient, why should I pray?" "If God knows my need before I ask Him, why should I bother to ask at all?" Have you ever been so overwhelmed in life that you felt like not praying because you thought it wouldn't make any difference?

Maybe Jeremiah felt this way and struggled with these questions. He was imprisoned for his ministry. He lived in difficult times of war with

Babylon. Many people were exiled to Babylon, as he predicted. Yet, even in prison, "the word of the Lord came to him a second time [saying], 'Call to me and I will answer you and tell you great and unsearchable things you do not know'" (Jeremiah 33:1-3).

Prayer is more than asking God for stuff; it is a word that describes our relationship to God as our Father. When we pray, He promises to answer. When God says, "I will answer you," He means more than just saying *yes*, *no*, or *later*. He means, *I will respond to you. I will minister to you. I will work in your life and situation.* He promises to tell us great and unsearchable things!

Have you ever felt like God has given up on you? Or, perhaps that God is not even mindful of what you are going through? God promises to show you His purpose and plan for your life when you call on Him. The Hebrew word for *unsearchable* means "things that are inaccessible, beyond the grasp of human knowledge and out of our reach." God was telling Jeremiah that those things which seemed beyond Israel's reach were now within their grasp if they would pray.

When God answers us, He opens our minds to see the way we need to go and decisions we need to make. "What no eye has seen, what no ear has heard, and what no human mind has conceived—the things God has prepared for those who love him—these are the things God has revealed to us by his Spirit" (1 Corinthians 2:9-10). Prayer is a time when God gives us creative ideas and new insights that can change our lives. Prayer is a time when God's Spirit gives us hope when we feel all is hopeless.

Call on the Lord today, and open your heart and mind to the great and unsearchable things He is going to show you for your life.

Prayer for the Day: *Lord, in the confusion of life, it is good to know that You have a plan for me. As I pray and listen for Your voice, I will wait for You to reveal the direction that will guide my journey with You. I praise and thank You.*

Day 46

PUSH BACK

When you face a personal or spiritual attack to your goals and dreams, you need to push back. Don't accept defeat. Don't let life push you around. You can overcome every enemy you face.

The psalmist said, "Through you we push back our enemies; through your name we trample our foes. I put no trust in my bow, my sword does not bring me victory; but you give us victory over our enemies, you put our adversaries to shame" (Psalm 44:5-7).

I like the phrase, "I put no trust in my bow, my sword does not bring me victory." That is a strong statement for a warrior to make. Obviously, a soldier in battle is not going to discard his weapons and enter a battle defenseless. We too need our natural talents and abilities and do the best we can do in life. We need to work hard for success. We need to fight for the things we want to achieve in life.

But we need to realize that victory takes more than self-effort. We cannot put our total trust in our own abilities. We need to trust the Lord for this power to be at work in us, through us, and for us.

That is why the psalmist says, "You give us victory over our enemies." God works with us. He doesn't do everything for us. So, push back against your enemies and use every spiritual and natural weapon you have at your disposal. But, trust the Lord to give you victory as He blesses you.

Don't accept defeat. Don't be intimidated. Push back as you fight the good fight of faith, and see the victory the Lord will give you.

Prayer for the Day: *Lord, show me where it is You want to use my God-given talents and abilities. I will push forward, seeking Your direction. I praise and thank You.*

Day 47

AT ODDS WITH THE WORLD

Do you ever feel at odds with the world? The world system advocates one thing but, as a Christian, you believe another. The world says something is OK but, in your heart, you believe it is wrong. Jesus told His disciples, "If the world hates you, keep in mind that it hated me first" (John 15:18).

The world system is fallen from grace. It is lost and misguided. It has turned away from the Lord. As followers of Jesus, we are the light of the world. We are to shine the light of Jesus Christ in the world to dispel the darkness of sin, fear, and deception. Following Jesus means we believe His Word, not the values of a fallen world. We obey His commands, not the secular trends of the day. We find our purpose in Him, not in fame, fortune, and pleasure.

Jesus tells why we are at odds with the world: "If you belonged to the world, it would love you as its own. As it is, you do not belong to the world, but I have chosen you out of the world. That is why the world hates you. . . . If they persecuted me, they will persecute you also. . . . They will treat you this way because of my name" (John 15:19-21).

Dr. Martin Luther King said, "The true measure of a man is not how he behaves in moments of comfort and convenience, but how he stands at times of controversy and challenges."

Persecution and rejection, regardless of how mild or severe it may be, is never a pleasant experience. It hurts when the media misrepresents the Christian faith, when a teenager is ridiculed for his or her faith, when a college student is accused of being irrational for his or her faith, or when a businessperson is challenged because of his or her Christian values. The name of Jesus is the most powerful name in the world. When we mention His name, people feel the pressure to make a choice about Him. Although Jesus is loved and respected, He is also controversial because He said, "I am the way and the truth and the life" (John 14:6).

So, when you find yourself at odds with the world, rejoice that you bear the name of Jesus. Remember to shine the light of His love into the darkness of the world that everyone may come to know Him as their Lord and Savior.

Prayer for the Day: *Lord, I am at odds with the world. But, knowing You are the way, the truth, and the life encourages me to shine that light so that others may hear the name of Jesus, too! I praise and thank You.*

Day 48

CHRIST IS ALL!

I was at the mall looking for earrings for Barbie. I had to find the exact pair she described to me, which can be an adventure if you have ever had to find the exact piece of jewelry the woman of your dreams wants. The woman waiting on me said, "You must be a Capricorn."

Now this sparked a response from me. "What do you mean?"

She began to talk to me about my astrological sign. She said she was good at guessing people's signs. I said, "No, I'm not a Capricorn." She said, "Then you must be a Scorpion."

I asked her why she thought that, and she said my personality gave her that impression. I said, "You know, astrology isn't true. It's based on ancient beliefs that the sun and planets revolve around the earth and that they influence world events. It's only based on five planets and other constellations because they couldn't see the other planets in our solar system. If you have someone read your chart here versus China, the results are different. It's not absolute. People read a sign and automatically see similarities with their lives."

She said, "Well, you must be a Sagittarius!"

I never did tell her my sign (which she never guessed, although she said she was good at guessing people's signs), but I gave her something to think about.

People search for a meaningful religious and spiritual experience through world religions, astrology, science, philosophy, New Ageism, mysticism, the occult, drug use, pleasure, wealth, and relationships. But for me, "Christ is all!" (Colossians 3:11). Everything I need spiritually I have found in Jesus Christ. He has given me everything I need for a life of peace, purpose, and power. He is everything to me.

Prayer for the Day: *Lord, thank You for being all I need for life and godliness. You are the reason I live without fear and with perfect peace. I praise and thank You.*

Day 49

TRUST HIM

Think of someone you trust completely. Why do you trust that person? Because you know them. We trust the people we know. The same is true of God. We trust Him when we know Him. Psalm 9:10 says, "Those who know your name trust in you, for you, Lord, have never forsaken those who seek you."

We are born with innate ability to trust. We naturally trust our parents and the world around us to provide for us and keep us safe. But it doesn't take long for us to begin to have feelings of mistrust. We learn not to trust through our experiences. Over time, fear replaces faith. Suspicion replaces trust. Doubt replaces belief.

Our parents teach us not to trust strangers because we don't know them. When our kids want to spend the night with a friend, we want to know the family before we let them go. When our daughter wants to date, we want to know the guy because we don't trust him.

Trust is the basis of our relationship to God. Adam and Eve were created to trust God. Then Satan appeared and asked, "Did God really say . . . ?" He convinced them that God had lied to them and they couldn't trust Him. He convinced them that God didn't have their best in mind and that they needed to disregard what He said and take matters into their own hands. They needed to do their own thing, listen to their own inner voice, and ignore the voice of God. Mistrust grew in their hearts toward God, and they disobeyed Him. That became the first sin and the essence of what sin is—to mistrust and, therefore, to disobey God.

When we are born again, we learn to live as God created us to live—by faith. How can we learn to trust God more fully? The psalmist gives us the key: "Those who know your name will trust in you." The name of the Lord in the Bible means His character, nature, and purpose. People have some strange ideas about who God is, so they fear Him, or avoid Him, or conclude He doesn't exist. But, once we know God as He truly is, we will trust Him.

Ask the Lord to reveal Himself to you more clearly and personally through the Scripture and through life's experiences. God created you in His image, and He cares about you. You can know His presence and purpose in your life. You don't need to live in fear and worry. You only need to trust Him because He is trustworthy!

Prayer for the Day: *Lord, life is unpredictable. Just when I think I have it all planned out, it throws me a curve ball. I'm glad I have You to trust in so that I don't lose hope.*

Day 50

YET WILL I TRUST

President John F. Kennedy wrote in his book *Profiles in Courage*, "Great crises produce great men and great deeds of courage." How do we respond when we face a great crisis? As Christians, how does our faith change how we respond to a great crisis?

One of the most well-known stories in the Bible is the story of Job. Job was a godly man who loved his family and was very wealthy and influential. But then tragedy came his way, and he lost everything. Instead of giving up his faith, he declared, "Yet will I trust Him" (Job 13:15 NKJV). He suffered bankruptcy. He faced the death of his children. He battled disease. He had marriage problems as a result of the other troubles. Everything went wrong, but he could say, "Yet will I trust Him!" What can we learn from Job about trusting God?

Trust God in spite of feelings. Job went through the same feelings of confusion, depression, and fear we go through when we suffer a tragedy, but he held on to his faith in God. "Yet will I trust Him" means in spite of my feelings, I will trust Him. Just because we trust God does not mean we are not going to be angry, disappointed, and depressed. It means we are not going to let those feelings control us and destroy us. We can rise above our feelings by our faith.

Trusting God doesn't mean your life is going to be perfect. "Yet" means life brings us both positive and negative: good times and bad times. Faith is not fantasy! We can face the realities of this life and still worship our God because He is with us in bad times as well as good. Faith doesn't always keep us out of the fire, but it always takes us through the fire, so we are refined as pure gold.

Trusting God is a matter of personal conviction based on your experience with God. "Yet will *I* trust Him" is a very personal statement. You cannot hitch a ride on someone else's faith! You must be able to say from your heart, "I will trust Him." No one can do that for you. As you experience God more and more in your life, your personal faith in Him will get stronger so that you can make it through anything life brings your way.

Trust God for a new chapter in your life. The Lord turned things around for Job and gave him twice as much as he had before his troubles. What you are going through right now is not your final chapter. God can turn things around for you just like He did for Job. You need only to look to Him and not let anything keep you from trusting Him.

Prayer for the Day: *Lord, I am at a place in my life where I am experiencing circumstances beyond my control. I have good days of belief and I have bad days of doubt. But, one thing I know, I am Yours and You are mine. So, I will trust You in all of it, knowing You will bring me through.*

Day 51
YOUR OPINION MATTERS

Have you ever had so many people advising you and telling you what they think you should do that you wanted to stand up and say,

"My opinion matters, too"? In fact, your opinion about your life matters most because you are responsible for your life! The two opinions about important decisions are God's and yours.

When making important decisions, start with what God says about it in the Bible. Consult scriptures that relate to the issue you are facing and the decision you are trying to make. Believe what God says about it and obey, and you will prosper! David said, "Your word is a lamp for my feet, a light on my path" (Psalm 119:105).

Then consider your thoughts and feelings about life's issues and decisions. What you think matters! We need to think for ourselves and not let other people do our thinking for us. When I was in high school, as the teacher was teaching on a subject, she used a word I didn't know. So, I raised my hand and asked, "What does that word mean?" She replied, "Do you know what a dictionary is? I want you to look up that word so that you will know what it means." That may sound rude to you, and maybe it was, but it taught me how to look up things for myself and how to think for myself. She also knew if I took time to look up the definition of the word, I would probably remember it because I had to work at it.

When Job was suffering, his friends had many views about his condition. He finally got frustrated listening to their analysis of his problems. He stood up for himself and told them, "What you know, I also know; I am not inferior to you" (Job 13:2). I am not saying not to listen to the counsel of others—we should. However, you also need to listen to your own heart and make your own decisions. After all, it is your life and it is up to you and to God how you choose to live it. Your opinion matters, so be true to yourself and true to the Word of God.

Prayer for the Day: *Lord, I have many highly opinionated people in my life who constantly give me their well-meaning advice. But, in the end, it's just You and me! Please give me wisdom to make good decisions based on Your plan for my life! I praise and thank You.*

Day 52

UNFAILING LOVE

One of the greatest challenges we face is living by faith instead of our feelings. This is especially true when we are going through difficult times. It is easy to feel as though God doesn't love us, that He has forgotten us or even forsaken us.

David battled such feelings when going through a tough time in Psalm 13. We don't know what the specific problem was he was facing, but he was defeated by his emotions. Four times he asked God, "How long?" We have all asked that question when dealing with personal problems, financial difficulty, sickness, marital stress, problems with our kids, or stress at work. *How long, O Lord, will this go on? Give me a break from these problems!* Then David proclaimed, "But I will trust in your unfailing love" (Psalm 13:5).

The only way to overcome the feelings of depression, hopelessness, fear, and the thoughts that God has forsaken you or forgotten about you is to trust His unfailing love. God's love is the focus of our trust. The Hebrew word *love (hesed)* combines three virtues into one: love, strength, and steadfastness. God's love is strong and powerful, enduring to the end. *Hesed* is translated as "loyal love, covenant love, steadfast love, loving-kindness, and tender mercies." When you trust in His unfailing love, you can say with the psalmist the rest of this psalm: "My heart rejoices in your salvation. I will sing the Lord's praise, for he has been good to me" (Psalm 13:5-6).

The Christian hymn "The Love of God" was written by three men over nearly one thousand years. The first lines of the hymn were written by Rabbi Mayer, who, in 1096, wrote a lengthy poem celebrating God's great love. Years later, a patient in an insane asylum was so moved after reflecting on Mayer's words, he wrote a line on the theme of God's love. After he died, his words were discovered. In the late 1890s, a pastor named Fred Lehman heard the patient's words quoted by a minister in a sermon. His heart was deeply moved. Twenty years later, Lehman was forced by circumstances into manual labor in California to survive financially. One day he propped up on a lemon box against the wall, sat down, and scribbled out two lines and a chorus to accompany the patient's words:

> Could we with ink the ocean fill
> And were the skies of parchment made
> Were ev'ry stalk on earth a quill
> And ev'ry man a scribe by trade
> To write the love of God above
> Would drain the ocean dry
> Nor could the scroll contain the whole
> Though stretched from sky to sky.
>
> O love of God, how rich and pure!
> How measureless and strong!
> It shall forevermore endure
> The saints' and angels' song.

Prayer for the Day: *Lord, when I ponder Your incredible love for humanity, it gives me great hope. Hope that gives me strength to love others the way You do. I praise and thank You.*

Day 53
WORK, NOT WORKS

The history of the world turns on the axis of great discoveries. Civilization develops to a new level with each new dynamic discovery.

In 1543, Polish astronomer Nicholas Copernicus discovered the sun is a motionless body at the center of the solar system, with the planets revolving around it. In 1664, Isaac Newton discovered the law of gravity.

In the 1860s, Louis Pasteur discovered disease came from microorganisms and bacteria could be killed by heat and disinfectant. His discovery led to vaccinations and pasteurization. Surgeons began to sterilize their hands and instruments. In 1928, Alexander Fleming discovered the first antibiotic, *penicillin*.

On February 28, 1953, James Watson and Francis Crick discovered the structure of DNA. In 1962, they were awarded the Nobel Prize for this discovery that helps us understand diseases and may someday prevent some illnesses like heart disease and cancer.

More recently, the names of Steve Jobs and Bill Gates will remain in history as the key innovators who discovered how to take computer technology and put it in the homes and hands of every person to make our lives easier and more efficient.

The greatest discovery you can make is the discovery Abraham made when he learned to trust God. "What then shall we say that Abraham . . . discovered in this matter? If, in fact, Abraham was justified by works, he had something to boast about—but not before God. What does Scripture say? 'Abraham believed God, and it was credited to him as righteousness.' Now to the one who works, wages are not credited as a gift but as an obligation. However, to the one who does not work but trusts God who justifies the ungodly, their faith is credited as righteousness" (Romans 4:1-5).

Abraham discovered if he trusted God, he would be right in the eyes of God. How can a person be right with God in spite of his sins? By trusting God's grace and power to save him and to forgive him of his sins. God's work of sending His Son Jesus to die for our sins is the basis of our eternal salvation. It is in trusting, not trying, that we are saved and given eternal life. I can truly say today that I trust Jesus and Jesus alone for my salvation.

In 1847, James Simpson discovered the anesthetic properties of chloroform resulted in the saving of untold numbers of lives. It was one of the major breakthroughs of medicine. Someone once asked Simpson what he considered to be his discovery, expecting him to say, "Chloroform." Instead, he said, "My greatest discovery was to know Jesus Christ is my Savior."

Prayer for the Day: *Lord, I have been walking with You for a long time. During our time together, I have learned to stop relying on my own gifts, abilities,* and strength alone, but to trust You! It is only what You accomplished on the cross that enables me to stand before You, a sinner saved by grace. I trust You with my eternal life. I praise and thank You.

Day 54

GET THROUGH IT

Two mountain goats met head to head on a narrow pathway. On one side was a chasm 1,000 feet deep; on the other, a steep cliff rising straight up. There was no room to turn around, and the goats could not back up without falling. What would they do? Finally, instead of fighting for the right to pass, one of the goats knelt down and became as flat as possible. The other goat then walked over him, and they both went on their way safely.

How should we, as Christians, handle conflict in our relationships? How should we handle ridicule, betrayal, false accusation, persecution, or mistreatment? Should we take revenge? Should we harbor resentment? Should we pray for God to judge them? The sufferings of Jesus teach us how to respond to conflict and mistreatment.

We need to follow Jesus' footsteps as He dealt with mistreatment. While our sufferings cannot compare to His, the Apostle Peter tells us to consider the way He handled mistreatment and to follow His example: "To this you were called, because Christ suffered for you, leaving you an example, that you should follow in his steps. 'He committed no sin, and no deceit was found in his mouth.' When they hurled their insults at him, he did not retaliate; when he suffered, he made no threats. Instead, he entrusted himself to him who judges justly" (1 Peter 2:21-23).

The Greek word for *example* (*hupogrammon*) is an outline sketch children use to learn to write letters and draw pictures. We need to copy Jesus' exact response to criticism, rejection, and false accusation.

Instead of lashing out, striking back, and harboring resentment, turn it over to God and trust Him to get you through it. Turn the other cheek. Go the second mile. Love your enemies. Bless those who curse you. You will continue to walk in the favor of God, and you will be blessed if you let it go and keep your faith in Him. Don't try to get even. Get ahead in life by moving on in faith.

Prayer for the Day: *Lord, relationships can be so difficult! Especially when there is conflict. When I try to fix it, I make it worse. So, What would Jesus do? I ask myself. Love them, bless them, and let You work out the rest. I praise and thank You.*

Day 55

BUILD TRUST

Our nation is experiencing a crisis of trust in business, financial, and political institutions and their leaders. Trust is on the decline. But we can always trust in our God, for He is faithful and true. Paul reminds us that the one who "[trusts] in him will never be put to shame" (Romans 9:33).

Author Stephen M. R. Covey, in an article, "How the Best Leaders Build Trust," talks about the financial costs to businesses caused by a lack of employee trust in senior management. There are tangible costs to a lack of trust and tangible benefits to creating an environment of trust. He says trust makes the world go around (*LeadershipNow.com*).

In the same way, there are costs to a lack of trust in God and there are benefits of trusting Him. Build your trust in the wisdom, power, and goodness of God. Trusting God means to depend on Him, to lean on Him, and to roll the weight of your problems and worries on to Him. Listen to how a prophet explained the costs and benefits of trusting the Lord: "Cursed is the one who trusts in man, who draws strength from mere flesh and whose heart turns away from the Lord. That person will be like a bush in the wastelands; they will not see prosperity when it comes" (Jeremiah 17:5-6). The word *cursed* in Hebrew means to forfeit the blessings of God and to experience the consequences of disobedience.

Now for the benefits of trust: "But blessed is the one who trusts in the Lord, whose confidence is in him! They will be like a tree planted by the water. . . . It does not fear when heat comes; its leaves are always green. It has no worries in a year of drought and never fails to bear fruit" (Jeremiah 17:7-8).

If we can trust God with our salvation, we can trust Him with our situation!

Prayer for the Day: *Lord, we live in a world filled with crime and violence, and with people who mislead and lie to us. So, whom can we trust but You! I trust You to care for me, provide for me, protect me, and give me wisdom. I trust You to do the same for my brothers and sisters in Christ. I praise and thank You.*

Day 56

KEEP ON STANDING

On April 18, 1521, Martin Luther faced a religious trial for heresy. He said, "It is neither right nor safe for a man to violate his own conscience. I cannot nor will not recant anything. Here I stand. I cannot do otherwise. God help me. Amen."

How do we respond when our trust in Jesus Christ is put on trial? Are we faithful or faithless? Are we courageous or cowardly? Do we speak up or remain silent? The Old Testament story of Shadrach, Meshach, and Abednego inspires us to trust God when our faith is on trial.

King Nebuchadnezzar, who ruled Babylon, built a massive gold image to honor himself, 90 feet high by 9 feet wide. They held a dedication service for the image of gold. The sound of music summoned all the leaders in his administration and all the people present to fall down and worship King Nebuchadnezzar (Daniel 3:5). The word *fall* reminds me of the saying, "If you don't stand for something, you will fall for anything! That is what the devil said to Jesus, "Bow down and worship me"; but Jesus said, "Worship the Lord, your God, and serve him only" (Matthew 4:9-10). The image of gold violated the law of God that forbids making idols and bowing down to them (Exodus 20:4; 1 John 5:21).

When the music began and everyone fell down, Shadrach, Meshach, and Abednego kept standing! We, too, will face pressure to bow down and conform to the world. But, when others fall down and worship the things of this world, we need to keep standing as witnesses of Jesus Christ as we seek to be His light in the world dispelling the darkness.

Your family and your friends need to see you standing up for what you believe as a living witness that Jesus is the way, the truth, and the life. Others need to see our commitment to Jesus instead of conforming to the pattern of the world. As the Apostle Paul reminds us, we are "letters [from Christ]" that are "known and read by everyone" (2 Corinthians 3:2). We would send emails today instead of letters, but the point is clear—Jesus Christ has sent us out as a witness to others of His saving grace.

The world of Babylon saw the witness of those three Hebrew men when they refused to fall down and worship the image of gold, and it made a difference. At the end of the story, Nebuchadnezzar gives praise to the God of Shadrach, Meshach, and Abednego. So, when the world is bowing down, keep on standing!

Prayer for the Day: *Lord, it's so easy to be silent in an environment where my faith is ridiculed. It's much more difficult to stand up and speak Your truth. But if we are silent, some may never know You and die in their sins. So, I will stand and speak and pray that Your truth will set the captives free. I praise and thank You.*

Day 57

FIGHT BACK

It has been said, "The price of freedom is eternal vigilance." Liberty undefended is liberty lost. So it is spiritually. Just as national freedom has to be defended, so does spiritual freedom. The Apostle Peter said, "Be self-controlled and alert. Your enemy the devil prowls around like a roaring lion looking for someone to devour. Resist him, standing firm in the faith, because you know that the family of believers throughout the world is undergoing the same kind of sufferings" (1 Peter 5:8-9).

You and I face a spiritual enemy. Peter calls him the *devil*, meaning "enemy, adversary," or "opponent." Evil is real, and we battle it every day. We are often tempted to conform to the ungodly standards of the world instead of conforming our lives to the standard of God's Word. The question we need to ask in order to overcome temptation is, "What does the Bible say?" We shouldn't concern ourselves with what talk radio says, or what TV commentators say about the issues of our day. We need to consider what the Bible says about life's issues and live our lives accordingly.

Also, Peter tells us to be self-controlled and alert. We need to be in control of our passions and feelings so we are not misled into spiritual error or even into sin. Peter himself denied Jesus when He was arrested and led to His crucifixion because he was caught off guard. He was spiritually unprepared. He got caught off guard, and he submitted to the temptation of denying Jesus rather than standing up for Him. Don't be ruled by your passions and your emotions. Be ruled by your faith and your commitment to Jesus Christ. We cannot follow every feeling we have, nor can we indulge every passion we have. We need to live disciplined lives so that we can overcome every temptation. It is not what we feel but what we will that is most important in life.

Peter then tells us to "resist" the devil. The gift of faith is free, but to live the faith is a fight! You and I will have to stand our guard and resist the enemy of our souls. *Resist* means to put our foot down and refuse to surrender any ground to the enemy. Don't give into doubt, fear, or temptation; resist the devil.

Your brothers and sisters in Christ are facing the same kinds of struggles you have. Find a battle partner who will stand with you in prayer and encourage you to remain strong in your faith. Put up a fight, and you will win! "Greater is he [the Holy Spirit] who is in you than he [the devil] who is in the world" (1 John 4:4 NASB).

Prayer for the Day: *Lord, I thought when I became a Christian that life would be easy. But I have learned that our journey is a series of battles. Some we win, some we lose. But because of Christ, whose Spirit lives in us, we can wage war against the enemy and fight back. I praise and thank You.*

Day 58

SATISFIED

When we finish a great meal, we often say, "I'm satisfied." We can have spiritual satisfaction. Jesus told a woman who was searching for real fulfillment for her spiritual void, "If you drink of the water I give you, you will never thirst. It will be in you a well of water springing up to eternal life" (see John 4:14). A true relationship with Jesus gives us satisfaction.

Spiritually, I have found all I need in Jesus. We are "complete in him" (see Colossians 2:9). Our spiritual search ends when we meet Jesus Christ. My deepest questions about God, life, and myself are answered in Jesus.

Sadly, people search for satisfaction through religion, philosophy, and mystical spirituality. Hebrews 13:9 says, "Do not be carried away by all kinds of strange teachings. It is good for our hearts to be strengthened by grace, not by eating ceremonial foods, which is of no benefit to those who do so." Why? Because, as verse 8 says, "Jesus Christ is the same yesterday and today and forever." Strange teachings today lead us away from our faith in Jesus and distract us spiritually.

Look out for strange teachings that say Jesus isn't enough. Look out for legalism that depends on ceremony and ritual instead of a relationship with Jesus. When you keep yourself anchored in Jesus, you won't be misled by strange teachings. Jesus is the same day after day. His love never changes. His truth never changes. His Word never changes. Stay close to Him. Listen to His voice. Practice His presence and you will be fully satisfied because you are made complete in Him!

Prayer for the Day: *Lord, I am amazed at the way people search for spiritual satisfaction: ghost hunting, New Age teaching, witchcraft, and even religious history that is devoid of God's truth. My searching ended when I realized You are God and I could have a relationship with You. I am satisfied because You have filled the hole in my heart with Your great love. I praise and thank You.*

Day 59

WHAT REALLY MATTERS

If I were to ask you why God created humankind, what would you say? In a word, God made us for a relationship with Him. This is what Paul means when he says, "I urge you . . . in view of God's mercy, to offer your bodies as a living sacrifice, holy and pleasing to God—this is your true and proper worship" (Romans 12:1). True worship is experiencing the presence of God. We innately worship God. Augustine called it a God-shaped hole within us. He wrote the prayer, "Our hearts were made for You, O God, and they will not rest until they rest in You." We naturally long for a relationship with the God who made us, but sin has ruined that relationship. Jesus came to forgive our sins and restore our relationship to God.

What is worship, and what does it matter? *Worship* means "worth-ship." It means to give God honor and glory because He is our Creator, Father, Savior, and Provider. William Temple, the renowned archbishop of Canterbury, said *worship* is "quickening the conscience by the holiness of God, feeding the mind with the truth of God, purging the imagination by the beauty of God, opening the heart to the love of God, and devoting the will to the purpose of God."

The most frequent words (*saha*, Hebrew; and *proskyneo*, Greek) used in the Bible for *worship* mean "to fall prostrate" or "to bow down." "Come let us bow down in worship, let us kneel before the Lord our Maker; for he is our God and we are the people of his pasture" (Psalm 95:6-7).

Personally, I define *worship* as our response of love to the love of God. We don't worship to get God to do something for us; we worship Him for who He is and for what He has already done for us! We don't worship God to get Him to bless us; we worship Him because He has blessed us! "We love [Him] because he first loved us" (1 John 4:19). The more aware we are of His love, the more we will express our love to Him. Worship doesn't initiate anything; it is the natural response of love and thanksgiving we have in our hearts because of God's great love for us.

"When the praises go up, the glory comes down" is bad theology. The truth is: When the glory comes down, the worship goes up! Jesus said, "Freely you have received; freely give" (Matthew 10:8). That is exactly why Paul said "in view of God's mercy," offer yourself to God in spiritual worship. Take time right now to give God praise for His love, mercy, and blessings, for He alone is worthy of our praise.

Prayer for the Day: *Lord, I want You to know how grateful I am for what You did on Calvary; giving up Your life so I would have the opportunity to know and love You. I worship You with my whole heart. I praise and thank You.*

Day 60

FADED GLORY

One day Moses met with God on the mountain. "Show me Your glory," Moses said to the Lord. God hid him in a cleft in the rock and caused His glory to pass by him. Moses saw the back side of God as He walked past him. The glory and light of God's presence was so brilliant that it left a glow on Moses' face. When he came down the mountain to share his experience with God, the people were afraid of the effects of the divine radiance on Moses' face. The Israelites were like a lot of people today who are afraid of God because they don't know He loves them. But "perfect love drives out fear" (1 John 4:18).

Because they were afraid, Moses put a veil over his face so they could not see God's radiance on his face. The first lesson of this story is that the radiance of Moses was associated with the giving of the Law that was to fade over time until the fullness of grace came in Jesus Christ. "If the ministry that [condemns men is] glorious, how much more glorious is the ministry that brings righteousness? . . . And if what was [fading away] came with glory, how much greater is the glory of that which lasts!" (2 Corinthians 3:9, 11).

Over time, however, the glory on Moses' face faded. But he kept the veil on! We, too, may experience the effects of God's presence; but if we don't stay in His presence, the glory fades. Do we hide the fact that the glory has faded, or do we return to the presence of God to see Him again? Do we have a temporary experience with God and then go our own way, or do we live in His presence every day?

Worship is the place where we experience the glory of God. So, "We are not like Moses, who would put a veil over his face [while the radiance was fading] away.... And we all, who with unveiled faces contemplate the Lord's glory, are being transformed into his image with ever-increasing glory, which comes from the Lord, who is the Spirit" (2 Corinthians 3:13, 18).

The age of the customs and ceremonies of the Law were designed by God for a season until Jesus Christ came. "Christ is the culmination of the law so that there may be righteousness for everyone who believes" (Romans 10:4). In the Old Testament they had the temporary glory of the Law; we now have the permanent glory of grace. As we worship the Lord, we reflect His glory. Instead of fading away, the glory of God can increase in our lives as we are transformed into His likeness. The word *reflect* in the Greek language also means to "contemplate" or "look at." As we keep our minds and hearts focused on the Lord in worship, we reflect His likeness with ever-increasing glory!

Prayer for the Day: *Lord, there is nothing more sacred to me than to be in Your presence. Not only on Sundays in Your sanctuary, but daily as I read Your Word and grow in Your grace and knowledge. I praise and thank You.*

Day 61

COST VERSUS DIVIDENDS

Keeping the peace in our relationships comes at a high price, but it pays rich dividends. When you sow seeds of peace, it is like putting money in wise investment that will later give you a great return. The Word of God instructs us to "make every effort to keep the unity of the Spirit through the bond of peace" (Ephesians 4:3). Getting along with others requires us to make *every* effort. Not some effort . . . not our best effort . . . not an occasional effort . . . but every effort! And they have to make every effort to get along with us—let us not forget that as well.

We must work hard at keeping the unity of the Spirit. The Holy Spirit, who lives in our heart, desires us to live in unity with others. God is not pleased with the bickering, fighting, striving, competing, undermining, complaining, and manipulating that often goes on in our relationships. The Lord calls us to make every effort to keep the unity of the Spirit in our relationships and, yes, it takes every effort to do so.

Unity comes through the bond of peace. The word *bond* refers to glue, adhesive, or cement. When we practice peace by loving others, overlooking their faults and forgiving them, we provide the adhesive that holds our relationships together. "Blessed are the peacemakers," Jesus said (Matthew 5:9). Peacemakers often sacrifice their own agenda for the good of their relationships. Our relationships have more to do with our success in life than anything else.

Are you struggling with some difficult people today? Do you have a strained relationship with someone? Then go out of your way to make every effort to live in unity and keep peace with them. It will cost you hard work, but it will be worth it in the end.

Prayer for the Day: *Lord, I guess I've become a bit of a peacekeeper. Over the years, You've taught me how to love when it was hard, to forgive when it was painful, and to make the most of every opportunity and use my words wisely instead of making my feelings known. You've allowed me to see people through Your eyes, and that has made all the difference. I praise and thank You.*

Day 62

UNWORTHY SERVANT

On a visit to the Beethoven museum in Bonn, a young student was fascinated by the piano on which Beethoven had composed some of his greatest works. She asked the museum guard if she could play a few bars on it; she accompanied the request with a lavish tip, so the guard agreed. The girl went to the piano and tinkled out the opening of "Moonlight Sonata." As she was leaving, she said to the guard, "I suppose all the great pianists who come here want to play on that piano." The guard shook his head no. "Padarewski [the famed Polish pianist] was here a few years ago, and he said he wasn't worthy to touch it."

Attitude is everything. Pride is an attitude that will ruin our relationships and rob us of our potential. "Pride goes before destruction, a haughty spirit before a fall" (Proverbs 16:18). Jesus taught His disciples to be on their guard against pride. "When you have done everything you were told to do, [you] should say, 'We are unworthy servants; we have only done our duty'" (Luke 17:10).

Why did He teach them the importance of this attitude? The apostles could have felt entitled or better than other people because of their high calling (Mark 3:13-15). They had a special relationship with Jesus that others did not have. They were given authority (Luke 10:17). They had a unique commission: The word *apostle* means "one sent with a special mission." There were only twelve apostles; the early church followed their lead after Jesus returned to Heaven (Acts 2:42).

Although the apostles were given such positions of leadership, Jesus said they should only say, "We are unworthy servants." When people try to praise you, say, "I am an unworthy servant." When people look up to you, say, "I am an unworthy servant." When people try to follow you, say, "I am an unworthy servant." When people try to put you up on a pedestal, say, "I am an unworthy servant." When people tell you how great you are, say, "I am an unworthy servant."

Three words need unpacking. *Unworthy* does not mean "worthless"; it means to know all you have is from God. It means not to take praise that belongs to God. It is proper to give honor to others and to encourage others. The word *servant* in Greek means a bond-servant—one who serves out of love, not out of obligation. We focus on leading, but Jesus focused on serving. Finally, the Greek word for *duty* also means "debt"— that which is owed. The best you can do is your duty; it's not to win great accolades.

When Harry Truman was thrust into the presidency by the death of President Roosevelt, a friend took him aside and gave him some sound advice: "From here on out, you're going to have lots of people around you. They'll try to put up a wall around you and cut you off from any ideas but theirs. They'll tell you what a great man you are, Harry. But you and I both know you ain't."

Prayer for the Day: *Lord, I am so grateful for all the gifts and abilities You have given me. I am also thankful that You have provided a church home where I can use them. I am honored to be called Your servant. I praise and thank You.*

Day 63
HOLD ON TO HOPE

Have you ever had something important or valuable and you told yourself you better hang on to it? Or, you may have said to someone, "You need to hang on to that!"

One of the greatest treasures you will ever have is *hope*. You need to hang on to hope. The power of hope that comes from God will get you through any difficulty you are facing. We often lose our battles because we give up. We give in to feelings of fear, helplessness, and despair. We tell ourselves such negative things as, "It won't get any better," "It's time to quit," or "Things will never change."

According to Dr. Snyder in *Handbook of Hope*, three elements are necessary for people to maintain a hopeful position in life: (1) We need to have a goal; (2) We need to believe we can attain the goal; and (3) We need to see a way to reach the goal.

Hope is the power of expectation based on the promises and power of God. The writer of Hebrews encourages us: "Let us hold unswervingly to the hope we profess, for he who promised is faithful" (10:23).

It is a terrible feeling when you feel like you are trapped and have no options. A guy came home depressed from the doctor's office. "What's the matter?" his wife asked.

He replied, "The doctor says I have to take one of these white pills every day for the rest of my life."

She then asked, "And what's so bad about that?"

He replied, "He only gave me seven pills!"

Why should we have hope? Because we have a relationship with the living God! Before we received Jesus Christ as Savior, we were "without hope and without God in the world" (Ephesians 2:12). Let that phrase sink in—*without hope and without God in this world.* That is where people live who don't have a relationship with the Lord. They live every day struggling to make sense out of life. They wonder how they are going to cope with the pressures of life. They feel like their problems are hopeless and unsolvable. But with God, we have hope because with God all things are possible. The world without God has a false hope—mere wishful thinking. But with God in our lives, we have true hope because we have His promises and His power. We have something to base our hope on. So, let us hold on to hope today because God "who promised is faithful" (Hebrews 10:23).

Prayer for the Day: *Lord, things have been tough lately. I have even thought of giving up. But, when I think back on all the ways You have provided for me, my hope rises up again. I believe in You to get me through. I praise and thank You.*

Day 64
GRATEFUL FOR GRACE

The longer we follow Jesus Christ as Lord, the more aware we become of His amazing grace. With that awareness, we grow more grateful for His grace. Grace means to give freely. Grace is God's unconditional love. Grace means our eternal salvation is based on His atonement, not our actions. All that we enjoy spiritually is a gift from God. "Not by works, so that no one can boast" (Ephesians 2:9). We move from self-sufficiency to Christ-sufficiency the more aware we become of His grace.

Humility means being totally dependent on God's grace. We can see the Apostle Paul's humility and reliance on God's grace in his writings. In his first letter, he introduced himself as "Paul an apostle" (Galatians 1:1). Later, at the height of his ministry, he wrote, "I am the least of the apostles" (1 Corinthians 15:9). During Paul's first Roman imprisonment, he wrote, "I am less than the least of all God's people" (Ephesians 3:8). In his last letters, shortly before his execution by Emperor Nero, Paul said, "I am the worst [of sinners]" (1 Timothy 1:15). The next time you feel like the worst of sinners, get your mind off your failures and get it on God's faithfulness!

Paul wasn't suffering from low self-esteem when he called himself the worst of sinners. He was coming to terms with the amazing grace of God. His testimony was simple: "By the grace of God I am what I am" (1 Corinthians 15:10). As the years passed, he became more deeply aware of his own inadequacy yet more confident of the sufficiency of Jesus in his life. He even wrote, "Christ is all" (see Colossians 3:4). On one hand, he said, "I am nothing." Yet, he claimed, "I can do all [things] through [Christ] who gives me strength" (Philippians 4:13).

It has been said the gate of Heaven is so low that no one can enter it except upon his or her knees.

Prayer for the Day: *Lord, "Amazing Grace, how sweet the sound that saved a wretch like me, I once was lost but now I'm found, was blind but now I see." I am nothing; Christ is everything. I am grateful for Your grace. I praise and thank You.*

Day 65
PURSUE HAPPINESS

In the year 2000, fifty books were published on the subject of happiness. In 2008, four thousand books were published on happiness. It seems we are chasing happiness these days with greater passion (*Psychology Today*, 2009). In 2020, new books on happiness included *The Art of Happiness* and *Perfect Happiness*. Even the Declaration of Independence states we have been "endowed with certain unalienable rights, that among these are Life, Liberty, and the pursuit of Happiness." To be *happy* means to be "content, satisfied, and pleased with one's place in life." There are two sides of the coin of happiness—positive emotions and satisfaction in life.

Several years ago, James Montier, a "global equity strategist," took a break from investing in order to publish a brief overview of existing research into the psychology of happiness. Montier learned happiness comes from three sources. First, about 50 percent of happiness comes from genetics—some of us are more naturally happy, cheerful, and optimistic than others. Second, about 10 percent of happiness comes from our circumstances. Our age, ethnicity, gender, experiences, and wealth only make up a tenth of our happiness. Finally, 40 percent of our happiness is based on choice, or what he calls "intentional activity."

Although we cannot control our genetics or all our circumstances, we can control our choices. Are you making wise choices in your life that will lead you to happiness? This is what the psalmist means when he writes: "Blessed [happy] is the one who does not walk in step with the wicked or stand in the way that sinners take or sit in the company of mockers, but whose delight is in the law of the Lord. . . . Whatever they do prospers" (Psalm 1:1-3).

When "the law of the Lord"—the Word of God as we have it in the Bible—is the source of our thoughts and actions, we will live according to the will of God, and that will always lead us to happiness.

Prayer for the Day: *Lord, thank You for helping me to understand that happiness is more than money, beauty, and success. Happiness is based on my ability to make wise choices and be content in life where I am right now. I praise and thank You.*

Day 66
THE POTTER'S HAND

Julie Gold wrote a popular song that says, "God is watching us from a distance." Nothing could be further from the truth! God is present and active in our lives. We all want to know how God works in our lives. What does He do? How does He involve Himself? In what ways does God "work together all things for our good" (see Romans 8:28)?

The relationship of the potter and the clay helps us understand how God works in us. "You, Lord, are our Father. We are the clay, you are the potter; we are all the work of your hand" (Isaiah 64:8). "Does not the potter have the right to make out of the same lump of clay some pottery for special purposes and some for common use?" (Romans 9:21). "We have this treasure in jars of clay to show that this all-surpassing power is from God and not from us" (2 Corinthians 4:7).

The potter chooses the clay. The clay has no part in its selection. Jesus said, "You did not choose me, but I chose you" (John 15:16). Paul wrote, "For [God] chose us in [Christ] before the creation of the world" (Ephesians 1:4). The potter sees the potential of the raw clay. The potter is an artist. He sees beyond the lump of clay to the finished product. The potter is the epitome of hope. The potter knows the shapeless lump of clay will eventually emerge as a useful vessel if it endures the long, tedious process of preparation. Clay is cheap, simple material, but the potter sees its potential to be a vessel of honor. We too are made from clay (Genesis 2:7). We are common but endowed with great potential. God looks beyond our fault and sees our potential. He looks beyond where we are to what we can become.

Once the clay has been chosen, it is now in the hand of the potter. The only job of the clay is to yield to the will of the potter. The potter will break the clay, remove stones and foreign particles, soften it with water to make it pliable, and let it rest in an air-tight container sitting in water for months, or even years. When it's conditioned, he will take it out of its state of rest, put it on the wheel, spin it around and around as he shapes it by the pressure of his hands, and paint and carve beautiful figures on the pot. But he's not finished. Finally, he puts his work in the kiln, where the fire completes the finishing touches. The fire causes the painted images to radiate with brilliant colors and makes the clay strong so it can be useful.

That is how God works in us. Like a potter, He is breaking us, removing things unlike Him, softening our wills, applying pressure as He forms us, bringing beauty as He molds our character, and putting us through the fire to make us strong. And what do we do in this process? One thing and only one thing—yield to the will of the Potter. The biggest struggle we all face is yielding to the will of God. If we yield to Him, He will do the rest!

Prayer for the Day: *Lord, the story of the potter and the clay has always baffled me since I am not very artistic. But I believe I understand the wisdom behind the metaphor. You are the Creator and I am the work of Your hands. If I yield to Your will, You will complete me and use me. I praise and thank You.*

Day 67

GO FORWARD

As I was reading the Book of Jeremiah, I was struck with God's word to Israel when the people were following false gods. The Lord said, "They went backward and not forward" (Jeremiah 7:24b). If we follow worldly values instead of Biblical virtues, we will always go backward in life.

Why were they going backward in the relationship to the Lord? Because they were living in idolatry and immorality, ignoring the prophets He sent, and "did not listen or pay attention" to the word of God (Jeremiah 7:24a). In verse 28, God says, "This is the nation that has not obeyed the Lord its God or responded to correction. Truth has perished; it has vanished from their lips."

Sounds like our times, doesn't it? Truth has certainly vanished from our lips. Truth has been silenced for politically correct speech. Yet, Jesus said, "The truth will set you free" (John 8:32). We all need to listen to and live by the truth given in the Bible, even though we may not want to hear it. If we don't, we will be like the people of Jeremiah's day, when God said, "They [are] harming themselves, to their own shame" (Jeremiah 7:19).

Let us go forward, not backward, in our faith as we follow the Lord with all our heart!

Prayer for the Day: *Father, help me today to go forward in my spiritual life. Protect me from the wrong influences that try to drag me away from You. I desire above all things to do Your will, to please You, and to live worthy of Your calling on my life.*

Day 68

GOD'S WILL

When I was a teenager, I began having an interest in knowing God's will for my life. I heard ministers and youth leaders talk about it, but the way they described it made me think it was difficult to know and easy to miss. They talked of the "perfect" will of God and His "permissive" will, so if you missed His perfect will, you were stuck with a somewhat less desirable life in His permissive will. My mother had a paperback book titled *God's Will for Your Life*. In it, I read a statement that continues to make an impression on me: "Inside the will of God there is no failure. Outside the will of God there is no success."

We need to understand how the term "the will of God" is used in Scripture. The will of God is about big things, not small things. The will of God is about God's purposes, not every specific detail of our life. God never intended to micromanage every detail of our life. Creation was the will of God. "You created all things, and by your will they were created" (Revelation 4:11). The cross was the will of God. Jesus prayed, "Not as I will, but as you will" (Matthew 26:39). The will of God is that every person is saved from his or her sins through faith in Jesus Christ. "[God is] not willing that any should perish, but that all should come to repentance" (2 Peter 3:9 KJV).

The will of God, for the most part, is the same for all of us. His will is that we live according to His Word, as He created us to live in right relationship to Him and to others. It is God's will for us not to be "conform[ed] to the pattern of this world" (Romans 12:2), to not be "unwise but . . . wise" (Ephesians 5:15), to live holy (1 Thessalonians 4:3), to be thankful at all times (1 Thessalonians 5:18), and not to be governed by "the lust of the flesh, the lust of the eyes, and the pride of life" (1 John 2:15-17). That is what we might call the *general* will of God that applies to everyone.

God also has a *specific* will for every person's life. That doesn't mean every detail of your life is preordained and you have to spend your life in fear trying to find it. You are free to make your own decisions as long as they glorify God and as long as you submit your plans to His will. But He does have a plan for your life, and the first step in knowing God's will is to desire it. Do you want to know God's will? I didn't ask if you were willing to do it but, rather, do you want to know God's will? Or, would you rather have the Lord stay out of your affairs and let you do your own thing? I trust that, as a child of God, you desire His will.

So, make this your prayer: "I desire to do your will, my God; your law is within my heart" (Psalm 40:8). David prayed that he would desire to do God's will because the Word of God was in His heart. He knew God had a will and plan for His life. When you come to important life decisions, pause and pray, "If it is the Lord's will" (James 4:15). Wait on the Lord to give a sense of inner peace that you are making a wise decision in line with His will for your life.

Prayer for the Day: *Lord, it is amazing to think that You have a plan and purpose for my life. That if I have a desire to do Your will and get to know You better through Your Word, You will direct my life. I praise and thank You.*

Day 69

OVERWHELMED

I was sitting at Starbucks one day and noticed a guy with two books to read: *Learn the Bible in 24 Hours* and *Ultimate Fighting Techniques*. What a combination! The Bible gives ultimate fighting techniques for the spiritual battles we face. Revelation 12:7 says, "War broke out in heaven." When there is war in the heavenly realm, there is conflict in the natural realm.

We live in a world of evil. The Lord's Prayer says, "Deliver us from the evil one" (Matthew 6:13). In his letter to the Ephesian believers, Paul said, "Put on the full armor of God, so that when the day of evil comes, you may be able to stand your ground, and after you have done everything, to stand" (Ephesians 6:13).

One of the most fascinating books ever written is the Book of Revelation. It was written nearly 1,900 years ago by the Apostle John.

Still today it inspires best-selling novels and movies. It tells us the drama of future history and assures us Jesus Christ will return at the end of this age.

Why was the Revelation of Jesus Christ given? It was written to encourage the people of God to be faithful to the Lord Jesus during difficult times: "This calls for patient endurance and faithfulness on the part of God's people" (Revelation 13:10).

A spiritual war rages, and we need to be faithful. We need to fight the good fight of faith. We need to be true to our faith. We need to be the light of the world to dispel the darkness. Even in our personal battles, we need to fight them with faith and know that we can overcome.

Christians are called "overcomers" by John in his writings. He tells us, "Everyone born of God overcomes the world. This is the victory that has overcome the world, even our faith" (1 John 5:4).

By faith, we can overcome deception, discouragement, temptation, and difficulties. We don't shrink from stress. We don't shrink from a challenge. We don't shrink from our fears. We don't shrink from threats. We have a commitment to Jesus to the end.

Hebrews 10:39—11:1 tells us, "But we [are not of] those who shrink back and are destroyed, but [of] those who have faith and are saved. Now faith is confidence in what we hope for and assurance about what we do not see."

Because we believe the promises of God, we can face every challenge and stand up instead of backing down. We can overcome instead of getting overwhelmed because we know "if God is for us, who can be against us?" (Romans 8:31).

Prayer for the Day: *Lord, life can really be overwhelming. Just the day-to-day challenges we face can sometimes do us in! I'm so glad to have You in my life and I am grateful for the strength and wisdom You give me just when I need it. I praise and thank You.*

Day 70

GIVE IT UP

Give up the right to be angry, bitter, and resentful. Stop punishing people. That is what Ephesians 4:31 says: "Get rid of all bitterness, rage and anger, brawling and slander, along with every form of malice." I talked to someone once who was angry because some family members had cheated her out of some of the family inheritance. She had been angry for several years and was considering legal action. I suggested that she forgive them and get past her anger and resentment (regardless of what she did about the money). She emphatically told me, "I have the right to feel this way!" I replied, "No you don't—not if you're a Christian." We surrender our rights to Jesus as Lord. He commands to forgive. The Scripture teaches us to "get rid of all bitterness."

I was talking to a friend one day about the need to get over hurtful experiences. He said to get over it before it happens! In other words, you need to know things are going to go wrong and you're going to get hurt in life. You must decide now that you are going to get over it and not stay stuck in that place of hurt, anger, and resentment. The people of Edom did not come to Israel's rescue when they were attacked and destroyed by war because they "harbored an ancient hostility" (Ezekiel 35:5). Don't keep stirring the pot. Let it go.

James A. Garfield was president of the United States for less than four months when he was shot in the back on July 2, 1881. While he remained conscious, the doctor probed the wound with his little finger, searching unsuccessfully for the bullet. Over the course of the summer, a team of doctors tried to locate the bullet. The president clung to life through July and August, but in September he died. He didn't die from the gunshot wound but from infection. The constant probing of the wound ultimately killed him. So it is with our hurts. The more we probe the past wounds, the more infection spreads throughout our souls and poisons our relationships.

Let's stop probing our emotional wounds and relationship wounds and let them heal.

Prayer for the Day: *Lord, relationships can be so wonderful and yet so difficult. I know we all get angry. I also know people will hurt us and we will hurt those whom we love. One thing I have learned is to forgive and move forward, to get rid of all anger and strife and seek peace. Life is too short to stay angry.*

Day 71

YES!

The Bible is the most amazing book ever written in the history of the world. It is the inspired, infallible, and inerrant word of God.

According to statistics from Wycliffe International, nearly 170,000 Bibles are sold or given away in the U.S. every day! The Bible can be read aloud in 70 hours. It contains 1,189 chapters, 6,468 commands, 3,268 verses of fulfilled prophecy, and 3,294 questions. More importantly, the Bible contains 3,500 promises!

A promise is an assurance by one person to another. A promise is the reasonable ground upon which we expect something to be done. The promises of God are the foundation of our faith. "For no matter how many promises God has made, they are 'Yes' in Christ" (2 Corinthians 1:20).

We have all been disappointed by broken promises. "Daddy, do all fairy tales begin with the words, 'Once upon a time'?" The little girl asked. "No," he replied. "A whole lot of them begin with the words 'If elected, I promise.'"

God never breaks His promise. His promises are always "yes in Christ." What does this mean? First, it means God gives the promises. They are based on the character of God, who is faithful and true—the One "who does not lie" (Titus 1:2). "It is impossible for God to lie" (Hebrews 6:18). "For he who promised is faithful" (Hebrews 10:23).

Second, "yes in Christ" means Jesus guarantees the promise. Spiritual promises are grounded in the ministry of Jesus Christ for the salvation for our sins. I know I am forgiven because Christ died for my sins. I know I have eternal life because He rose again. I know I am saved because He promised eternal life. I know I am reconciled to God because He made peace through the cross. I know I can come to God with confidence because He lives to make intercession for me. I know I can do all things because He strengthens me. I know I can make it through life's difficulties because His grace is sufficient. I know I can survive hard times because He will supply all my needs according to His riches in glory.

The promises are yes to me because I believe in Him. The phrase "in Christ" appears 172 times in Paul's writings to speak our relationship to Him. "If anyone is in Christ, he is a new creation" (2 Corinthians 5:17 NKJV). As the song writer said, "My faith is built on nothing less than Jesus' blood and righteousness. I dare not trust the strongest frame but wholly lean on Jesus' name! On Christ the solid rock I stand, all other ground is sinking sand."

Prayer for the Day: *Lord, I have learned over the years to never make a promise. Why? Because if I'm unable to keep it, I don't want to let anyone down. It is good to know that You are the promise-keeper and that You never let anyone down! You can be trusted to fulfill Your word.*

Day 72

SET YOUR FOOT

We live in a world of broken promises. God gives us promises that never fail. "Not one word has failed of all [His] good promises" (1 Kings 8:56). When you face problems, get a promise of God in the Bible. Keep your thoughts on the promise, not the problem.

God's promises need to be possessed. It feels great when someone says to us, "I promise." We know we can count on them. But, just because God makes a promise to us does not necessarily mean we are going to receive it. There is a difference between having a promise and possessing a promise. Some of God's promises are conditional on us. We have a part to play.

When Joshua led Israel into the Promised Land, God told him: "I will give you every place where you set your foot, as I promised Moses" (Joshua 1:3). Some of God's promises come with a prescription. We all want God to provide for us, but, like Joshua, we must set our foot. That means taking action. Remember, "Faith by itself, if it is not accompanied by action, is dead" (James 2:17).

Joshua and the people of Israel could claim their inheritance and possess the land if, and only if, they set their foot on it. Our feet represent direction, action, and movement. Our feet take us everywhere we can possibly go. They had to get moving and take the land. Every promise has to be possessed. Many of the promises of God never come to pass because we don't do what is necessary on our part to possess the promises. God gave the people the land, but they had to possess it.

We need to believe the promises of God. We also need to act on what we believe and do what is required on our part. We, too, must set our feet on the promise for it to be a reality. Real faith is active, not passive. Real faith gets moving; it does not sit around and wait for God to do everything. God gives the promise, but we must possess it by taking action. Set your foot and get moving!

Prayer for the Day: *Lord, I am glad to know that I have a part in seeing Your promises fulfilled in my life. I am not a robot, I am a person made in Your image. I can determine my own destiny. I have decided to do what is necessary in order to possess Your promises.*

Day 73

FAITH WALK

Bill Irwin, with his seeing-eye dog named Orient, is the only blind person to have completed the 2,168-mile Appalachian Trail. His historic hike began in Georgia and ended almost nine months later in north central Maine. This amazing odyssey was the single most publicized human endeavor that year, and an inspiring example of overcoming the odds for all! He walked by faith, not by sight, being led by the guidance of his companion. We walk (or live) by faith, not by sight, being led by the guidance of the Holy Spirit and the Word of God.

The phrase *by faith* best describes the Christian life. Everyone has faith at some level and in something. God has given us "the measure of faith" (Romans 12:3 KJV). We need the right faith. Paul means faith in God and in Jesus Christ as Lord. Christians are called *believers*. Faith is belief, trust and confidence. Faith is more than a *feeling*, measuring our relationship to God by how we feel. Faith is more than a *force* by which we control people and circumstances. Faith is more than *functions*, a set of religious activities. Faith is more than *facts*, mere intellectual agreement to Christian truth. Faith is not *fantasy*, living in denial of reality. Faith is not blind, but it is based on the fact of God's existence, that Jesus Christ is real, and His Word is trustworthy.

Some people have symbols of faith but no substance. They practice religious rituals, but they have no relationship with the Lord. While teaching children about world religions, a teacher asked her students to bring a symbol of their family's faith to class. The next day the kids got up and made their presentation. The first child said, "I'm Muslim, and this is a prayer rug." Next, a little boy said, "I'm Jewish, and this is a Star of David." Another girl said, "I'm Catholic, and this is my Mom's rosary." Finally, a little boy said, "I'm a Baptist, and this is a casserole."

"We live by faith, not by sight" (2 Corinthians 5:7). The Greek word for *live* is "walk" and means to live the entire sphere of one's life in faith. My relationship to God shapes everything about my life. Faith influences every aspect of life. When we live or walk by faith, every area of our life is influenced by our relationship to the Lord. We are Christian in every area of life. Faith informs every decision we make. We ask for God's guidance when we face important decisions. Faith inspires every challenge we face. By faith, we overcome anxiety, depression, circumstances, temptation, and stress. "Greater is He who is in [us] than he who is in the world" (1 John 4:4 NASB).

Prayer for the Day: *Lord, it can be difficult walking by faith when we live in such a visual world. When trying times come, I have learned to close my eyes and say, "I live by faith, not by sight." In other words, regardless of what I see around me, I trust God to take care of me.*

Day 74

NOT BY SIGHT

We need to "live by faith, not by sight" (2 Corinthians 5:7). Sight is a wonderful gift of God, but our sight is limited. We cannot live by faith and live by sight at the same time. We must choose one or the other. It is important to know what you believe and what you do not believe—how you live and how you do not live. We cannot do both.

Faith sees spiritually, not just naturally. We have spiritual eyes as well as natural eyes. When we live "not by sight," we look beyond the problem to the promise! We look beyond the present to the future! We look beyond the temporary to the eternal! "So we fix our eyes not on what is seen, but on what is unseen, since what is seen is temporary, but what is unseen is eternal" (2 Corinthians 4:18). We need to "fix our eyes" on what is permanent, not what is temporary. Every situation you are going through today is temporary. Nothing in this world will last. Get the focus of your life on the things that will last instead of being overly worried about the things that will change over time and pass away.

There are reasons we are to live "not by sight" (5:7). First, sight is limited. Many things in our world cannot be seen. We cannot see air, but we breathe it. We cannot see atoms, yet they are the building blocks of life. We cannot see electricity, but we use it. We cannot see X-rays, but they can save our life. We cannot see radio waves, but we enjoy the radio. We cannot see the internet and cell-phone signals, yet we enjoy global communications. The person who says "I only believe what I can see" is foolish. We draw the wrong conclusions about things, circumstances, and even people when we look at them only with sight. That is why Jesus said, "Stop judging by mere appearances" (John 7:24).

Whatever problem or challenge or opportunity you are facing today, don't be limited by what you see at the moment. Things change over time. Look past the problem to the promise of God. Look at it from a spiritual view, not just a natural view. Look past what is going on to what can go on by faith. If we live by faith, we have to give up living by sight.

Prayer for the Day: *Lord, help me today to look past what I see to what the future holds in You! Help me to remember that my situation is only temporary, but You are eternal and You have my life in Your hands.*

Day 75

CAN YOU SEE?

As we consider what it means to "live by faith, not by sight" (2 Corinthians 5:7), there are two more reasons why we cannot trust everything we see naturally. The second reason we live "not by sight" is because sight can be misleading. God told the prophet Samuel, "People look at the outward appearance, but the Lord looks at the heart" (1 Samuel 16:7). We look at the outward appearance of everything and often draw the wrong conclusions about what we see. Magicians use sleight of hand to convince their audience that magic is real. Also, charlatans rip people off for money every day with investment schemes because people are misled by what they see.

Finally, sight is subjective. When people witness an accident and give a report, there are conflicting stories because the eyewitnesses mentally interpret what they saw. They are called "eyewitnesses," yet their eyes cannot be trusted because they interpret what they saw and that interpretation is unique to people. Several people can witness the same traffic accident and yet interpret differently what took place. One of my favorite stories in Jesus' ministry is His conversation with the woman at the well. He told His disciples, "Open your eyes," look at things differently (John 4:35).

George Washington Carver was a devout Christian. He maintained daily devotions, usually beginning his prayer with the word *Behold!* He said to himself, "Behold! What will God show me?" It was his way of opening his mind to God's Word and to his world. One day he was holding a sweet potato. God said to him, "Behold! What can you do with it?" Today, at the Tuskegee Institute in Alabama, you can see samples of the 118 things Dr. Carver did with the sweet potato. He saw the creation from a new perspective and, in doing so, unlocked some of God's secrets. Now when I look at a sweet potato, all I see is butter and cinnamon! But he saw more because his mind was opened to new possibilities.

So, live by your faith in God. Make a decision to live "not by sight." There is more going on in your world and in your situations than what you can see with your natural eyes and what is going on in the present. "Open your eyes" spiritually and ask God to help you see things from a different perspective. You will make better decisions when you look at things spiritually, not just naturally, and when you look at them eternally, not just immediate.

Prayer for the Day: *Lord, open my eyes to see the possibilities I have in You. Give me spiritual eyes to see truth and the ability to make good decisions based on my knowledge of Your Word and trust in Your providence.*

Day 76

CONFIDENCE CODE

If you look under the "Self-Help" heading on *Amazon.com*, there are about 5,000 books listed under the subheading "Self-Esteem." Self-image is the picture we have of ourselves. Self-esteem is the value we place on ourselves. Quite often, we struggle with a sense of low self-esteem and a negative self-image, and that makes us feel inadequate. We don't feel we have what it takes to reach our goals, to be successful, to get the job done, or to take the challenge. We back down from opportunities, challenges, and competition.

That was Jeremiah's struggle. He was a young Levitical priest. He was a timid man, given to self-analysis and self-criticism. When God spoke to him, he felt inadequate for the challenge and unworthy of the calling. He responded to God by saying, "I do not know how to speak; I am only a child." He writes of his experience: "The word of the Lord came to me, saying, 'Before I formed you . . . I knew you, before you were born I set you apart; I appointed you as a prophet to the nations'" (Jeremiah 1:4-5).

We hear that and say, "So what? I'm not a prophet; I'm just an ordinary person." Just as Jeremiah was called by the Lord, we have been called. God has a purpose and plan for everyone. Our self-esteem is derived from God's Word to us. He said, "The word of the Lord came to me."

When you hear God's word to you about who you are, you will also have confidence. God wants you to know three things about who you really are. First, God formed you. David said of the Lord, "You created my inmost being: you knit me together in my mother's womb. I praise you because I am fearfully and wonderfully made" (Psalm 139:13-14).

Second, God says, "I knew you." The Hebrew word *knew* means "I chose you." When someone chooses you, it validates you. How much more to know God chooses you! He has a calling on your life.

Finally, God says, "I set you apart; I appointed you." To be *set apart* means to be dedicated for God's purpose, to make holy and special. It was a great revelation to me the day I learned that *holy* means "special" and "unique." The Bible is called *holy* because it is a special book unlike any other. We are called *holy* because we are special to God. We are also appointed. Paul said, "For he [God] chose us in [Christ] before the creation of the world" (Ephesians 1:4). Let that sink in the next time you feel you don't have what it takes to be successful in life.

You are formed, chosen, set apart, and appointed by God for great things!

Prayer for the Day: *Lord, I am called and appointed! That's big! Just to know that You know me personally and have a purpose and plan for my life gives me hope and direction!*

Day 77

FIRST STEPS

Winston Churchill, prime minister of England during World War II, said, "Success is not final, failure is not fatal: it is the courage to continue that counts."

The first motor skill we learn as infants is to walk. We are so proud as young parents when we see our children take their first steps. We were thrilled when our first child, David Paul, crawled! For some strange reason he preferred crawling backward, but we were happy that he was moving. When he took his first steps, he got up on his own and held himself against the case opening between the family room, where we were sitting on the couch, and the kitchen. We went nuts when we saw him standing there! Then he took his first steps and hit the floor. Of course, we ran over and picked him up and cheered his accomplishment.

I think we spend our lives learning to walk. It seems we never really master it. We all fall down at times. When we do, we need someone to pick us up. We want to walk by faith, but we fall into doubt. We want to walk in the Spirit, but we fall into the flesh. We want to walk in the light, but we stumble in the darkness. But we can overcome our failures. We can say with the prophet Micah, "Do not gloat over me, my enemy! Though I have fallen, I will rise" (Micah 7:8).

Failure is not final. Or, I should say failure doesn't have to be final or fatal. It is up to you to get back up! If you fail a course in school, you can take it again. Life is the same way. It is up to you to decide to get back up when you fall. Make this declaration: "I will rise!" I will rise because with God all things are possible. I will rise because I can do all things through Christ. I will rise because God's grace is sufficient for me. I will rise because the mercies of the Lord are new every morning. I will rise because there is no condemnation to those in Christ Jesus. I will rise because in all things God works for my good. I will rise because if God is for me, who can be against me? I will rise because nothing shall separate me from the love of God. I will rise because the Lord will never leave me or forsake me.

If you have fallen, get back up today. Don't let the enemy of fear, failure, or disappointment gloat over you and keep you down. Face your failures and say, "I will rise!"

Prayer for the Day: *Lord, life has a way of knocking us down. The choice is whether we are going to stay down or get back up. If we plan to live, there is no other choice but to rise up and keep moving. This time I'll take Your hand and go where You lead.*

Day 78

HEALTHY HEARTS

The human heart is an amazing organ. It is a hollow muscle about the size of your fist that weighs between 8 and 12 ounces. The heart stays in a state of perpetual motion, supplying blood to the body systems through its own circulatory system, which is between 60 and 100 miles long, including 50 feet of arteries and veins and 62,000 miles of capillaries!

A normal adult heart pumps at a rate of 70 to 75 times per minute and beats 4,200 times an hour, 36 million times a year, and more than 2.5 billion times in your lifetime! As tough and endurable as the heart is, it must be maintained with utmost care. Heart disease is our number one health problem and the leading cause of death in the U.S. Most heart attacks occur in the morning between 6 a.m. and noon, and they happen most often on Mondays.

Just as we have a natural heart, we also have a spiritual heart. The spiritual heart is the center of our thinking and feeling, our perspectives, and our passions. "As a man thinks in his heart so is he" (Proverbs 23:7). Paul prays that the "eyes of your heart may be enlightened" (Ephesians 1:18). Jesus said, "Out of the overflow of the heart the mouth speaks" (Matthew 12:34). Paul said to "set your hearts on things above" (Colossians 3:1).

Just as we need to maintain a good diet, rest, and exercise for the physical heart, we need to take care of the spiritual heart. "Above all else, guard your heart, for [it is the wellspring of life]" (Proverbs 4:23). The phrase *wellspring of life* means everything we do comes from the heart.

I was having lunch with my good friend Mike Parker at a breakfast place. He ordered steel-cut oatmeal and soaked it in honey. I said, "Looks like you put all that honey on it to hide the bland taste." He said, "Yes, but oatmeal is good for your heart." I replied, "But it's still gross."

Well, we need to keep our spiritual heart healthy by a steady diet of the Word of God, which is soaked in honey! David said the Scriptures are "sweeter than honey, than honey from the honeycomb" (Psalm 19:10). As you take time to feed your spiritual hearts by reading and reflecting on the Word of God, you will have a healthy heart.

Prayer for the Day: *Lord, sometimes I hear people say "Trust your heart" when making decisions. But, unless a person is born again, their hearts cannot be trusted. Today I want to thank You for saving my soul and giving me a new heart that fully trusts in You.*

Day 79

COME TO YOUR SENSES

Leo Tolstoy said, "Everyone talks about changing the world, but nobody talks about changing himself." Change comes from insight. Change starts in the mind. "Be transformed by the renewing of your mind" (Romans 12:2).

Sometimes people around us tell us we need to change, but we don't. We try to help others change by pointing out issues in their lives, but they don't listen. Change occurs when a person gains insight. Change doesn't come because other people tell to us change. It occurs when we tell ourselves we need to change. Lasting change and growth comes when we get insight. As long as we are blind to the issues in our lives or we justify the way we are, we stay the same. But when the light comes on and we see it for ourselves, we are on the road to change.

As a counselor, I understand this. The difference between counseling and advice boils down to one thing. When someone gives you advice, they are telling you what to do. Counselors lead you on a path of discovery until you see things for yourself and then you tell yourself what to do!

Jesus teaches the principle that insight leads to change in the parable of the prodigal son. He leaves his family, takes his inheritance, and goes off in rebellion against everything he has been taught. Sometime later, after having lived the party lifestyle, he runs out of money and finds himself alone and working on a pig farm. He is so hungry he wants to eat the cornhusks given to the pigs. There "he came to his senses" (Luke

15:17). He said, "I will go home to my father."

His personal insight motivated him to make a change. He started the long walk home. When his father saw him on the road, he ran out and met him with a big hug. The son only asked his father for a job as a servant, but his father restored him as his son. Things turned out for better for him than he asked or even thought possible because "he came to his senses."

When you come to your senses, you will make new decisions. Those decisions will lead you with new direction. And that will take you to your destiny! Get on the right road today and it will take you where you need to be.

Prayer for the Day: *Lord, I need to make a change in my life. Please give me wisdom and insight now that I have come to my senses. Don't allow me to be blind, but transform me by the renewing of my mind.*

Day 80

SOW IT, REAP IT

When God created the universe, He established laws to govern it. Laws govern everything from atoms to attitudes, radar to relationships, protons to people. A *law* is "a rule or principle that brings about a certain result when obeyed." Laws are fixed, absolute, and predictable. Laws give our world order and peace. We toss an object into the air; it falls to the ground and we call it the *law of gravity*. We board an airplane, it rises into the clouds, and we call it the *law of aerodynamics*. We research the relationship between heat and other forms of energy, and we call it the *law of thermodynamics*. We observe the relationships of matter, motion, and energy, and we call them the *laws of physics*.

Life not only operates by natural laws; it also operates by spiritual laws. One of the most important laws is the law of sowing and reaping. There are 66 verses in the Bible that deal with the law of the harvest. "A man reaps what he sows" (Galatians 6:7). "As I have observed, those who plow evil and . . . sow trouble, reap it" (Job 4:8). "Those who sow in tears will reap with songs of joy" (Psalm 126:5). Those who "sow the wind . . . reap the whirlwind" (Hosea 8:7). Jesus said, "Give, and it will be given to you" (Luke 6:38).

A basic law of physics states that for every action there is an equal and opposite reaction. We get out of life what we put into it. Life is a series of investments and returns. If we don't like what we're getting out of life, let's change what we're putting into it. Give tithes, receive blessings. Invest money, accumulate savings. Work hard, prosper in life. Study diligently, achieve an education. Train for athletic competition, win the prize. Take care of your body, live healthy. We can choose the life we want by sowing the right seeds. When we plant the right seed, we will get the right harvest!

I once read: Sow a thought—reap a word. Sow a word—reap an action. Sow an action—reap a habit. Sow a habit—reap character. Sow character—reap your destiny.

Prayer for the Day: *Lord, I have realized today that I'm not putting into life what I expect to get out of it. I can't expect You to pour blessings into my life unless I'm pouring blessings into the lives of others. Thank You for refreshing my spirit with this truth as I give so I shall receive.*

Day 81

IF

The biggest little word in our vocabulary is the word *if*. In Scripture we read, "If anyone is in Christ, he is a new creation" (2 Corinthians 5:17 NKJV). The word *if* means when certain conditions are met, the desired results will naturally follow. The condition of faith must be met. A person must accept Jesus' invitation to believe in Him and follow Him as Savior and Lord in order to truly be His disciple.

Jesus said, "*If* anyone wishes to come after Me, he must deny himself, and take up his cross daily and follow Me" (Luke 9:23 NASB). Again, He invites us, "Let anyone who is thirsty come to me and drink" (John 7:37). The Apostle John assures us, "*If* we confess our sins, he is faithful and just and will forgive us our sins and purify us from all unrighteousness" (1 John 1:9). Paul shows us the way of salvation: "*If you declare with your mouth, 'Jesus is Lord,' and believe in your heart that God raised him from the dead, you will be saved*" (Romans 10:9).

Listen to Jesus' gracious invitation: "Here I am! I stand at the door and knock. *If* anyone hears my voice and opens the door, I will come in and eat with that person, and they with me" (Revelation 3:20). God is no respecter of persons, which is why He says "if anyone." God's grace and blessings are available for everyone, if we meet with the condition of faith in Him. His promises are sure *if* we believe Him.

What *if* do you need to fulfill today in order to accomplish your goals, fulfill your dreams, and reach your potential? The only thing standing between you and your success is the word *if*.

Prayer for the Day: *Lord, if is a strong but powerful word. As I study Your Word, I will be looking for the "ifs" to fulfill, that I may reach my full potential in You.*

Day 82

THE MIRACLE OF PROVISION

The cycle of blessing applies to all areas of life. Take the gift of *encouragement*. Those who sow it, reap it. Have you ever been in a planning meeting with a group of positive people? They generate plans and ideas. They bring out the best in others. However, it is very discouraging to get around a group of negative people and listen to their pessimistic outlook.

The same is true of *faith*. Faith breeds faith. Think about the miracle of Jesus feeding the five thousand with five loaves and two fish. The miracle required the partnership of a little boy who had "five small barley loaves and two small fish" (John 6:9). The miracle of provision required two things—the power of Jesus, and the boy's lunch. The boy's lunch wasn't much until he placed it in Jesus' hands. Then his lunch fed a multitude. But first, he had to give it.

There were twelve baskets left over. I wonder if the boy got to take the leftovers home. Now, that would have been a sight to see the look on his mother's face when she said, "Did you eat your lunch?' and he responded, "Yes, but I could not eat it all."

Not only did the boy have his needs met, but he also met the needs of many others because he gave what he had. He had put it in the hands of Jesus, and it multiplied. The more-than-enough principle goes into effect when we partner with Christ through Kingdom giving.

Prayer for the Day: *Lord, I know Your Word says You love a cheerful giver. Please help me to cheerfully give from my blessings back to You, and then please use my gifts to bless others.*

Day 83

LOOK UP

Pandemic. Terrorism. Mass shootings. Hurricanes. Racial violence. What else can go wrong? It feels like the world is coming apart at the seams. Global unrest. War. Financial uncertainty. Ecological disasters. The persecution of God's people. These are the exact signs Jesus foretold of His return in Luke 21.

Jesus said the world in the days right before His return would be terrifying. "People will faint from terror, apprehensive of what is coming on the world, for the heavenly bodies will be shaken" (Luke 21:26). Yet, He tells those who have faith in Him, "Stand up and lift up your heads, because your redemption is drawing near" (Luke 21:28).

When Jesus was taken from this earth into heaven, two men dressed in white (apparently angels) said: "Men of Galilee . . . why do you stand here looking into the sky?" (Acts 1:10-11a). They were gazing into the sky looking for His return, and so should we!

When you hear terrifying news, don't look down in discouragement. Don't look out in fear. Don't look around in confusion. Look up in hope! "This same Jesus, who has been taken from you into heaven, will come back" (Acts 1:11b). So, look up!

Prayer for the Day: *Lord, we live in terrifying times! People are afraid. But I have hope in knowing that You spoke of such times and told us to prepare. So, I will look up knowing Your return is near!*

Day 84

ROLL WITH IT

One of my favorite songs is Bob Dylan's classic, "The Times They Are a Changin'." Although written many years ago, the lyrics are as relevant as ever. Change happens more rapidly than ever because of technology. It's unnerving because we don't know what will change next in our world. The support systems we use today will be obsolete tomorrow. Less than 40 percent of us even have a landline for our phones.

The Bible teaches we are "foreigners and [strangers in the world]" (1 Peter 2:11). During the international travels Barbie and I have enjoyed, I am reminded that life itself is like being a tourist. Life is always in a state of transition. We are either going into a time of change or just coming out of one!

As threatening as change can feel, it gives us new opportunities. Leon Martel, in *Mastering Change*, says there are three things that keep us from making the changes we need to make. (1) We believe yesterday's solutions will solve today's problems, but they won't. We need new solutions to meet today's challenges. (2) We assume present trends will continue, but they won't. Whatever is new and innovative today will be old and obsolete tomorrow. (3) We neglect the opportunities offered by change. Like the people in Jesus' day, we don't "recognize the time of God's coming to [us]" (Luke 19:44).

Do you accept the changes you are facing with faith and hope in God? Or, are you fearfully resisting change, telling yourself everything will go on like it is? Don't miss the opportunities that transition brings. Don't get stuck where you are. When life changes, change with it!

Prayer for the Day: *Lord, just when I get used to something and begin to feel comfortable, it changes. I now realize this is just how life is. So, help me not to get stuck and miss valuable opportunities, and enjoy whatever life brings!*

Day 85

VOCABULARY

Today we are in the habit of making up new words. Sometimes we hear or read a word and ask, "Is that really a word?" Let me introduce you to an old word that we need to add to our vocabulary—*repentance*.

It could be said that *repentance* is the first word of the message of hope Jesus proclaimed. "Repent, for the kingdom of heaven has come near" (Matthew 4:17). The first of the *95 Theses* Martin Luther nailed to the door of the Wittenberg Church during the Protestant Reformation read: "When our Lord and Master Jesus Christ said 'Repent,' He willed that the entire life of believers be one of repentance."

When you hear the word *repentance*, what comes to mind? Perhaps you picture Jonah, fresh out of the belly of a whale, walking into Nineveh covered with seaweed and smelling like a fish, declaring, "Repent!" Or, maybe John the Baptist preaching in the Judean wilderness, dressed in camel's hair, with eyes of fire confronting everyone from religious aristocrats to the common person with the challenge, "Repent!" Or, maybe a man on the street corner carrying a sign over his shoulder bearing the word "Repent!"

What does it mean for us to repent? The word *repent* comes from the Greek word *metanoeo*, and it means to "change the mind." You could translate *metanoeo* as "to perceive afterward." *Repentance* means to change your mind after you have perceived and come to an understanding of what God is saying to you.

In the Bible, *repentance* is always used for changing our mind for the better. We turn away from unbelief to faith; from sin to righteousness; from the wrong road to the right road. Once we change our mind, the rest of our lives change as a result. So, when we repent, we change our whole course of life. Jesus once told a crowd, "Unless you repent, you too will all perish" (Luke 13:5).

Repentance gives us a fresh start in life as we put off old destructive ways of thinking and living and put on the new life God desires for us.

Prayer for the Day: *Lord, repentance sounds so old and religious that I forgot just how important it is to understand. It means to change the wrong way I'm going, to the right way I should be going. I repented when I gave my heart to You, but now I realize I need to repent of wrong attitudes, unbelief, and even sin when it creeps in uninvited. Thank You for reminding me.*

Day 86

NOT A CHANCE

Where did the universe come from, and why are we here on this earth? The way we answer that question determines our sense of purpose. Faith rests on the foundation that God is our Creator. "In the beginning God created the heavens and the earth" (Genesis 1:1). We believe in a Creator, not in chance!

British astronomer Sir Fred Hoyle, famous for his research on the origins of the universe, claims that believing the first cell originated by chance is like believing a tornado could sweep through a junkyard filled with airplane parts and form a Boeing 747!

In a letter to a botanist friend in February 1860, Charles Darwin expressed concern over the marvelous construction of the human eye that defied his evolutionary scheme of gradualism. He wrote, "To this day, the eye makes me shudder."

At some point, evolution and science part company. *Science* is limited to research on empirical data; therefore, it cannot postulate philosophically as to how life originated. *Evolution* is a philosophical worldview about the origin of the universe and the origin of life.

In *Evolution: A Theory in Crisis*, Michael Denton (an Australian biologist and self-described agnostic) challenges Darwin's assumptions. He asks, "Is it really credible that random processes could have constructed a reality, the smallest element of which—a functional protein or gene—is complex beyond our own creative capacities, a reality which is the very antithesis of chance, which excels in every sense anything produced by the intelligence of man?"

While the Bible's account of Creation does not tell us everything about the amazing mysteries and wonders of how God created the universe, it does make it clear He created it by His will, by His power, and for His purpose. "For from him and through him and for him are all things" (Romans 11:36).

Faith begins with knowing God as our Creator. Let us live this day in praise to Him: "You are worthy, our Lord and God, to receive glory and honor and power, for you created all things, and by your will they were created and have their being" (Revelation 4:11).

Prayer for the Day: *Lord, I am grateful to know that I am not just an animal that has evolved with time, but that I am created in Your image for Your purpose. I trust You to reveal that purpose so that I might fulfill it.*

Day 87

LITTLE BY LITTLE

Life is often measured by our achievements. Major achievements are milestones that tell the story of our lives. It starts early in life with performances before our parents and class in school. We have graduations from kindergarten through graduate studies. We earn degrees, certificates, and awards. We win trophies and recognitions. We get married and have children. We start businesses, build churches, support charities, write books, produce music, create arts, build houses, erect skyscrapers, develop technology, and create resources. We collect photos and videos to tell the story of our achievements. Every accomplishment is a milestone in our lives.

The difference between fulfillment and frustration is often whether or not we achieve what we set out to achieve. After all, success is simply reaching our goals. How do we set and reach our goals? Let's learn an important principle taught in Scripture. Moses instructed the people of Israel as they prepared to possess the Promised Land: "The Lord your God will drive out those nations before you, little by little. You will not be allowed to eliminate them all at once, or the wild animals will multiply around you" (Deuteronomy 7:22). They would achieve the goal of the

Promised Land "little by little." The reason is important—or the wild animals would multiply around them. In other words, they would create more problems if they tried to take too much too fast. If they did, they would upset the ecosystem, which would destroy them. Too much success too fast, or trying to accomplish too much too fast, will destroy us.

I like the word *eliminate*. It reminds us to get rid of things little by little. We fight attitude problems, financial problems, health problems, family problems; we fight enemies of circumstances. We change things little by little, not all at once. Several times in the New Testament we are told to get rid of things (see Ephesians 4:31; James 1:21; 1 Peter 2:1).

A guy asked me recently about getting in shape. He said, "I'm gaining weight—feel like my metabolism is slowing down. What can I do?" Then he started mentioning all kinds of things he knew he could do—eat better, start exercising. I said, "Pick one. Just one thing."

"Like what?" he asked. I said (and I'm not a nutritionist or fitness coach, but I eat right and exercise a lot), "Don't eat anything white—no white bread, white flour, white sugar, white rice, white potatoes—white ain't right!"

When you do one thing successfully, it builds confidence that you can do more. That is how you eventually reach your goals—little by little.

Some of the best advice I got to start a project was to start small, go deep, and then think big. Don't start off thinking big; start small. Don't expand too fast; go deep. Get firmly established before you start expanding. Get better before you think about getting bigger. Finally, think big. Then, what you build will have a strong foundation and you will be able to stand the strain of expansion.

You can accomplish your goals little by little. If you try to do too much too fast, you will create other problems, disrupt your life, and quit. But you can do it little by little.

Prayer for the Day: *Lord, because we live in a fast-paced, instant society, the idea of moving "little by little" seems to work against everything we've learned in our age of technology. But it actually makes perfect sense! Anything done in a hurry is never done right. Help me to slow down and trust You more!*

Day 88

PROUD OF IT

Don't you love it when someone calls you and says, "Guess what? I have good news!" Especially if it's your lawyer, your banker, your doctor, or the IRS!

Jesus began His ministry with good news. "Jesus went into Galilee, proclaiming the good news of [the kingdom of] God. 'The time has come,' he said. 'The kingdom of God has come near. Repent and believe the good news'" (Mark 1:14-15).

The Apostle Paul said, "I am not ashamed of the gospel, because it is the power of God that brings salvation to everyone who believes" (Romans 1:16). The word *gospel* means "good news." Paul preached the good news of Jesus in Jewish synagogues, Greek lecture halls of philosophy, Roman universities, and public marketplaces. He testified of the Gospel before judges, governors, and kings! He was not ashamed of the simple and powerful message about the Lord Jesus Christ.

Paul was writing to people in Rome, the world's superpower of the day. A city that prided itself on its philosophy, learning, and sophistication. Rome was the world's great political, economic, and military power. It would be easy to think the message of Jesus would seem irrelevant to these people. But Paul was not ashamed of the good news of Jesus. He boldly proclaimed its truth in the face of intellectualism, self-reliance, and sophistication. In the last letter Paul wrote, he said: "[I am not ashamed], because I know whom I have believed, and am convinced that he is able to guard what I have entrusted to him until that day" (2 Timothy 1:12).

Have you ever felt ashamed of something on the news where some crazy person misrepresented Christianity? I am ashamed of what some people have said and done in the name of Christ who are not Christian. I am ashamed of churches and denominations when they depart from Christian truth. I am ashamed of any misrepresentation of Christ. But when it comes to Jesus Christ, I can say what Pilate said, "I find no fault in Him!"

I am not ashamed of the Gospel because of its nature. The message of Jesus is not bad news. Nothing He said or taught is bad. It is fundamentally good, and it is good for you! It brings the world good, not harm. The Gospel teaches us how to live the good life. The way of Jesus Christ is the more excellent way to live. The fruit of the Gospel is new life for those who believe it.

Prayer for the Day: *Lord, in an age of multiple religions and New Age philosophy, I can stand up and say I am not ashamed of the good news of the gospel of Jesus Christ! Your Word heals, frees, restores, changes the heart, saves the soul, and is eternal truth. All that is good news because You are good! I am proud to share that truth with others, that they may experience Your goodness!*

Day 89

FORGET NOT

One day in 1883, the sun did not rise in New England! The people awoke in total darkness. They went outside to work in silence without the normal sounds that greeted the day—to roosters crowing on the farms, the sound of birds chirping. In apprehension, people gathered to question what was happening. As fear increased, people went to the churches to pray. By noon, every church was filled with people praying to God.

The next morning, crowds of people gathered on their farms and in the towns hoping to see the sun rise. Finally, as the sun rose, people started shouting, clapping, and dancing in praise to God. What had happened the day before? The volcano Krakatoa in Indonesia had erupted, sending a huge cloud of dust and ash into the atmosphere. The black cloud, carried around the world by the jet stream, covered entire areas of the world. Who would have thought a volcano halfway around the world could eclipse the light of the sun? Yet for many people, it was the first time they really gave thanks to God for light and warmth of the sun we all take for granted.

The psalmist said, "Praise the Lord, my soul, and forget not all his benefits" (Psalm 103:2). We all like benefits at work. Benefits are the extras that come along with our salary. We talk about fringe benefits. Every day we live on the benefits of God's grace and provision. It is important that we remember to take things with gratitude and not take them for granted.

Our experiences with God add up over time, thus we can trace His hand at work in our lives. We "taste and see that the Lord is good" (Psalm 34:8). We need to journal our experiences with God so we don't forget all His benefits. When we stop to think about our lives, we can see God at work in the details to remind us of the ways He intervened when nothing else could help us.

The first lesson of math we learned in school is how to add. Faith grows as we add up our experiences with God. Take time today to add up the ways God has protected, provided, and guided you. Let us be thankful and always be careful to forget not all His benefits.

Prayer for the Day: *Lord, as I look back over my journey with You, I can see Your love, care, and protection for me. I can never forget how You saved my soul. I am grateful for the relationship I have with You!*

Day 90
LIVE THE MOMENT

The Latin phrase *carpe diem*, meaning "seize the day," was made popular in the movie *Dead Poets Society*, starring Robin Williams. What a sad irony that he ended his life by suicide.

One of the most important principles for living a full life is living in the moment. Some of us live in the future with our plans and anxieties. Others of us live in the past with memories, traditions, or regrets. The psalmist has the right attitude toward life when he says, "This is the day" (Psalm 118:24 KJV). He embraces today with faith, hope, and love. He lives the day with gratitude and praise. How can we live fully in the moment?

Let us rejoice! Receive this day with thanksgiving. There is no such thing as a bad day. There is only a bad attitude about the day. Whatever the circumstances, rejoice, for the joy of the Lord is your strength! Get your mind on today. For the people who worry about tomorrow, Jesus says, "Do not worry about tomorrow" (Matthew 6:34). For people who dwell on the past, the Lord says, "Forget the former things; do not dwell on the past" (Isaiah 43:18).

Get your actions and energy focused on today. When I was a boy, I got up before everyone and stayed up as late as I could. My mother told me once that it was like I was afraid I was going to miss out on something. Today is all we have. Time stops for no one. The Bible places a strong emphasis on today. "Today is the day of salvation" (2 Corinthians 6:2 NLT). Don't waste the moment. Take full advantage of the day. Don't waste today by regretting the past or by being a couch potato. Dream your dreams, use your gifts, and work hard to make this day the best day of your life.

Conquer the tragedies, trials, and temptations of this day. Jesus made this statement facing the cross: "In this world you will have trouble. But take heart! I have overcome the world" (John 16:33). The day of our salvation was at hand, but it was the day of His suffering on the cross. Yet, He could say He had overcome the world. Be larger than life. If life hurts you, or someone disappoints you, or things don't turn out like you plan, rise above it in victory. Conquer the challenges of the day, and don't let them conquer you!

Live this day for the glory to God. As you rejoice in this day, resolve to bring honor and glory to God, and to be the salt of the earth and the light of the world. Yesterday is not the day. Tomorrow is not the day. This is the day the Lord has made!

Prayer for the Day: *Lord, I will put the past with its regrets in the past. I will not be anxious about what tomorrow holds. I will trust You, rejoice in today, and be led of Your Holy Spirit tomorrow!*

Day 91
WHEN DARKNESS COMES

When Jesus was arrested in the Garden of Gethsemane, He said something very interesting: "This is your hour—when darkness reigns" (Luke 22:53). Even though He had all authority and power, He lived through a season of darkness as He suffered for our sins. But then came the light of His resurrection to dispel the darkness! Up from the grave He arose as Lord of all!

I like the fact that He said, "This is your hour." In other words, when we go through a time in our lives when darkness reigns, we have the assurance that it will only last "an hour." Jesus told the crowd of religious and political leaders who arrested Him that their day would not last. They thought they were getting rid of Jesus, but they were just pawns on the divine chessboard as He laid down His life for us. Jesus endured the cross because of "the joy [that was] set before him" (Hebrews 12:2). Even when darkness reigned, He had joy because He could see by faith the final outcome of the cross—the salvation of the world!

When you are going through a time in your life when darkness reigns, remember it will only last an hour; it won't last forever. The darkness of sin, failure, fear, sickness, financial darkness, and family problems won't last. As you put your trust in God, the same way Jesus did when He faced the cross, you can be certain the darkness will give way to the light of God's healing, deliverance, and salvation.

So, don't despair when darkness reigns. Commit the situation to God in absolute trust and praise Him as you go through the season of darkness, knowing it will only last for a while. Take God's promise to heart: "But for you who revere my name, the sun of righteousness will rise with healing in its rays" (Malachi 4:2). Praise Him in the darkness, declaring by faith, "The Lord turns my darkness into light" (2 Samuel 22:29).

Prayer for the Day: *Lord, I have never liked the dark. I guess it's because I have been in dark places and prefer the light, where You abide. I know there may be more darkness ahead but, as David said in Psalm 23:4,*

"Even though I walk through the darkest valley, I will fear no evil, for you are with me."

Day 92
JOY TO THE WORLD

A recent MSN homepage carried the line, *Would Winning Jackpot Lottery Bring Joy?* Followed by the words, *Not Really.* The odds of winning the grand prize are somewhere around 1 in 176 million. Most lottery winners don't end up any happier. Studies conducted over the years show that after the initial euphoria wears off of winning and getting those big checks, the winners end up no happier than they were before they won. One study showed the lottery winners took "significantly less pleasure" in the simple things like chatting with a friend, reading a magazine, or receiving a compliment. Psychologists believe hitting an especially huge jackpot may alter that happiness baseline, making it harder to see the joy in everyday things.

So where does joy come from? How can we have it and keep? On the first Christmas, the angels told the shepherds in the field of Bethlehem, "I bring you good news [of] great joy. . . . A Savior has been born to you; he is Christ the Lord" (Luke 2:10). Joy is based on your salvation, not your situation! Handel H. Brown said, "The early Christians did not rejoice because of better things to come. They rejoiced because Christ had come. God's unspeakable gift was not provisional. They rejoiced because it was final." Joy overcomes adversity and problems! Joy is an intense feeling of happiness, gladness, and contentment.

Spiritual joy is a gift from God. We all have feelings of discouragement, sadness, and depression. Joy is not euphoria. It is, however, that inner sense of gladness because we know we are held in the palm of God's hand and He will never leave or forsake us. Joy sustains us in the tough times. The joy God gives us is our inner source of strength that makes us strong enough to handle anything life throws at us. Spend Christmas rejoicing in the salvation we have in Jesus Christ, regardless of whatever situation you may be facing.

Prayer for the Day: *Lord, sometimes the holidays can be difficult. Spending time with family members who don't understand my relationship with You and all the gift-giving can be stressful! But I have a joy inside my soul that gives me great strength. You are that joy, Lord!*

Day 93

UNCERTAINTY

One of the greatest fears we battle is the fear of uncertainty. David felt this way when he penned these prayerful words: "My times are in your hands" (Psalm 31:15). Israel was surrounded by nations that wanted to destroy the nation the way terrorist groups, radical religions, and tyrannical governments threaten us today. David talks about being surrounded by his enemies. We face personal, economic, and spiritual enemies as well.

We all face personal uncertainties with our circumstance and things going on in our life. We face national uncertainty with changing political climate, economic instability, and secular attacks to our faith as Christians. Yet, we too can say with confidence, "My times are in Your hands, Lord. My future is in Your hands. It is not in my hands or in the hands of others or in the hands of my enemies, but everything about my life is in Your hands!"

This is a statement about the providence of God. The time of my life and the times and seasons and the very time frame in which I am living is in the hands of God! My birth, the seasons of my life, and even the moment I see Him face-to-face. I belong to Him! The question of us is, How are we using the time God gives us? David says his days were written in God's book before one of them came to be (Psalm 139:16). Paul says we were chosen in Christ "before the creation of the world" (Ephesians 1:4).

This is also a declaration of purpose. The circumstances of my life are in God's hands. God is able, with His hands, to work everything together for my good. This is why Paul could say he had learned to be content, whatever the circumstances, and why Job could endure a season of great suffering—they believed their times were in God's hands and He was at work. God pursues His purpose for us in every time and season of our lives. At no point is your life outside of God's hands if you belong to Him.

This is also a place of peace when you can say, "My times, O Lord, are in Your hands." I can rest safely in His hands. When the Lord disciplined King David for numbering the army, David said, "[Please] let us fall into the hands of the Lord, for his mercy is great; but do not let me fall into human hands" (2 Samuel 24:14). I can live every day at peace because I know my times are in His hands!

Prayer for the Day: *Lord, although the circumstances of my life may be hard right now, I still have peace, knowing You have my life in Your hands. Whatever I go through, I know You will go with me. I am never alone!*

Day 94

STARS

The Bible has a lot to say about the stars and how God shows Himself in the heavens. God made the stars (Genesis 1:16). The universe is 30 billion light years across. It consists of 100 billion galaxies, each containing hundreds of billions of stars. God calls each of the stars by name (Isaiah 40:26). Our galaxy, the Milky Way, has billions of stars, each with its own set of planets. The closest star to Earth is Alpha Centauri. The brightest star is Sirius, the Dog Star, which is nine light years from Earth. (In case you're interested in traveling, one light year equals six trillion miles!)

The star Epsilon is larger than the orbit of Pluto. If it were hollow, it would contain 23 billion of the earth's suns! No wonder David proclaimed in praise, "The heavens declare the glory of God; the skies proclaim the work of his hands" (Psalm 19:1)!

When I ponder the universe, I think, *God is so great and I am so small!* Yet, God has numbered the hairs on my head and knows my thoughts before I think them. He is familiar with all my ways. Before I was born, He knew me even as I was being formed in my mother's womb.

The God who inhabits the universe, who calls each star by name, knows each of us and lives in us when we put our trust in Him. God has so much to think about today, but remember He always thinks about you!

Prayer for the Day: *Lord, it is nice to know that You, who made the universe and holds it together, hold me together too! When I feel alone and am hurting, You are there to comfort me and remind me that I am Yours and You are mine.*

Day 95

SYNERGY

Synergism refers to two or more things functioning together to produce a result not independently obtainable. The word *synergy* comes from the Greek word *synergia*, meaning "working together." The early church had the power of the Holy Spirit, and they had the power of synergism that made them an unstoppable force. "All the believers were together and shared everything in common" (see Acts 4:32). Jesus said, "A kingdom divided against itself cannot stand" (see Matthew 12:25). But a kingdom united cannot fall.

The Tower of Babel teaches us the power of unity. God said of the people who built that tower for ungodly purposes: "If as one people speaking the same language they have begun to do this, then nothing they plan to do will be impossible for them" (Genesis 11:6). If they used the power of speaking and acting as "one people" to do their own thing, how much more can we use the power of unity to accomplish what God has called us to do?

God scattered them and confused their language to stop their efforts. But He empowers us when we unite to do good! Unity creates synergy that makes everything possible. "Make every effort to keep the unity of the Spirit through the bond of peace" (Ephesians 4:3). When we act as one people with one purpose and speak one language, nothing is impossible.

Treasure your relationships. Resolve every conflict that arises ASAP. Conflict scatters us like it did at the Tower of Babel and defeats our efforts. The word *Babel* means "confusion," and that is what conflict creates in our relationships. Don't wait for others to resolve the conflict; resolve the hurt feeling, or clear up the confusion. You take the initiative today and "make every effort" on your part "to keep the unity of the Spirit through the bond of peace" (Ephesians 4:3).

Prayer for the Day: *Lord, if there is conflict in my life with anyone, I pray You will reveal it so that I may make amends. I want to be at peace with everyone so that I can hear Your voice clearly!*

Day 96
COME TOGETHER

Pastor Eric Daniel Harris pled guilty to a 1996 arson that burned down the Missionary Baptist Church in Saline County, Arkansas. A federal prosecutor said Harris did it because "there was a division among church members, and they needed a project to unify them" (*News of the Weird*, March 30, 2000). He tried to reach the right goal by the wrong means!

God calls us to live in unity. The word *unity* means to be "one in mind, thought, and purpose." We are told, "Make every effort to keep the unity of the Spirit through the bond of peace" (Ephesians 4:3). As Christians, we are called to spiritual unity. Not political unity, or cultural unity, or unity of preference (music, art, food), nor to unity of personal convictions. We are not called to financial unity like socialism, nor are we called to the loss of individuality or personality like a cult.

Unity is not *uniformity*. We can be brothers without being twin brothers. Unity also creates division. We don't sacrifice truth on the altar of unity. If I unite with Christ, I am at odds with this world. Jesus said, "Do not think I came to bring peace but a sword" (Matthew 10:34 NKJV). When we stand together, we also stand against certain things. You cannot be united with things you fundamentally disagree with. Real unity is based on the truth of Jesus Christ and the Word of God.

"How good and pleasant it is when God's people live together in unity! . . . For there the Lord bestows his blessing, even life forevermore" (Psalm 133:1-3). When we live in unity, there is a good and pleasant atmosphere. Disunity and division bring an unpleasant atmosphere. The word *blessing* means "God's favor." God is pleased when we live in unity, and He pours out the blessings of His grace on us.

So, whatever relationship problems you may experience, settle matters quickly and keep the unity of the Spirit!

Prayer for the Day: *Lord, living in unity with other Christian brothers and sisters can be difficult because we are all so different. Please help me to honor differences without altering my faith! Belief and trust in the truth of Your Word keeps us unified.*

Day 97
WHAT IS YOUR LIFE?

As I was out running one day, I began to think about this scripture (I get a lot of inspiration when I run.): "What is your life? You are a mist that appears for a little while and then vanishes" (James 4:14). There are two great truths given to us here.

First, realize how insignificant you are. (I don't mean to be negative or to diminish our self-worth.) When you think of yourself in light of world history and the vastness of this universe, you cannot help but realize how insignificant you are! You are just a mist, and there is not much substance to a mist. So, what is the point? This truth delivers us from pride. Prideful people think they are all that and parade around like the world is dependent on them. They don't realize they are only a mist that appears for a little while. When we come to terms with this fact, we will live a life of humility.

Now for the good news! The second truth is to realize how significant you are! Since you only appear a little while, make it count! Live up to your potential. Use what God has given you. Get better, not bitter. God has created you in His image, called you to serve Him, and commissioned you for a life of ministry. Time is valuable—don't waste it. Time is a great treasure that we need to invest. "Making the most of every opportunity" (Ephesians 5:16).

When time finally vanishes away for all of us and we stand before the Lord in eternity, let's live in such a way that we hear Him say to us, "Well done, good and faithful servant!" (Matthew 25:21).

Prayer for the Day: *Lord, most of us live as though our life on earth will never end. We waste time, money, and live selfishly. Please remind me that my time on earth is short and I should make the most of it for Your glory!*

Day 98

BUILD A BRIDGE

Author E. Stanley Jones said, "Bitterness comes to all; sours some, sweetens others. I will use it to sweeten my spirit." When someone offends you and apologizes to you, let it go. Don't hold on to the hurt. Also, when you do or say something wrong and then you apologize, let that go as well and stop beating yourself up over it. Jesus said, "If your brother or sister sins against you, rebuke them; and if they repent, forgive them. Even if they sin against you seven times in a day and seven times come back to you saying, 'I repent,' you must forgive them" (Luke 17:3-4).

One of Aesop's Fables is the story of a farmer who had a family that argued frequently. After trying in vain to reconcile their differences with words, he showed them an example. He called his sons and told them to gather a pile of sticks before him. Then, tying the sticks into a bundle, he told them to lift the bundle and break it. They all tried but failed. Then, untying the bundle, the farmer gave his sons the sticks to break one-by-one, which they broke with ease. He then told them, "My sons, as long as you remain united, you are a match for all your enemies, but when you are divided, you will be easily conquered."

We need to build bridges, not walls, just as Jesus did. "He himself is our peace, who destroyed the dividing wall of hostility . . . thus making peace" (see Ephesians 2:14-17). The word *priest* in Latin means "a bridge-builder." Jesus is our High Priest, and He calls us to be priests to others. "[He] has made us to be a kingdom and priests" (Revelation 1:6).

The famous prayer, "Lord, make me an instrument of Your peace," teaches us to let it go.

Prayer for the Day: *Lord, make me an instrument of Your peace. / Where there is hatred, let me sow love. Where there is injury, pardon. / Where there is doubt, faith. Where there is despair, hope. / Where there is darkness, light. And where there is sadness, joy.*

Day 99
PEACEMAKER

The motto of the *Apollo II* mission was, "We come in peace for all mankind." This motto is on the plaque left there on the surface of the moon, where the astronauts landed on the Sea of Tranquility. Astronauts Neil Armstrong and Buzz Aldrin found themselves in a peaceful place on the moon because there were no people living there!

Our relationships are the greatest treasure we have, yet they are often tough to maintain. We are called to "keep the unity of the Spirit through the bond of peace" (Ephesians 4:3). The word *bond* means "close unity; a band; a ligament; like a family bond." We often say, "My word is my bond." A bond is the glue that holds us together.

We need always work for peace and try to relieve conflict, tension, and strife when we encounter it. It is possible to do a right thing in the wrong way. The process is as important as the outcome. That is why James 3:18 says, "Peacemakers who sow in peace reap a harvest of righteousness." We get results when we sow in peace. You can sow a good idea with a contention and not get any results when working with others. It is only when we sow in peace that we get a harvest of righteousness.

Just like the first astronauts, let's make it our goal to always come in peace for the benefit of others. We need to take seriously the challenge of Jesus: "Blessed are the peacemakers" (Matthew 5:9). Nowhere in Scripture does He say, "Blessed are the troublemakers."

Prayer for the Day: *Lord, just as my relationship with You is of great value, so is my relationship with others. Please remind me to always be a peacekeeper, so that they may see Christ through me.*

Day 100

ONE STEP AT A TIME

Everyone would like to know the future, but God expects us to walk by faith. We are to trust Him to unfold His plan for us one step at a time. Sometimes the Lord will give you a glimpse of something that will happen to you somewhere down the road, maybe years in advance. If He does, treasure it in your heart. God will bring it to pass at the proper time.

Think of the call of Abraham. When God called him to go to Canaan, he "obeyed and went, even though he did not know where he was going" (Hebrews 11:8). That is a strong statement—*even though he did not know where he was going!* Abraham knew the general direction, but he had to take the first step before God showed him the next one.

In order to know the Lord's direction, we need to fully surrender our lives to His will and purpose. Surrendering to God is risky. He doesn't always tell us what is around the next corner, or the next year, or ten years from now. He expects us to walk by faith and not by sight. God's will unfolds one page at a time. Life with God is always an adventure.

In *Indiana Jones and the Last Crusade,* Indiana is in search for the Holy Grail. He comes to a cavern he must cross, yet there is no way. The man of wisdom told him, "Take the leap of faith." As he steps out onto what seems to be nothing, his footsteps land on a narrow bridge spanning the camouflaged chasm. Once you and I take the first step of faith God is leading us to take, He will reveal the next step until we get to our destiny!

Prayer for the Day: *Lord, thank You that my steps are ordered by You. I don't need to know the future; I just need to take one step at a time and trust You!*

Day 101

PAY FOR IT

One of the leaders in our church told me that when he and his wife were first married, they attended a small Baptist church in Tennessee. One day the pastor of the church invited him to lunch. "I notice that you are not tithing," he told my friend. Then the pastor said, "I challenge you to start tithing, and if you don't do well after three months, then I will give you the money back." So, he started, and he has prospered ever since.

One of my favorite stories in the Bible is the story of David insisting on purchasing the threshing floor of Araunah to offer a sacrifice of worship to God (2 Samuel 24:18-24). The site of the threshing floor later became the foundation site for the Temple in Jerusalem. Araunah wanted to give King David the threshing floor free of charge, but the king insisted on paying for it. That day David offered the burnt offering, which expressed the total consecration of the worshiper to God, followed by the fellowship offerings of praise and restored fellowship with God after his time of repentance. David's attitude is challenging to all of us: "No, I insist on paying you for it. I will not sacrifice to the Lord my God burnt offerings that cost me nothing" (v. 24).

True worship involves the total person, including the giving of our finances to support the ministry of the gospel of Christ. Remember, always "honor the Lord with your wealth" because "God loves a cheerful giver" (Proverbs 3:9; 2 Corinthians 9:7).

Prayer for the Day: *Lord, help me to remember all money is not the same. The first tenth belongs to You, the second tenth should be saved for emergencies, and the rest is to live on wisely. If I am consistent with this, I will be blessed and prosper.*

Day 102

RUN TO THE BATTLE

Psychologist Alfred Adler, in his theory of personality, said we all strive for superiority—not over other people, but to conquer the basic inner sense of inadequacy with which we struggle.

I am sure young David felt that way the day he first encountered a Philistine giant named Goliath. Everyone knows and loves the story of David and Goliath. However, the real giant he faced that day was not Goliath, but the giant of fear. Fear is the greatest obstacle we face to success and victory in life. How could we stand up to the inner giant of fear and inadequacy and take on such a great challenge?

David knew he was not alone; God was with him. As David drew near his enemy, he declared, "You come against me with sword and spear and javelin, but I come against you in the name of the Lord Almighty . . . the Lord will deliver you into my hands." I like what happened next: "As the Philistine moved closer to attack him, David ran quickly toward the battle line to meet him." And the result? "So David triumphed over the Philistine" (1 Samuel 17:45-50).

Tom Rusk, in *Get Out of Your Own Way!* says, "When you try new things, you may be frightened. But afterward you will feel a surge of self-respect, and you will have gained competence and confidence. You will also have taken a step toward self-acceptance and the elimination of self-doubt."

Prayer for the Day: *Lord, fear is the most devastating emotion we deal with. Nevertheless, I'm glad to know that what we normally fear never happens. When I'm afraid, I will look to You and place that fear in Your hands, knowing You are able and have my best interest at heart.*

Day 103

OUTWARD AND INWARD

The other day I got to thinking about this scripture: "Therefore we do not lose heart. Though outwardly we are wasting away, yet inwardly we are being renewed day by day" (2 Corinthians 4:16). Life comes down to managing what's going on outwardly around us and inwardly within us.

We live in a material age that puts too much emphasis on the outward: style, fashion, appearance, and getting as much stuff as we can. But Paul reminds us that outwardly we are wasting away. Not a very pleasant thought, I might add, but true nonetheless. The outer world, including our physical bodies, is in a state of decay. Things wear out and we throw them away. The joy of material gifts fade over time. Only what is internal and spiritual has lasting value. I'm not saying material things are unimportant. I'm only saying we need to live our lives from the inside out, and what is going on in us spiritually takes priority over what is going on around us.

True happiness, joy, and purpose come from within. You cannot get those things just by material possessions or personal experiences. We often make the mistake of putting too much emphasis on the outer life. We improve our lifestyle, but not our souls. Even though we experience the wear and tear of the world around us, we can be renewed inwardly day by day through our relationship with the Lord. The psalmist said of the Lord, "He restores my soul" (Psalm 23:3 NKJV). He also reminds us that in His presence is the "fullness of joy" (see 16:11). We need to take time to read and reflect on the Word of God daily and to spend time in His presence so we can be "transformed by the renewing of [our] mind[s]" (Romans 12:2).

Take a soul check today. Don't measure your success and security by what is going on around you, but by what is going on within you spiritually. As you practice the presence of the Lord, you will be "renewed day by day."

Prayer for the Day: *Lord, living in a material world can sidetrack us if we're not careful. Keeping up with the Joneses to fit in and be accepted is temporary. Only the richness of our soul being fed by Your Word is permanent. Thank You, Lord, for Your Word that renews my mind and feeds my soul!*

Day 104

IMPOSSIBLE POSSIBILITY

During a counseling session, I came to see a scripture in a new light. A couple was having tremendous problems in their marriage. One of them asked me after I heard about their problems if I thought there was any hope. I have seen many couples survive pain, betrayal, and failure in marriage. On the other hand, I have seen pressures and problems tear marriages apart. I shared with them the words of Jesus: "With man this is impossible, but . . . with God all things are possible" (Mark 10:27).

Many things with us are impossible. We need to come to terms with that fact. There is a limit to what we can handle. We all have a breaking point. It is important to not let ourselves get pushed too far or to allow our relationships to get overloaded with problems.

We are only jars of clay that can break under pressure. That is an important lesson with our time management, our work, our finances, and our relationships. Take care of yourself and your relationships, and protect them from getting to the place you feel like it is impossible for you to handle the pressures of life. Know your breaking point, and try to avoid getting pushed to the place that you break under the pressure.

Now for the good news—with God all things are possible! When you are defeated by life's battles, depressed by life's concern, and discouraged by life's unfairness, you can get up and go on. Brokenness can be followed by blessing. Defeat can be followed by victory. Hurt can be followed by healing because with God, all things are possible.

Nothing is hopeless in your life unless you believe it's hopeless. Trust the Lord today for a turnaround and dare to believe that with God, all things are possible.

Prayer for the Day: *Lord, I want the world to know I serve a "possible" God! The pressures of this life, in this broken world, certainly come. But I serve a God who is able to bring victory to any defeat!*

Day 105

LIVING LETTERS

Barbie has several hat boxes filled with every letter, card, song, and poem that I have written to her since the day I met her. Letters, emails, and texts tell the stories of our lives. What we write reveals our passions and priorities. In the same way, Paul tells us that, as followers of Jesus Christ, we are "letter[s], . . . known and read by everyone" (2 Corinthians 3:2).

In the days of Moses, God wrote the Ten Commandments on two tablets of stone. The people of God saw the chiseled tablets and could read God's laws. Now, God writes the story of His love and grace on the tablet of our hearts so other people can read our life and see God's work in us, through us, and for us. "You are a letter from Christ . . . written not with ink but with the Spirit of the living God, not on tablets of stone but on tablets of human hearts" (2 Corinthians 3).

Your life as a Christian is a living letter from Jesus Christ to your family and friends. Don't keep the letter, the email, and the text of your faith private, but let them read your mail—share openly with them the story of your relationship with the Lord Jesus Christ. Today, people are worried over intrusion of privacy by hackers and by the government. Let us not be private about our faith, but openly share the story of God's grace that we experience with others.

Prayer for the Day: *Lord, living in America allows me to share my faith wherever I go without fear of persecution. I pray I can always be a living letter to all I encounter for Your glory.*

Day 106

TURN RIGHT

I am embarrassed to tell you this story, but I did a music performance with my band on a Saturday in Statesboro, Georgia. We ate dinner at a Mexican restaurant, and then I headed north on a state highway because I was scheduled to speak at a church in Augusta the next morning. The trip should have taken me two hours max. I came to some roadwork construction and had to take a detour. Then I had to get on two-lane country roads.

The sun set, and it got dark with no streetlights. I drove forever. I talked on the cell phone to my brother Tim and to my friend Mike, who had performed with me. They made it back to Atlanta while I was still driving! Their trip was three hours, and I should have arrived at my hotel an hour before they did, but I was still driving in the dark. I stopped at a couple of convenience stores in the middle of nowhere, and they gave me directions to Augusta that I followed.

I kept on driving until I felt like I was in an episode of the *Twilight Zone*! I had now been on the road for nearly four hours when I saw a sign that read "Statesboro 25 miles"! I was right back where I had started, so I had to turn around and drive another two hours. This time I paid more attention to the detour and didn't go in a circle. I arrived at my hotel after midnight.

Life is often like my trip. We waste our time when we get on the wrong road. The wrong road always takes us the wrong direction and heads to the wrong destination. Listen to God's Word about the right road: "Set up road signs; put up guideposts. Take note of the highway, the road that you take" (Jeremiah 31:21).

What road are you on? The right road goes the right direction, and it will lead you to the right destination. Be sure you take the right road.

Prayer for the Day: *Lord, I have learned that every time I got off the right road, it was because I was distracted and not seeking Your direction. May I always stop, listen, and follow Your voice on the road to eternal life.*

Day 107

FREELY GIVE

Rabbis have used the two main seas in Israel to describe two types of people. The Sea of Galilee receives the fresh water from three fountainheads that flow into it. Its outlet then forms the head of the Jordan River that flows south through Israel until it empties itself into the Dead Sea to the north. The Sea of Galilee is surrounded by lush vegetation and teaming with fish.

The Dead Sea, however, has no vegetation growing around it and no fish, because of its 33 percent salt and mineral content. The reason for this is because it has an inlet but no outlet. There is no flow of the water, so the minerals have built up a deposit over time.

Like the Sea of Galilee, there are people who give and allow what they receive to flow through their lives and out to others. Other people are like the Dead Sea—they keep life's blessings for themselves.

This is what Jesus meant by saying, "Freely you have received; freely give" (Matthew 10:8). Everything we enjoy is a gift from God. We don't really own anything. So, we should not hold on to things so tightly. God has freely given us everything we enjoy, not because we deserve it, but because He is good and generous! When we give away freely, no strings attached, even what we give comes back "a good measure . . . shaken together and running over" (Luke 6:38).

So, give something away today, even if it's just a compliment, a word of encouragement, or an expression of gratitude. Always measure your success in life by what you give away, not by what you get, and your life will count for something great.

Prayer for the Day: *Lord, I praise You today and thank You for always providing everything I need. Please make me sensitive to know how and when to share with others what I have so generously been given as they have a need!*

Day 108

LOOKING FOR GOD'S WILL

I was having lunch with a friend when he asked me, "How can you know you're in the will of God? It is different for people in business than for people in full-time ministry. For you, it's easy. You know you are called to preach. You are called to be a pastor. But for us it's not so easy. The will of God is something we are always looking for, but it seems it's always just around the corner, just out of reach."

He went on to tell me how tempting it is to look at successful people and feel as though he hasn't accomplished enough, or that God has something great for him to do but he doesn't know what it is. I told him, "The will of God is more about *being* than it is about *doing*. It is more about who we are than it is what we do."

Paul said, "Each one should test their own actions . . . without comparing themselves to someone else, for each one should carry their own load" (Galatians 6:4). He also told the Corinthians that those who compare themselves with others are not wise.

The will of God starts with being the person God wants you to be. The will of God starts with being faithful in the duties and responsibilities you have right here and now. God is more concerned with *who* we are than *what* we do.

I told my friend, "You're looking for something that isn't lost. Opportunities to do the will of God are all around you, and you can't see them because you're looking for something grandiose to accomplish."

The will of God is to serve Him right here, right now, where you live and the people God has placed in your life. Do the will of God that you already know to do today with a humble heart, and God will lead you to where you need to be tomorrow.

Prayer for the Day: *Lord, I delight to do Your will. Help me to do what I know is Your will for my life and to take advantage of the opportunities I have today to share Your grace with others. I let go of anxiety about tomorrow because I know You will lead me where I need to go tomorrow if I do what You give me today!*

Day 109

A DROP OF WATER

Can you prove the existence of God? I see God in big things and little things. I cannot conceive of God not existing when I consider the universe and the world in which we live. I agree with the psalmist, "When I consider your heavens, the work of your fingers. . . . Lord, our Lord, how majestic is your name in all the earth!" (Psalm 8:3, 9).

When I gaze up in the sky, I sing with the psalmist, "The heavens declare the glory of God; the skies proclaim the work of his hands" (Psalm 19:1). Paul reminds us, "Since the creation of the world, God's invisible qualities—his eternal power and divine nature—have been clearly seen . . . so that people are without excuse" (Romans 1:20).

Let me give you one example. The molecules in one drop of water, if they became grains of sand, could build a highway one-half mile wide, one-foot thick, from New York to San Diego! That is incredible, and that is our God. Even in a little drop of water, you can see the evidence of the eternal power and the divine nature of our God.

When people say, "Show me the evidence that God exists," I say, "Show me the evidence that God does not exist!" You cannot logically explain anything in the vast universe without an omnipotent God who created it all. I look above and I see God in creation. I look around and I see God is with me. I look within and see God at work in me, for "I am fearfully and wonderfully made" (Psalm 139:14).

Faith is not blind. Atheism is blind. Faith has its eyes wide open to the wonders of God. Atheism has its eyes tightly closed like a little child who thinks if they keep their eyes closed, no one can see them. Open your eyes today and see the evidence of God at work above you, around you, and within you!

Prayer for the Day: *Lord, when the world says "God is dead," I want to shake them and say, "Open your eyes and see, open your ears and hear!" God's fingerprint is on and in everything. His voice is sounded around the earth.*

Day 110

PLANS AND PURPOSE

One of the keys to success is having a plan. Decide where you are going and how to get there. "Many are the plans in a person's heart, but it is the Lord's purpose that prevails" (Proverbs 19:21).

Our plans and God's purpose must coexist; we need both to live a full life. As you make plans, keep them flexible because things change. Adjust your plans when necessary. All accomplishments are the results of a master plan. Plan your work; then work your plan. Look out for distractions that get you off course. When Mother Teresa was once asked why she thought people lost their spiritual passion, she replied in one word: "Distractions."

As important as plans are, they must be submitted to God's purpose, for it "prevails." If we pursue our own plans but miss God's purpose, we miss the point of living. Growing up in the Presbyterian Church, I learned the *Westminster Shorter Catechism* as a boy. The first question is, "What is the chief end of man?" Answer: "The chief end of man is to glorify God and to enjoy Him forever."

God created us with a purpose. If we don't know God's purpose for our lives, we feel empty and life feels meaningless. You are not here by accident. God created you with a divine purpose. "'I know the plans I have for you,' declares the Lord" (Jeremiah 29:11).

Submit your plans to the Lord and pray, "Father, not my will but Yours be done." When you trust Him with your plans, you can be assured that "He shall direct your paths" (Proverbs 3:6 NKJV). He will lead you and guide you, giving you an inner sense of direction of the way you are to go in life as you face important decisions.

Prayer for the Day: *Lord, I am so guilty of making significant plans without seeking You first. Help me to remember that direction comes from You and that I will be a happier person if first I seek Your plan for my life!*

Day 111

GET PAST IT

When Israel was stuck between Pharaoh's army and the Red Sea, Moses prayed for God's direction. God told Moses to tell the people, "Move on" (Exodus 14:15). The answer to what you need is not going back to the way things were but to move on. The past is over. The answer for your life is ahead of you, not behind you.

God's way is never the way of retreat. If you go back, you will forfeit the opportunities ahead. Just as God said He would lead the Hebrews to the Promised Land, He has given us great promises. We, like them, have to move forward to possess His promises. The past often holds us back from the promises of God and from reaching our potential.

There are three ways the past can affect us:

1. The past can become a museum where we walk up and down the halls in our mind and remember great times of the past. But we need to be dreaming new dreams for today.

2. The past can become a mausoleum. We let our dreams die because we are disappointed or hurt by what happened to us in the past. The pain of the past keeps us from enjoying the present. Don't write your own obituary, and don't plan your own funeral! Instead, start a new chapter in your life.

3. The past can be a mentor. Learn life lessons from your past experiences. Let your past make you a better person, not a bitter person. Your past experiences, both good and bad, are rich with wisdom to help you move forward. Take God's Word to heart today and move on!

Prayer for the Day: *Lord, memories often keep us stuck in the past, unable to move forward. I pray that You will use those memories to teach me and move me forward into the good life You have ahead for me.*

Day 112

GET SOME REST

What do you do when you face a crisis? This is when you need to pray the prayer of commitment.

Prayer is more than simply asking God to change our circumstances. There is more to prayer than changing the world around us. Prayer changes the world *within* us—the inner world of our attitudes, feelings, values, and beliefs.

Turn the stressful situation you are facing today over to your heavenly Father. Relinquish control and release your worries about it. When you have done everything you can do, it is time to turn it over to God and enter into His rest. The psalmist David wrote, "He leads me beside the still waters; He restores my soul" (Psalm 23:2-3 NKJV).

Walking by faith, not by sight, means to rest in the power and providence of God who alone can do for you what you cannot do for yourself. When you turn things over today to God in complete trust, you will enter His rest. "Now we who have believed enter that rest. . . . For anyone who enters God's rest also rests from their works" (Hebrews 4:3, 10). The spiritual rest God gives you will free you from worry and the need to control everything.

This is what the Apostle Paul meant when he wrote these words from a prison cell: "Don't worry over anything whatever . . . tell God every detail of your needs in thankful prayer, and the peace of God, which surpasses human understanding, will keep constant guard over your hearts and minds as they rest in Christ Jesus" (Philippians 4:6-7, Ph.).

Turn the problem over to God and trust Him to work things out for you. Cease from the hard work of worry and trust Him. When you do, you will enter God's rest.

Prayer for the Day: *Lord, I admit I tend to worry about things that I have no control over. What I need to do is pray and allow You to work out all the details of my life! Thank You for reminding me to turn these things over to You, knowing only You have the best solution.*

Day 113

TREMBLE OR TRUST

The concept of "the fear of the Lord" is intriguing in all its facets and carries with it a natural tension. For example, when Moses came down from Mount Sinai with the Law of God, he told the people, "Don't be afraid." Yet, we are taught to fear the Lord, for it is "the beginning of knowledge" (Proverbs 1:7).

The writer of Hebrews said: "You have not come to a mountain that can be touched and that is burning with fire; to darkness, gloom and storm.... The sight was so terrifying that Moses said, 'I am trembling with fear.' But you have come to Mount Zion, to the ... heavenly Jerusalem ... to thousands upon thousands of angels in joyful assembly, to the church of the firstborn, whose names are written in heaven. You have come to God, the Judge of all ... to Jesus the mediator of a new covenant, and to the sprinkled blood that speaks a better word than the blood of Abel" (Hebrews 12:18-24).

We don't stand at the foot of Mount Sinai and tremble in fear. We stand at the foot of the cross of Jesus Christ where He finished the work of redemption in trust. "The law was given through Moses; grace and truth came through Jesus Christ" (John 1:17). The old covenant has been fulfilled by the new covenant, for "Christ is the culmination of the law so that there may be righteousness for everyone who believes" (Romans 10:4). As Christians, we should learn from the Old Testament but live by the New Testament as followers of Jesus (Romans 15:4; 2 Timothy 3:16-17). Jesus has fulfilled and completed everything in the Old Testament. The old has given way to the new!

I'm trusting today, not trembling! How about you?

Prayer for the Day: *Lord, there was a day when I trembled in fear before You, being a sinner in need of salvation. Today, as I serve You wholeheartedly, I don't tremble with fear, even if I have sinned. I trust You to forgive me and lead me into Your truth. I praise You.*

Day 114

HEALING TIPS

God revealed Himself through names in Old Testament times. One of the most meaningful names of God is *Jehovah-Rapha*. "If you listen carefully to the Lord your God and do what is right in his eyes, if you pay attention to his commands and keep all his decrees, I will not bring on you any of the diseases I brought on the Egyptians, for I am the Lord, who heals you" (Exodus 15:26). *Jehovah-Rapha* means "I am the Lord who heals you." What a powerful promise!

Illness can be the most stressful situation we face. Yet, we have the assurance that He is Jehovah-Rapha. There are thirty accounts of divine healing in the Old Testament and thirty-eight accounts in the New Testament. One-fifth of the Gospels focus on Jesus' healing ministry. The word *heal* means "to save, mend, restore, cure, and cleanse." Healing is for the total person—spirit, mind, and body (see 1 Thessalonians 5:23).

Healing involves two things: God's part ("I am the Lord who heals you") and our part ("if you listen carefully to the Lord and do what is right"). God gave them dietary and health guidelines in the Mosaic Law. Now we don't have to live by all the dietary laws of the Old Testament. But those laws were for the Hebrews' health. The point is that how we take care of ourselves physically has a lot to do with our overall health.

Did you know that every year the body completely regenerates itself? All the cells in the body are regenerated. The food you eat determines the quality of cell growth. You are a new person every year! Paul even told Timothy, "Stop drinking only water, and use a little wine because of your stomach and your frequent illnesses" (1 Timothy 5:23). He needed to take something for his physical problem. Even though Paul was a powerful apostle, he told Timothy to take care of himself.

Here are two practical steps you can take today to live a healthy life: Trust God to heal you, and take care of yourself!

Prayer for the Day: *Lord, Your Word once again reminds me that healing is for me, but I have a part in my healing. I need to take care of my body by eating right, exercising regularly, obeying Your Word, and leading a life of forgiveness.*

Day 115

LOVE TO THE END

One of the most troubling stories in the Bible is the betrayal of Jesus by Judas Iscariot. Jesus selected Judas as one of the twelve apostles who made up His inner circle. He prayed all night before selecting him (Luke 6:12). Jesus taught and mentored him for four years. Jesus and Judas were close friends. Judas went into towns and villages and told people Jesus was the promised Messiah and that He provided the way of eternal salvation. Yet, in the end, Judas betrayed Him.

Why did Judas betray Jesus? Perhaps it was for political persuasion—trying to provoke a confrontation between Jesus and the powers of the day so Jesus would display His power, mobilize His followers, and overthrow the Roman domination of Israel. Whatever his motive, one thing is certain—Judas had come to the place that he followed Jesus for his own purpose and no longer served God's will.

The prayer of Jesus with His disciples at the Last Supper included a prayer of release: "None [of them] has been lost except the one doomed to destruction so that the Scripture would be fulfilled" (John 17:12). As Jesus and His disciples went to Jerusalem for the Passover, "then Satan entered Judas" and he betrayed Jesus for thirty pieces of silver (Luke 22:3). But Jesus still didn't give up on him. That night He told them all: "Satan has asked to sift all of you as wheat. But I have prayed for you" (Luke 22:31-32). Did Judas repent in the end? Did Jesus' prayer save him in the end? I don't know, but I hope so.

If Jesus didn't give up on Judas, how much more do we know He will never give up on us? Even after Judas sold Him out, led the mob to find Jesus in the Garden of Gethsemane, and betrayed Him with a kiss, Jesus still prayed for him. The Apostle John said Jesus "loved them to the end" (John 13:1).

While the story of Judas troubles us, it also contains a great promise—Jesus will love us to the end. He will never give up on us, for nothing can separate us from His love!

Prayer for the Day: *Lord, I am blown away by Your love for Your creation. To think that You would pray for us even when we are working against You is beyond the love that I can understand. Thank You for being patient and never giving up on us.*

Day 116

MEASURE IT

We use measurements every day. We measure our lives by time. Chefs measure ingredients for cooking. Engineers measure buildings for construction. Accountants measure money for balancing finances. Tailors measure the body for clothing. Measuring things requires us to have an absolute standard such as 12 hours in a day, 12 inches in a foot, and 100 cents in a dollar.

What standard do you and I use to measure our life? Paul wrote of those who use the wrong measurement: "When they measure themselves by themselves and compare themselves with themselves, they are not wise.... For it is not the one who commends himself who is approved, but the one whom the Lord commends" (2 Corinthians 10:12, 18).

As followers of Jesus, we measure our lives by Him. Our goal is to please Him. Our desire is to be like Him. Our purpose is to do His will. Jesus gives us the highest standard by which to measure ourselves. Avoid the trap of measuring yourself by other people's lifestyle, accomplishments, or even their expectations of you. Set your sights higher and aspire to "the whole measure of the fullness of Christ" (Ephesians 4:13). Stop measuring your worth by the things of this world. Rise up to the high calling of God and measure yourself by the standard of Jesus Christ.

Prayer for the Day: *Lord, I must admit I have been following the measurements of this world and of others for too long. Today, I am starting over with brand-new guidelines to measure myself and my life by Your standards.*

Day 117

TWO ROADS

As a high school senior in a literature class, I found myself deeply interested in the poetry of Robert Frost and wrote a paper on his life and work. His poem "The Road Not Taken" still makes a strong impression on me:

> Two roads diverged in a wood,
> And I took the one less traveled by,
> And that has made all the difference.

We come to crossroads in life, and the road we take determines where we will end up. A decision today determines our destiny tomorrow. God speaks to us, "Stand at the crossroads and look; ask for the ancient paths, ask where the good way is, and walk in it, and you will find rest for your souls" (Jeremiah 6:16). Sometimes the best road is the ancient path of time-tested wisdom. New is not always better. Don't get misled because something is trendy. Ask for the ancient path and stay on the road that leads to a blessed life.

Jesus said, "Enter through the narrow gate. For wide is the gate and broad is the road that leads to destruction, and many enter through it. But small is the gate and narrow the road that leads to life, and only a few find it" (Matthew 7:13-14). What a powerful reminder not to take a road just because "that's what everyone is doing"! Don't follow the crowd but follow the will of God, the leading of the Holy Spirit, and your own conscience. Have the courage to be yourself and go against the grain. Resist the urge to follow the crowd when you know they are on the wrong road.

I have learned the right road always leads to the right place. You determine your destiny by choosing the right road today and staying on it. Sometimes it is the less-traveled road that will get you where you should be.

Prayer for the Day: *Lord, thank You for always directing my footsteps! When I look back over my life, I can see Your nudging me away from the roads of the world and guiding me back to Your path that leads to life as I should live it.*

Day 118

NOAH'S ARK AND YOU

Noah courageously served God in his generation. "By faith Noah, when warned about things not yet seen, in holy fear built an ark to save his family" (Hebrews 11:7a).

Noah was a man in tune with the voice of God. He knew calamity was coming at some point in the future, although God didn't give him a time frame. He didn't know the specifics, only that he was to get ready today for what was coming.

God will never tell us much about the future because He wants us to live by faith in Him each day and not worry about the future. But when He shows us something, we need to take action today and get ready for it so we are not taken by surprise.

Noah warned his generation. He preached the Word of God to them (2 Peter 2:5). He cared about them and pointed the way to safety. What we build needs to help others along the way. The name *Noah* means "comfort, encouragement."

Just like Noah, God often speaks to us about our future. He gives us a plan or a task, and He expects us to do the work. God blesses what we build according to His plans.

Noah built an ark to save his family. By doing so, Noah "became heir of the righteousness that is in keeping with faith" (Hebrews 11:7b).

What we build today will carry us tomorrow. We determine our destiny by what we are building today. Don't worry about the future, but get busy building today!

Prayer for the Day: *Lord, forgive me for always wanting to know the future. Sometimes I can't live in the moment because I am looking ahead trying to figure out what You're doing. Help me to rest in knowing that it will prepare me for whatever tomorrow brings.*

Day 119

STONE CUTTERS

Michelangelo described the art of sculpture as "the making of men." He said his role was to free men and women from the prison of stone. Instead of trying to fashion the image of a man from stone, he chiseled away the excess stone that kept the image hidden. He had the ability to look at a piece of marble and envision such great works of art as *David*, the *Pieta*, *Moses*, and the *Bacchus*.

His work illustrates how the Holy Spirit works in us to conform us to the image of Jesus. In the beginning, we were created in God's own image, but sin has ruined that image. Jesus came to save us from our sins and restore in us the image of God.

Sometimes Michelangelo quit working on a sculpture out of frustration. He left the statue of *Saint Matthew* half-finished. He said the stone refused the release of the prisoner. Four of his most magnificent statues (*the Slaves*) are unfinished. Not so with the Holy Spirit. God promises to finish what He started in us the moment we received Jesus as Savior.

Someone asked the famous painter Rembrandt at what point a painting is complete. He replied, "A painting is finished when it expresses the intent of the artist."

So, cooperate with God, letting Him chip away the excess stone so the image of Jesus can be seen more fully in you. Be encouraged to know that "he who began a good work in you will carry it on to completion" (Philippians 1:6).

Prayer for the Day: *Lord, please keep chipping away at the stone of my heart! I am excited to see what I can become when You are finished with me.*

Day 120

LEFTOVERS

One of the greatest stories in the Bible is about a woman named Ruth, who became the great-grandmother of King David. She grew up in Moab, south of Israel, where people worshiped idols. She met a Jewish woman named Naomi and her family, who had moved to Moab during a famine. Ruth married one of Naomi's sons, and for ten years they lived together in Moab. Then both Naomi's husband and Ruth's husband died.

Steeped in grief, Naomi decided to go back home to Bethlehem. She told Ruth to stay in Moab and get married again, but Ruth refused to leave Naomi's side. So she went back to Bethlehem with her. Naomi's neighbors were overjoyed to see her, but she said, "Don't call me *Naomi* [meaning 'pleasant'] anymore, but call me *Mara* because the Lord has made my life very bitter" (see Ruth 1:20).

The family house and property had been lost ten years earlier through the famine and bankruptcy. Naomi's husband and two sons had passed away. She returned home broke and bitter. But Ruth wanted to help her. "Let me go to the fields and pick up the leftover grain behind anyone in whose eyes I find favor" (Ruth 2:2).

What do you do when you are living on leftovers? Three things turned their famine into fortune, and they will turn your life around. First, Ruth worked hard, doing whatever she could find to do. Second, she found favor through her hard work and faithfulness to Naomi. Third, she trusted God to open a new door of opportunity and provision.

Boaz, who owned the fields and was a wealthy relative, noticed Ruth. She fell in love with him, and they got married. They had a baby boy, Obed, who became King David's grandfather. Naomi changed her name back to "pleasant" when God restored everything to her. Her grandson gave her new joy and purpose. "Then Naomi took the child in her arms and cared for him" (Ruth 4:16).

Instead of living on leftovers, get to work, look for favor, and trust God!

Prayer for the Day: *Lord, I have been living on leftovers. Well, no more! I am throwing the leftovers in the trash and am trusting You for new opportunities.*

Day 121

VALIDATED!

Psychologist Alfred Adler coined the term *inferiority complex*. He believed we are driven to overcome a basic sense of inadequacy and to achieve a sense of superiority. He did not mean superiority over others but over our own sense of inadequacy.

We tend to have a low opinion of ourselves. We often battle feelings of unimportance and insignificance. After learning about the calling of God, a teenager remarked, "I used to feel invisible to others, but now I know God has a purpose for my life." You matter to God, to your family, and to this world.

If you go for a job interview and they call you back, it makes you feel important. There is a validation when you get called. If you apply for college and they send you a letter of acceptance, you feel important. When you get an award, you feel valued and special. If you are a man who asks a woman to marry you, and to your surprise she says yes, you feel validated (and blessed). More importantly, you have the high calling of God on your life!

When you and I become followers of Jesus Christ, there are not just the spiritual benefits of forgiveness, healing, and salvation; there are also psychological benefits. When we hear and answer the call of Jesus Christ to follow Him, we suddenly realize we matter in this life and God has a purpose for our lives.

So, "forgetting those things which are behind . . . press toward the goal for the prize of the upward call of God in Christ Jesus" (Philippians 3:14 NKJV). There is a high calling on your life.

Prayer for the Day: *Lord, there was a time in my life when I didn't know who I was or why I was even alive. When I found You, that all changed! Now I know I am Your child. You placed me here, and I have purpose. Thank You for Your validation.*

Day 122

COMMON DENOMINATOR

When working with math fractions, we use the highest and lowest common denominator. The calling of God is the highest common denominator that will raise your life to the highest level. Don't follow the crowd or your own sinful desires down to the lowest common denominator. Instead, "[walk] worthy of the calling you have received" (Ephesians 4:1).

In Proverbs 1:10 we read, "[When sinners] entice you, do not give in to them." Following the crowd leads us down the wrong road to the wrong destination. Remember, "the person who walks with the wise grows wise, but a companion of fools suffers harm" (Proverbs 13:20). I am sure we have all gotten in trouble at some point in our lives because we hung out with the wrong people and followed the crowd that brought us down to a low level.

Jesus Christ comes by and says, "Follow Me, and I will make you fishers of men" (Matthew 4:19 NKJV). He promises to make something special of us and do something great with us if we will follow Him. The way of the crowd leads us downward; the way of Jesus leads us upward.

The calling of God will keep you focused on living for the glory of God. Don't do anything that violates the calling of God on your life. You don't live by chance or coincidence but by the calling of God.

Let's walk worthy of the high calling of God we have received. Let's answer that calling every day with new faith and commitment. Let's live up to our potential and seek to honor the Lord in all we think, do, and say. Face life today knowing Jesus Christ has called you to represent Him to the world!

Prayer for the Day: *Lord, I look around this world and see a lot of people living low lives. They don't realize that in You there is so much more. Thank You for Your calling upon my life. I pray I will always walk worthy of it.*

Day 123

WHAT'S THE THEME?

While reading Psalm 22, I was struck with the impact of this phrase: "From you [God] comes the theme of my praise" (v. 25). Movies, books, plays, and music are built around a theme. In literature, music, and art, writers and artists have to keep the theme central.

What is the theme of my praise? What am I thankful for? What do I acknowledge as most important? Where do I get my life principles? What do I honor and respect? The psalmist reminds us our God needs to be the theme of our praise. My praise is about Him—not about me or about the temporary situation of my life.

Some people make their situation and circumstance the theme of their praise. If the situation is good, then they are good. As long as their circumstances are up, they are on cloud nine. But if things are down, they are down. They rise and fall on their circumstances. They are victims of their situation.

My praise is based on the changelessness of my God who loves me with an everlasting love, who keeps me by His grace, and who watches over me with His power, provision, and protection. He alone is the theme of my praise. Today I give Him praise, honor, and glory for who He is, what He has done, what He is doing, and what He will do. Even though things around me may change, He never changes!

Prayer for the Day: *Lord, You and You alone are the reason I have any praise at all! Your love, Your salvation, Your healing, Your Word, and Your relationship with Your children are all reasons to make You the theme of my praise.*

Day 124

THE FEAR THAT CURES ALL FEARS

Robert Louis Stevenson said, "Keep your fears to yourself; share your courage with others." Fear is one of the most toxic emotions we feel.

It has a paralyzing effect on us. We battle different kinds of fears and phobias.

One night during a thunderstorm, a mother tucked her little girl into bed. As she turned off the light, her little girl said, "Mommy, will you sleep with me tonight?"

She gave her little girl a big hug, reassured her she was OK, and said, "I can't, sweetheart. I have to sleep with Daddy."

As she turned to leave the room, the little girl muttered, "That big sissy!"

What would you think if I told you there is a fear that cures all fears? "The fear of the Lord is the beginning of knowledge, but fools despise wisdom and instruction" (Proverbs 1:7) The fear of the Lord is not the unhealthy fear of worry, anxiety, and panic. "For God has not given us a spirit of fear" (2 Timothy 1:7 NKJV). First John 4:18 says, "Perfect love drives out fear." God does not want us to be afraid of Him.

The fear of the Lord is a sense of awe, reverence, worship, and trust in God that cures us of all fears. When we fear the Lord, we have nothing else to fear because we live under His care, provision, and protection.

The first Biblical reference to the fear of the Lord is when God tested Abraham's faith. When Abraham passed the test, the angel said to him, "Now I know that you fear God" (Genesis 22:12). That is the same as saying, "Now I know that you completely trust the Lord." The fear of the Lord is total trust in Him that He will provide, and that gives us peace instead of anxiety and worry. Circumstances will always change, but God never changes and we can depend on Him. The fear of the Lord will cure you of all your fears.

Prayer for the Day: *Lord, before I asked You into my heart, I was a fearful person. I worried over everything. As I have learned to trust You, my life isn't perfect, but I don't worry as much, knowing that my life is in Your hands.*

Day 125

RUSTED OUT

The *Queen Mary* was the largest ship to cross the oceans when it was launched in 1936. Forty years later she was retired and anchored as a floating hotel and museum in Long Beach, California. During the renovation work, the three massive smokestacks were removed so they could be scraped down and repainted, but they crumbled on the dock. Nothing remained of the three-fourth-inch steel plate from which the stacks had been built. The only thing that remained was thirty coats of paint which had been applied over the years. The steel had completely rusted away!

The ship only had the appearance of strength. Its weakness was revealed when it was shaken and fell apart. God promises, "Once more I will shake not only the earth but also the heavens. The words 'once more' indicate the removing of what can be shaken—that is, created things—so that what cannot be shaken may remain" (Hebrews 12:26-27).

We must not allow our lives to be built on things that can be shaken—that is, created things, physical things, and material things. The *Queen Mary* looked like its structure was solid steel, but the smokestacks crumbled. We need a real faith in God—not just the appearance of faith.

We need to build our lives on things that cannot be shaken—faith, hope, and love—so when we are shaken by the problems, pressures, and pain of life, we won't crumble. Instead, we will remain "strong, firm and steadfast" (1 Peter 5:10).

Prayer for the Day: *Lord, thank You for reminding me that the things I value and the world I live in is temporary. Once again, I realize that my only true value is You. This world may fall apart and everything in it rust out, but You remain.*

Day 126

KEEP MOVING

My favorite street sign is one you will see on turn lanes that simply reads, "Keep Moving!" We had one near our house, but people would stop right in front of it! Blowing my horn was not rude and was not road rage because I was helping them obey the law. Several months ago, Barbie called me and said, "They got rid of your sign. It's no longer there."

Why would they do that? I couldn't believe it. For almost a year, that turn lane got bogged down because they got rid of that sign. I told Barbie that they needed to put the sign back up. Then I was on cloud nine the day I saw they put up a brand-new "Keep Moving" sign. They even moved it to a better location to send the message loud and clear, although I saw an SUV stop right in front of it the other day. The drivers behind them were going nuts, and I knew everyone in their cars was yelling, "Keep moving!"

The ability to keep moving is one of the most important principles for a healthy and productive life. Difficulties and disappointments can cause us to bog down. Discouragement and setbacks tend to make us want to quit. Fears and anxieties can paralyze us. Questions and confusion can get us to the point that we cannot make a decision about anything. Then the Lord speaks to us like He did when the Israelites faced the Red Sea and said, "Move on" (Exodus 14:15). Move on in faith. Move on with courage. Move on toward your destiny. Your Red Sea will part when you take the first step to move on.

If you are stuck today, get yourself unstuck by moving. Don't sit where you are, and don't stay like you are. Dr. Martin Luther King Jr. said, "If you can't fly, then run; if you can't run, then walk; if you can't walk, then crawl; but whatever you do, you have to keep moving forward."

Prayer for the Day: *Lord, there have been discouraging times in my life when all I wanted to do was stop and give up. Life had become too hard, and I felt like things would never change. But I picked myself up and kept moving forward, and You, in Your great mercy, pulled me out of my despair. I praise You!*

Day 127

LISTEN UP

My mother used to tell me God gave me two ears and one mouth, so I should spend twice as much time listening as I did speaking. Proverbs 19:27 teaches us to listen so that we can become wise: "Stop listening to instruction, my son, and you will stray from the words of knowledge."

Teaching won't benefit us unless we listen. Our ears have 3,500 tiny hair cells and 25,000 sound receptor cells that distinguish 300,000 tones. Every sound has its own number of vibrations that activate the eardrum. For example, middle C on a piano is molecules oscillating 256 times per second. We can distinguish between 20 and 20,000 vibrations. That is why we can hear the differences between buzzing, a word, a musical note, and the blowing of the wind.

Listen . . . learn . . . live! No matter how much we know, we can learn more. "Let the wise listen and add to their learning" (Proverbs 1:5). When someone is talking to us, we need to listen closely and not get ahead of them. "To answer before listening—that is folly and shame" (Proverbs 18:13).

When we read or hear God's Word taught, we need to tune in and listen. Jesus said, "Whoever has ears, let them hear" (Matthew 11:15). Most importantly, we need to live out the Word of God we listen to. "Do not merely listen to the word. . . . Do what it says" (James 1:22).

May we have the attitude of Samuel when he prayed, "Speak, [Lord] your servant is listening" (1 Samuel 3:10). Listen up! God is speaking to you.

Prayer for the Day: *Lord, I haven't always listened when You were speaking to me. I ignored Your Word and pursued my own way. That was foolish! Today I say, "Speak, Lord, Your servant is listening." I choose to pursue You.*

Day 128

TAKE THE FIRST STEP

Many people want to know the future. But God wants us to walk by faith and trust Him with the future. He unfolds His plan for us little by little, one step at a time. Otherwise, it would be like watching a movie the second time—you know what's going to happen next. The adventure is gone.

I took Barbie to a movie I had already seen. At every suspenseful scene she would whisper, "What's going to happen next?" Every time I would say, "Watch the movie!"

We ask God in prayer, "What's going to happen next in my life?" God says, "Watch the movie! Enjoy the adventure of your life!"

Think of the call of Abraham. God called him to leave his home and go to the unfamiliar land of Canaan. He "obeyed and went, even though he did not know where he was going" (Hebrews 11:8). He knew the general direction, but he had to take the first step and trust God to lead him to the next step. God only told him to leave. Just one word—*leave*. He obeyed, "even though he did not know where he was going!"

Abraham went on adventure with God. When he left, God showed him the next step. But not until he took the first step by faith. God doesn't always show us what lies around the next corner. He expects us to walk by faith, not by sight. God's will unfolds one step at a time in a great adventure.

We often want a guarantee before we take the step of faith, but *God* is the guarantee. He doesn't give a guarantee; *He* is the guarantee because His word never fails. So, take the first step and trust God to lead you to the next step. Stop trying to know the future; just live the present fully!

Prayer for the Day: *Lord, I am going to walk with You daily. When You say go left, I will go left. When You say go right, I will go right. I will listen and obey because I trust Your way.*

Day 129

PACE YOURSELF

This is a common saying about archery: "Do not keep the strings pulled back all the time or the bow will break." That is an important lesson for life. When I visited Germany, I noticed how much better the people paced themselves than we do in America. At 5 p.m., everything abruptly shuts down! People went to dinner and hung out for hours.

I was in a store looking to get a souvenir in the old town of Rothenburg. They had this huge cuckoo clock in the town square. At 5:00 that clock went off and every store started immediately to close their doors. An employee told me, "We're closing, so if you are going to get something, you need to do it now."

We are a driven people; we are driven to succeed, and that is a great quality about us. But, do we drive too hard and too fast? Are we always living in the fast lane? Or, do we know how to get off at the rest stops of life?

Learning to pace yourself is vital to reaching your goals and achieving success. The Bible says, "Go to the ant, you sluggard; consider its ways and be wise! . . . It stores its provisions in summer and gathers its food at harvest" (Proverbs 6:6-8). Ants prepare for the future. They look ahead. They keep an eye on the future seasons and pace themselves. Ants are long-range thinkers, as are successful people. They think about where life is heading and get ready in advance so life doesn't take them by surprise.

We are often too short-sighted, burning ourselves out trying to do everything *now*. We do too much too fast, and "Haste makes waste," as my mother used to tell me.

Life moves in seasons. First are *seasons of gathering*, which means work, activity, and productivity. Second comes *seasons of storing*, and that is when we rest from our work. We hang out with friends. We spend time in worship. We enjoy our hobbies and personal interests.

Don't push yourself (or others) so much that the Lord "makes [you] lie down in green pastures," as Psalm 23:2 says. Make yourself lie down and rest. Pace yourself. When it's gathering time, work with all your heart. When it's time to enjoy what you have stored up and worked for, then do it with as much joy as you do when you work. Life is a marathon, not a sprint, so remember to pace yourself.

Prayer for the Day: *Lord, thank You for the reminder to pace myself rather than wear myself out. Too often I work myself too hard. Success won't come overnight but by me being diligent and faithful. I will work and I will rest.*

Day 130
GOLD RING IN A PIG'S SNOUT

In *King Henry IV*, Shakespeare said, "Discretion is the better part of valor." Proverbs 11:22 says, "Like a gold ring in a pig's snout is a beautiful woman who shows no discretion." What a graphic picture—a gold ring in a pig's snout. How out of place! So, it is with indiscretion. *Discretion* has the meaning of "acting on one's own authority and judgment."

The discreet person avoids causing offense, keeps information private, and takes appropriate action. This person knows the right thing to say and do in a situation. We see labels and signs like: "Viewer Discretion Advised," "Parental Discretion Advised," and a new one, "Voter Discretion Advised!" I saw a T-shirt that read: "Welcome to my life—viewer discretion advised."

The Proverbs were written for "giving . . . knowledge and discretion. . . . Discretion will protect you, and understanding will guard you" (Proverbs 1:4; 2:11). As David was about to become the next king, he said to Solomon: "May the Lord give you discretion and understanding when he puts you in command over Israel, so that you may keep the law of the Lord your God" (1 Chronicles 22:12).

The Apostle Paul said, "Be careful, however, that the exercise of your [freedom] does not become a stumbling block to the weak" (1 Corinthians 8:9). He also said of his own ministry, "For we are taking pains to do what is right, not only in the eyes of the Lord but also in the eyes of man" (2 Corinthians 8:21). Many people say, "I don't care what people think." When we practice discretion, we will care what people think and always try to do what is right, not only in the eyes of the Lord but also in the eyes of others.

We all need to think more before we speak, consider the outcome of our actions, protect the secrets of others, and aim to do what is the best thing for others in every situation we face.

Prayer for the Day: *Lord, once again Your Word speaks loudly to my heart! I will make it my aim to be more discreet, to guard what comes out of my mouth, and to be sensitive of others' feelings.*

Day 131
KEEP A SECRET

At the end of a recent conversation, the other person said, "Please don't say anything to anyone." I replied, "As a pastor and a counselor, I don't repeat anything to anyone." I have spent a lot of time and money in my training as a counselor learning how to be confidential.

The Bible says, "A gossip betrays a confidence, but a trustworthy person keeps a secret" (Proverbs 11:13). Can we keep a secret?

One of the greatest ways we can help people is to provide a safe, trustworthy place where they can tell us anything and we will keep their secret, pray for them, and not judge them. Emotional healing is experienced when someone listens and loves us unconditionally.

This is what the Apostle James meant when he wrote, "Therefore confess your sins to each other and pray for each other so that you may be healed" (James 5:16). Confessing our sins, failures, mistakes, faults, and hurts can only happen in a safe, trusting environment.

We should never say something about a person, regardless of how true it is, if it will hurt them. Remember, a gossip betrays a confidence. People who gossip don't think of it as gossip if what they're saying about someone is true. Gossip can also be telling the truth for the purpose of hurting someone. "A gossip betrays a confidence; so avoid anyone who talks too much" (Proverbs 20:19).

Our words should build others up, not tear them down. The best way to build someone up is to not say anything that would hurt them. The Apostle Paul spoke of "the authority the Lord gave me for building you up, not for tearing you down" (2 Corinthians 13:10). We also have that same authority.

President Calvin Coolidge said, "I've never been hurt by something I didn't say." Neither has anyone else. So, keep a secret.

Prayer for the Day: *Lord, I'm so convicted by Your Word on keeping a secret. Sometimes I share information I shouldn't. I realize this is gossiping. Please keep a guard over my lips and remind me to keep the secrets entrusted to me.*

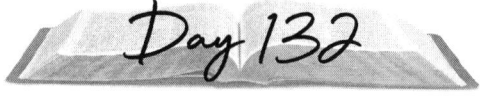

Day 132

PLEASANT WORDS

We know how powerful words are in our relationships. Words make us or break us in terms of the words we speak and the words we hear. With social media we are using more words than at any time in history. It is important that we speak gracious words.

Proverbs 16:21 says, "Gracious words promote instruction." This proverb can be translated from Hebrew, "Pleasant words make a person persuasive." The idea of *promoting instruction* means when we use persuasive words, people listen to us and take to heart what we are saying. If we say the right thing with unpleasant words, people tune us out.

If you want to influence people, don't criticize them, pressure them, or control them with words, but use pleasant words. When Joseph was restored to his brothers after they abused him, he did not retaliate. Instead, he "reassured them and spoke kindly to them" (Genesis 50:21). Do the same, even to the people who hurt you.

Proverbs 16:24 says, "[Pleasant] words are a honeycomb, sweet to the soul and healing to the bones." I love honey. It goes with just about anything. Honey not only tastes sweet, it gives energy. I like to eat honey before I speak or exercise because of the burst of energy it gives. Pleasant words are easy to listen to, "sweet to the soul," and give people strength for life, "healing to the bones." King David said of Holy Scripture, "How sweet are your words to my taste, sweeter than honey to my mouth!" (Psalm 119:103).

It is a simple, yet powerful gift we can all give to others—the gift of pleasant words. As we go about this day, let us focus on speaking gracious words and know they make us persuasive, attractive, and influential.

Prayer for the Day: *Lord, I so agree with Your instruction on using pleasant words rather than harsh words. It seems we have a world of people using harsh words to make their points and get their way. It doesn't work and never will. We can accomplish so much with kindness.*

Day 133

HE KNOWS THE WAY I TAKE

One of the worst feelings in the world is feeling like people have forgotten about us. I think that is why social media is so important to people. It gives us a way to stay connected and not be forgotten. It is great to hear from friends and family, for people to check up on us, to share our dreams and accomplishments with them. When we are going through tough times, it means everything to us for people to call us, text us, message us, and even drop by to see us (if the house is not a wreck!). Nobody wants to be forgotten.

Sometimes we feel like God has forgotten about us. When we go through dark times of discouragement and depression, we wonder, *Where is God?* I am sure that is how Job, whose story is made famous in the Old Testament, felt when he went through a horrific season of life. He experienced financial loss, the death of loved ones, illness, and tension in his marriage. In spite of all of that, he said, "He [God] knows the way that I take; when he has tested me, I will come forth as gold" (Job 23:10).

Amazing, isn't it! Instead of turning away from God, Job turned to Him. Instead of telling himself (we all talk to ourselves) that God had forgotten about him, he told himself God was at work in his life. He saw the difficulties of life as a test, and I don't think he was blaming God for his problems or suggesting God had caused his problems. He meant that what happens to us in life is always a test of what we truly believe. He chose to believe God knew everything he was going through and would bring him through. He would emerge as a better man, not a bitter man. He would come forth as gold refined by fire.

Well, if God knows the way that I take, why doesn't He come down here and do something about it? God's role is not to live life for us or to fix all our problems. That is just fantasy thinking. God created the world and allows it to take its natural course. One day in the future He will make a new heaven and a new earth, but for now we are stuck down here. God has not abandoned us. He knows the way that we take. He walks with us through every experience and every season of life, good and bad. We must trust Him to be with us, strengthen us, to bring us through every experience as gold!

Prayer for the Day: *Lord, sometimes I forget You are always with me, especially when times are hard. Thank You for leading and guiding me, for carrying me when I can't move on, and never forsaking me.*

Day 134

WITHDRAW

I heard a man remark, "I got out of the rat race; the rats won!" When people put great demands on Jesus, He "often withdrew to solitary places to pray" (see Luke 5:16). Studies show that when we're alone, quiet negativity decreases and alertness, calmness, creativity, and energy increases.

I talked to a friend who had just been released from the hospital after having brain surgery for cancer. He has fought six battles with cancer. As we talked, his faith in God was radiant. I called to encourage him, but he encouraged me! I told him I was sorry to hear of his struggles, but he told me of the peace, joy, and victory he enjoyed. He focused on his Creator, not on his cancer. A survey conducted by the National

Opinion Research Center showed Americans who had suffered divorce, unemployment, death of a loved one, or serious injury or disability—but had a strong faith in God—had greater joy than those who had no faith.

Take time to withdraw and worship. You will find new strength for life's journey if you do. Remember, "If you do not stand firm in your faith, you will not stand at all" (Isaiah 7:9). Our faith is renewed in the presence of the Lord when we withdraw and worship Him. Strength is often found in solitude.

Prayer for the Day: *Lord, please help me to remember to withdraw to a quiet place when the struggles of life press in—a place where I can feel Your presence and hear Your voice, a place where I can worship You.*

Day 135

KEEP IT TOGETHER

Many people these days are falling apart. Marriages, finances, and businesses are falling apart. The world around us is falling apart. But you can keep it together!

The Bible says Jesus is "sustaining all things by his powerful word" (Hebrews 1:3). This means He holds the universe together. The word *sustain* means "to carry along." Jesus holds all things together by His powerful word. He guides history, or carries it along, toward its final goal. He sustains all things! Nothing is excluded from His providence.

What Jesus does for the world around us, He can do for the world within us! He will hold us together. He will hold our families together. He will hold His church together. When we trust Him completely, we won't come apart in fear, stress, and depression because He will keep us together "by his powerful word."

That is the key to keeping it together—build your life on Christ's powerful word. Don't build your life, your marriage, your family, your finances, and your career on the ways of this world, but on Him. Live by the promises and principles of Scripture and you will be able to keep it together. "The word of God is alive and active" (Hebrews 4:12), so when you read it, believe it, and act on it, the truths of God will be alive and at work in you!

Don't be unsettled by the world today. Keep it together by listening to, learning from, and living out the Word of God.

Prayer for the Day: *Lord, I long for Your return! But until then, I will build my life on Your Word and do everything humanly possible to hold it together. When things begin to fall apart, I will look to You for strength and wisdom, knowing You keep Me in the palm of Your hand!*

Day 136

LISTEN TO YOUR HEART

There are two things the Holy Spirit does to help protect us. First, He gives us a sense of unrest when we are about to go the wrong way or make the wrong decision. He gives us a feeling of concern. We have an intuition to avoid a situation, a place, or a relationship. We have an innate sense that something is wrong. We need to listen to His voice of caution to keep us from making a mistake. The Holy Spirit doesn't just comfort us; He troubles us for our own protection.

Second, the Holy Spirit gives us a sense of peace when we are going the right way and doing the right thing. I believe we should only make a decision when we are at peace, not when we are in conflict. If your decision causes you unrest, anxiety, and confusion, then you are making the wrong decision. When we make the right decision and do the right thing, we will experience peace.

Weighing the pros and cons of a decision is important. But at the end of the day, after all the research is done, it may be best to follow your heart, if Christ is living there. "Let the peace of Christ rule in your hearts" (Colossians 3:15).

Prayer for the Day: *Lord, I praise You for the Holy Spirit who guides and directs my life. I haven't always listened to His voice and made mistakes because of it. I am determined to always pray and seek Your way before going forward. I will listen and wait for Your peace.*

Day 137

BLAME OR BLESS?

Have you ever met someone who is angry at God? Or have you ever been angry with God? Provers 19:3 speaks to such anger: "A person's own folly leads to their ruin, yet their heart rages against the Lord."

We are often the victims of our own decisions. Sometimes we experience the consequence of bad decisions we made many years ago. Have you ever made decisions that ruined your life or at least messed you up for a while? I have. So, we don't need to blame God for our decisions.

Projection is a way we cope with our negative feelings. Instead of taking ownership of our feelings and choices, we like to blame others. Sometimes we blame God. Maybe it's not our bad decisions that are ruining our lives. It can also be the impact of other people's decisions on us. A family member, a close friend, a business associate, the company you work for, or politicians and their laws make an impact on us, and sometimes it's for the worst!

But we should not "rage against the Lord." We should always praise God and trust Him. Turn to Him, never away from Him, in times of trouble. Don't blame God for your decisions or the decisions of others that affect your life and circumstances. Instead of blaming God, bless Him! "Bless the Lord, O my soul; and all that is within me, bless His holy name!" (Psalm 103:1 NKJV).

Prayer for the Day: *Lord, I have made some poor decisions that have negatively impacted my life. I have also listened to bad counsel that affected my life. Starting today, I'm creating healthy boundaries from well-meaning advisers, and I'm going to live my life by Your Word and seek Your wisdom.*

Day 138

WHICH WAY SHOULD I GO?

In Lewis Carroll's classic *Alice in Wonderland*, Alice comes to a fork in the road. She meets the Cheshire Cat and says somewhat timidly, "Cheshire Puss, would you tell me, please, which way I ought to go from here?"

"That depends a good deal on where you want to get to," says the Cat.

"I don't much care where."

"Then it doesn't matter which way you go."

"So long as I get *somewhere*," Alice adds as an explanation.

"Oh, you're sure to do that," says the Cat, "if you only walk long enough."

We all want to know the way to live a happy and meaningful life. We stand at crossroads of major decisions and ask which way we should go. The answer lies in where we want to end up. Our decisions determine our direction, and that leads to our destination or destiny. About that—the words *destination* and *destiny* have the same meaning. Proverbs 16:25 cautions us: "There is a way that appears to be right, but in the end it leads to death."

There is always "a way" to get to where you want to go. God will make a way where there is no way if you will follow Him. He said, "I am making a way in the wilderness" (Isaiah 43:19). Our problem is that we want to take shortcuts, but there is no shortcut to God's blessings. You have to choose the right way, and that is always God's way for your life.

Be cautious in making major decisions—"there is a way that *seems* right," but it isn't right. Everything that seems right is not always right. We get misled by false advertisement, secular media, bad counsel, and by our own heart! Test everything by the Word of God and by the leading of the Spirit after you pray and seek wise counsel.

Let those words echo in your mind—"in the end it leads to . . . ." Your decisions lead to something in the end, either good or bad. Shortsighted thinking will get you in trouble. Ask yourself, *What is the end result of my decision?*

A young couple came to see me for counseling. The husband said, "I've tried doing the right thing, but it doesn't work out."

I replied, "That's impossible! If you do the right thing, it will turn out right. If you do the wrong thing, it will turn out wrong." Our decision determines our destiny!

Prayer for the Day: *Lord, when I come to a crossroads, it is safer to stay there until I hear from You. I want to make good decisions that will lead to where You have called me to go. Speak to me through Your Word and through godly counsel!*

Day 139

JUST HIT "DELETE"

My favorite feature on a computer is the delete button. You undo all your mistakes and remove all the clutter from your computer at the touch of a button. Computers run faster when the files are cleared out. In the same way, we need to learn to clear our minds. "Be alert and of sober mind so that you may pray" (1 Peter 4:7).

The human brain is the most complex and powerful computer in the world. The brain is divided into two hemispheres: *right brain* (visual imagery, art, music, spatial relations) and *left brain* (language, logic). The *mind* is a psychological term describing the functions of the brain—thought, feeling, and choice. Our ability to think, reason, and decide is what makes us unique. We are always free to choose!

What do I need to clear my mind of? First, *past failures*. God says, "Forget the former things; do not dwell on the past" (Isaiah 43:18). Delete the files in your brain that remind you of your mistakes, sins, poor decisions, and failures. Call it "history" because it's over!

Second, clear your mind of *present frustrations*. "Do not let the sun go down while you are still angry" (Ephesians 4:26). It's OK to get angry, frustrated, and disappointed in life, in situations, and even with other people; but get over it quickly. Get your mind back on your purpose for today and not all the things around you that frustrate you. Accept the imperfections of life without letting your frustrations get the best of you.

Third, clear your mind of *future fears*. Stop worrying about what *might* happen to the economy, your personal situation, or the world. In speaking about the time of His second coming, Jesus said, "Be careful, or your hearts will be weighed down with carousing, drunkenness and the anxieties of life" (Luke 21:34). Live in the moment and let God take care of tomorrow.

If your mind is cluttered with the files of past failure, present frustrations, or future worries, just hit "delete"!

Prayer for the Day: *Lord, please help me to be clear-minded and self-controlled so I can hear Your voice and pray. Clear my mind of the past I can do nothing about; the present, knowing You will work out all things for me; and future fears that may never ever happen.*

Day 140

THE RIGHT WORD

A foreign ambassador attended a special dinner in Washington, D.C. His English was very poor. The senator seated next to him struck up a conversation. The senator asked him, "Do you have any children?" Trying to explain that his wife could not bear children, he said, "No, we don't have any children; my wife is impregnable."

The senator looked puzzled, so the ambassador added, "What I mean is my wife is inconceivable." The senator looked even more puzzled. "What I meant to say is that my wife is unbearable!"

The right word is so important. Proverbs 25:11 says, "A word fitly spoken is like apples of gold in settings of silver" (NKJV). We need the right word for the situation. The right word can make a difference in winning a negotiation, solving a problem, healing a relationship, making a sale, or getting a job.

According to *Compton's Encyclopedia*, the total number of words in the English language is around 750,000. Of that number, we habitually use 500 to 2,000 at the most. In *Roger's Thesaurus*, there are more than 3,000 words describing various emotions. Two-thirds of these words describe negative emotions.

Proverbs 10:19 says, in effect, "When words are many, sin is not absent, but he who holds his tongue is wise." Learning to monitor our words, conserve our words, and wisely use our words is key to success. The Lord's Prayer contains 56 words; the Gettysburg Address, 266 words; the Ten Commandments, 297 words; the Declaration of Independence, 300 words; and a U.S. government order setting the price of cabbage, 26,911 words! It is not how long we talk, but what we say that is important.

Always search for the right word in your conversations and communications. The right word can make all the difference!

Prayer for the Day: *Lord, please put Your words in my mouth and give me the ability to use them wisely. In all my conversations, may I listen carefully and respond with love and the right words.*

Day 141

YOU GOTTA SEE IT

The great missionary William Carey, who preached the good news of Jesus in India, said, "Expect great things from God. Attempt great things for God." We live in the age of mediocrity where the average is celebrated as greatness, where there are no winners in the game, and where trying is the same as doing. Mediocrity exists because people have no real vision for their lives.

Proverbs 29:18 says, "Where there is no vision [no revelation of God and His word], the people are unrestrained; but happy and blessed is he who keeps the law [of God]" (Amp.). Happiness comes from keeping the law of God, and that means to have a vision for your life based on Scripture.

What is your vision for the kind of person you want to be? What is your vision for your life and career? What is your vision for your marriage and family? What is your vision for ministry? Where there is no vision, we are unrestrained—we live without boundaries. We drift off course. We fall apart at the seams!

What you see is what you get! Your vision determines everything about who you are and what you will accomplish with your life. Jesus told His disciples, "Open your eyes and look at the fields! They are ripe for harvest" (John 4:35). He wanted them to see things differently than they had ever seen them. If you want to get your life on track and accomplish everything you have the power to accomplish, get a vision for your life based on Scripture. Then go for that vision with all your effort.

When Jesus faced the cross, He had a vision of the salvation of the world. "For the joy [that was] set before him he endured the cross" (Hebrews 12:2). The joy before Him was our salvation through His death and resurrection. You and I can endure the challenges of life when we, too, have a joy (a vision) set before us. Before you seize it, you've got to see it.

Prayer for the Day: *Lord, open my eyes and show me the vision You have for my life. Keep me in Your Word and on the right path that leads to the fulfillment of my calling based on Your destiny for me.*

Day 142

THE REAL YOU

Plato said, "The unexamined life is not worth living." The Word of God challenges us, "Examine yourselves to see whether you are in the faith; test yourselves" (2 Corinthians 13:5). Who you are? Are you real with yourself? Do you have objectivity about yourself? Can you laugh at yourself? Do you ever step outside of yourself and evaluate yourself? Or, do you take yourself too seriously? If you're really honest with yourself, you will be able to laugh at yourself and not get so defensive. You won't be threatened by every criticism or negative comment you hear. Sometimes you may even agree with the critics!

To know yourself, you must be aware of three aspects of the self: (1) your *real self*—the person you truly are; (2) your *projected self*—the self-image you show others; (3) your *ideal self*—the person you would like to be. For Christians, the ideal self is the image of Jesus in us. The more the real self and the projected self are the same, the healthier we are. We need to be free of trying to manage our self-image so others will like us, and just be who we are. There is great liberty in being true to yourself.

My undergraduate degree is in psychology. During college I was at a friend's house. His dad was a Christian psychologist. He had me take the MMPI, which is the mother of all personality inventories with five hundred questions of self-examination. When the results came back, he told me I failed it!

"How can I fail a personality test?" I asked.

He answered, "The MMPI has a built-in *lie scale*." Over the five hundred questions, certain ones track whether or not the person is being consistent. I was trying to make myself look good instead of honestly answering the questions. Was I intentionally lying? No, but I was intuitively trying to manage and protect my image.

One of the marks of a mature person is being realistic. Immature people live in a fantasy world. Get real with yourself and be honest about your strengths and weaknesses, successes and failures. Know what you need to work on. Get real with God and get real with others. Be genuine and sincere. Besides, people will like the real you better!

Prayer for the Day: *Lord, I want to always be honest and open with You. You know all things anyway! I also need help being myself with others rather than being what I think they want me to be. I want to be genuine.*

Day 143

PRIDE WATCH

"Pride goes before destruction, a haughty spirit before a fall" (Proverbs 16:18). What is *pride*, and what does it destroy in our lives? Is it possible to have healthy pride? The pride that "goes before destruction" is an attitude of arrogance, conceit, selfishness, superiority, and no dependence on God.

Pride caused the downfall of Lucifer: "How you have fallen from heaven, morning star, son of the dawn! . . . You said in your heart, 'I will ascend to the heavens; I will raise my throne above the stars of God. . . .'

But you are brought down to the [grave], to the depths of the pit" (Isaiah 14:12-15). Pride caused the downfall of King Uzziah. "But after Uzziah became powerful, his pride led to his downfall. He was unfaithful to the Lord his God" (2 Chronicles 26:16).

Moses cautioned Israel, "When you have eaten and are satisfied, praise the Lord your God for the good land he has given you. Be careful that you do not forget the Lord your God. . . . Then your heart will become proud" (Deuteronomy 8:10, 14). We are taught, "Do not be proud, but be willing to associate with people of low position. Do not be conceited" (Romans 12:16). The early Christian reformer Martin Luther said, "Nothing puts us further from the devil's reach than does humility."

Prayer for the Day: *Lord, please help me to resist taking pride in my accomplishment, when the glory and honor belong to You alone.*

Day 144
A GOOD NAME

People were asked what they thought of the two leading presidential candidates of both parties. What one word came to mind when they thought of them? For one candidate the most frequent word was "liar," and the second candidate was "arrogant." It is going to be hard to get elected when that is what people think of you. Warren Buffet said, "It takes twenty years to build a reputation and five minutes to ruin it. If you think about that, you'll do things differently." A good name is one of the greatest assets you have. "A good name is more desirable than great riches; to be esteemed is better than silver or gold" (Proverbs 22:1).

My mother told me something early in my ministry that has helped me: "David, who you are is more important to God than what you do. Your maturing is more important than your ministry. Your personal walk with God is more important than your public work for Him."

I wrote a paper in a class on the Holy Spirit my senior year at college. I disagreed with the theology of the professor and told him that in class. I wrote a paper refuting his interpretation of Scripture. He gave me an *A* and wrote, "You have an equal talent for writing and research [because I had proved him wrong]. Keep yourself humble and you will go far." Those last words challenge me to this day. I was making the right point, but I was making it in the wrong way. The way we carry ourselves and the way we treat others is just as important as what we are doing.

Having a good name has more to do with our success and promotion in life than anything else. A good name is more important than ability, aptitude, and appearance. Remember, "A good name is more desirable than great riches."

Prayer for the Day: *Lord, a good reputation is the most important character trait of a godly person. I thank You for reminding me to be aware that everything I do or say is measured by my claim to be Your child. My good name is the most valuable possession I own.*

Day 145

SERVE, DON'T LEAD

One of the most remarkable individuals in the Bible is King David. His name and his legacy live on to this day. He was a man after God's own heart. What does that mean? It means he served God's purpose for his life and not his own agenda. His legacy is summed up in these words: God "made David their king. God testified concerning him: 'I have found David son of Jesse, a man after my own heart; he will do everything I want him to do'" (Acts 13:22). What a legacy—for God to call us people "after [His] own heart"! What does that mean? It means being willing to do everything He wants us to do. God's pleasure is our purpose!

David "served God's purpose in his own generation" (Acts 13:36). God has a plan and a will for our lives—to *serve* Him. That is different from running the show and doing your own thing. There is no way to fulfill God's purpose without possessing the heart of a servant. A servant is the one who does the will of another. David saw himself as a servant, not as a king. He wrote, "Truly I am your servant, Lord; . . . you have freed me from my chains" (Psalm 116:16).

Mary, the mother of our Lord, saw herself as a servant of God's will when the angel appeared to her: "I am the Lord's servant. May it be to me as You have said" (see Luke 1:38). Jesus saw Himself as serving God's will, not His own. "'My food,' said Jesus, 'is to do the will of him who sent me and to finish his work'" (John 4:34).

Serving God's purpose means surrendering your will to the purpose of God for your life. A servant has lost their will to the will of the one they serve. I constantly come back to the place of surrender to God's purpose in my life. I often pray, "Not my will, but Yours be done."

I am increasingly uncomfortable with the word *leadership*. Yes, we all have influence on others and want to help them live the best life they can. Personally, I find myself more at home with the word *serve* than *lead*. I want to serve my family, my church, and my community. If that is leadership, then so be it. Just like King David, I want to serve God's purpose, not do my own thing or try to get God to promote my agenda. It is in serving God's purpose that we discover the true purpose for living.

Prayer for the Day: *Lord, never let it be said that I'm a good leader, but rather that I'm a true servant of the Lord. You lead me, and I will serve those You put in my path.*

Day 146

IT'S HOW YOU LOOK AT IT

The famous "Pale Blue Dot" is a photograph of Earth taken on February 14, 1990, by the *Voyager 1* space probe from a record distance of 3.7 billion miles. In the photograph, Earth's apparent size is less than a pixel. Earth appears as a tiny dot against the canopy of the vastness of space. It appears we are a meaningless, insignificant speck, all alone in the universe.

Voyager 1 had completed its primary mission and was leaving the solar system when NASA commanded it to turn its camera around to take one last photograph of Earth across a great expanse of space, at the request of astronomer and author Carl Sagan. The problem with the photo is that we're looking back at Earth. The perspective is wrong, so the conclusion is wrong. When you look back at Earth from space, it appears to be a tiny blue dot. But we don't live in heaven, we live on earth.

We look up at the heavens and see the wonders of God in the universe He has created. When we look up, we see the glory of God. "The heavens declare the glory of God; the skies show forth his handiwork" (see Psalm 19:1).

When we look up, we see the characteristics of God: "For since the creation of the world, God's invisible qualities—his eternal power and his divine nature—have been clearly seen, being understood from what has been made, so that people are without excuse" (Romans 1:20).

When we look up, we see the providence of God. "For from him and through him and for him are all things" (Romans 11:36), and "in him all things hold together" (Colossians 1:17).

When we look up, we see the sovereignty of God: "The Lord has established his throne in heaven, and his kingdom rules over all" (Psalm 103:19).

When we look up, we see the purpose of God: "When the times will have reached their fulfillment—to bring all things in heaven and on earth together under one head, even Christ" (see Ephesians 1:10).

It is how you look at it that matters. Take time today to look up to the heavens and see the greatness of God who made you, saved you, and cares for you. We are not lost in space. We are strategically put exactly in the space God made for us, safe in the palm of His hand.

Prayer for the Day: *Lord, the universe is immense and our earth is overpopulated, yet You know me and call me by name! I will not fear, knowing I am in the palm of Your hand.*

Day 147

DESTINY DISCOVERED

The quality of our lives is largely determined by great discoveries in science, medicine, and technology. In 1821, Michael Faraday published his research that led to the development of the electric motor. In the 1860s, Louis Pasteur discovered that bacteria could be killed with heat.

In 1905, Albert Einstein published the theory of special relativity, which changed the way we understand physics. In 1913, Niels Bohn discovered the structure of the atom. In 1928, Alexander Fleming discovered penicillin that enabled us to treat infections. In 1953, James Watson and Francis Crick discovered DNA structure.

In 1984, Luc Montique and Robert Gallo, discovered HIV virus as the cause of AIDS.

The greatest personal discovery you can make is to discover God's purpose for your life. Until we know God's purpose, we battle feelings of meaninglessness and anxiety. Solomon struggled to find meaning: "Everything is meaningless," he declared (Ecclesiastes 1:2). Job struggled to find purpose in his suffering: "Mortals, born of woman, are few of days and full of trouble" (Job 14:1). The key to a life of peace is discovering your purpose. Mark Twain said, "The two greatest days in a person's life is the day they were born and the day they discover why."

God has a purpose and a plan for your life. "When David had served God's purpose in his own generation, he fell asleep; he was buried with his ancestors" (Acts 13:36). Take out the name *David* from this verse of Scripture and insert your name. Now read it with your name in it. Let this verse of Scripture become your personal life mission. Say it every day. Discover that God has a purpose for your life, and make it your goal every day to serve His purpose.

Prayer for the Day: *Lord, my life on earth is short compared to eternity. Please direct me to discover my purpose for being here so that I may fulfill it for Your glory.*

Day 148

WHY ARE YOU HERE?

There is a story involving Yogi Berra, the well-known catcher for the New York Yankees, and Hank Aaron, who, at that time, was the chief power hitter for the Milwaukee Braves. The teams were playing in the World Series. As usual, Yogi was keeping up his ceaseless chatter, intended to pep up his teammates on the one hand, and distract the Milwaukee batters on the other. As Aaron came to the plate, Yogi tried to distract him by saying, "Henry, you're holding the bat wrong. You're supposed to hold it so you can read the trademark."

Aaron didn't say anything, but when the next pitch came, he hit it into the left-field bleachers. After rounding the bases and tagging home plate, Aaron looked at Berra and said, "I didn't come up here to read."

Do you ever ask yourself, *Why am I here? What is my purpose for existence?* Many people live with no meaning and no destiny. Henry David Thoreau said, "The mass of people live lives of quiet desperation."

The Bible says we are here by the creative will and work of God, and that gives us purpose. "Many are the plans in a person's heart, but it is the Lord's purpose that prevails" (Proverbs 19:21). We are free to make our plans, but we need to submit them to God's purpose. David said, "The Lord will fulfill His purpose for me" (see Psalm 138:8). God is faithful to fulfill, which means to complete and to work out every detail of His purpose in my life.

Proverbs 16:4 says, "The Lord works out everything to its proper end—even the wicked for a day of disaster." Are you glad God works things out? God is orchestrating human history, working behind the scenes for His own purpose. Don't ever think things are out of control for God. He is in control of everything, and our world is heading toward the fulfillment of His purpose.

God has a purpose for you. When you receive Jesus Christ as your Savior and follow Him as Lord, God's purpose is at work in you. "We know that in all things God works for the good of those who love him, who have been called according to his purpose" (Romans 8:28). While you go about making your plans, remember to keep God's purpose first and foremost in your life.

Prayer for the Day: *Lord, because I belong to You, I know there is a reason for my life. Show me the path You have chosen for me and I will walk it, run it, and complete it for You.*

Day 149
GET STARTED

We talk a lot about purpose, but we also need to consider the importance of plans. If we don't make plans, we won't fulfill our purpose! Isaiah 32:8 says, "The noble make noble plans, and by noble deeds they stand."

Getting started with a plan is the most difficult step. When a young woman gets engaged, she starts planning immediately; she doesn't procrastinate. Then her mother weighs in, and the plans really get off the ground! A wedding is a big event because it takes so much time to plan. The longer the engagement, the more the plans and the bigger the wedding. I have met many couples who say, "We just want a small, low-key, intimate wedding for family and friends." But then the plans start. When all the family and friends help make the plans, the wedding ends up being a big event.

Write down sequential steps to help your mind get focused on what you will need to do in order to reach your goals. Plans take time. When we build a house, planning is the most important part of the process. Procrastination is the number one enemy to fulfilling your purpose. Planning also keeps us from being hasty. "The plans of the diligent lead to profit as surely as haste leads to poverty" (Proverbs 21:5). A well-thought-out, detailed plan is the difference between profit and poverty!

Sometimes we don't plan because we think (falsely, I might add) planning is unspiritual. We expect everything to come to us from God in a vision, a dream, or a word of prophecy. Such thinking will paralyze us, but the Lord expects us to make plans. The Apostle Paul's prayer for the Thessalonians teaches us the importance of planning: "We constantly pray for you, that our God may count your worthy of his calling, and that by his power he may fulfill every good purpose of yours and every act prompted by your faith. We pray this in order that the name of our Lord Jesus Christ may be glorified in you and you in him according to the grace of our God and the Lord Jesus Christ" (see 2 Thessalonians 1:11-12).

So, get started today with your plans!

Prayer for the Day: *Lord, getting started is the most difficult part of making a plan. But I know You have the best plan, so I will not make mine until I know Yours. I'm listening, Lord!*

Day 150

OPEN DOORS

While doing my personal devotions one day, 2 Corinthians 2:12 leaped off the page: "Now when I went to Troas to preach the gospel of Christ [I] found that the Lord had opened a door for me." Paul was describing his experience of traveling from city to city preaching the gospel of Christ. He didn't go to Troas because he had a vision from the Lord; he went there because he and his team had worked out a plan to go to cities that needed to hear about Jesus. As they implemented their plan, the Lord "opened a door."

Planning does not control the future. Change your plans and modify them when you hit obstacles or find a better way of doing something. Don't be OCD (or CDO to get it right!) about your plans. When change comes your way, are you a "yes" person or a "no" person? Do you embrace the new or hold onto the old? Do you accept change with enthusiasm or resist it with resentment? Just because we make a good plan doesn't mean everything in the plan is going to happen just like we expect. Your understanding of the future is limited, so you have to be flexible.

Paul did not find an open door in Troas until he took action and went there. That simple statement changed my life. I know God expects me to develop a plan as I pursue His purpose for me. As I implement my plans, He will direct my steps.

Paul went to Troas because of a general call to preach the Gospel. He was active in his ministry, and God opened a door. Later, God closed the door into Bithynia and led him to Macedonia (Acts 16:6-10). God's closed doors are as important as His open doors! I thank Him for unanswered prayers as much as I do for answered prayers.

When you and I are active in our plans, God will direct our steps. Your future has both challenges and opportunities that you cannot see now. You cannot plan for everything. When God closes a door, don't stand in front of it and bang on it to open! Keep moving, and God will open the right door for you.

Prayer for the Day: *Lord, so many open doors! I pray that You will close the doors You don't want me to walk through. Direct me into the open doors that give opportunity for me to use my spiritual gifts to expand Your Kingdom.*

Day 151

PRODUCTIVE LIVING

Henry David Thoreau said, "It is not enough to be industrious; so are the ants." What are you industrious about? You need two things to succeed—a *why* (purpose) and a *what* (plan). Our purpose is the source of our passion in life. But, how do we fulfill our purpose? We need plans in order to accomplish our purpose.

Consider Proverbs 21:5: "The plans of the diligent lead to profit as surely as haste leads to poverty." Without a good business plan, a business fails. Jesus is looking for spiritual profit—"fruit that will last" (John 15:16).

How can we produce such fruit? Jesus said: "I am the vine, you are the branches. If you remain in me and I in you, you will bear much fruit; apart from me you can do nothing" (John 15:5). In verse 4, Jesus says just as a branch cannot bear fruit if it is detached from a vine, so we cannot bear spiritual fruit if we do not "remain" in Him. If we disconnect from Him, we will dry up and die. However, if we remain in Christ, we can "ask whatever [we] wish, and it will be done for [us]" (John 15:7). Such purposeful and productive living will bring glory to the heavenly Father and show us to be genuine disciples of Christ (John 15:8).

As Christians, our ultimate purpose (our *why*) is to glorify God. The plan (our *how*) to accomplish this is to stay connected to Christ, the Vine.

Prayer for the Day: *Lord, my plan is to pursue You. Only that will profit and bring glory to You.*

Day 152
IF THE LORD IS WITH US

Sorting out suffering is the most difficult challenge of life. When we go through a time of suffering or we watch someone else suffer, we wonder why God allows it. We wonder how we can get through and what causes it.

The Old Testament leader Gideon asked the same questions when Israel was being attacked by the Midianites. Midian invaded their land; attacked their towns, villages, and farms; and terrorized the people. The angel of the Lord called Gideon to lead the people to victory, but Gideon asked the angel, "But if the Lord is with us, why has all this happened to us?" (Judges 6:13).

The angel never answered the question, but replied, "Go in the strength you have and save Israel out of Midian's hand" (Judges 6:14). Gideon felt inadequate to lead the charge and said, "How can I save Israel? My clan is the weakest in Manasseh, and I am the least in my family" (v. 15). (Talk about an inferiority complex!) In verse 16, the Lord answered him, "I will be with you, and you will strike down all the Midianites."

While the Lord does not give us all the reasons suffering exists, He calls us to fulfill our purpose in life to help others. We, too, are to go and save others. Jesus came to "seek and to save the lost" (Luke 19:10), and so are we in His name. Instead of losing our faith, we need to strengthen our faith. Instead of withdrawing from the battle of life, we need to fight the good fight of faith. Instead of quitting the race, we need to press on to win the prize for which "God has called [us] heavenward in Christ Jesus" (Philippians 3:14).

Regardless of what you are facing in your life and family, God is with you like He was with Gideon. The Lord promised Gideon, "I will be with you." Together with the Lord and together with the support of others, you and I can conquer the doubt and discouragement that come with suffering.

Prayer for the Day: *Lord, I know You are with me! I feel Your presence; I hear Your voice speaking gently to my heart. I may not fully understand the difficult circumstances of my life, but I trust You will help me and never leave me.*

Day 153

USE IT

In his book *Profiles in Courage*, President John Kennedy said, "Great crises produce great men and great deeds of courage." I once read a book called *Don't Waste Your Sorrows*. God doesn't cause our problems or send suffering to His people, but He works in our lives in spite of our circumstances. He is with us in this broken world. Not only is God with us, but He works in our lives and in our situations, regardless of the causes of our problems.

Someone told me about a difficult time they were going through and then added, "I know God is going to use this in a powerful way." I agreed, but I asked him, "How are *you* going to use it?"

The psalmist David reflected on how he used suffering to grow spiritually: "Before I was afflicted I went astray, but now I obey your word. You are good, and what you do is good; teach me your decrees" (Psalm 119:67-68). Notice, he did not blame God for his trouble or even suggest God caused it. To the contrary, David affirmed how good God is and said everything God does is good. But he used his afflictions to learn obedience. Then he wrote, "It was good for me to be afflicted so that I might learn your decrees" (Psalm 119:71).

When we go through difficult times, do we become bitter or better? Do we become faithful or faithless? Do we overcome or are we defeated?

We don't get to choose what happens to us in this life, but we do choose how we will respond. Decide to trust God even in your suffering, and depend on Him to bring you through the experience a better person than you were before you went through it.

Prayer for the Day: *Lord, I may not always respond to the crisis in my life the way I should. But if You will show me how to use it to become a better person, I will embrace it and grow through it.*

Day 154
MAKE IT HAPPEN!

There are three kinds of people in the world: (1) Those who make it happen, (2) those who let it happen, and (3) those who ask, "What just happened?" While we depend on God for His grace, He also expects us to use the grace and gifts He has given us to make it happen. The Apostle Paul said, "We are God's handiwork, created in Christ Jesus to do good works, which God prepared in advance for us to do" (Ephesians 2:10). The key word here is *do*!

Be a doer, not just a dreamer. "Be doers of the word, and not hearers only, deceiving yourselves" (James 1:22 NKJV). We deceive ourselves when we think things are going to happen by themselves, or problems are going to fix themselves, or God is going to do everything for us. God does work in wonderful ways, but He also expects us to do our work. "Faith by itself, it is not accompanied by works, is dead" (James 2:17).

Don't be passive, sitting in the grandstands, and watching things happen. Get out of the bleachers and get in the game! Don't let things happen or, worse, be one of those people who asks, "What just happened?" Make things happen!

Zig Ziglar said, "If it's going to be, it's up to me!" If you face a problem, you can fix it. If you set a goal, you can reach it. If you face an obstacle, you can overcome it. If you take on a challenge, you can do it. If you fail, you can get over it. How? Paul said, "I can do all this through [Christ] who gives me strength" (Philippians 4:13).

Prayer for the Day: *Lord, sometimes I'm guilty of waiting on You when You are waiting on me to use the strength and wisdom You have given me to overcome the obstacles of life. Help me to know the difference.*

Day 155
BEHIND THE SCENE

Life is often determined by what goes on behind the scenes. I am thinking of the Biblical account of the Israelites being attacked by the army of the Amalekites to stop them from entering the Promised Land. The Israelites were fresh out of Egypt and had very little military experience. Yet, Joshua led them in battle to defend themselves, and something incredible happened. While Joshua fought in the valley, Moses prayed on the mountain.

Prayer and action go hand in hand. Prayer is not passive. Moses took Aaron and Hur with him to the mountain to pray. "As long as Moses held up his hands, the Israelites were winning, but whenever he lowered his hands, the Amalekites were winning" (Exodus 17:11). Why did he raise his hands? He raised his hands in prayer to God. "I will praise you as long as I live, and in your name I will lift up my hands" (Psalm 63:4). "I want people everywhere to lift up holy hands in prayer, without anger or disputing" (see 1 Timothy 2:8).

We, like the soldiers on the battlefield, are so engrossed in our battles that we might be unaware of the people praying for us. Most of them had no idea Moses was praying for them, but his prayers were the source of their victory. Prayer can be tiring for both the mind and the body. Moses' hands got tired. So, Aaron and Hur gave him a rock to sit on when his knees got tired and his hands dropped. What a lesson for us!

We need to rest on the rock of Christ Jesus and on His finished work on the cross for our salvation.

Earlier in Moses' life, he would have never dreamed of trying to win a battle through prayer. He would have been the first to garnish the sword and enter the fight as he did in his youth. Now he used a more powerful weapon—*prayer*. As we grow up spiritually, we learn more of the power of prayer. "The prayer of a righteous person is powerful and effective" (James 5:16).

After the battle was won, the Lord told Moses, "'Write this on a scroll as something to be remembered' . . . . Moses built an altar and called it The Lord is my Banner" (Exodus 17:14-15), which means "the Lord is my victory!"

Don't try to win your battles only by fighting. It is the prayer behind the scene that makes victory possible. You and I can lift up our hands in prayer to God today in confidence that He is "able to do immeasurably more than all we ask or [even think possible]" (Ephesians 3:20).

Prayer for the Day: *Lord, thank You for reminding me that the power behind everything we do is prayer. Teach me to pray first and act after I know Your will.*

Day 156
DO WHAT YOU CAN

One day Jesus attended a dinner party in the town of Bethany at the home of Simon the Leper. Bethany is only a couple miles from Jerusalem by way of the Garden of Gethsemane. It was also the town where Lazarus lived, and he was at the dinner along with his sisters, Martha and Mary. Eating dinner with a leper was an odd thing, so apparently Jesus had healed Simon of leprosy.

During the evening, Mary took an expensive box of perfume, worth a year's income, and poured it on Jesus' head. The fragrance filled the room. But Judas Iscariot and others complained she had wasted the perfume and criticized her extravagance, saying the perfume "could have been sold for more than a year's wages and the money given to the poor" (Mark 14:5). Mary loved Jesus and worshiped Him with an extravagant love.

Jesus defended Mary, saying, "The poor you will always have with you, and you can help them anytime you want. But you will not always have me. She did what she could" (Mark 14:7-8). That is all God requires of you and me—to do what we can. You don't have to be the most talented or have the most resources to be what God calls you to be and make a difference in this world. Don't ever focus on what you can't do; do what you can. The Apostle Peter, who was present at that dinner, wrote, "Each of you should use whatever gift you have received to serve others, as faithful stewards of God's grace in its various forms" (1 Peter 4:10).

Mary teaches us the way of real success and significance—she did what she could. Jesus added, "Wherever the gospel is preached throughout the world, what she has done will also be told in memory of her" (Mark 14:9). She left a lasting legacy because she did what she could. And so can we.

Prayer for the Day: *Lord, sometimes I feel like doing what I can isn't always enough. Looking again at what Mary did reminds me that we all have gifts and a part to play in the body of Christ.*

Day 157
WHO CAN YOU HELP?

When we go through difficult times, we can use it to help others. The season of difficulty will come to pass. A new season will begin for you. When you come through it, be on the lookout for others going through similar problems. You may be the difference between them living in victory or defeat. Paul said, "We can comfort those in any trouble with the comfort we ourselves receive from God" (2 Corinthians 1:4).

When Gideon questioned why God was allowing Israel to go through suffering, the Lord told him, "Go in the strength you have and save Israel out of Midian's hand. Am I not sending you?" (Judges 6:14). Don't focus on why suffering exists; focus on saving others out of their suffering. Suffering has a way of eclipsing everything in our lives. It demands our full attention. But we don't have to let it dominate our lives. We can serve even in suffering.

Jesus served in suffering. "Because He Himself [in His humanity] has suffered in being tempted, He is able to help and provide immediate assistance to those who are being tempted and exposed to suffering" (Hebrews 2:18 Amp.). Just as Jesus is able to help others because of His suffering, we can help others because of our experiences. We can share with others our story of God's faithfulness to help them get through tough times.

The Apostle Paul shared this truth about his imprisonment: "What has happened to me has actually served to advance the gospel.... Because of my chains, most of the brothers and sisters have become confident in the Lord and dare all the more to proclaim the gospel without fear" (Philippians 1:12-14). He saw his imprisonment for preaching the Gospel as something that advanced the Gospel. He found purpose in his pain. He discovered success in suffering. He turned imprisonment into inspiration!

So, be on the lookout for someone struggling to get through the season of suffering that you made it through. Put your arm around them and remind them that with man this is impossible, but with God all things are possible.

Prayer for the Day: *Lord, help me to use the seasons of difficulty I've experienced to help others going through the same thing. With You, all things are possible!*

Day 158

GOD, PUMPKINS, AND YOU

When I graduated from college and started in the ministry, I went to California as an evangelist preaching in a different church every week. The denomination held a ministers' conference. One afternoon the overseer for the Church of God in Scotland brought the message. He told of his call to the ministry starting with a street ministry in Los

Angeles and youth crusades with great results. Then he went to Scotland. Everything he tried failed. After a year, he had seen little results of his ministry. In frustration, he prayed and told God how disappointed and upset he was that he had gone to Scotland. He shouted to God, "What kind of ministry are You trying to make?"

There was silence. Then the Lord spoke to his heart: "I'm not making a ministry. I am making a man."

God makes men and women. He has from the very beginning. God said, "Let us make mankind in our image" (Genesis 1:26). He still is in the business of making individuals in His image. God's greatest purpose in your life is not about what you do but who you are. I have learned that God puts you somewhere primarily not to help others, but because that is the best place where He can conform you to the image of His Son. What God is doing in you is far more important than what He is doing through you.

This is what Paul meant when he spoke of God's greatest purpose: "In all things God works for the good of those who love him, who have been called according to his purpose. For those God foreknew he also predestined to be conformed to the image of his Son" (Romans 8:28-29).

We are created in God's image. Sin marred that image, "for all have sinned and fall short of the glory of God" (Romans 3:23). Sin makes us less than what God created us to be. Sin reduces us, but grace enhances us! Jesus came to save us from sin and to restore us to the image of God in us. Once you become a disciple of Jesus, God works in all things to conform, shape, and mold you in His image so others see a little bit of Jesus in you.

A boy asked his mother, "What does it mean to be a Christian?" She replied, "It's like being a pumpkin. God picks you from the patch, brings you in, and washes all the dirt off you. Then He cuts off the top and scoops out all the yucky stuff. He removes the seeds of doubt, hate, and greed, and then He carves you a new smiling face and puts his light inside of you to shine for all the world to see."

Prayer for the Day: *Lord, it gives me great comfort to know You are always working on me. Who I am is more important than what I do.*

Day 159

GOD SO LOVED

The children's Sunday-school teacher noticed a little boy drawing a picture of an old man during their art time. "Whose picture are you drawing?" she inquired. "I'm drawing a picture of God," he said assuredly.

Teacher said, "But no one has ever seen God. No one knows what God looks like." The boy replied, "Well, they will know when I finish this picture!"

When Jesus came into the world, people finally knew what God is like. Jesus is "the image of the invisible God" (Colossians 1:15). In John 3:16, Jesus explained what God is like: "God so loved the world that He gave His only begotten Son, that whoever believes in Him should not perish but have everlasting life" (NKJV). Let the words "God so loved" sink deep into your heart.

There are many ideas about who God is. To the ancient Egyptians, God was immortality. To the Hindu, God is truth and bliss. To the Buddhist, God is the cosmic force of life in all things. To the ancient Greeks, God was wisdom. To the Muslim, God is authority. To the humanist, God is the innate human potential. To the scientist, God is natural law. But in the Christian faith, God is love!

Any picture of God we have in our mind that doesn't look like Jesus is the wrong picture of God. We must see all the attributes of God through the lens of love. We tend to project our sinful and imperfect attributes on to God and assume He is like us, but He is not. "God is not human, that he should lie" (Numbers 23:19). God loved each of us so much that He gave His Son to provide the way for our eternal salvation.

When you know you are loved by God, it will break the bondage of fear, inadequacy, and low self-esteem off your life and set you free. Live this day knowing God "so loves" you!

Prayer for the Day: *Lord, because I know You love me, I can go where You lead, pray with authority, and love unconditionally. Thank You for the Cross—the ultimate proof of Your love.*

Day 160

HE GAVE IT

I have a friend who serves as missionary to Muslims in the Middle East. One day he went to a Syrian restaurant for lunch. After placing his order, the waiter said to him, "Can you tell me how to become a Christian?" Believing the waiter to be insincere in his request, thinking he only wanted to get a U.S. visa, my friend asked him, "Aren't you a Muslim? Why do you want to become a Christian?" The waiter replied, "I want to be a Christian because yours is the religion of love."

Without question, the most important statement made in the Bible, the most influential and popular book ever written—consisting of 66 books, 1,189 chapters, 31,173 verses, and more than 770,000 words—is this: "God so loved the world that He gave His only begotten Son" (John 3:16 NKJV).

God so loved the *world*? Jesus made the world flat with that statement. He did not say God "so loved" the good people, the religious people, or the righteous people in the world. We share a common problem—sin. The only solution is the saving grace of God that came to us in the gift of Jesus because God so loved the world.

God so loved the world that He *gave*. The most important word in the Bible is *grace*, which means to "give freely." *Grace* describes the nature and character of God. Jesus is God's gift to the world. A gift is given because someone cares about us, and all we have to do is receive the gift! This is how we become a Christian—by receiving the free gift of salvation through faith in Jesus.

Not only did God give Jesus; Jesus then gave Himself for us on the cross. Jesus said He came "to give his life as a ransom for many" (Mark 10:45). A *ransom* is the money you pay to get someone back who has been kidnapped or, in the ancient world, the money paid to buy a slave and then set them free. No one took Jesus' life the day He died on the cross—He gave His life for our salvation. He took our sin on the cross and offers us His forgiveness today if we will only receive the gift.

A chaplain was speaking to a combat soldier in a hospital. "You have lost an arm in the great cause of freedom," he said. "No sir," replied the soldier. "I didn't lose it; I gave it." Jesus didn't lose His life; He gave it. He gave it for us.

Prayer for the Day: *Lord, I have received many gifts over the years, but the gift of Your life for mine is the greatest gift anyone could ever receive. You exchanged Your perfect life for my sinful life that I may live with You forever. I'm eternally grateful.*

Day 161

SET YOUR FOOT

Just as God had a Promised Land for the people when they were delivered from slavery in Egypt, He has a promised life for you. *Promise* means your potential, your ability, your goals, your dreams, and God's will for your life.

A promise *given* and a promise *received* are two different things. God's promises will go unfulfilled in you, if you don't take action. God told Joshua as he led the people into the Promised Land, "I will give you every place where you set your foot, as I promised Moses" (Joshua 1:3). If they didn't walk on it, they would never have it. You too must set your feet and get moving toward the promised life by taking action.

First, *get off the land you're on right now*. You must be tired of being where you are and living like you're living before you can move forward to your promise. The comfort zone will keep you where you are. If you don't step on new land, what you have now is all you will ever have. Change starts when you get tired of being where you are.

Second, *move by faith*. Fear will keep you where you are; it will keep you looking at the promise but not living in it. It is a long and arduous journey to get to any promise. Just as Israel faced giants in the land, you will also face giant obstacles. But, by faith, they can be defeated.

Third, *get grounded in the promises of God*. There are over 3,500 promises of God in the Bible. God told Joshua, "As I promised Moses."

Moses was the first author of Scripture, writing the first five books of the Bible. God's promises are found in His written Word.

Live by faith in the promises of God and you will be able to push past your problems and into the promises God has for you.

Prayer for the Day: *Lord, I have faced many giants in my life and fear that disabled me. But, claiming Your promises and stepping out in faith has made the difference of being paralyzed and walking into the Promised Land.*

Day 162

BREAK OUT!

Are you stuck in your life? Systems theory shows that things tend to stay the way they are. A system naturally maintains *homeostasis*—the status quo. It is difficult to change. Things and people tend to stay the way they are unless changes are made intentionally.

Why do we get stuck where we are? Why do we stay the same, even when we don't like it? *Poor self-esteem* keeps us where we are. We don't think we deserve any better. Every time you read the Bible and learn about who you really are in your relationship to God, you will make a deposit into your "self-esteem" bank. Scripture says, "[Build] yourselves up in your most holy faith" (Jude 20). Don't put yourself down; build yourself up!

Perfectionism keeps us where we are. We think everything has to be perfect before we do anything. Since perfection is impossible, it keeps us where we are. We overanalyze and over-criticize everything as we strive for perfection. We get stuck where we are, micromanaging our lives instead of fulfilling our dreams and reaching our goals. We must keep our eyes on our goals and not get distracted by all the details.

Procrastination keeps us stuck. We procrastinate because we are afraid of failure. We must be discontented with the way things are before we have the desire to change and live a better life.

Jesus said, "Unless you change and become like little children, you will never enter the kingdom of heaven" (Matthew 18:3). We must change in order to enter the best life God has for us. It is time to break out!

Prayer for the Day: *Lord, I have learned that change is good, especially if You are the One bringing that change. I want Your best, Lord! I want to grow in Your grace and knowledge as I move forward into Your will for me.*

Day 163

ABOVE US AND AROUND US

The Bible is a book about God, first and foremost. What we call *theology* simply means "the understanding of God." The Bible begins with the words, "In the beginning God." God wants you to know Him and have a relationship with Him. One of the unique aspects of God we see in the Bible is that He is both transcendent and imminent. These big words simply mean God is "above us" (*transcendent*) and God is "with us" (*imminent*). Most religions present God as transcendent, distant, and unreachable. But in the Bible, God comes to us, lives with us, and dwells in us!

God tells us this truth about Himself: "I live in a high and holy place, but also with the one who is contrite and lowly in spirit, to revive the spirit of the lowly and to revive the heart of the contrite" (Isaiah 57:15). Think of that! The God who created the universe and who dwells in Heaven comes down here to where we are and lives with us. God wants to walk with you and talk with you every day. God wants you to know His presence and experience His provision.

God lives with those who are "contrite and lowly in spirit." That means being humble enough to admit our need for God and to trust Him for all we need. *Pride* means being self-sufficient, falsely believing we can make it on our own and that we don't need God. Things go better with God at the center of our lives. Augustine, an early Christian minister (AD 354-430), said, "Our hearts were made for You, O God, and they will not rest until they rest in You."

You are never alone. God is with you, He is for you, and He is in you. Keep God at the center of your life and you will experience incredible blessings.

Prayer for the Day: *Lord, the peace of knowing I am never alone is overwhelming to my soul. You are at the center of my life. I listen to hear You speak and reveal Your truth to me.*

Day 164
TOMORROW

Dr. Charles Mayo once said, "Half the hospital beds are filled with people who worry themselves there." Worry is often caused by the tyranny of tomorrow. We look ahead and worry what might go wrong. We imagine all the possibilities of negative things that could happen, and then we start to believe they will happen.

Tomorrow can fill our lives with anticipation or anxiety. We can look forward with faith or with fear.

The answer is to trust God with our tomorrows. As David declared to God, "When I am afraid, I put my trust in you" (Psalm 56:3). There are times we are afraid. When fear comes, we must put our trust in God. Jesus said, "Do not worry about tomorrow, for tomorrow will worry about itself. Each day has enough trouble of its own" (Matthew 6:34).

Prayer for the Day: *Lord, I recognize You are the God of yesterday, today, and tomorrow. When I am tempted to fret about tomorrow, help me to remember You are already there, waiting for me.*

Day 165
HIT "REFRESH"

When our computer bogs down, we hit "refresh" to fix system problems. The same is true spiritually. The Apostle Peter preached, "Repent, then, and turn to God, so that your sins may be wiped out, that times of refreshing may come from the Lord" (Acts 3:19). Look at those two words—*repent* and *refresh*. Repentance leads to refreshing!

What is *repentance*? Dr. Martin Luther King Jr. said, "We will have to repent in this generation not merely for the hateful words and actions of the bad people but for the appalling silence of the good people." In the Old Testament, *repent* in Hebrew means to "turn." So, we turn away from sin and we turn to God. In the New Testament, the Greek word for *repent* means to "change your mind," and it always refers to change your course of life for the better according to God's will.

When we repent, our "sins [will] be blotted out, so that times of refreshing may come from the presence of the Lord" (NKJV). Ancient writing was written on papyrus, and the ink had no acid in it. It didn't soak into the papyrus like modern ink does; it just laid on top of the papyrus. You could erase the ink by wiping a wet cloth over the dried ink as though no words were ever written on it. God says when we repent, He takes the cloth of His grace and wipes our sins away. The word *times* refers to crisis moments. The word *refreshing* means a cooling like a rain on a hot day. The word *presence* refers to the face of God or the favor of God. Refreshing only comes from God, not from anyone or anything else.

You can have a definite crisis moment with God in your life today and be refreshed. Hit "delete" by repenting of your attitudes and actions and turning to God. Receive His grace, forgiveness, and cleansing so times of refreshing may come from the Lord in your life.

Prayer for the Day: *Lord, as I repent of my sins, I also start over anew, following after You. I leave the old behind and look to You for a better and more peaceful life. I thank You for the cleansing and refreshing that is given as confirmation of Your forgiveness.*

Day 166
REBUILD THE RUINS

One of the greatest tragedies in American history was the terrorist attack of 9/11. Two planes were flown into the twin towers of the World Trade Center and brought it crashing to the ground. Yet, the people of New York City rebuilt on the ruins.

When we suffer tragedy, we can either leave our lives in ruin or we can rebuild. We can leave the tragedy as is or overcome the tragedy with triumph. We can rebuild. The Lord's word to the Jewish people after the city of Jerusalem and the Temple was destroyed by the Babylonians is also His word to us: "I will restore you to health and heal your wounds. . . . I will restore the fortunes of Jacob's tents and have compassion on his dwellings; the city will be rebuilt on her ruins" (Jeremiah 30:17-18).

What a powerful message of hope from God himself! What He did for ancient Israel, He will do for us. Let His Word give you hope that you, too, can rebuild on your ruins. You may tell yourself that your marriage is ruined, your finances are ruined, or your career is ruined, but, with faith in God, you can rebuild on your ruins. Get your mind off the ruins and get a vision of the new life you want to build.

You may ask, What can I do to get started rebuilding? Bring your ruins to God and ask Him to help you get past the hurt, disappointment, and frustration and to get on with the work of rebuilding. The promise of God in Jeremiah 30 includes His asking a question: "Who is he who will devote himself to be close to me?" (v. 21). God has great plans for your life, even though you may be experiencing a season of ruin. A new season is on the way! Devote yourself to be close to God, depend on His strength, and get started rebuilding.

Prayer for the Day: *Lord, I have some ruins in my life that I need to build on. Give me the strength to get up and start all over again, rebuilding strong life that is dedicated to You.*

Day 167

CAN I HELP?

We often ask our friends and family how we can help them. One way we can help them is through prayer. Paul said, "We have set our hope that he [God] will continue to deliver us, as you help us by your prayers" (2 Corinthians 1:10-11). Prayer is very powerful. It changes people and circumstances.

I'm not saying prayer is the only thing we can do to help. Prayer does not take the place of action. But, action without prayer is not enough.

When we pray, God leads us into the right action to take so we don't waste our time with the wrong action. Prayer brings about a change in people and circumstances.

Sometimes people are away from us by distance so we can't get to them, or situations are bigger than our ability to get involved. That is when we can help by praying. Paul also told his friends, "Join me in my struggle by praying to God for me" (Romans 15:30). We are never left without an option in any situation, crisis, or decision. We can always help others through the power of prayer.

Is there someone you are concerned about today and feel you can't do anything about it? Pause right now and bring that person and situation before the Lord. Call on Him to intervene and to intercede on their behalf, and believe He "is able to do immeasurably more than we ask or imagine, according to his power that is at work in us" (Ephesians 3:20).

Prayer for the Day: *Lord, sometimes I forget how powerful prayer is when prayed by a righteous person. Help me to always pray for others when You lay them on my heart. Remind me, Lord, that prayer is the first step and action is the second! They work together.*

Day 168

FOCUS

The United States is the only nation in the history of the world that has "the pursuit of happiness" in its mission statement. How can we have real joy in life? Where can we find it? If we are going to pursue it, we want to find it. Here is the secret: "The joy of the Lord is your strength" (Nehemiah 8:10).

God wants us to be joyful, not sad or somber. Spirituality can be a pitfall of making us feel guilty and inadequate. That is because the more we look at God's holiness, the more we are aware of how unholy we are. When we pursue God's will, we cannot help but notice we fall short of His will. We want to be like Jesus, but almost daily we see the ways we are not like Him. It can lead you to quit pursuing godly goals because you feel like you will never reach them.

If you focus on yourself and your shortcomings, you are going to feel like you don't measure up, and that will rob you of your joy. Focus on the Savior, not on yourself, and you will have great joy.

Many people grow up with a religion that makes them anxious and depressed, feeling like they fall short of God's glory. Romans 3:23 does say, "For all have sinned and fall short of the glory of God," but that is not the end of the sentence. Read verse 24: "And are justified freely by his grace through the redemption that came by Christ Jesus."

Some people have half of a religion. It is not enough to say all have sinned and fall short. It is also true that everyone who has faith in Jesus is *justified* (that means "made righteous in God's sight") freely by His *grace* (that means salvation is a free gift, not something you work for) through the *redemption* (referring to His death on the cross for our sins) that came by Christ Jesus (that means the Son of God who loves you and gave Himself for you).

If you only focus on "fall short," you will be spiritually depressed. If you instead focus on "justified freely by his grace," you will have joy, and that joy will give you strength. *Guilt* will weaken you, but *grace* will strengthen you so you can experience "the joy of the Lord [as] your strength."

Prayer for the Day: *Lord, help me to keep my eyes focused on You as I live out my Christian faith. Don't let me get bogged down in the past, but remind me of Your redemption, grace, and unconditional love so I have joy unspeakable and full of glory.*

Day 169

FEELING FAITH

Can *faith* and *feeling* travel together? God created us with feelings, which serve an important place in our life. We are emotionally rich. When we feel good, we will be more positive and effective in everything we do.

Some people de-emphasize emotions in spirituality. "You can't follow your feelings," they object. Or they like to say, "You can't base your faith on your feelings." I agree with that, but if they are dismissing feelings altogether, I don't agree with that. If you have faith, you will feel better. If you have hope, you will be optimistic. If you have love, you will be healthy. Feeling is an indispensable part of faith. If you take feeling out of faith, then you have an incomplete faith.

If you trust, you will feel peace. God will give you "perfect peace" if you will steadfastly trust in Him (Isaiah 26:3). If you draw close to God, you find "fullness of joy" in His presence (Psalm 16:11 NKJV). If you obey God, you will feel happy: "May the righteous be glad and rejoice before God; may they be happy and joyful" (Psalm 68:3).

I went to a Christian high school (which I loved), but they were legalistic and didn't have a lot of emotion in worship. I used to hear preachers say *emotionalism* was bad and we needed to avoid it. Looking back on it, I realize I liked stirring up certain emotions in worship. They stirred up feelings of fear of consequences and judgment. They stirred up feelings of guilt about sin.

They didn't have a problem will emotionalism; they only had a problem with joy. Don't get too excited or be too happy in worship, they taught us. But God created us to express our emotions in worship: "Clap your hands, all you nations; shout to God with cries of joy. . . . God has ascended amid shouts of joy" (Psalm 47:1, 5).

You cannot have faith without feeling. You cannot experience redemption without rejoicing. You cannot have justification without joy. The Great commandment is to love the Lord with all our heart, mind, and strength. Worship involves all of life, including our feelings! Psychology has proved that what you believe affects what you feel. Feelings are rooted in beliefs.

In *Celebration of Discipline*, Richard J. Foster wrote: "Superficiality is the curse of our age. The doctrine of instant satisfaction is a primary spiritual problem. The desperate need today is not for a greater number of intelligent people, or gifted people, but for deep people. . . . Joy is the keynote of all the disciplines. . . . Singing, dancing, even shouting characterize the disciplines of the spiritual life."

Prayer for the Day: *Lord, as I follow You and obey Your Word, my emotions line up with Your will for my life. It wasn't always this way, but now I am truly free to have feelings in my faith, knowing You keep them in check.*

Day 170

TRIPPED UP

At the 1984 Summer Olympics in Los Angeles, U.S. runner Mary Decker was on pace to win the 3,000-meter race and take the gold medal. Everything was going great until the last lap. As Mary rounded the final turn, a native South African running for Great Britain—a barefoot runner named Zola Budd—came up behind Mary, who tripped on Zola's foot. They both fell, and then finished without winning any medals.

That event reminds me of the Apostle Paul's caution: "You were running a good race. Who cut in on you to keep you from obeying the truth?" (Galatians 5:7). Don't let anyone trip you up as you run the race of faith. Instead, "run with perseverance the race marked out" for you (Hebrews 12:1). The Galatians were tripped up by legalism—trying to add their works to God's grace in order to be saved.

In 2 Timothy 4:10, Paul wrote about how a young man named Demas had forsaken him, "having loved this present world" (NKJV). Paul's heart must have broken to see Demas fall in his race of faith. I am sure Paul prayed often for Demas to get back up from his failure, to forsake the world and return to the calling of God on his life.

We can get tripped up because we don't like what God says to us in His Word. One day Jesus taught that He is "the bread of life" (John 6:35). He was comparing Himself to the manna God gave the Israelites in the desert. Some of His followers were offended by what He said. "From [that] time [on] many of his disciples [but not the Twelve] turned back and no longer followed him" (John 6:66). In our day, we must choose between political correctness and Biblical truth. Are we going to follow Christ or culture?

Disappointment can also trip us up. Asaph wrote, "Surely God is good to Israel, to those who are pure in heart. But as for me, my feet had almost slipped; I had nearly lost my foothold. For I envied the arrogant when I saw the prosperity of the wicked" (Psalm 73:1-3). He was disappointed that people who didn't even serve God had a better life than he did. Then he went to the house of God to worship and got his mind right. He told the Lord, "You hold me by my right hand. You guide me with your counsel. . . . My flesh and my heart may fail, but God is the strength of my heart and my portion forever" (Psalm 73:23-24, 26).

Prayer for the Day: *Lord, in the past I have quit running the race of faith. I got tangled up in the things of this world and lost my way. Now I see the race before me, and, with Your strength, I will keep my eyes on the prize, which is You!*

Day 171

TURN IT OFF!

Thomas Edison, who invented the telephone, attended a banquet where he was the featured speaker. The emcee of the banquet introduced Thomas Edison and listed all his inventions and contributions to the world. He remarked that Edison was the first person to invent a talking machine.

As Edison came to the lectern to give his address, he responded, "I appreciate the kind introduction tonight. But, I need to make one correction. I'm not the first man to invent a talking machine. God invented the first talking machine—the human tongue. I am the first person to invent a talking machine that can finally be shut off."

Words are powerful, and sometimes we need to turn our tongues off! That includes social-media talking. The Word of God tells us: "Anyone who is never at fault in what they say is perfect, able to keep their whole body in check" (James 3:2). "When words are many, sin is not absent" (see Proverbs 10:19). Jesus said, "Everyone will have to give an account on the day of judgment for every empty word they have spoken" (Matthew 12:36).

When we are spiraling out of control with a verbal barrage toward someone, let us grab the switch on our tongue and turn it off!

Prayer for the Day: *Father, I yield my words to You and pray that what I say today will bring glory to You, benefit others, and bring out the best in me. May the words of my mouth and the meditations of my heart be pleasing in Your sight.*

Day 172

WORSHIP YOUR WAY TO HEALTH

According to a Vanderbilt University study, people who did not attend church at all were twice as likely to die prematurely as those who had attended a worship service in the last year (*Today.Com*, 6/3/2017). A 2018 report by *Sleep Health* found "religious adults in particular exhibit healthier sleep outcomes than their less religious counterparts."

Worship is directly connected to our emotional and physical health! When we center our lives on our Creator, all of life functions in an orderly way. God to us is like the sun to the planets. The planets revolve around the sun. For centuries, people falsely believed the sun revolved around the earth! Too many of us make the mistake of putting ourselves at the center of life and expect everything to revolve around our wants and needs.

God created us to worship Him. When we do, we live the best life God has for us. Think of this great truth: "Those who wait on the Lord shall renew their strength" (Isaiah 40:31 NKJV). The word *wait* means to trust in God instead of yourself or other people or institutions. Waiting on God means letting go of your anxieties and taking hold of His promise to provide for you. When you wait on Him, you can let go of your fear, worry, and anxiety that weakens you. You become strong in faith and, as a result, you become healthier. Worry will make you sick. Waiting on God will make you strong.

We see this principle in Malachi 4:2: "But for you who fear my name, the sun of righteousness will rise with healing in his wings. And you will go free, leaping with joy like calves let out to pasture" (NLT). If we fear God, we will "go out" instead of being shut up in a world of depression and defeat. If we honor God in worship, we will "leap like calves," which means we will have new energy.

Getting together on the Lord's Day to worship God with His people is also vital to our spiritual health. "[Let us not give] up meeting together, as some are in the habit of doing, but encouraging one another—and all the more as you see the Day [of Christ's return] approaching" (Hebrews 10:25).

Prayer for the Day: *Lord, I praise You every day that I can worship You in spirit and in truth. And thank You for the opportunity to worship with fellow believers, which brings me joy and gives me wisdom and strength for the week ahead.*

Day 173

COMPARING GOD

When we try to explain something to someone, we will often use a comparison, saying, "Well, *this* is like *that*." Jesus used parables for this purpose: "The kingdom of heaven is like . . ." He would begin. He compared the Kingdom to something people knew so they would better understand it.

Can we use comparisons to help us comprehend God? Isaiah 40:18 asks, "With whom, then, will you compare God?" If we reduce God in our comparisons, we will limit our understanding of Him. We must not confuse God with people who have hurt us or disappointed us. Nor must we compare Him to a puppeteer who manipulates his puppets on a string. God allows us to make decisions, live our own lives, and manage the world that He gave us.

The best comparison we can make is to compare God with His Son, Jesus, who is "the image of the invisible God" (Colossians 1:15). Jesus is "the Word" of God (John 1:1). A *word* is an expression of a thought. A private thought becomes a public statement with words. The way a word reveals a thought is the way Jesus reveals God. Jesus said, "Anyone who has seen me has seen the Father" (John 14:9). Any picture you have of God that doesn't look like Jesus is the wrong picture of God. Go back and read the Gospels to understand what God is like as you see Him in Jesus.

Alfred Lord Tennyson was an old man when someone asked him, "What do you need?" He replied, "I need a new vision of God."

Prayer for the Day: *Lord, I can never compare You to anything or anyone other than Jesus, Your Son. He represents all You are—displaying Your great love and mercy and individual care over each of us. He listens and answers our prayers and provides every need. You and Jesus are God, forever the same.*

Day 174

PATIENT PROMISES

As great as our promises are to each other, the promises of God are greater. A promise is a declaration to do something, a legal contract, a binding oath; and it provides the basis on which we expect something. God's promises require two things of us—*faith* and *patience*. "We do not want you to become lazy but to imitate those who through faith and patience inherit what has been promised" (Hebrews 6:12).

The word *lazy* means to be "disinterested, slack, and sluggish." In the Greek language, it means to have "no push." Instead of being lazy, we are to mimic people who model faith and patience. *Faith* means to believe God's promises and personalize them for your life. Faith pleases and honors God. He promises to reward us when we diligently seek Him.

Now for the difficult part—we also need patience. In Greek, *patience* literally means "long-burning," like a slow-burning fuse. When you go through setbacks, disappointment, and delays regarding God's promises, continue to trust Him. Don't lash out at God in anger, impatience, or doubt. Having patience means to never give up.

God's Word is filled with promises we can possess through faith and patience. So, don't stop short of the promises! Through faith and patience, we will inherit what God has promised.

Prayer for the Day: *Lord, I promise to trust You through everything I live through, knowing that You hold me in the palm of Your hand. I promise to be patient, knowing Your timing and ways differ from mine. You are the promise-keeper.*

Day 175

SEEING JESUS

I heard about a young girl whose parents were atheists. When she was five years old, her father snapped. He shot his wife and then killed himself before her eyes.

The girl went to live with a Christian family. They took her to Sunday school, where a teacher showed the kids a portrait of Jesus. "Does anyone know who this is?" the teacher asked. The little girl said, "I know! That Man held me the night my parents died."

When Jesus was in Jerusalem for Passover, some Greeks came to His disciples and said, "We would like to see Jesus" (John 12:21). They told Jesus about it, and He said, "The hour has come for the Son of Man to be glorified" (John 12:23). I hear the same spiritual desire from people today as they search for meaning in life. People have had enough of formal religion, Christian marketing, and denominational politics. They want to see Jesus. Is Jesus hidden from people's vision by the structures of religion? The greatest gift a Christian can give another person is to introduce them to Jesus.

On our first mission trip to Trinidad, Barbie and I ministered in a small, rustic church in a mountain village. The pastor was a former Hindu priest! After the service, we had dinner at his home next to the church. We sat spellbound as he shared this story of meeting Jesus. He had served as a Hindu priest in that village for thirty years. One night he was reading a Hindu book (which he showed us) and pointed to this statement in the book: "The Word became flesh and [lived] among us. We [saw] his glory" (John 1:14). He pondered the meaning of the statement. That night he prayed, "God, show me who is 'the Word that became flesh'?"

During the night, he had a dream of Jesus calling him. When he awoke, he committed his life to Jesus, found a Bible, and began to read it. He became a preacher of the good news of Jesus. He was persecuted heavily in the village for his newfound faith, even to the point of being attacked by a mob who stoned him. He was hospitalized and barely survived. The little, rustic church I had preached in that night was formerly the Hindu temple where he had served in that village.

As Christians, we need a fresh vision of Jesus. If you don't really know Hm, I pray you will see Jesus, believe in Him, and find abundant life in Him.

Prayer for the Day: *Lord, I only want to see Jesus, serve Him, love Him, and be like Him. I want others to see Jesus in me. Give me a fresh vision of Jesus that I may share Him with others.*

Day 176

SPRING CLEANING

We often do spring cleaning in our homes. We also need to do some "spring cleaning" in our heart and mind, whatever the season might be. We need to clean out the past so we can live in the present. The past continues to influence us in ways we are not even aware. Psychology calls it *unconscious motivators of behavior*. Past hurts, fears, and failures can scar us with feelings of anxiety, inadequacy, and resentment. As a result, we fail to live up to our potential today.

After spending four decades in the desert, Joshua told the Israelites it was time to possess the Promised Land. They needed to erase the memories of their wanderings and move forward. The people answered him, "Wherever you send us we will go" (Joshua 1:16). Ahead of them was new opportunity. Their future was not behind them, and neither is yours. Just like ancient Israel, God has a place and a mission for you.

Are you being held back by past hurts, fears, or failures? It is time for cleaning. Purify your mind of past failures and fill your mind with new dreams, plans, and expectations. Stop looking back and start looking forward, telling the Lord, "Wherever You send me, I will go."

Prayer for the Day: *Lord, my past hurts, fears, and failures have hindered me. But I am letting them go as I start looking forward to the new opportunities You have for me. Cleanse my heart and mind of all that is past, and help me focus on a better future with You.*

Day 177

NOT TALK BUT POWER

People, businesses, news reports, and marketers are constantly talking to us through texts, emails, and social-media posts. The words never stop. But there is more to life than words. Paul wrote, "The kingdom of God is not a matter of talk but of power" (1 Corinthians 4:20). God's work in our lives and the work we do for Him consist of more than talking.

Sometimes we talk about things as a substitute for doing anything about them. Words should never be a substitute for action. Words should not be used to impress people or manipulate them. People are often misguided spiritually by high-sounding spiritual words.

God gives us power that makes a difference in our lives and enables us to make a difference in the world. The Greek word for *power* is *dunamis*, from which we get the word *dynamite*. It means strength, energy, and authority that God will gives us. Jesus promised, "You will receive power when the Holy Spirit comes on you" (Acts 1:8).

Stay in a place of dependence on the Holy Spirit so His power can flow in us and through us. There is no power without the ministry of the Holy Spirit.

Ask God for new power every day. Power to witness for Him without fear. Power to stand for your convictions. Power to love others as God loves you. Power to overlook an offense. Power to forgive as Jesus forgave. Power to bend under pressure but not break. Power to resist temptation. Power to live as more than a conqueror.

The power of the Holy Spirit gives us the ability to be more than we could be, accomplish more than we could ever accomplish, and handle more than we could ever handle on our own. The key to power is to remain dependent on Him. It's not about talk but power!

Prayer for the Day: *Lord, I need Your power, not mine, every day and in everything. I can only be what You have called me to be with the power of the Holy Spirit on and in me. I am dependent on You and Your power alone.*

Day 178

WHEN GOD WONDERS

Can you imagine God wondering about anything, since He knows everything? Yet, the Bible says God "wondered that there was no intercessor" (Isaiah 59:16 NKJV). An *intercessor* is one who intervenes to help others. *Intercessory prayer* means praying for others, and seeking

God's blessings and salvation for them. Such prayer comes from our compassion and concern for their spiritual welfare.

When we intercede, we share in the ministry of Jesus, who "always lives to intercede for [us]" (Hebrews 7:25). While God honors intercessory prayer, He is not limited by our lack of prayer. Read all of Isaiah 59:16: "He saw that there was no one, he was appalled that there was no one to intervene; so his own arm achieved salvation for him, and his own righteousness sustained him."

I am glad that God is not hindered by our prayerlessness. But I am equally encouraged by His promise to hear and answer our prayers. *Prayer* is a ministry God has given to us so we can share in the needs of others. Why pray? God has given us prayer so we are His partners in His work in the world. What God does on earth, He usually works in partnership with us.

John Wesley said, "God will do nothing apart from the prayers of His people." Intercessory prayer is Samuel saying, "God forbid that I should sin against the Lord by ceasing to pray for you" (see 1 Samuel 12:23). Intercessory prayer is Jesus praying, "Father, forgive them, for they do not know what they are doing" (Luke 23:34). Intercessory prayer is the Apostle Paul saying, "I have great sorrow and unceasing anguish [for my people Israel]" (Romans 9:2).

God wondered there was no intercessor. Who do you know today who needs the grace of God in their life? Take time today to intercede for them and watch God work through the power of prayer.

Prayer for the Day: *Lord, teach me to be an intercessor. Help me to pray for the world, the nation, my church, my family, my friends, and my neighbors, and all whom You lay on my heart.*

Day 179

SPIRITUAL GRAVITY

A father tried to explain Newton's law of gravity and how it holds things together to his son. His son asked, "Well, Dad, how did things hold together before they passed this law?"

We don't pass the laws that govern life; we discover them. God's laws are woven into the fabric of the universe and every aspect of life. We live in a spiritual world as well as a natural world. God gave us an inner moral compass we call "conscience" that helps us know right from wrong. Romans 2:15 says God's laws are written on human hearts.

A *law* is a fixed or absolute rule that, when obeyed, yields certain results. When God created the world, He established fixed and absolute laws to govern it. This is why we can study the world scientifically. We see order, pattern, and predictability. God's laws govern our health, our happiness, and our relationships. The Bible itself is called "the law of God" because it gives us the principles we need to live a healthy, happy, and holy life.

When we keep the law of God—which means to live by His principles found in Scripture—we will be able to keep it together. You don't have to fall apart emotionally and come unglued by stress and worry. Your marriage doesn't have to come apart with fighting and bickering. Your career doesn't have to end in failure because of poor decisions. Your dreams don't have to end in disillusionment because of disappointment. Live by God's laws, and you can keep it together. "But whoever looks intently into the perfect law that gives freedom, and continues in it—not forgetting what they have heard, but doing it—they will be blessed in what they do" (James 1:25).

Prayer for the Day: *Lord, I love the way You help me keep it together. When I follow Your ways and trust in You, my life doesn't fall apart. When I pray and read Your Word, I'm able to overcome fear and anxiety, knowing You will hold me and never let go.*

Day 180
DOWN AND OUT

Discouragement sucks the life out of us and leaves us with no passion or purpose. Moses got discouraged, even though he was used by God in such powerful ways. When Moses confronted Pharaoh with

God's message, "Let my people go" (Exodus 5:1), Pharaoh threw him out of the royal court. Pharaoh then turned on the Hebrew slaves and subjected them to harsher work conditions. The leaders of Israel blamed Moses for their hardship and said, "May the Lord look on you and judge you!" (Exodus 5:21). When the people you are trying to lead want God to judge you, that's bad!

Pharaoh resisted Moses' demands, and the people rejected his leadership. Any way you look at it, Moses was down and out. He was discouraged with the outcome, disappointed in himself, and probably a bit disillusioned with God who sent him on this apparently pointless mission. Discouragement is the gap between our expectations and achievements. If we have high expectations but low achievements, we feel discouraged.

When we are discouraged, we have three poor options: (1) Lash out in anger toward God, other people, and life itself, declaring "Life's not fair!" (2) Retreat in fear of our assignment. Moses' biggest challenge was going back to face Pharaoh again. (3) Give up in defeat. Moses could have concluded he didn't have the leadership qualities and skill necessary to do the job.

But there is a fourth option, and that is the one Moses chose: "Moses returned to the Lord" (Exodus 5:22). That is the way out of discouragement. Return to the Lord in prayer to find new power and new courage to face life's challenges and do what God has called you to do. When we pray, we get a new perspective on our situation, we get new peace for our fears, and we get new power to carry on with our dreams, goals, and ambitions. We rise from prayer with new assurance that "if God is for us, who can be against us?" (Romans 8:31).

Prayer for the Day: *Lord, I may be discouraged now, but I'm looking to You for the strength and courage to face the challenges that come with Your plan for my life.*

Day 181

GONE ASTRAY

Have you ever wondered why the Bible compares people to sheep? I once went to a sheep farm so I could better understand this analogy. The first thing I noticed was how dirty the sheep were! They had thick white wool, but they were covered in dirt. They didn't look like those angelic animals I had seen in pictures.

I think the main reason we are like sheep is because we need constant care from the Shepherd. We cannot make it on our own. We are not as independent as we think we are. But if the Lord is our Shepherd, we "lack nothing," David said (Psalm 23:1). During the days of Moses, God led His people "like a flock" (Psalm 77:20).

Sheep have no inner guide, so they wander away from the shepherd and from the herd. We, too, have no built-in sense of direction. "We all, like sheep, have gone astray, each of us has turned to our own way" (Isaiah 53:6). Another prophet said, "Strike the shepherd, and the sheep will be scattered" (Zechariah 13:7).

When we lose sight of the Shepherd, we get lost. We must let the Scriptures become our moral compass to keep us on track in a secular world. We must stay close to the Shepherd, not losing sight of Him.

The movie *The Edge* portrays a story of three men who survived the crash of a small plane in Alaska. As they travel for days in the freezing snow hounded by a grizzly bear, one of the men panics, feeling like they are lost. He takes out his compass and shakes it, trying to get a sense of direction. The one who knew the way to safety calmed the man down and said, "Just because you feel lost doesn't mean your compass is broken."

When you feel lost, confused, and anxious, God's Word within your heart will lead you to safety if you trust it.

Prayer for the Day: *Lord, sometimes I feel so lost in this world. Please keep Your Holy Spirit nudging me in the right direction and into a safe place with You.*

Every Day With God

Day 182

DON'T GET CAUGHT LOOKING

When Jesus said, "Go into all the world and preach the Good News to everyone" (Mark 16:15 NLT), He didn't give us just the Great Commission; He gave us the *only* commission! It is the one thing Jesus has called us and empowered us to do. His commission is our purpose. We are called to lead people to know Jesus Christ as their Savior. "You will be my witnesses," Jesus said (Acts 1:8). We are the only witnesses He has! A witness in a trial is a person with firsthand knowledge, experience, or expertise. As Christians, we are personal and expertise witnesses of God's grace.

As I prepared to speak at a conference on the importance of Christian education, the Lord revealed His commission to me in a new way. The commission of Jesus to us is not just evangelism (telling the good news of salvation), but also education. He said, "Go and make disciples of all nations . . . teaching them to obey everything I have commanded you" (Matthew 28:19-20). Telling and teaching go hand-in-hand so people know how to live as Jesus taught us to live for Him.

At the end of His ministry on earth, Jesus' disciples stood with Him on the Mount of Olives and watched Him ascend into Heaven. As they stood there still looking into the sky even though He was gone, two angels stood by them and asked them (and us) a thought-provoking question: "Why do you stand here looking into the sky?" (Acts 1:11). They had just witnessed a miracle. Now they needed to get on with Jesus' mandate.

You, too, can get caught standing when you should be going, looking when you should be acting. Instead, you need to look at the needs of the people around you. You are God's missionary where you live—to your family, friends, and neighbors. Don't get caught standing instead of going, or looking instead of living. You have a message and a mandate. Share your story. Get on the witness stand and tell others of God's amazing grace in your life, and He will do the rest.

Prayer for the Day: *Lord, I'm so guilty of looking up and wondering why You are taking so long to return. Instead, I should be looking at the people around me who desperately need You. Thank You for refocusing my eyes!*

Day 183

TIMES AND DATES

Jesus' disciples wondered about the future and asked, "Lord, are you at this time going to restore the kingdom to Israel?" Jesus answered, "It is not for you to know the times or dates the Father has set by his own authority" (Acts 1:6-7). The word *set* means "predetermined." The future belongs to God, and He alone is in charge of it. The one thing I appreciate about my Presbyterian background is the emphasis on the sovereignty of God!

The word *sovereignty* means God has all power and all authority the way a king, or a sovereign, does. I don't need to know times and dates because God "works out everything in conformity with the purpose of his will" (Ephesians 1:11). I don't need to know the future because I know the One who controls the future and final outcome of all things in this magnificent world He has created. I trust the sovereignty of God because, "The Lord has established his throne in heaven, and his kingdom rules over all" (Psalm 103:19).

When I was in college learning theories of the return of Jesus, I got into a discussion with my dad about the return of Jesus Christ. I was reading popular books on the Second Coming, signs of the times, and the rapture of the Church, and I thought I knew all things. I got frustrated with him because I couldn't convince him that I had Bible prophecy figured out and he needed to agree with me. Finally, he said, "I don't believe in pre-millennialism or post-millennialism; I'm a pan-millennialist." "What's that?" I asked. He replied, "I believe in the sovereignty of God and it's all going to pan out the right way in the end!"

Join the worship of Heaven today and declare, "Hallelujah! For our Lord God Almighty reigns. Let us rejoice and be glad and give him glory!" (Revelation 19:6-7).

Prayer for the Day: *Lord, forgive me for being impatient about Your return! I only see my reasons and do not see the full world scope of things. You are sovereign and You know best.*

Day 184

REPAY IT

Paying our bills and our debts is an important and, yes, stressful, part of life. But what about how we repay others emotionally? How should we repay people when they hurt us, insult us, or harm us? The word on the street is, "Pay them back!"

As God's people we follow a higher ethic. The Word of God says, "Do not repay evil with evil or insult with insult, [but] with blessing, because to this you were called so that you may inherit a blessing" (1 Peter 3:9). Peter mentions two things we are going to face at times—evil and insults. Evil is done against people in many ways. We all get insulted from time to time for our appearance, performance, and even our beliefs. Don't repay with what you get. Instead, pay back evil and insults with blessing.

The word *blessing* means to "speak well of." We need to continue to speak well of people instead of broadcasting their wrong actions. We can also bless people by praying for them. It takes a lot of restraint not to get on social media and let everyone know how we got mistreated. We need to show restraint. We don't have to tell the world about every bad thing that happens to us.

God calls us to be a source of His blessing to others, even in the face of evil and insult. Here's the good part—"so that you may inherit a blessing." If we show restraint and do not lash out in anger, even though people may deserve it, the Lord promises to send a special blessing our way. Let us put ourselves in a position to get a blessing from the Lord by blessing the very people who hurt us. Pay back the bad with blessing!

Prayer for the Day: *Lord, thank You for reminding me not to lash out to those who hurt me but, rather, find some way to bless them. It is so easy to run my mouth or blast a text message when I should just stop and pray. Teach me not to overreact but to respond with love and kindness.*

Day 185

GET WELL SOON

Mark Twain said, "The only way to keep your health is to eat what you don't want, drink what you don't like, and do what you'd rather not do." We are living in a health craze in America, but are we becoming healthy? We like to shop at a health-food grocery store. The only problem is we are met with four isles of dark chocolate when we enter. Everyone is filling up bags of dark chocolate-covered nuts, raisins, and whatever, because it's in a health store!

Jesus is the Great Physician, and a big part of His ministry was making people well. During Pentecost, Jesus visited the Pool of Bethesda in Jerusalem. *Bethesda* means "house of mercy." The pool was surrounded by five covered porches and fed by underground springs deep enough to swim in. People who were sick gathered at the pool. They believed that occasionally an angel would stir the waters and the first person in the pool would be healed. Among the people that day was a man who had been crippled for thirty-eight years. He came every day hoping to be healed.

Jesus asked the man a strange question: "Do you want to get well?" (John 5:6). Instead of answering Jesus' question, the man made an excuse that he had no one to help him in the water when it was stirred. Jesus, in turn, ignored the man's response and proceeded to give him three steps toward wellness: Get up, pick up your mat, and walk.

Jesus did not ask him if he wanted to get healed and walk. The word *well* Jesus used means to "make whole." Jesus came to make us whole, not just to heal us. Healing is temporary; wellness is permanent. Healing is instantaneous; wellness is progressive. Healing is partial; wellness is complete. Healing treats symptoms; wellness addresses the root cause.

We focus on healing instead of wholeness. We pray for healing, but we don't talk about lifestyle changes. We care for the poor, but we don't empower them to make a living for themselves. We pray for a financial miracle, but we don't learn to manage money. We want a miracle for our marriage, but we don't go to counseling or make changes. Jesus didn't come to solve problems; He came to save people. *Salvation* is more than the forgiveness of our sins. It means to make whole, free, and complete in every area of life.

While doing hospital visitation, Barbie and I saw a woman with severe breathing problems. She carried an oxygen tank when she went outside to smoke. A nurse told us it is common for patients to continue their bad habits that are the root cause of their illness even while getting treatment.

Do you want to get well? Get up, pick up your mat, and walk! Begin to make the changes you need to make so you can live your best life.

Prayer for the Day: *Lord, I have some unhealthy habits that need to be changed. I can't keep living like I am without consequences. Give me the wisdom and the desire to make these changes so that I walk in wellness of body, mind, and spirit.*

Day 186
STAY ON TOP OF IT

If you don't stay on top of it, it will come out from under you! Carelessness leads to making a lot of mistakes and creating a big mess. Things come out from under us when we don't stay on top of them. Perhaps you've heard the saying, "The price of freedom is eternal vigilance."

The Bible constantly challenges us to stay on top of things. "Be alert and of sober mind. Your enemy the devil prowls around like a roaring lion looking for someone to devour" (1 Peter 5:8). "So, if you think you are standing firm, be careful that you don't fall!" (1 Corinthians 10:12). "Be on your guard so that you . . . [do not] fall from your secure position" (2 Peter 3:17). Jesus said, "Watch and pray so that you will not fall into temptation" (Matthew 26:41).

Marriages fail because couples get careless in their relationship. Businesses lose customers because they don't pay attention to customer service. Churches lose their impact because they don't stay true to Christ's mission. Governments waste resources because they don't revise programs and services. Individuals fail to reach their potential because they don't manage their time and priorities.

Staying on top of things means to be a good manager of your time, talent, and treasure. Barbie and I used to tell our kids, "Your life is God's gift to you. What you do with your life is your gift back to God." Stay on top of everything and everyone important to you so things don't come out from under you and you end up losing the things that matter the most. As Jesus said, "To whom much is given, much more is required" (see Luke 12:48).

Prayer for the Day: *Lord, I have ignored some things that really need my attention. I didn't pray and didn't follow up when I needed to stay on top of things. In the future, I will be on my guard and more alert, not allowing things to slide.*

Day 181

DON'T LOOK AT THE OBSTACLES

Hannah More (1745-1833) was an English playwright and philanthropist who worked to abolish slavery and raise the literacy of the poor. She said, "Obstacles are those frightful things you see when you take your eyes off the goal."

I like to go running on trails, in parks, and at the national battlefield at Kennesaw Mountain. Running down a mountain trail with sharp rocks, a jagged path, and fallen tree limbs can be risky. I learned the only way to keep my footing is to not look at the obstacles but, instead, to look at the place I want my feet to land. Look at the safe spot, not at what I want to avoid. I discovered my feet naturally go to what my eyes see. If I look at the rocks, limbs, or holes I want to avoid, I run the risk of stepping there.

What a great lesson for life! Don't look at the obstacle; look at the opportunity. Don't look at the problem; look at the solution. Don't look at the failures; look at the successes!

Isn't this what Jesus taught us? Jesus "steadfastly set His face to go to Jerusalem" (Luke 9:51 NKJV). He was a Man on a mission. The phrase "steadfastly set His face" means "like a flint." The way a flint rock was carved into a sharp point in the ancient world is the way Jesus looked forward to accomplishing His mission. The writer of Hebrews spoke of this quality of Jesus' life: "For the joy set before him he endured the cross, scorning its shame, and sat down at the right hand of the throne of God" (Hebrews 12:2). Jesus kept His eyes on the joy that was set before Him, not the past problems or the present obstacles.

If you will keep your eyes on God's goal for your life, you won't see the obstacles, and you too will receive the joy He sets before you.

Prayer for the Day: *Lord, I have spent most of my life trying to overcome obstacles when I should ignore them and focus on the goals You have for me. I will learn from my failures and keep moving forward as You lead.*

Day 188

WE FOLLOW, HE MAKES

A Christian is a person who believes in Jesus and who follows Him as Lord of their life. It's that simple. Jesus says to each of us, "Follow Me, and I will make you . . ." (Matthew 4:19 NKJV). Look at His promise: *I will make you.* We can't make ourselves better. Only He can do that. If we will follow Him, He will make us. We follow; He makes!

Thomas à Kempis coined the term *The Imitation of Christ* in his famous book by that title. Being a disciple of Jesus is more than a decision; it is a direction. Following Jesus means to go the same direction He is going, to submit our will to Him, and to remain loyal to Him. Sometimes we follow at a distance, like Peter did when Jesus was arrested. He watched the trial of Jesus from a distance. Sometimes we quit following because we get distracted, discouraged, or defeated. We need to follow Him fully. The Apostle John describes Christians this way: "They follow the Lamb wherever he goes" (Revelation 14:4).

Jesus is the Way, so follow Him. He doesn't show us the way. He doesn't teach us the way. He *is* the Way to an abundant and eternal life. He says, "Follow Me." He doesn't say, "Follow the church" or "Follow My followers" or "Follow your feelings" or "Follow the trends of the day." He says, "Follow Me!" If we follow Jesus, He will make us into the person we want to be and that He calls us to be.

E. Stanley Jones, missionary to India, tells of two Hindu men traveling on a train. One tells the other that he has become a Christian. "Why did you convert to Christianity?" the other asked. "Why do you not remain a Hindu and work to improve our religion?" The man replied, "I don't want a religion that I can improve; I want a religion that can improve me." Follow Jesus, and your life will improve!

Prayer for the Day: *Lord, during my life I have followed after many things. No more! I will keep my eyes focused on You, the author and finisher of my faith, knowing that any other path is a dead-end and leads to destruction.*

Day 189

I DIDN'T RECOGNIZE HIM

In an episode of *The Twilight Zone*, an American on a walking trip through Europe gets caught in a storm. He arrives through the pouring rain to a medieval castle where a brotherhood of monks takes him in. That night, he finds a cell with a man locked inside. An ancient wooden staff bolts the door. The prisoner claims he is being held by the insane head monk, Brother Jerome, who tells him the prisoner is Satan himself, "the father of lies" (John 8:44), who is being held captive by the staff of truth—the one barrier he cannot pass.

The man is convinced Jerome is insane, so he removes the staff and releases the prisoner. Immediately, the prisoner transforms into a frightening demon and disappears in a misty cloud. Jerome tells the terrified American, "I'm sorry for you, my son. All your life you'll remember this night and the evil you have turned loose on the world." "I didn't believe you," the man replies. "I saw him but didn't recognize him." Jerome says, "That is man's weakness and Satan's strength."

Our world no longer recognizes evil for what it is and, as a result, is often mislead. The prophet Isaiah said, "Woe to those who call evil good, and good evil" (Isaiah 5:20). Paul said that in the last days, people will be under "a powerful delusion [and] believe the lie" (2 Thessalonians 2:11). The Apostle John described Satan as the one "who leads the whole world astray" (Revelation 12:9).

Our culture has lost its moral and spiritual compass as a result of not recognizing truth from error. The only answer to deception is discernment that comes from God. We need to pray like young Solomon, "Give [me] a discerning heart . . . to distinguish between right and wrong" (1 Kings 3:9). When we have a wise and discerning heart, it will keep us safe and guide us in the way we should go.

Prayer for the Day: *Lord, give me a wise and discerning heart. I'm tired of being deceived and falling for the lies of Satan. Open my eyes that I may see Jesus.*

Day 190

SHOCK WAVES

A small northern Pennsylvania community constructed a city hall and fire station. All the citizens were so proud of their new red brick structure—a long-awaited dream had come true. Not too many weeks after moving in, however, strange things began to happen. Several doors failed to shut completely, and a few windows wouldn't slide open very easily. As time passed, ominous cracks began to appear in the walls. Within a few months, the front door couldn't be locked since the foundation had shifted, and the roof began to leak. By and by, the little building that once was the source of great civic pride had to be condemned. An intense investigation revealed that deep mining blasts several miles away caused underground shock waves that weakened the supporting earth beneath the building's foundation, resulting in its destruction.

The underground shock waves of secularism and spiritualism have weakened our faith. We need to shore up the foundation of our faith in God and refuse to be worldly. Remember, "If you do not stand firm in your faith, you will not stand at all" (Isaiah 7:9).

When we stand firm in our faith in God, we can overcome every problem, win every battle, and accomplish every goal. Our faith is anchored in the character of God "who does not lie" (Titus 1:2). We can trust His promises, for "not one word has failed of all the good promises he gave" (1 Kings 8:56). For "no matter how many promises God has made, they are 'Yes' in Christ" (2 Corinthians 1:20).

One truth I have learned about faith is that God honors it. He searches the world looking for people who will dare to believe Him. "The eyes of the Lord range throughout the earth to strengthen those whose hearts are fully committed to him" (2 Chronicles 16:9). Don't let the shock waves of the world's pressures, life's stresses, or uncertainty of the times move you from your foundation of faith in God.

Prayer for the Day: *Lord, help me to stand firm in my faith when everything around me is falling apart. Help me to anchor myself to You alone that I may rest in Your sovereignty.*

Day 191

FACT, NOT FANTASY

"Reason is itself a matter of faith," said G. K. Chesterton, "It is an act of faith to assert that our thoughts have any relation to reality at all."

The Christian faith will always be attacked by skeptics. The Apostle Peter said, "In the last days scoffers will come, scoffing and following their own evil desires" (2 Peter 3:3). We can be confident our faith in God is based on reality, not fantasy. "We did not follow cleverly devised stories when we told you about the [power and] coming of our Lord Jesus Christ," Peter wrote, "but we were eyewitnesses of his majesty" (2 Peter 1:16). One of the qualifications for the apostles was that they had personally seen and known the Lord.

Be inspired, not intimidated! Be confident, not cowardly. Be passionate, not passive. As a Christian, your faith is based on fact, not fantasy. Let us be courageous in our witness for Jesus, because everyone we meet needs to know Him as their Savior. He is the only answer to their problems. He is "the way and the truth and the life" (John 14:6).

The world where you live is your mission field, so let your light shine. When you have the opportunity to share your personal faith and to talk with others about spiritual matters, be confident! "Always be prepared to give an answer to everyone who asks you to give the reason for the hope that you have. But do this with gentleness and respect" (1 Peter 3:15). The reason for the hope you have of eternal life is based on fact, not fantasy: Jesus Christ lived a sinless life, died for our sins on the cross, arose on the third day, and lives forever as King of kings!

Prayer for the Day: *Lord, when I hear people share their beliefs in spiritual things that aren't true, give me the confidence to share the truth based on the historical fact You lived, died, and rose from the dead to save us and give us eternal life.*

Day 192

DO IT NOW!

In his book *Rich Habits*, Tom Corley says successful people do not procrastinate; they are goal-oriented and accomplish things. Breaking the bad habit of procrastination is crucial to success. When the thought of putting something off enters your mind, immediately conquer the thought by saying, "Do it now." "Repeat these three words a hundred times a day if necessary," Corley writes.

If it's worth doing, it's worth doing now! "Today, if you hear [God's] voice, do not harden your hearts" (Hebrews 4:7). Maybe we don't harden our hearts against God, but we can harden our hearts against our responsibilities, desires, and goals, and fail to take action. When opportunity knocks, get up and answer the door! Time is a wonderful gift from God that we need to treasure and never waste. We should strive to make "the most of every opportunity, because the days are evil" (Ephesians 5:16).

Why do we procrastinate? It may be because we lack discipline and confidence to act with intention and immediacy. Procrastination is just a bad habit that develops over time. Tell yourself, "Do it now," when important things arise. The main reason we procrastinate is because we are afraid of failure. We delay taking action because we fear failure. This line of thinking develops when we are children, and it becomes a deeply ingrained habit of procrastination when we are adults.

There is a legend about three apprentice demons who were coming to earth to complete their apprenticeship. They met with the Satan, who questioned their tactics to tempt and destroy humankind. The first demon said, "I will tell him there is no God." Satan said, "That will not deceive many of them, for they can readily discern there is a God." The second demon said, "I will tell them there is no hell." Satan replied, "Very few will believe, for they know there is a hell for sin." The third demon said, "I will tell them there is no hurry." "Go," said Satan, "You will destroy them by the thousands." The most dangerous delusion of all is that there is plenty of time.

William Barclay said, "The most dangerous day in a person's life is when he or she learns that there is such a word as *tomorrow*." Conquer the fear of failure, take the risk, rise to challenge, and do it now!

Prayer for the Day: *Lord, forgive me for putting off what I know needs to be done today. Because You are with me, I do not need to fear, for You will direct my footsteps.*

Day 193
LOOK FOR A PROMISE

One of the most successful people in American history is Dr. George Washington Carver. Carver described his work as getting up every morning at 4:00 going into the woods to look for specimen and to listen to what God would say to him. After his morning "talk with God," Carver went to his laboratory to work on experiments which he called "carrying out God's will."

One day, Carver asked God to explain to him the purpose of the universe. He said God told him, *You want to know too much for such as little mind as yours. Ask for something your size.* So, he asked the Lord, *What was man made for?* Again, God, whom he called the Creator, told him, *You are still asking too much. Bring down the extent of your request.* Finally, he prayed, *Tell me then, Creator, what the peanut was made for.* Carver wrote, "Then the great Creator taught me how to take the peanut apart and put it together again. And out of this came all these products which the Creator taught me to make."

Dr. Carver developed about three hundred different products from the peanut and over one hundred products from the sweet potato. He explained the secret of success: "It is not we little men who do the work, but it is our blessed Creator working through us. . . . Other people can have this power, if they only believe. The secret lies right here [touching his Bible] in the promises of God. They are real, but so few people believe them to be real" (*George Washington Carver: God's Ebony Scientist*, by Basil Miller).

When we read the Bible, let's learn to look for a promise. There is one in it for every situation, problem, and challenge we face. The promises of God are backed up by God's faithfulness. "For no matter how many promises God has made, they are 'Yes' in Christ. And so through him the 'Amen' is spoken by us to the glory of God" (2 Corinthians 1:20).

The word *amen* comes from the Hebrew language. When Moses read the Law of God, the people responded by repeatedly saying, "Amen" (Deuteronomy 27). *Amen* is the Hebrew word for "faithfulness." When we say "Amen," we declare God's Word is true and God is faithful to keep His word!

Look past your problem today and look at the promise of God, who is faithful to do more than you even think possible if you will trust Him.

Prayer for the Day: *Lord, I'm always looking for answers when I should really be focusing on Your promises. I will pray, trust, and rest in those promises which provide the answers.*

Day 194

HIDE YOURSELF

We live out in the open these days. Security cameras record our movements. People take pictures and videos of us on their cell phones without our knowing it. We stay connected 24/7 with our smart phones and on social media. Satellites monitor our homes from the sky. If you get lost driving, call *Siri*—she knows right where you are. There is nowhere to hide!

There are times when we need to hide. Health requires hiding at times. When Elijah faced great danger, God told him, "Leave here, turn eastward and hide in the Kerith Ravine, east of the Jordan. You will drink from the brook, and I have directed the ravens to supply you with food there" (1 Kings 17:3-4).

Sometimes we need to take the advice to hide. We need to turn off the phone, disconnect from the crowd, and cancel the schedule. Sometimes we need to hide away to refresh our minds, renew our strength, and replenish our joy. We will burn out if we don't stop to hide away. It may be for thirty minutes in the middle of the day or for a short vacation.

Our health requires us to hide. God will feed us spiritually when we get away in His presence. He supplies us with spiritual food as He reveals His Word to us and refreshes us by the ministry of the Holy Spirit. As long as our minds are cluttered and our hearts are racing, we cannot focus on what God is wanting to speak to us. But when we get still, we get strong! "They that wait upon the Lord shall renew their strength" (Isaiah 40:31 KJV). Maybe God is saying to you the same thing he said to Elijah: "Get away from here and hide yourself, and there I will supply your every need."

Prayer for the Day: *Lord, today I am taking Your advice. I am going to hide myself that I may refresh, renew, and replenish my joy and spiritual strength.*

Day 195

VICTORY IN THE VALLEY

We use the term "mountaintop experiences" to describe great experiences of life. We have mountaintop experiences in our personal life, our work life, our family life, and also spiritually when the Spirit of God does a great work in us. When we're on the mountain, we naturally want to stay there. But life requires us to keep moving. Eventually we come down from the mountain and find ourselves in a valley. A *valley* is a low point between two mountains. We cannot stay on the mountain. We must go back down and cross the valley to the next mountain. We might feel God has left us, or is punishing us, or that we have done something wrong when we are in a valley, but He is the God of the valley as well as the God of the mountain.

This was God's message to the king of Israel when they faced an invading army: "Because the Arameans think the Lord is a god of the hills and not a god of the valleys, I will deliver this vast army into your hands, and you will know that I am the Lord" (1 Kings 20:28). There are five Hebrew words in the Old Testament for *valley*, ranging from small dry riverbeds called "wadis" to a great mountain cleft. We too go through small valleys and deep, treacherous valleys in our life journey. Don't make the same mistake the king of Aram did when he thought God only worked for His people on the mountains.

Don't quit when you're in a battle in the valley; believe the report of the Word of God. The king of Israel had to trust that God would be faithful in the valley. You can get through every valley because God promises to fight for you. God says, "I am going to deliver you from this vast army." Persevere through the valley to the mountain! Declare by faith, "I am going to get through this valley. I'm not going to get stuck in it!"

At the height of World War II, General Dwight D. Eisenhower sent this message to the U.S. troops as they prepared to storm the beaches of Normandy and defeat Nazi Germany: "I have full confidence in your courage, devotion to duty, and skill in battle. We will accept nothing less than full victory." Accept nothing less than full victory in the battles you face in the valleys of life.

Prayer for the Day: *Lord, I look forward to the mountain-top times with You, but I always dread the valleys. I have been looking at this the wrong way! The valley is where I grow and learn to trust You. Help me to press through and grow through the valley that I may be refreshed on the mountain.*

Day 196

LIKE IT, DON'T LOVE IT

I have a simple rule I use when it comes to material things: I don't use the word *love* in relationship to them. Someone asked me if I loved my new guitar. I replied, "No. I like it, but I don't love it."

Love is a word I reserve for the Lord and people. I like things, but I love God. I like my house, but I love my family. I like my church facility, but I love the people.

Like it, don't love it! First John 2:15 says, "Love not the world, neither the things that are in the world" (KJV).

"Things" are an important part of life. We need food to eat, clothes to wear, a job to do, money to spend, a car to get around in, a house to live in, health care to maintain, insurance to protect us, and so on. Jesus told us if we trust God, we will always have the things we need: "But seek first [God's] kingdom and his righteousness, and all these things will be given to you as well" (Matthew 6:33).

There are also things we want and enjoy but don't necessarily need—vacations, hobbies, sports, travel, jewelry, toys, eating out, movies, art, music, and so on. The Bible says, "Hope in God, who richly provides us with everything for our enjoyment" (1 Timothy 6:17).

Things are important to us. God wants us to have things we need and want. Many of the things we possess serve an important place in our lives and in our families. People often pass down valuable things for generations. I have a solid silver pocket watch that has been in my family since the 1700s, along with a ledger with the name of every person who has ever owned it.

But things are just things, and they will perish with time. "The world and its desires pass away, but whoever does the will of God lives forever" (1 John 2:17). So, like it, but don't love it. Love should be reserved for God and for people.

Prayer for the Day: *Lord, there is a big difference between* liking *and* loving. *I have You, Your Word, Your people, and my family and friends. May I never have an attachment of love to something that can pass away.*

Day 197

UNASHAMED

I often wonder what it will be like to see Jesus for the first time in Heaven. The Apostle John wrote, "Continue [to live] in him [Jesus], so that when he appears we may be confident and unashamed before him at his coming" (1 John 2:28).

There is a part of me that is excited about seeing Jesus. I want to see His nail-scarred hands, like Thomas did, and thank Him for going to the cross to take away my sins. But there is another part of me that is afraid to see Him. He is holy, but I have done unholy things. He is the perfect Messiah, but I am imperfect. He does all things well, but I make some mistakes over and over.

When I see Jesus, I believe I will be overwhelmed as Isaiah was when he saw the Lord in all His glory and said, "I am ruined! For I am a man of unclean lips . . . and my eyes have seen the King, the Lord Almighty" (Isaiah 6:5). I think I will feel like Peter did when he first met Jesus and said, "Go away from me, Lord; for I am a sinful man!" (Luke 5:8). I imagine fear will overtake me as it did John, when He saw Jesus in all His glory and wrote, "I fell at his feet as though dead" (Revelation 1:17).

Yet, John assures us that we can be "unashamed" before Christ. How is that possible? How can we ever stand before a holy God and be unashamed? Because He has taken away our sins and has given us His righteousness as a gift! That's what the Bible calls "justification." God has pardoned us of our sins and credited to us the righteousness of Jesus.

Our spiritual "bank account" was on zero, but God paid off all our debts and deposited into our account the righteousness of Jesus, making us spiritual millionaires!

So, let us continue to live faithfully in Jesus with confidence, knowing we are unashamed before Him. Unashamed before Him when we pray. Unashamed before Him in His presence. Unashamed before Him when He returns.

Prayer for the Day: *Lord, how will I be able to stand before You when I see You face-to-face without feeling ashamed? You have forgiven me of so much, and I know I will be overwhelmed by Your presence. But, because of Your gift of righteousness, I will do my best to stand in Your presence unashamed!*

Day 198

ADMIRED

We all want to be admired and to be an inspiration to others. The ancient poem *Beowulf* declares, "Behavior that's admired is the path to power among peoples everywhere."

We don't need fame, fortune, or power in order to make an impact on others; we simply need to live in such a way that our behavior is admired, and when it's admired, it will inspire! This is the point made to Christian women trying to inspire their husbands to follow Jesus Christ: "Wives, in the same way, submit yourselves to your own husbands so that, if any of them do not believe the word, they may be won over without words by the behavior of their wives" (1 Peter 3:1).

Submission means to serve someone in love, rather than being dominated by someone. We are all called to that kind of submission. "Submit to one another out of reverence for Christ" (Ephesians 5:21).

Consider Peter's phrase "won over without words." Words are important, and we are to share the Word of God with others; but our behavior must back up our words. We are taught, "Let us behave decently, as in the daytime" (Romans 13:13). Proverbs 11:30 says, "The seeds of good deeds become a tree of life; a wise person wins friends" (NLT). The power of good deeds wins friends and inspires others.

My dad gave me this poem by Edgar A. Guest:

I'd rather see a sermon than hear one, any day;
I'd rather one would walk with me than merely tell the way;
The eye's a better pupil and more willing than the ear.
Fine counsel is confusing, but example's always clear,
And the best of all the preachers are the men who live their creeds,
For to see good put in action is what everybody needs.
I soon can learn to do it if you'll let me see it done;
I can watch your hands in action, but your tongue too fast may run.
And the lecture you deliver may be very wise and true,
But I'd rather get my lessons by observing what you do.
For I might misunderstand you and the high advice you give.
But there's no misunderstanding how you act and how you live.

Prayer for the Day: Lord, teach me how to live out my life before others that they see You and desire to follow You. Help me to be an inspiration to all who cross my path for Your glory.

Day 199

DON'T GO THROUGH IT; GROW THROUGH IT

We often tell people what we're going through. Don't go through it, grow through it! We want God to deliver us from our problems, but He never delivers from problems without developing the person. When you are going through challenging circumstances, ask yourself, *How can I grow through this experience? What can I learn? How can I improve?*

Simon Peter was writing to Christians undergoing persecution when he said, "Grow in the grace and knowledge of our Lord and Savior Jesus Christ" (2 Peter 3:18). I'm not a negative person who thinks God sends adversity or that we learn more in difficult times than easy times. We need to be learning all the time!

In *Peanuts*, Charlie Brown complains that his baseball team always loses. Lucy tries to console him by saying, "Remember, Charlie Brown, you learn more from your defeats than you do from your victories." Charlie replies, "That makes me the smartest man in the world."

When you get through the challenge, come out better as a person than when you started. Come out anointed, not angry. Come out better, not bitter. Come out confident, not confused. Come out dynamic, not defeated.

Come out empowered, not empty. Come out faithful, not faithless. Come out grateful, not guilty. Come out hopeful, not hopeless. Come out inspired, not inferior. Come out joyful, not judgmental. Come out loving, not losing. Come out magnificent, not mediocre.

Come out new, not negative. Come out overcoming, not overwhelmed. Come out praising, not panicking. Come out qualified, not quavering. Come out revived, not ruined. Come out stronger, not stressed.

Come out triumphant, not troubled. Come out understanding, not unhinged. Come out victorious, not victimized. Come out winning, not whining. Come out zealous, not zapped!

Don't just go through it; grow through it!

Prayer for the Day: *Lord, please show me how to grow through this situation so I don't have to go through it again. I am willing and teachable.*

Day 200

WITHOUT A SWORD

Individuality is one of the great freedoms we have. While we need to learn from others and sometimes imitate them, we also need to find our own way in life and do things our way.

We are often compared to others. When we assume a position from someone, our style and methods may be compared to theirs. "You don't do it the way they did," people may observe or object.

Shakespeare's advice is good advice: "To thine own self be true." The Bible story of David and Goliath illustrates this: "David triumphed over the Philistine with a sling and a stone; without a sword in his hand he struck down the Philistine and killed him" (1 Samuel 17:50).

"So David triumphed." What enemy or challenge or problem do you face that you need to triumph over? David defeated Goliath "without a sword." Even King Saul tried to put his armor on David when he went to face Goliath. Saul was the tallest man in Israel, and his armor was too big for David to wear. David told the king, "'I cannot go in these ... because I am not used to them.' So he took them off" (1 Samuel 17:39). As you discover yourself, you may take off some of the ways of working, leading, and living that others said were necessary in order to succeed.

David took his shepherd's staff and sling, chose five smooth stones from the brook in the valley, and went out to face Goliath. When Goliath verbally abused David, he replied, "All those gathered here will know that it is not by sword or spear that the Lord saves; for the battle is the Lord's" (1 Samuel 17:47). The rest is history!

So, David triumphed without a sword—without the conventional method. He triumphed his way, using his talents and the weapons he had mastered. Above all, he trusted God to anoint his talent, and that is the secret to victory. God's anointing on our lives and His power makes the difference.

Prayer for the Day: *Lord, sometimes it is hard to be myself when compared with others. I can only use what You have given me and ask that You make up the difference. I will develop and grow to be what You see in me.*

Day 201

NO RECORD

One of the greatest things that can happen to a person who has a criminal record is to have their record *expunged*. That means there is no record of their past offenses. God promises to expunge the record of our sins if we will confess them to Him and receive His forgiveness. God's grace can give us a guilt-free conscience.

The psalmist sang about this: "If you, Lord, kept a record of sins, Lord, who could stand? But with You there is forgiveness, so that we can, with reverence, serve you" (Psalm 130:3-4). This reminds me of

1 Corinthians 13:5: "[Love] keeps no record of wrongs." Just as we are taught to keep no record of the wrongs we endure from others, God promises to keep no record of our wrongs if we confess them.

If God kept a record of our wrongs, how could we ever stand before Him? The record of our sins would condemn us. But we can stand before a holy God in faith because He keeps no record of wrongs! David wrote, "Who may stand in his holy place? The one who has clean hands and a pure heart" (Psalm 24:3-4). The only way to have clean hands (actions) and a pure heart (attitude) is to receive God's forgiveness and cleansing. God not only promises to forgive our sins, He also promises to "purify us from all unrighteousness" (1 John 1:9).

In Revelation 6:17, we read of God's judgment coming to the Antichrist system: "The great day of their wrath has come, and who can withstand it?" We don't ever have to worry about facing judgment for our sins if we confess them to God, receive His forgiveness, and accept His salvation. "Since we have now been justified by his blood, how much more shall we be saved from God's wrath through him!" (Romans 5:9).

Prayer for the Day: *Lord, what an amazing thing—You keep no record of wrongs! When we confess our sins, You cleanse us and forgive us, allowing us to start new. You are a great God!*

Day 202

LEARNED OBEDIENCE

Life is about learning. One of the most important lessons we learn is to *obey*. We learn to obey our parents when we are young. We learn to obey those in authority over us. We learn to obey the rules in athletics. We learn to obey the laws of the land. Without obedience, life and society experience anarchy.

Above all, we need to learn to obey God. When Moses told Pharaoh the word of God, "Let my people go!" (Exodus 5:1), Pharaoh responded in arrogance, "Who is the Lord, that I should obey him?" (Exodus 5:2). Pharaoh learned the hard way the answer to his question after the punishment of the Lord came on Egypt for the sin of slavery. The human heart in its rebellion resists God's will and asks, *Who is the Lord that I should obey Him?*

Obedience to God is the key to living a blessed life. "All these blessings will come on you and accompany you if you obey the Lord your God" (Deuteronomy 28:2). Jesus said, "If you love me, [you will] keep my commands" (John 14:15). The early Christians believed, "We must obey God rather than human beings!" (Acts 5:29).

Obedience, however, doesn't come naturally; it has to be learned. Meditate on this extraordinary statement about Jesus: "Although he was a son, he learned obedience from what he suffered" (Hebrews 5:8). Even Jesus, in His humanity, learned obedience through the difficult experiences of life.

Arabian horses go through rigorous training in the deserts of the Middle East. The trainers require absolute obedience from the horses and test them to see if they are completely trained. The trainer makes the horses go without water for the maximum number of days they can endure. Then he turns them loose, and they immediately run toward water. As they get to the edge and are ready to plunge in, the trainer blows his whistle. The horses who have been completely trained will stop. They stand there shaking, wanting water, but they wait because they have learned obedience. When the trainer is sure he has their obedience, he gives them a signal to go back to drink. This severe training is vital for survival in the hot desert sands of Arabia. Learned obedience to God is the key to not only survival but also success in this life.

Prayer for the Day: *Lord, learning to be obedient in life has taught me to be obedient to You. When I obey Your Word, it provides me with safety and blessing.*

Day 203

ANCHORED

The human ear consists of 20,000 tiny hairs that distinguish 300,000 tones. What we listen to is very important. Information becomes thoughts, thoughts become words, words become actions, and actions become our destiny.

False teachers will try to turn our "ears away from the truth and turn aside to myths" (2 Timothy 4:4). We often don't like truth because truth is absolute. We would rather make up our own rules instead of following God's rules. The secular values of the American culture today are, in the words of the English historian Macaulay, "all sail and no anchor." Our generation is drifting in a state of spiritual and moral confusion lost at sea, because we are not anchored to unchanging truth found in Jesus Christ and the Bible. We need to be careful that we are not influenced by secular education, misguided spiritual teachers and the media, and find ourselves turning away from the truth. We need to turn to the truth, not away from it. Only the truth will set us free.

Listening to false teaching will cause us to turn to myths instead of truth. Our culture readily accepts anything called science, anyone who calls himself an expert, and whatever the media tells us. We believe in ghosts, magic, astrology, reincarnation, atheism, moral relativism—you name it, we accept it. We accept fiction like it is fact. It is like we are willing to accept anything as fact as long as it isn't in the Bible.

What is the answer? Stay anchored to the Bible. Read it, receive it, and live it. God's Word will keep you on track. The faith we have in Jesus and the unchanging truth of Scripture is "an anchor for the soul, firm and secure" (Hebrews 6:19). If you're anchored, you won't turn away or turn aside.

Prayer for the Day: *Lord, thank You for Your Word that anchors me to the truth. May I never be distracted by myths and fables but hold securely to the truth of Your Word, which keeps me free from bondage.*

Day 204

MAKE AN IMPACT

One of the most challenging passages of Scripture reminds us, "It is appointed once for a person to die and after that, the judgment" (see Hebrews 9:27). How will our lives be judged, evaluated, and measured in Heaven and on earth?

We can make an impact on others. We can leave a lasting legacy. When we arrive in Heaven, we can hear the Lord say, "Well done, good and faithful servant! You have been faithful over a few things; I will put you in charge of many things. Come and share your master's happiness!" (Matthew 25:21).

Make an impact with who you are. Years ago, the communist government in China commissioned an author to write a biography of Hudson Taylor with the purpose of distorting the facts and presenting him in a bad light. They wanted to discredit the name of such a dedicated missionary for Christ. As the author was doing his research, he was increasingly impressed by Taylor's saintly character and godly life, and he found it extremely difficult to carry out his assigned task with a clear conscience. Eventually, at the risk of great punishment, he put aside the project, renounced atheism, and received Jesus as his personal Savior. Our lives leave an impact one way or the other.

News commentator Dan Rather has a good way of keeping his professional goals in mind. He carries with him a question he looks at often that he's written on three slips of paper. He keeps one in his billfold, one in his pocket, and one on his desk. The probing question, "Is what you are doing now helping the broadcast?"

The real question for us is, "Is what we're doing now helping others, and will it matter in eternity?"

Prayer for the Day: *Lord, I want to make an impact on those You bring across my path. Please eliminate anything in me that would hinder that process. Thank You.*

Day 205

COST OR CONVENIENCE?

When David Livingstone was working in Africa as a missionary, a group of friends wrote him: "We would like to send other men to you. Have you found a good road into your area yet?"

According to a member of his family, David Livingstone sent this message in reply: "If you have men who will only come if they know there is a good road, I don't want them. I want men who will come if there is no road at all."

Early in my ministry, I read a book by Dr. Charles Stanley, *Confronting Casual Christianity*, that made a great impact on me. Instead of asking, *What am I getting out of being a Christian?*, we need to ask, *What am I giving up to follow Jesus as Lord?*

Tithing costs money. Church attendance costs time. Serving in ministry costs effort. Yet, what we give comes back to us "a good measure, pressed down, shaken together" (Luke 6:38). Dr. Paul Walker used to say, "The price of church growth is the willingness to be inconvenienced." That statement has stuck with me.

The cost of discipleship is challenged by a culture of convenience. We have convenience stores where we are willing to pay more for items to avoid waiting in a long line. We want things fast and easy, which is fine when it comes to buying a snack at store, but not when it comes to the important things in life.

Jesus still challenges us, "If anyone [would] come after Me, let him [or her] deny [themselves], and take up [their] cross daily, and follow Me" (Luke 9:23 NKJV).

Prayer for the Day: *Lord, may I never turn away from Your calling on my life because of cost or convenience. I will seek Your will daily and follow where You lead.*

Day 206

FIVE SMOOTH STONES

When David went into the valley to face Goliath, he stopped at the brook and picked up five smooth stones and put them in his shepherd's bag. Goliath couldn't believe his eyes when he saw a young shepherd coming to fight him. So he cursed David by his false gods.

David replied: "You come against me with sword and spear and javelin, but I come against you in the name of the Lord Almighty. . . . This day the Lord will deliver you into my hands. . . . All those gathered here will know that it is not by sword or spear that the Lord saves; for the battle is the Lord's" (1 Samuel 17:45-47).

Then David ran toward Goliath, reached into his bag, selected one stone, and put it in the sling. Before Goliath could draw his sword, David hurled the stone, striking Goliath in the forehead. The stone sunk deep into his head and he fell to the ground. David stood over Goliath, drew the giant's sword from its sheath, and cut off his head. When he did, the Philistines fled for fear. The Israelite army pursued the enemy and won a great victory.

The five smooth stones teach us that David used what he had. What are your five smooth stones . . . or even your one or two stones? What gifts and talents has God given you? Use what God has given you, and trust Him to do the rest. God will make up the difference if you will do your part.

Prayer for the Day: *Lord, please develop the gifts and abilities You have given me to be used for Your kingdom. Where I am weak, You are strong.*

Day 207
CHOOSE WHAT'S BETTER

After getting married, a young couple decided he would make all the major decisions and she would make the minor ones. At their 25th anniversary, he was asked how this arrangement had worked. "Great! In all these years, I've never had to make a major decision."

Our lives turn on the axis of our decisions. Our decisions determine our destiny. If you want to know how your life will turn out in the future, just look at the small decisions you are making today. God created us with the freedom and power of choice. We are created in God's image. We are higher than the animal kingdom.

We did not evolve from a lower life form. We were made by the hand of God and given the power to think, dream, create, and decide. We function by intellect, not instinct; by choice, not conditioned response. Our choices, not our circumstances, are the major determining factor in the quality of our lives.

Jesus commended a worshipful woman named Mary, saying, "Mary has chosen what is better" (Luke 10:42). Mary chose what was better—not what was easy or convenient, popular or selfish. The choice that brings honor to God and fulfills His will always lead to the best life. When it comes to our day-to-day decisions, let's choose what is better.

Prayer for the Day: *Lord, please give me the insight to make good decisions based on what You have called me to do. As Mary did, may I also choose what is better.*

Day 208

ERASE RACISM

The day was November 13, 1956. The place was Montgomery, Alabama. The decision was Rosa Parks' refusal to give up her seat on the bus. The result was the birth of a civil rights movement. Her courage began the process of erasing racism.

What is *racism*? It is when one group of people believe they are superior to another group of people. Racism exists where people are discriminated against, looked down on as inferior, or treated unfairly just because of their ethnicity.

So, how do we erase it? Racism is sin—just old-fashioned pride. We must repent of the sin of racism and receive God's forgiveness. Only the grace of God at work in our hearts can erase racism. Jesus came to save us from our sins, including racism. Politics, legislation, and economics alone cannot erase racism because it is a heart issue. Jesus is exalted above culture, race, and ethnicity. When we come to know Him, He lifts us up to higher plane of living.

The Bible declares, "There is neither Jew nor Gentile, neither slave nor free, nor is there male and female, for you are all one in Christ Jesus" (Galatians 3:28). As Christians, we are part of a new culture and a new community in which we no longer discriminate against, categorize, or label others. We are one in Christ! We have unity because we have equality. We can now show the world through our unity that Jesus Christ gives a more excellent way to live.

Prayer for the Day: *Lord, may I always be sensitive to the issue of racism and how it effects Your children. May I always show others that through You, we are all equal in the body of Christ.*

Day 209

STORED UP

Everyone needs storage space these days. Huge storage centers are being built everywhere. Computers need to be upgraded at times for more storage space. We buy smart phones with maximum storage space for all our photos, games, and music. People often buy a house with an unfinished basement just for the storage space.

Jesus talked about the need for spiritual storage space: "Make a tree good and its fruit will be good, or make a tree bad and its fruit will be bad, for a tree is recognized by its fruit. . . . For the mouth speaks what the heart is full of. A good man brings good things out of the good stored up in him, and an evil man brings evil things out of the evil stored up in him" (Matthew 12:33-35).

Our life's fruit is the result of what is stored in our heart and mind. If we store up good things—*faith*, *hope*, and *love*—we will do good things, say good things, and accomplish good things. But if we store up bad things—fear, depression, and resentment—we will produce bad things.

Take Jesus' challenge to heart by storing up good things. When bad things happen, or you hear negative words or you fail, don't store it up. Deal with it and move on. Store up the Word of God in your heart. Store up the encouragement you get from others. Store up the experiences you have with God. Good things will happen to you and through you!

Prayer for the Day: *Lord, reveal to me the bad things I've stored in my heart that I may rid myself of these things through Your forgiveness. Teach me to store up Your Word that I may grow spiritually and help others to do the same.*

Day 210

I AM

Here are ten words that will change your life: "I can do all things through Christ who strengthens me" (Philippians 4:13 NKJV).

People recite this Bible verse because it gives a sense of confidence, and we all need confidence. A few verses earlier, Paul wrote, "Brothers and sisters, whatever is true, whatever is noble, whatever is right, whatever is pure, whatever is lovely, whatever is admirable—if anything is excellent or praiseworthy—think about such things" (Philippians 4:8). How you think about yourself is important.

It is not enough to know God believes in you, your parents believe in you, or your friends believe in you; you must believe in yourself. We all battle self-doubt, feelings of inadequacy, and a lack of confidence. But when you say, "I can do all things through Christ," you feel empowered to face your problems, tackle your challenges, and reach your goals.

Jesus said, "I Am" to describe Himself. He said, "I am the bread of life" (John 6:35); "I am the light of the world" (John 8:12); "I am the good shepherd" (John 10:11).

What do you say about yourself? We too need some "I am" declarations! Declare these "I am" statements today:

"I am able. I am blessed. I am confident. I am dynamic. I am empowered. I am faithful. I am gifted. I am His. I am inspired. I am joyful. I am kind. I am loving. I am motivated. I am noble. I am optimistic. I am powerful. I am quickened. I am reliable. I am strong. I am true. I am unshakable. I am victorious. I am a winner. I am excited. I am yielded. I am zealous for the Lord Jesus Christ."

Prayer for the Day: *Lord, thank You for showing me I can do all things as You strengthen me. Help me to focus on the positive "I am's" as Your grace in my life.*

Day 211

GAINS AND LOSSES

Investors measure success by gains and losses. When we invest money, we want gains, not losses. So it is with life. Jesus asked, "What profit is it to a man if he gains the whole world, and loses his own soul?" (Matthew 16:26 NKJV). We can gain the wrong thing and lose the wrong thing if we're not careful.

The word *soul* means "life." Jesus says if we only invest our time, efforts, and resources in the things of this world, we will waste our lives. So, He goes on to say, "For the Son of Man is going to come in his Father's glory with his angels, and then he will reward each person according to what he has done" (v. 27).

When we meet the Lord in Heaven, it is what we have done for Him and for others that will really matter. All the stuff we accumulate will then be gone. "The world and its desires pass away, but whoever does the will of God lives forever" (1 John 2:17). Let us make a commitment to lose the things in life that don't really matter, and gain the things that matter the most.

Prayer for the Day: *Lord, the longer I walk with You, the more I realize what is and what is not valuable. I am understanding what will last and what will not. Today I make a new commitment to pursue a deeper walk with You and better relationships with family and friends, knowing that is what lasts forever.*

Day 212

WALK WITH GOD

While on a long walk, I thought about an Old Testament person named *Enoch*, who "walked faithfully with God; then he was no more, because God took him away" (Genesis 5:24). Apparently, he and God went for a long walk and God said, "Hey, Enoch, we're closer to My house than we are yours. Come on home with Me." And God took him to Heaven. When we walk with God, God always takes us to new places, and one day He will take us to Heaven.

Going for a "walk" with God means to enjoy a close relationship with Him. You can carry on a conversation with someone if you walk with them, but not if you run. You can walk with someone at the same pace, but everyone runs at their own pace. Don't get caught up in religion; keep a close relationship with the Lord. That is what it means to walk with God.

Walking with God also means to be in agreement with Him for His will in our lives. "Do two walk together unless they have agreed to do so?" (Amos 3:3). When we walk with God, we need to always let Him take the lead and decide where we're going. "Since we live by the Spirit, let us keep in step with the Spirit" (Galatians 5:25). When we are in the center of God's will, we will experience the greatest life possible. "Whoever does the will of God lives forever" (1 John 2:17).

Don't run ahead of God and decide to do things your own way. Don't lag behind Him by resisting Him. Following Jesus is a journey. Don't sit still in life. Go on regular walks with God and allow Him to lead you in the plan He has for your life.

Prayer for the Day: *Lord, walking with You through life is my greatest pleasure. I love the fact that I'm never alone and that You speak to me and guide me. I never have to be afraid, for my life is in Your hands.*

Day 213

COME HOME

When our kids were very small, we had to watch them constantly when we were out anywhere because they would wander off. We even kept our son on a leash when he was about three because he would just take off running!

We, too, have the tendency to wander off. We wander off from our faith and values, sometimes from our relationships, and even from God. We get distracted or deceived by something and lose our focus.

Jesus told a story about wandering off: "If a man owns a hundred sheep, and one of them wanders away, will he not leave the ninety-nine on the hills and go to look for the one that wandered off? And if he finds it, truly I tell you, he is happier about that one sheep than about the ninety-nine that did not wander off. In the same way your Father in heaven is not willing that any of these little ones should perish" (Matthew 18:12-14).

Have you wandered off? Come home today to the Lord and His calling on your life. God is not willing that you be lost in this life or the life to come. Come home today.

Prayer for the Day: *Lord, please keep me from being distracted by the things of this world and wander off away from You. Please keep a short leash on me as I walk with You through this life, knowing You alone know what's best for me and You will keep me safe.*

Day 214

70 X 7

We have all been hurt by other people and have asked how many times we should forgive them. Simon Peter asked Jesus, "How often should I forgive someone who sins against me? Seven times?" (Matthew 18:21 NLT). Jesus shocked him with His response: "No, not seven times . . . but seventy times seven!" (v. 22 NLT).

That is a lot of forgiving! Yes, but forgiveness is the key to freedom. Forgiveness frees us from anger, bitterness, and resentment, leaving us free to love others and enjoy life. Bitter people are miserable. Unforgiveness only makes us bitter, and who wants to hang out with bitter people? No one!

We do ourselves and others a big favor when we forgive. What does it mean to forgive? *Forgiveness* simply means to "cancel the debt." In the Lord's Prayer, we are taught to pray, "Forgive us our debts, as we forgive our debtors" (Matthew 6:12 NKJV). Forgiveness is not a feeling; it is a choice. Just as it comes as a big financial relief when someone cancels a debt we owe, so it's a big relief when we cancel the debt of hurt, injustice, and harm others have done to us.

The only part of the Lord's Prayer Jesus commented on was the prayer of forgiveness: "For if you forgive other people when they sin against you, your heavenly Father will also forgive you. But if you do not forgive others their sins, your Father will not forgive your sins" (Matthew 6:14-15).

Let us refuse to live in bondage to bitterness, and instead live in the freedom of forgiveness. E. Stanley Jones said, "Forgiveness is the fragrance of the rose left on the heel that crushed it." Forgiveness fills our marriages, families, and relationships with the beautiful fragrance of grace.

Prayer for the Day: *Lord, it is so hard sometimes to forgive those who hurt us, especially when it is a family member or a Christian brother or sister. Because forgiveness frees us, I will forgive as You command, seventy times seven.*

Day 215

PASS THE SALT

We read of a *covenant of salt* in the Old Testament. In ancient times, eating salt during a covenant made it legally binding. Two parties would eat salt in the presence of witnesses to bind their contract. In a time of civil unrest, Abijah, the king of Judah, said to the people of Israel: "Don't you know that the Lord, the God of Israel, has given the kingship of Israel to David and his descendants forever by a covenant of salt?" (2 Chronicles 13:5).

Jesus says to us, His disciples, "You are the salt of the earth" (Matthew 5:13). Barbie always puts salt on eggs. She puts the salt in her palm (enough for an ant) then sprinkles it on her eggs. Salt adds a little flavor. You don't need a lot of salt to make a difference between bland and tasty foods. In the same way, we don't have to overdo praise and encouragement so that it sounds cheap or overboard. A little salt goes a long way. We don't have to overdo sharing our faith in the Lord Jesus with others. A little grace and truth go a long way, just like salt does.

On the other hand, my dad loved salt. He put salt on everything. As a kid, my favorite supper meal was navy beans, black-eyed peas (with syrup), and cornbread. Mother gave Dad scallion onions on the stalk to go with beans. He would pour a pile of salt on the table next to his plate and dip the onion in the salt to eat with his vegetables. (As his son, I imitated him.) So, he didn't believe a little bit goes a long way. He went overboard with the salt.

So, there are times when we know someone is really down and out, defeated and discouraged, that we need to be like my dad and pour out the salt instead of sprinkle it. Pour out encouragement with an extravagant love. Whether you need to sprinkle the salt of love or pour it out, always remember to pass the salt!

Prayer for the Day: *Lord, give me the wisdom to know whether to sprinkle the salt of encouragement or pour out the salt of encouragement on Your children.*

Day 216

SOUND MIND

When our son David Paul was about three years old, he was terrified of the vacuum cleaner. Every time the vacuum cleaner was turned on, he would go into hysterics, run across the house seeking refuge. He just knew it was going to suck him up like a piece of lint.

One Saturday morning, Barbie headed out for the grocery store. "Please vacuum while I'm gone," she asked. I assured her I would. She left and I proceeded to vacuum the family room, where my son happened to be watching cartoons. That was a big mistake. As soon as I flipped the switch on, he went berserk, ran to the corner of the room, hid behind a recliner, and screamed uncontrollably. I wondered, *How can I get him over his fear?*

Suddenly, it dawned on me that he loved the lawn mower. He loved to put his hands on the handle of the push mower and help me cut the grass. "David Paul," I called over his screaming little voice. "This isn't a vacuum cleaner; it's a lawn mower!" Almost immediately, he grew calm and looked at me with a puzzled look. "It's a lawn mower," I said enthusiastically. "Come over here and help me mow the carpet." His face lit up with excitement. Running across the room, he put his tiny hands on the handle and off we went across the carpet.

Fear is a problem of perception. "God has not given us a spirt of fear, but of power and of love and of a sound mind" (2 Timothy 1:7 NKJV). The Greek word for *sound* means "self-discipline" or "self-control." It comes from the root *sophron*, meaning "saving the mind." It is the ability to control your thinking in the face of panic or passion. Fears are learned, and we have to unlearn them.

How do we do that? We "take captive every thought and make it obedient to Christ" (2 Corinthians 10:5). When you are afraid, think of a promise God has given in Scripture, focus on it instead of the panic, and you will overcome your fear. Remember President Roosevelt's famous challenge during the Great Depression: "There is nothing to fear but fear itself." Believe the promise of God, not the panic in your mind, and you will live in peace.

Prayer for the Day: *Lord, keep me from being taken captive or overcome with fear, and remind me that there is nothing to fear as long as You are holding me in Your hand. I will be free of fear and have a sound mind.*

Day 217

ONE THING

One day a man asked Jesus, "What good thing must I do to get eternal life?" (Matthew 19:16). This guy was young and successful, but he worried about life after death. Jesus said, "If you want to enter into life, keep the commandments" (v. 17). Then he asked Jesus which commands to obey. Jesus cited the Ten Commandments and added, "Love your neighbor as yourself" (v. 19).

The rich businessman said he had kept all these commandments since his youth. Can you believe that? He thought he was sinless and perfect. When we hear the Ten Commandments, the first thing most of us think is how we have broken some of them. The purpose of the Law is to reveal our sin so that we seek God's grace and forgiveness. Also, seeing how we are all selfish, we know we have broken the command, "Love your neighbor as yourself."

The young man then asked, "What do I still lack?" (Matthew 19:20). The question gave Jesus opportunity to show him his need of saving grace. Jesus replied, "If you want to be perfect, go, sell your possessions and give to the poor, and you will have treasure in heaven. Then come, follow me" (v. 21).

Jesus put His finger on the real issue—the businessman only lived for this life. The young man needed to come to the end of himself, admit his need of God (even though he didn't need anything materially), and give his life to Jesus as Lord. The word *perfect* means to "finish what you need to complete." Our good works and morality are not enough to give us eternal life. We need to trust Jesus as our Savior and follow Him as Lord if we want eternal life.

Maybe you "still lack" something—saving faith in Jesus. The Bible promises, "Whoever believes in him shall not perish but have eternal life" (John 3:16).

Prayer for the Day: *Lord, I love and serve You, but what do I still lack? What area of my life do I need to grow in? What do I need to let go of? I will wait patiently as You, by Your Spirit, reveal these things to me.*

Day 218

DON'T THROW YOUR BRAIN AWAY

When the ancient Egyptians embalmed the pharaohs, they removed the vital organs from their bodies and put the organs in jars that were buried with the mummies so they would have them for the afterlife. The Egyptians thought the heart was the central organ that controlled the body and that the brain was an unimportant organ (the way we think about the appendix today). So, when they prepared the body for embalming, they removed the brain and threw it away! So, if the pharaoh came back, he would have everything he needed except the main thing—his brain!

Many people are throwing away their brains these days by what they read, listen to, watch, and the counsel they get from others. One organization uses the slogan, "The mind is a terrible thing to waste." Yet, people are wasting their minds. We live in the day of shallow thinking where we naively believe every sound bite from the media and politicians. We ignore facts for our feelings. We let other people do our thinking for us. We worship at the altar of the expert instead of carefully examining things for ourselves and making up our own minds.

Proverbs 23:7 says, "As he thinks in his heart, so is he" (NKJV). Our level of living never rises above our level of thinking. The freedom to think for ourselves and not let other people do our thinking for us is the greatest freedom we have. Don't fall into the trap of "group think." That is when we think like the group we're in just because it's how everybody else thinks. We feel pressure to conform to the group, whether it is our family, friends, church, or community. Regardless of what the group thinks, think for yourself. Maybe you will agree with the group, but make sure you think things through for yourself.

While we cannot control the events in our world, we can control how we think. We can think godly thoughts in an ungodly world. We can think positive thoughts in a negative world. We can think pure thoughts in an impure world. And we can think for ourselves. "Whatever is true, whatever is noble, whatever is right, whatever is pure, whatever is lovely, whatever is admirable—if anything is excellent or praiseworthy—think about such things" (Philippians 4:8).

Prayer for the Day: *Lord, thank You for this incredible brain You gave me so I can understand Your Word and make good choices. May I never let another person think for me.*

Day 219

STORMS

Barbie and I had planned a short vacation to the Georgia coast. Unfortunately, a storm came in with powerful winds and heavy rains, preventing us from going on our vacation. Life is like that. We make our plans, set our goals, dream our dreams, and then life happens! A storm comes ripping through, creating a disaster. A family crisis. A health emergency. An emotional breakdown. A financial downturn.

How can we have stillness in the storm? The key is to never let the storm on the outside get on the inside! When there's chaos around us, we want calmness within us. When there's fear around us, we want faith within us. When there's stress around us, we want stillness with us. Hurricanes have an eye in the middle of every storm, and that is where we can stay if we trust God in the storm.

Toward the end of his ministry, Paul was arrested and being taken by ship to Rome. While at sea, the ship was caught in a furious storm with "a wind of hurricane force" (Acts 27:14). The ship was at the mercy of the raging storm, being carried wherever the storm willed. The crew tied ropes around the ship to keep it from breaking apart. Then they threw the ship's cargo overboard. "When neither sun nor stars appeared for many days and the storm continued raging, [they] finally gave up all hope of being saved" (Acts 27:20).

Then the scene changed. Paul addressed everyone on board: "Keep up your courage, because not one of you will be lost; only the ship will be destroyed. Last night an angel of the God to whom I belong and whom I serve stood beside me and said, 'Do not be afraid, Paul. You must stand trial before Caesar; and God has graciously given you the lives of all who sail with you.' So keep up your courage, men, for I have faith in God that it will happen just as he told me. Nevertheless, we must run aground on some island" (Acts 27:22-26).

That is how we find stillness in the storm. Keep up your courage. Don't give in to fear, panic, and discouragement. Surround yourself with people who will encourage your faith, just like Paul did for the men on the ship.

Then, confess your faith in God. Don't confess your frustrations, disappointments, and worry. Confess your faith, because words are powerful. They can lift us up or put us down; they can calm us down or hype us up. They can impart fear or faith in others.

Finally, live by the "nevertheless" principle. In spite of setbacks caused by the storm, we can trust God to bring us through.

Prayer for the Day: *Lord, help me to be still and know You are God when the storms of life come against me. May I remember that Your watchful eye is upon me.*

Day 220

THINK INSIDE THE BOX

Barbie and I bought some organic cereal that has the slogan, "Think inside the box." Think about what is in the box before you eat it because it will affect your life. The Bible gives us guidelines, and we need to accept the truth that is in it and live by it if we want the best life. We are constantly having to choose between Christ and culture for our beliefs, attitudes, and values.

When we put our faith in Jesus, we know Him as Savior. Then we need to know Him as Teacher. He teaches us to live the way God designed life to be lived. He says, "Come to me, all you who are weary and burdened, and I will give you rest. Take my yoke upon you and learn from me, for I am gentle and humble in heart, and you will find rest for your souls. For my yoke is easy and my burden is light" (Matthew 11:28-29).

Paul wrote about people who are "always learning but never able to come to a knowledge of the truth" (2 Timothy 3:7). They study religion, philosophy, and spirituality but never come to the personal knowledge of Jesus Christ as Lord. Why? Because they don't accept the truth found in Scripture. They challenge and resist the Word of God. We have to accept the Scriptures as did one church Paul commended: "When you received the word of God, which you heard from us, you accepted it not as a human word, but as it actually is, the word of God, which is indeed at work in you who believe" (1 Thessalonians 2:13).

Aldous Huxley was considered one of the greatest intellectuals of the twentieth century. He wrote the famous novel *A Brave New World*. In spite of his interest in spirituality and mysticism, he was an agnostic. He once attended a weekend getaway with some friends at a country house. On Sunday the guests went to church at a small chapel nearby, except for Huxley. However, he asked one man who had a strong Christian faith to stay behind and talk with him about his faith in Christ. The man said, "I am no match for you intellectually. I can't win an argument with you about faith." Huxley said, "I don't want to argue with you. I just want you to tell me about your faith and why you are a Christian." So, the man stayed behind and told Huxley about his personal experience with the Lord. Huxley listened attentively and was moved deeply. Then, with tears in his eyes, Huxley said, "I would give anything if only I could believe what you believe."

It takes humility to think inside the box and accept God's Word as true. Jesus said, "Unless you are converted and become as little children, you will by no means enter the kingdom of heaven. Therefore, whoever humbles himself as this little child is the greatest in the kingdom of heaven" (Matthew 18:3-4 NKJV). Let's read the Bible with humble hearts and open mind, accepting it as truth.

Prayer for the Day: *Lord, may I never get outside the box of Your protection to seek spiritual truth in the world. Rather, may I think inside the box of Holy Scripture, which is the only way to truth and life.*

Day 221

STRONG TO THE END

It is not how we start but how we finish that counts. This is especially true spiritually. The Lord will "keep you [strong] to the end, so that you will be blameless on the day of our Lord Jesus Christ" (1 Corinthians 1:8). One day we will be declared blameless in God's sight and welcomed into the kingdom of Heaven. That is God's promise to us—to keep us strong to the end—and "God is faithful, who has called you into fellowship with his Son" (1 Corinthians 1:9).

God has called us into fellowship with Jesus. We don't use the word *fellowship* much anymore, but we use the word *relationship,* which means the same thing. Your personal relationship with Jesus is the most important thing in your life. Spend some time with the Lord each day. Practice His presence throughout the day by reminding yourself He is always with you. Be conscious of His presence, speaking and listening to Him as you go about your day.

We are also called into fellowship with other believers. When we have close spiritual relationships, we will be strong to the end. When we get out of fellowship, we grow spiritually weak. We need each other for encouragement, safety, and support. Even though early Christians were persecuted, they remained strong because they stuck together as "they devoted themselves . . . to fellowship" (Acts 2:42).

When animals travel in a herd, lions will attack the weak one that gets separated from the herd. Once the animal is isolated, the lion attacks. The Bible describes Satan as "a roaring lion looking for someone to devour" (1 Peter 5:8). Don't get separated from other believers and find yourself fighting your spiritual battles alone. Stick with the herd—the family of God—and you will be strong to the end. We are vulnerable when we are alone, but we are victorious when we are together.

Prayer for the Day: *Lord, may I never drift away from Your Word but always be focused on our personal relationship. Give me the strength to get back up when I have been knocked down, and to stay faithful and strong to the end.*

Day 222

SURVIVE THE STORM

Several years ago, when we were living in an apartment, a tornado ripped through north Atlanta. We were on the second floor when the tornado came roaring over us. We all huddled in the bathroom. The noise and the shaking were overwhelming. We thought the roof would come off the building and that we would be taken up in the fierce wind.

The next morning, we got in the car and drove around to see what had happened. All around us was debris. Large steel billboards were twisted like thin wire. Buildings were gone. But we had been kept safe in the storm. We had the Lord to protect us, and we had each other.

Family storms come in many forms—financial, physical, legal, medical, spiritual, relational. How do we survive the storms? We can follow Noah's example when his family faced a great storm: "By faith Noah, when warned about things not yet seen, in holy fear built an ark to save his family" (Hebrews 11:7).

Noah was warned of a great flood, so he built an ark to save his family. The key words are "by faith Noah." The name *Noah* means "comfort." He lived through in a day of great evil and violence, when God's heart was filled with pain over the corruption of humankind. God warned Noah of the coming storm and gave him the plans to build the ark, so he and his family got to work. It takes everyone in the family to build a strong home.

Noah was a spiritual leader for his family. "Noah was a righteous man, blameless among the people of his time, and he walked faithfully with God" (Genesis 6:9). Research shows that families who practice their faith and attend church together are happier and stronger through adversity. We need unity to get through a storm. Noah's family trusted him and the word God gave him. They could have doubted God's warning, but they didn't. They could have rebelled against Noah's leadership, but they didn't. When a family comes together in faith and prayer, they can get through any storm.

So, gather your family together and declare, "By faith we will get through our financial problems. By faith we will get through counseling. By faith we will get through this health crisis. By faith we will get through the legal problems." Just as Noah and his family built an ark, you can build a strong family of faith.

Prayer for the Day: *Lord, I thank You that no matter what kind of storm hits my life, You are always there. No storm is too great as long as You are there and hold me in the palm of Your hand.*

Day 223

YOU RECEIVED IT

Cicero, the Roman poet, said, "Gratitude is not only the greatest virtue, it is the parent of all virtues." Whatever you have, your talent and your treasure, is a gift from God. The Apostle Paul asked, "For who makes you different from anyone else? What do you have that you did not receive? And if you did receive it, why do you boast as though you did not?" (1 Corinthians 4:7).

What makes each of us different? What gives us our uniqueness? It is God's special abilities, talents, and traits given to us. I was talking with someone about music and playing the guitar, and he told me, "There's no substitute for talent." He loves the guitar and works hard at it, but he still struggles after many years. He owns a number of guitars, but said he knew he would never be great at it. He told me, "You're very talented guitarist, and I wish I had that talent."

I replied, "You are a very talented businessman." I encouraged him to celebrate the gifts God has given him. We are all great at something! And where does that creative greatness come from? It comes from God.

Paul's question is thought-provoking: "What do you have that you did not receive?" We should stop comparing ourselves with other people. When someone tells you they wish they had the talent you have, tell them they have the talent God wanted them to have. If someone tells you they want to be like you, tell them to be like themselves! Be who God created you to be.

We should be grateful and humble for the abilities we do have. They are God's gifts to us. Your talents are God's treasure to you so you can succeed. "And if you did receive it, why do you boast as though you did not?"

We need to be good stewards of what God has given us. Talents and abilities come in their raw form, and it is up to us to develop what God has given us so we go from good to great. "Now it is required that those who have been given a trust must prove faithful" (1 Corinthians 4:2). God trusted you with your talents, so be trustworthy in the way you use them as you strive for excellence for His glory!

Prayer for the Day: *Lord, I am grateful for every gift and ability You have given me. May I always seek to develop them in excellence for Your glory.*

Day 224

RUN AWAY

When I was eight years old, one night after dinner I told my parents I was leaving. I just wanted their attention, so I was shocked when they asked me where I was going and they let me walk out the door! I walked slowly down the street, occasionally looking back to see if they would run after me. By the time I got to the end of the street, I turned around and went back home. Later that night, I got sick with stomach pains and was rushed to the hospital to save my life! I never ran away again.

Sometimes we run away from the Lord. We run away from our calling and our challenges. When we do, it creates more problems. That is the story of the prophet Jonah. God called Jonah to go to Nineveh, the capital city of Assyria—the archenemy or Israel. "But Jonah ran away from the Lord" (Jonah 1:3).

When Jonah ran, God ran after him. Jonah got on board a ship and headed for Tarshish, a city on the southern coast of Spain located 2,500 miles away from Nineveh. "Then the Lord sent a great wind on the sea, and such a violent storm arose that the ship threatened to break up" (Jonah 1:4). God may send a storm around us to disrupt our circumstances, or

He may send a storm inside us to disrupt our conscience. God comes after us when we run. His love is a love that will not let us go.

I have heard many people say it is easy to miss the will of God. Apparently, Jonah teaches us it is difficult to miss God's will. Even if we run away from God's will, He sends a storm, if necessary, to get us to the place of full surrender to Him. At the end of the story, Jonah surrendered and went to Niveveh.

If you are running away from God's plan for your life, stop running. Surrender your life to Him, and watch God do amazing things as you wholeheartedly do His will.

Prayer for the Day: *Lord, it is so easy to just run away from my problems instead of allowing You to get me through them. When I feel that urge to run like Jonah did, give me the strength to stay put and wait on You.*

Day 225

STILL HOLDING ON

At the lowest point of Job's life, his overwhelmed wife asked him, "Are you still [holding on to] your integrity? Curse God and die!" (Job 2:9). Suffering pushes us to our limit. What is the limitation to our faith? Do we have a limitless faith? Can we endure to the end? I like the words "holding on." When you are going through tough times, tell people, "I'm still holding on!" Instead of telling people how bad things are, tell them how you expect things to turn around for the good.

After his season of suffering, God blessed the latter part of Job's life more than the first (Job 42:12). Because Job kept holding on, God blessed him. His wife told him to give up, but he kept holding on. Job held on to his faith in spite of financial disaster, grief, marriage stress, personal questions about God, and criticisms of his friends who even blamed him for his troubles. He battled depression and sickness, but he held on to his faith in God!

Job released his feelings of despair and unanswered questions regarding his sufferings: "After this, Job opened his mouth and cursed the day of his birth" (Job 3:1). He said, "What I feared has come upon me" (Job 3:25); "Mortals, born of woman, are of few days and full of trouble" (Job 14:1). He cried out, "My spirit is broken, my days are cut short, the grave awaits me" (Job 17:1); "I am reduced to dust and ashes" (Job 30:19).

In spite of those thoughts and feelings, Job held on to his faith and declared, "Though [God] slay me, yet will I [trust] him" (Job 13:15); "When he has tested me, I will come forth as gold" (Job 23:10); "I know that my redeemer lives" (Job 19:25).

Are you still holding on? I pray that you are, because you will see God turn your situation around for His glory and for your good!

Prayer for the Day: *Lord, sometimes the stress of life is so overwhelming that I feel like giving up. But if Job could trust You through his horrible season of suffering, so can I!*

Day 226

SELFIES

We live in the culture of the selfie. We constantly take pictures of ourselves and send them to others. There's nothing wrong with that, but psychologists have observed there is a growing focus on ourselves to the exclusion of our concern for others. There always exists that tension between individualism and community.

One of the most important principles of leadership is learning to serve. When the angel told Mary she had been chosen to bring Jesus the Messiah into the world, she submitted to God's will, saying, "I am the Lord's servant.... May your word to me be fulfilled" (Luke 1:38). What a portrait of submission to God's will!

When we say we are the servants of the Lord, we stand in good company. In the kingdom of God, it is the highest honor to be called the servant of the Lord. Jesus said, "Whoever wants to become great among you must be your servant" (Mark 10:43). Jesus even said of Himself, "I am among you as one who serves" (Luke 22:27).

There are two Greek words for *servant*. *Doulos* means the "bond-servant" who serves out of love. *Diakonos* means "minister." *Diakonos* literally means to "walk through the dust," and was used of camel drivers of caravans. Human beings were created from the dust of the ground. You cannot be a servant of the Lord unless you are willing to get dusty from walking with others in their life experiences. You cannot stay in the penthouse or the corporate office and delegate the work of the ministry. You and I have to get out there and walk with people through the dusty experiences of life.

We don't serve because we're forced to, but because we love the Lord and we want to continue His ministry in this world.

Martin Luther said every Christian is called to be Christ to his neighbor. Walk through the dust with someone today and you will discover the power of saying, "I am the Lord's servant."

Prayer for the Day: *Lord, I am honored to be called Your servant because I serve You out of love. May I never fear getting among those in need and getting dirty. I will focus on being like Christ and sharing Your truth in all situations.*

Day 227

ATHEISTS IN HEAVEN

One day Jesus told His disciples He was going to prepare a place for them in Heaven. One of the Twelve, Thomas, asked the Lord, "How can we know the way?" (John 14:5). Jesus answered, "I am the way and the truth and the life. No one comes to the Father except through me" (John 14:6).

A woman once asked me how she could share her faith with her father who was an elderly atheist. He had recently told her that he wondered where he would go when he dies. So, she asked me, "Where will he go?" I told her, "I'm not in the place of God, so I don't know about anyone's eternal destiny. I do, however, know the way to Heaven is through Jesus Christ, because He promised eternal life to believers."

She then asked, "What would you say if an atheist asked you where he would go when he dies?"

I answered, "The first thing I would ask him is why is he so concerned if he doesn't believe in God. That is a contradiction—an atheist worrying about where he will spend eternity. Apparently, he has more faith than he thought he had. He should stop and consider where that concern comes from. It comes from the fact that he longs for a relationship with God and, until he has that relationship, he won't be at peace. If his atheism has brought him nothing but anxiety, perhaps it is time for him to take Jesus' advice in John 20:27: 'Stop doubting and believe!'

"Then I would ask him, 'Where do you want to go?' If he said, 'Heaven,' then I would tell him I know one way to get there—through the saving grace of Jesus Christ. He is the only One who has graced the stage of human history and guaranteed eternal life to those who believe in Him.

"If you ask me where's the Varsity, or the original Chick-Fil-A, or the governor's mansion, or the Coca-Cola Museum, I can guarantee you the way to get there because I was born and raised in Atlanta. And if you ask me how you can get to Heaven, I can definitely tell you, Jesus is the Way! Trust Him and you will have eternal life."

Prayer for the Day: *Lord, please bring about circumstances in unbelievers' lives so they turn their heart to You and receive salvation for their soul and healing for their mind. Open their eyes to see Jesus!*

Day 228

WONDERFUL

Charlie Brown was talking with Linus about his feelings of inadequacy. "You see, Linus," Charlie moaned, "it goes all the way back to the beginning. The moment I was born and set foot on the stage of life, they took one look at me and said, 'Not right for the part.'"

We all struggle with our self-image. *Who am I? Where did I come from? Why am I here?* The real question is, Do you like yourself? The way we see ourselves determines how we live. The only cure for low self-esteem is to know we are made in God's image. The psalmist said, "I praise you because I am fearfully and wonderfully made; your works are wonderful, I know that full well" (139:14). We are the wonderful works of God. That means you are wonderful! You are filled with the wonders of spirituality, creativity, intelligence, talent, gifts, and ability. Your dignity and your destiny come from the fact you are fearfully and wonderfully made by God!

You are not an evolutionary accident; you are a wonderful work of God. The renowned astronomer Johannes Kepler made a model of our solar system. An agnostic scientist saw it and commented, "That is a fantastic model of our solar system. Who made it?"

Kepler replied, "Nobody made it."

His friend said, "What do you mean, nobody made it? Someone had to make it. That model of our solar system couldn't just appear by itself."

Kepler said, "Let me ask you something. Why can I not convince you that no one created this little model of our solar system yet you are convinced that the grand design of our solar system from which this model comes happened by itself? By what kind of incongruous logic do you arrive at such a conclusion?"

Prayer for the Day: *Lord, thank You for making sure Psalm 139 was forever anointed and canonized into Your Word. At my lowest points in life, it has lifted me up and reminded me that I am wonderfully made in Your image.*

Day 229

CAUGHT BY SURPRISE

We often tell people to "stay in touch." Communication is key to everything. The most important thing is to stay in touch with God so you never get caught by surprise.

God told Noah to build an ark in order to save his family. Noah didn't know the specifics of what was going to happen when the Flood came. He was only told to get ready today for what was coming in the future.

We need to take action today so we are prepared for what will happen tomorrow and not get taken by surprise. The people of Noah's day were caught by surprise when the Flood came because they were out of touch with God. Noah called them to salvation, but they didn't listen so they were caught off guard. "They knew nothing about what would happen until the flood came and took them all away" (Matthew 24:39).

God will never tell us much about the future because He wants us to trust Him, stay focused on the present, and not worry about the future. If we trust God, we won't worry about the future. Jesus said, "Therefore do not worry about tomorrow, for tomorrow will worry about itself" (Matthew 6:34).

Noah is an example that we need to act on what we know and not worry about what we don't know. God gives us the word, but we have to do the work to get ready. God gave the plan, and Noah built the ark.

Stay in touch with God in prayer, trust Him with the future, and do what He tells you to do. You will never get caught by surprise, and you will be ready to face anything the future may bring.

Prayer for the Day: *Lord, I don't ever want to be caught by surprise when it comes to fulfilling Your will. May I take the time to listen and hear You speak, "This is the way; walk in it" (Isaiah 30:21).*

Day 230

START OVER

We can get a fresh start. We can have a new beginning. We can redo what we've done. We can restore relationships that are fractured. We can return to God like the Prodigal Son did. This was Jesus' challenge to the believers in Ephesus. While He commended them for their hard work, perseverance, and standing up for the truth, He had one thing against them—they had left their "first love" (Revelation 2:4). He did not say they had *lost* their first love, but that they *left* it, which means to "neglect, desert, or abandon."

He told them (and tells us) how to start over. First, "Consider how far you have fallen" (Revelation 2:5). We need to look back before we can go forward. We need to take an honest stock of ourselves and see where we got off track. Then we need to *repent*, which means to change our minds and our course of action to get in line with God's will. "Godly sorrow brings repentance that leads to salvation and leaves no regret" (2 Corinthians 7:10). You will never regret repenting for your sins and errors, but you will regret it if you don't repent. Jesus said, "Repent, [or] you too will perish" (Luke 13:3).

Jesus also told the Ephesian believers, "Do the things you did at first" (Revelation 2:4). It can also be translated, "Do your first works over." Go back to when your faith in God was fresh and vibrant, and do the things you did at first. Put those first spiritual disciplines back into your life. If you are going the wrong direction, you can start over today by the grace of God.

Prayer for the Day: *Lord, although I never want to walk away from Your path, it is good to know You will always redirect me back and I can start over. Keep me strong, keep me focused, keep me forever.*

Day 231

GREAT EXPECTATIONS

Israel's Benjamin Disraeli said, "What we anticipate seldom occurs; what we least expect generally happens." The feeling of disappointment comes from the gap between our expectation and our achievement. Disappointment can make us cynical. We tell ourselves the best way to not be disappointed is to not expect anything. The word *expectation* means "a strong belief that something will happen or be the case in the future; a belief that someone will or should achieve something."

God calls us to great expectations. Jesus heard two blind men call out to him in a public place to heal them. He went inside to a house in privacy and asked them, "'Do you believe that I am able to do this?' 'Yes, Lord,' they replied. Then he touched their eyes and said, 'According to your faith let it be done to you'" (Matthew 9:28-29). That is his message to us—according to your faith, it will be done to you.

Raise your expectations about your destiny, your potential, and the power of God in your life. Don't allow disappointment to make you cynical. Faith feeds on expectation. That is what *hope* means—"confident expectation." Hebrews 11:1 says, "Faith is the substance of things hoped for, the evidence of things not seen" (NKJV). It is the substance of things we expect to happen and to be achieved.

When I was in ninth grade, I developed a sense of inadequacy because I was doing so poorly in algebra. I studied all the time, and my mother had my older brother tutor me (who is a math genius with a degree in physics!). He grew impatient with me. As my mother and my brother quizzed me for an exam, I continued to not know the answer to the questions. In frustration I said, "I can't do this; I'm stupid."

My mother came unglued! "Don't you ever say you're stupid again as long as you live! Do you understand me? You are smart, and you can do this." We got back to work on the endless quizzing for my math exam. I was failing the course, but I made an *A* on the final exam, and that brought my grade to a *C* (which was great for a guy who doesn't like math). She was right. I could do it. I was selling myself short. I just needed someone to raise my expectations of myself.

Are you selling yourself short? Are you selling God short, doubting His power? Your success comes in accordance with *your* faith, not someone else's faith. Do you have faith in God and in yourself? Raise your expectations and you will see the incredible power that faith will have in your life.

Prayer for the Day: *Lord, increase my faith! I need to have hope and expectation of what You can do when I can't see past my nose. I believe in You; I trust You.*

Day 232

THE BEST IN YOU

When automaker Henry Ford was asked who was his best friend, he replied, "My best friend is the one who brings out the best in me." That is what 1 Corinthians 15:33 means: "Do not be misled: Bad company corrupts good character." I think we have all been misled at some time by someone we thought was a good influence on us but turned out to be a bad influence. Just as bad company corrupts good character, so good company changes bad character.

We need boundaries in our relationships. When we are in a relationship that affects us in negative ways, we need to draw the line. That is why the Scripture says, "Do not be misled." It is easy to tell ourselves we are going to change someone by being a good influence on them, but we need boundaries so we don't end up being ruined by them!

We need to choose good friends. As parents, we need to protect our kids from bad influences. Parents need to not only know where their kids are but who they are with. Once our children start attending school, getting involved in activities outside the home, and developing their own identity, peer pressure becomes the number one influence in their life. Peers are more influential than parents, the older our kids get. I remember my parents not letting me hang out with certain friends at school or in our neighborhood. They couldn't monitor everyone I was with, but they could control a lot of my relationships by where I went and how long I was gone. I realized they cared about me, although I didn't always like it.

Wholesome character comes from keeping good company. Jesus told His disciples, "I have called you friends" (John 15:15). Jesus shaped the character of His disciples by keeping them close to Him. They became more like Him by being with Him all the time. Jesus "appointed twelve that they might be with Him and that He might send them out to preach" (Mark 3:14 NKJV). Jesus knew the "with Him" principle of shaping people's character.

Parents need to keep their kids with them as much as possible; that is key to good parenting. Married couples need to be with each other because that is the secret to a good marriage. We need to be with godly people who exhibit faith, hope, and love in every situation of life so we grow to become all that God has created us to be.

Make a commitment to set boundaries in relationships that have a negative effect on you. Hang out with people who will bring out the best in you.

Prayer for the Day: *Lord, I haven't always surrounded myself with people who bring out the best in me. Remind me how important it is to have boundaries so I establish healthy relationships, keeping the stress in my life to a minimum.*

Day 233

LOST IN SPACE

One billion itself is a staggering number. If we wanted to make a book with a billion dollar signs, printed 1,000 per page printed on both sides, the book would be 500,000 pages long. A billion seconds ago, it was the 1960s. A billion minutes ago, Jesus was alive.

Scientists tell us the Milky Way galaxy contains over 100 billion stars. One billion is 1,000 times one million, and 100 billion is 100 times that. It would take 3,000 years to count out loud to 100 billion!

Incredibly, God "determines the number of the stars and calls them each by name" (Psalm 147:4). "Lift your eyes and look to the heavens: Who created all these? He who brings out the starry host one by one and calls forth each of them by name. Because of his great power and mighty strength, not one of them is missing" (Isaiah 40:26).

Just as God knows each of the stars by name, He knows you by name and He has a plan for your life! "Fear not, for I have redeemed you; I have called you by your name; You are Mine" (Isaiah 43:1 NKJV). Jesus tells us, "Even the very hairs of your head are numbered. So do not be afraid" (Matthew 10:30-31). The psalmist said of the Lord, "You see me when I travel and when I rest at home. You know everything I do" (Psalm 139:3 NLT).

Tonight, look up at the stars, seeing the wonder of this vast universe, and remember you are not lost in space. God knows everything about you, and He created you with a powerful purpose and a divine destiny!

Prayer for the Day: *Lord, until You found me, I was lost in space, lost on this earth, and lost in my soul. You have re-created me, called me by name, and given me purpose. I can look at the starry host and say, "I am no longer lost!"*

Day 234

DIFFERENT IS GOOD

Different is good. Differences give our world variety and richness. Aren't you glad life is in color, not black and white? Being different doesn't mean being difficult to get along with or being divisive in our relationships. It means celebrating our uniqueness and respecting other people's uniqueness.

One of the greatest principles for a good marriage is accepting and respecting each other's differences instead of trying to change each other. Marriages are ruined by a husband or wife constantly demanding their spouse to change. Unconditional love accepts people's God-given uniqueness and sees the beauty of God's creative work in each person.

Parents fail their kids when they pressure them too much to be like them and don't celebrate and encourage their children's uniqueness. All parents who have more than one child quickly discover how different they are and how they have to be parented in different ways.

The Apostle Paul gives us insight into the importance of our uniqueness: "The sun has one kind of splendor, the moon another and the stars another; and star differs from star in splendor" (1 Corinthians 15:41). Every person God creates has their own splendor. Let's learn to see, celebrate, and respect the splendor God has created in every person, and remember that different is good.

Prayer for the Day: *Lord, I used to wonder why I'm so different from my family. When You saved me and began to direct my life, I realized and understood I am different because I belong to You and am called by You. Different is good.*

Day 235

PROVEN TRUE

Trust is at an all-time low in our world. People don't trust the media, the polls, the news, corporations, or politicians. A news report recently asked if it was true that one of our branches of government was denying a report about their actions when it was obvious to everyone that they did what was being reported. I asked myself, *When did the word* deny *replace the word* lie?

In a world of half-truths, denials and, yes, lies, there is one thing we can count on—God's Word. The psalmist reflected on a man of integrity named *Joseph*. Joseph's brothers hated him and sold him as a slave, but God exalted him to second in command of Egypt. What God promised Joseph came to pass. Joseph was sold as a slave. "They bruised his feet with shackles, his neck was put in irons, till what he foretold came to pass, till the word of the Lord proved him true" (Psalm 105:18-19).

God gave Joseph a dream, but then came a long season of pain in his life. Nonetheless, Joseph kept trusting God and believing God's promise. His pain led to his promotion; his endurance led to his exaltation; his steadfastness led to his success.

The Lord will always prove us true when we believe His Word. If we govern our lives according to the Scriptures, we will always be proven true in what we believe. We can count on the unchanging truth of God's principles, precepts, and promises in a world of relative morals and shading of the truth. Jesus promised, "Heaven and earth will pass away, but my words will never pass away" (Matthew 24:35). Trust God and His Word, and He will prove you true.

Prayer for the Day: *Lord, it is difficult living in a world that doesn't always recognize its Creator—a world that is out of line with Your Word and will. I long to see You return and establish Your kingdom on earth and prove true Your Word.*

Day 236

MY TIMES ARE IN YOUR HANDS

We live in uncertain times that makes us feel anxious, worried, and afraid. We face uncertainly in personally, nationally, and globally. David felt the same way, yet He declared, "I trust in you, Lord; I say, 'You are my God. My times are in your hands'" (Psalm 31:14-15). He knew his life was in the hands of God.

What safer place could we be but in the hands of God? My life is not in my hands or in the hands of other people, but in God's hands. The Bible speaks of God's hands as a symbol of His protection and provision. David wrote, "Though he [a righteous person] stumble, he will not fall, for the Lord upholds him with his hand" (Psalm 37:24). David thanked God, saying, "You lay your hand upon me" (139:5). We read of the prophet Ezekiel, "There the hand of the Lord was on him" (Ezekiel 1:3). When John saw Jesus in a vision, he said, "He placed his right hand on me and said, 'Do not be afraid'" (Revelation 1:17).

All the circumstances, events, and experiences—good and bad—in our life are in God's hands. God is able to work everything together for good with His hands. Your faith has to be greater than your feelings to deal with ups and downs of life. You have a divine destiny, and God promises to direct the course of your life if you trust Him.

Jesus prayed to His Father from Psalm 31:5 when He gave His life on the cross for us: "Into your hands I commit my spirit" (Luke 23:46). When you are going through difficult times, pray this prayer of release: "Father, into Your hands I commit my need, my family, my illness, my problem, my sin, my failure, my fear, my addiction, my financial need." Confess by faith, "My times are in Your hands. My healing is in Your hands. My deliverance is in Your hands. My provision is in Your hands. My future is in Your hands."

Prayer for the Day: *Lord, although we live in uncertain times, there is one thing I know—my life is in Your hands. That strengthens my faith and gives me such peace.*

Day 237

BIOGRAPHY

Did you know God has a library? The Bible often uses the imagery of God's books. He even has a book about your life. David wrote, "All the days ordained for me were written in your book before one of them came to be" (Psalm 139:16). Your biography has already been written, containing God's perfect plan for your life.

You are here because of God's purpose; you are not an accident. Your parents may have told you that you were an accident. You may have been a complete surprise to them when you came along, but you were not a surprise to God. David describes God's miracle of creation of every child in the mother's womb: "For you created my inmost being; you knit me together in my mother's womb. I praise you because I am fearfully and wonderfully made" (Psalm 139:13-14).

God told Jeremiah, "Before I formed you in the womb I knew [chose] you, before you were born I set you apart; I appointed you as a prophet to the nations" (Jeremiah 1:4-5). The Apostle Paul tells us this same truth: "For he [God] chose us in [Christ] before the creation of the world to be holy and blameless in his sight" (Ephesians 1:4).

When I got out of college and stared my ministry, my mother told me a story about my life. She was bedridden for most of her pregnancy with me, and the doctor thought she would lose me. My mother had experienced three miscarriages and was not supposed to have any more children. When she was six months pregnant with me and wondering if she would lose me, the Lord spoke to her about my calling. He told her she would carry me to full-term and I would be healthy.

Live today with confidence, seeking to know God's will for your life because all the days ordained for you were written in God's book before one of them came to be.

Prayer for the Day: *Lord, how awesome it is to know You oversee my life and know every detail of it. You direct my footsteps and have a book of "me." Knowing this gives me confidence to know You better.*

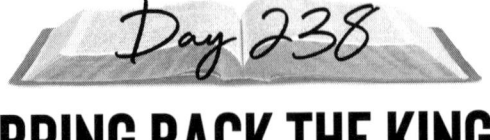

Day 238

BRING BACK THE KING

During the reign of King David, Jerusalem was attacked, and he had to flee the country. When Israel defeated the enemy, David was still out of the country. The people asked, "Why do you say nothing about bringing the king back?" (2 Samuel 19:10).

Why do we as Christians talk so little about the King coming back? Jesus promised He would return to this world to reign as King of kings and Lord of lords. The second coming of Jesus is the final hope for this world. We are to live "wait[ing] for the blessed hope—the appearing of our great God and Savior, Jesus Christ" (Titus 2:13).

When the King returns, "They will beat their swords into plowshares and their spears into pruning hooks. Nation will not take up sword against nation, nor will they train for war anymore" (Isaiah 2:4).

When the King returns, "The wolf will live with the lamb. . . . The cow will feed with the bear, their young will lie down together, and the lion will eat straw like the ox. The infant will play near the cobra's den, and the young child put its hand into the viper's nest. They will neither harm nor destroy on all my holy mountain, for the earth will be filled with the knowledge of the Lord as the waters cover the sea" (Isaiah 11:6-9).

When the King returns, "There will be no light, cold or frost. It will be a unique day, without daytime or nighttime—a day known to the Lord. When evening comes, there will be light. . . . The Lord will be King over the whole earth. On that day there will be one Lord, and his name the only name" (Zechariah 14:6-9).

When the King returns, "The heavens will disappear with a roar; the elements will be destroyed by fire. . . . But in keeping with his promise we are looking forward to a new heaven and a new earth, where righteousness dwells" (2 Peter 3:10, 13).

Let's celebrate, for the King is coming back!

Prayer for the Day: *Lord, how I long for Your return! I long for sin to be destroyed, illness to be eliminated, and the world to be at peace. Maranatha! Come, King Jesus!*

Day 239

STAND STRONG

When you hear the term *spiritual warfare*, what comes to your mind? A direct assault by demons? An irresistible temptation to sin? Unexplained and inescapable feelings of depression and anxiety?

Spiritual fatigue that leaves you powerless? Attacks against your family, your possessions, or your health? All of these are part of spiritual warfare.

We are engaged in spiritual warfare on three fronts: our sin nature, the world, and the devil. God gives us His armor to defend ourselves and to win every battle we face: "Be strong in the Lord and in the power of His might. Put on the whole armor of God, that you may be able to stand against wiles of the devil. . . . Take up the whole armor of God, that you may be able to withstand in the evil day, and having done all, to stand" (Ephesians 6:10-11, 13 NKJV).

This is the challenge to stand:
- Stand for Christ.
- Stand against evil.
- Stand alone if necessary.
- Stand together in unity.
- Stand up in the power of the Holy Spirit.
- Stand, and having done all, stand!

Prayer for the Day: *Lord, I realize I am facing spiritual warfare against my sinful nature, our sinful world, and the devil. I commit to wearing the spiritual armor You provide so I can stand strong!*

Day 240

TAKE TIME TO BE HOLY

When I was a young boy, one of my favorite hymns was, "Take Time to Be Holy." It was written by C. Michael Hawn in the 1800s when he was inspired by the words of 1 Peter 1:16, "Be holy, because I am holy." The melody was inspiring, and the thought of taking time to be holy intrigued me as to what it really meant. I still think about that phrase.

Maybe that is what Jesus meant when He said, "If anyone desires to come after Me, let him deny himself, take up his cross daily, and follow Me" (Luke 9:23 NKJV). Following Jesus is not a weekend pastime; it is daily. The word *daily* is important. We read of the early believers: "Day after day, in the temple courts and from house to house, they never stopped teaching and proclaiming the good news that Jesus is the Christ" (Acts 5:42).

The word *holy* means to be "set apart and consecrated to God's sacred purpose for our life." Jesus took time to be holy. "Very early in the morning, while it was still dark, Jesus got up . . . and went off to a solitary place, where he prayed" (Mark 1:35). If we are going to follow Jesus, we need to follow Him to a solitary place to pray.

If we don't take time to be holy, what will we become? When we take time to be holy, it brings out the best in us. When we take time to be holy, we live godly, joyful, and victorious lives.

Take time to be holy, speak often with your Lord
Abide in Him always, and feed on His Word.
Make friends of God's children, help those who are weak
Forgetting in nothing His blessing to seek.

Prayer for the Day: *Lord, the word* holy *is strange and archaic word for most people. I, however, desire to take the time to read Your Word, pray, and be holy. Walking with You daily keeps my faith strong.*

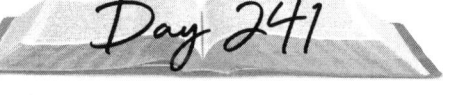

Day 241

PUT A LID ON IT

Barbie fixed me a great dinner with fresh organic vegetables. She brought me a plate filled to overflowing. I said, "Thanks. That's great. But it's too much food."

She replied, "You don't have to eat it all. Put a lid on it and save some for later."

What a great principle for life—put a lid on it!

Let's put a lid on our words. We don't need to say (text or tweet) every thought that pops into our heads. The news media has gone crazy today reporting every piece of information, including fake news, they hear. Too many "journalists" are merely spreading gossip.

Let's pray, "Set a guard over my mouth, Lord; keep watch over the door of my lips" (Psalm 141:3). Just as we muzzle a dog so he doesn't bite someone, we should put a lid on our words so we don't bite and injure people with our words.

We also need to put a lid on our appetites. When Barbie handed me that delicious plate of food, I wanted to eat all of it, but I knew I needed to be disciplined. We have appetites for both healthy and unhealthy things. It takes discipline not to overindulge our cravings. "Do not get drunk on wine which leads to debauchery. Instead, be filled with the Spirit" (Ephesians 5:18). We can get intoxicated on anything—money, sex, power, substances, pride, food, shopping, habits, entertainment—so we need to put a lid on it.

The only thing we don't need to put a lid on is the Holy Spirit. "Do not grieve the Holy Spirit of God" (4:30). We cannot get too much of God's grace, power, and presence. So, let's be filled with the Spirit and put a lid on everything else.

Prayer for the Day: *Lord, help me to put a lid on those things in life that tempt or intoxicate. May I rather be filled with Your Spirit and walk in wisdom and power.*

Day 242

GIVE THE GIFT

Ignace Jan Paderewski, the famous Polish composer-pianist, was once scheduled to perform at a great American concert hall for a high-society extravaganza. In the audience was a mother with her fidgety nine-year-old son. Weary of waiting, the boy slipped away from her side, strangely drawn to the Steinway on the stage. He sat down at the stool and began playing "Chopsticks." The crowd began to yell, "Get that boy off the stage!"

When Paderewski heard the uproar from backstage, he grabbed his coat and rushed over behind the boy. Reaching around him, the master began to improvise a counter-melody to "Chopsticks." As the two of them played together, Paderewski kept whispering in the boy's ear, "Keep going. Don't quit, Son . . . don't stop . . . don't stop."

Paderewski gave the greatest gift that day—the gift of encouragement. This gift imparts courage, strength, and confidence. Encouragement is the least expensive, but most valuable, gift we can give.

Barnabas was a Levitical priest who became a leader in the early church. His birth name was *Joseph*; his fellow Christians nicknamed him *Barnabas*, meaning "son of encouragement" (Acts 4:36-37). *Barnabas* comes from the Greek word *paraklete*, which is the name Jesus used for the Holy Spirit (John 14:16). The Holy Spirit is the divine Encourager, Comforter, Intercessor, and Counselor.

Barnabas was so full of the Holy Spirit that the greatest attribute of his life was encouragement. Who do you know today that needs encouragement? Reach out to them. Send them a text or a Facebook message, buy them a gift, give them a call, or take them to lunch. Give the gift!

Prayer for the Day: *Lord, please give me the gift of encouragement so I can pass it on to others. Make me sensitive to their needs, that I may impart courage and confidence.*

Day 243

SENT

Going somewhere and being sent somewhere are two different things. *Going* is passive; *being sent* is active, intentional, and purposeful. Jesus sends us into our world every day to share His good news of eternal life and to call people to accept Him as their Savior.

Jesus came "to seek and to save the lost" (Luke 19:10). He came into "the world to save sinners—of whom I am the worst" (1 Timothy 1:15). He calls us to share His purpose. We are sent by Him just as He was sent by God. "As the Father has sent me," Jesus said, "I am sending you."

Oliver Cromwell was Lord Protector of the Commonwealth of England, Scotland, and Ireland during the civil war of the 17th century. During his administration, the treasury ran out of silver to mint coinage. Cromwell sent delegates throughout the empire to collect silver for the treasury to use. They reported back to him that the only silver they could find was in the statues of the saints in the churches and cathedrals. "What should we do?" they asked.

Cromwell replied, "Melt the saints down and put them into circulation."

That is what needs to happen to us. We need to be melted down by the fire of the Holy Spirit, molded into the image of Jesus, and then be put into circulation so others may see "Christ in [us], the hope of glory" (Colossians 1:27).

We must not spend our life in church; we must be put it into circulation. The famous columnist Erma Bombeck said, "When I stand before God at the end of my life, I would hope that I would not have a single bit of talent left but could say, 'I used everything You gave me.'"

Every day, let us pray the prayer of Jim Elliot, who gave his life carrying the Gospel to the Auca Indians: "Lord, make me a crisis man. Not just a signpost on the highway of life, but a fork in the road so that people who meet me will come to know Jesus Christ!"

Prayer for the Day: *Lord, when I meet and converse with unbelievers, may they see Christ in me through what I say, what I do, and how I live. Melt me down and put me into circulation.*

Day 244

ACT OF KINDNESS

Aesop was a Greek storyteller who lived six hundred years before Christ. He was a slave but later freed. Aesop said, "No act of kindness, no matter how small, is ever wasted."

The first miracle of the early church took place in Jerusalem when Peter and John went to the Temple to pray. A beggar asked them for money, but he gave him more. Peter said, "In the name of Jesus Christ of Nazareth, walk" (Acts 3:6). Peter took the man by the hand and "helped him up, and instantly the man's feet and ankles became strong. . . . Then he went with them into the temple courts, walking and jumping, and praising God" (Acts 3:7-8).

That night, religious leaders arrested Peter and John. They went to court the next day and were asked how they had performed the miracle.

Peter replied, "If we are being called to account today for an act of kindness shown to a man who was lame and are being asked how he was healed, then know this, . . . It is by the name of Jesus Christ of Nazareth, whom you crucified but whom God raised from the dead, that this man stands before you healed. . . . Salvation is found in no one else, for there is no other name under heaven given to mankind by which we must be saved" (Acts 4:9-12).

Acts of kindness are wonderful, and they become powerful when they are followed by sharing the good news of salvation with those to whom we are kind. Look for opportunities to do acts of kindness, but don't stop there—tell about Jesus.

Prayer for the Day: *Lord, as I reach out to those in need, may I always bless them in Your name and be willing to pray for them as You direct me. Help me to see what act of kindness is needed, and allow me to be Your hands extended.*

Day 245

BIRTHRIGHT

Jacob and Esau were twin brothers, the sons of Isaac. Abraham, the man of faith, was their grandfather. When they were born, Esau had the birthright and the blessing of his father, since he was the firstborn.

When they were young men, one day Esau came home from hunting and was famished. Jacob was a great cook, known for his Brunswick stew (I made that part up). Actually, it was lentil stew. Jacob said, "Sell me your birthright for a bowl of lentil stew." (That's a bad deal.) Years later, Isaac transferred the family blessing to Jacob instead of Esau because Esau had sold his birthright and, thereby, gave up his blessing.

Why did Esau sell his birthright on a whim for a bowl of stew? Because "Esau despised his birthright" (Genesis 26:35). A birthright is a privilege and possession to which a person is entitled by birth. Jacob, on the other hand, valued the birthright and his father's blessing. We lose what we don't value, even if we are entitled to it.

Living with a sense of entitlement is one of the surest ways of losing our blessings. When we are born again through faith in Jesus, we too have a birthright. "If we are children, then we are heirs—heirs of God and co-heirs with Christ" (Romans 8:17). The temporal things of this world, like the bowl of stew, appeal to our desires and tempt us to compromise our faith and values. If we don't value our birthright of faith, we may lose it in a moment of weakness.

If your parents raised you in a Christian home and taught you the way of faith, treasure it and value it. It is your birthright that will lead to your blessing. Don't hunger for the temporal pleasures of this world like Esau did. "The world and its desires pass away" (1 John 2:17). Rather, hunger and thirst after righteousness. Treasure your birthright and you will enjoy its blessings!

Prayer for the Day: *Lord, May I never take for granted but always treasure my birthright of salvation. It has provided me with healing, wisdom, and provision. It is a privilege to be a child of the King.*

Day 246

LOL

According to research from the University of Wisconsin, children laugh an average of four hundred times a day, while adults laugh about four times a day. Jesus taught us to receive the Kingdom as a little child. Laughter increases our joy, lowers our stress, and rejuvenates our energy. Laughter is connected to mental, emotional, and physical health. "A cheerful heart is good medicine, but a crushed spirit dries up the bones" (Proverbs 17:22).

Sometimes a good laugh is the best medicine you can take for a heavy heart. What can you do to laugh more? First, *lighten up*. The joy of the Lord is your strength, so lighten up in life and don't let stress and worry rob you of your joy. Don't take everything so seriously, and don't overreact to problems.

Second, *laugh at yourself*. Perfectionism will keep you wound tight as a drum trying to live up to everyone's expectations and your own idealistic goals. You are going to fail and make mistakes. You are not going to reach all of your goals. So, learn to laugh at yourself and your shortcomings and to recognize you are just human like the rest of us.

Third, *find humor even in troubled times.* Books, movies, and plays often intertwine the contrasting themes of tragedy and humor. Even in tough times, you can often find something to laugh about.

Prayer for the Day: *Lord, when I become overwhelmed with stress and trouble comes my way, remind me to give that over to You so that my heart and soul aren't crushed. Teach me how to lighten up even in the toughest of situations.*

Day 247
WALK IN THE LIGHT

Barbie and I were having dinner in a dimly lit restaurant. The waiter handed us the menu and, as we looked it over, she said, "What are you going to have?"

I replied, "I don't know . . . I can hardly read the menu; it's so dark in here."

"Do you want my glasses," she asked.

"No, I need light."

I thought of the Scripture verse, "But all things become visible when they are exposed . . . for it is light that makes everything visible" (Ephesians 5:13-14 Amp.). Light is also associated with life. Everything depends on light to grow and be healthy. Light is associated with a life of moral integrity, truth, and honesty.

Barbie proceeded to take out her smartphone and turn on the flashlight app that lit up not only the menu but the entire restaurant! When she turned on the light, I could see everything on the menu. Take out your spiritual flashlight today, the Bible, and let God's light shine in your life, your marriage, and your relationships. God's Word is "a lamp to my feet and a light to my path" (Psalm 119:105).

Don't walk around in the darkness of sin, fear, or foolishness and end up making a mess of your life. "Walk in the light, as he [God] is in the light" (1 John 1:7). Everything you are facing is visible in the light of God's Word. His Word will show you clearly how to live in a way that pleases Him and bring you His blessings.

Prayer for the Day: *Lord, there have been times in my life when I have walked in darkness and fear. Teach me to stay on the road of light that I may give that light to all that cross my path.*

Day 248

BOUNDARIES

Our relationships make us or break us, so we need to choose our friends carefully. The person we marry is the greatest decision we make in human relationships. Not only do we need to choose our relationships carefully, we also need to clearly define our relationships. Confusion comes in friendships, work relationships, marriage, and our relationship to our children if we don't clearly define our relationships.

Jesus told His disciples, "I no longer call you servants but friends" (John 15:15). He was redefining their relationship and taking it to a new level. Relationships need to be clearly defined for them to be peaceful and productive. When we are unclear about the definition of a relationship, there is stress, tension, and misunderstanding between us.

We need to set boundaries in our relationships. All relationships require balancing closeness and distance. We need to know when to be together and when to be apart. We need to know what to say and what not to say. We need to know what to reveal and what to keep secret.

We need to know when to be part of the group and when to be an individual. We need to know when to share our thoughts and feelings and when to keep our privacy.

Our relationships have more to do with who we become and what we accomplish than any other single factor. So, we must choose them wisely, define them carefully, and set the proper boundaries.

Prayer for the Day: *Lord, I haven't always been very good at setting boundaries. This lack of discipline has brought me great trouble. Give me the courage to keep a balance between closeness and distance so I have healthier relationships.*

Day 249

WHAT DO YOU SEE?

Moses stood on Mount Sinai and said to God, "Show me your glory" (Exodus 33:18). Barbie and I have climbed to the top of Mount Sinai in time to see the sunrise. We saw the glory of God surround us in creation that morning. We saw the glory of God in the mountain-scape, the light of the sun, and the fresh morning air. Moses asked to see God's glory, but he missed the glory of creation.

We, too, ask to see God. We want God to show Himself to us in some special way, but if we will look around, we can see His glory in His creation. We can see who He is and what He is like. "The heavens declare the glory of God; the skies proclaim the work of His hands. Day after day they pour forth speech; night after night they display knowledge. There is no speech or language where their voice is not heard" (see Psalm 19:1-3). There are 6,500 spoken languages, and the creation speaks to every person that God exists and He is our Creator.

Atheism is intellectual laziness. It is easy and takes no mental energy to merely dismiss the evidence of God in nature and science. It is easy to get upset with the hardships of life and the problems of the world and just say God doesn't exist. Atheism doesn't take any effort. "The fool has said in his heart, 'There is no God'" (Psalm 14:1). It's foolishness to observe the universe, nature, and science and say it's all an accident that happened by chance.

Just look around you. What do you see? "For since the creation of the world God's invisible qualities—his eternal power and divine nature—have been clearly seen, being understood from what has been made, so that people are without excuse" (Romans 1:20).

Nature reveals God's power, presence, and wisdom. We all struggle to understand the mysteries of life and why God permits the world to continue in this current state of imperfection as we wait for the day He restores it all to its original condition of perfection. We are better served to trust Him instead of denying Him.

Take a look around you today and see the glory of God.

Prayer for the Day: *Lord, I don't understand those who deny Your existence. All we have to do is look at creation and see Your amazing handiwork. Hardships can blind us, but I choose to trust You and see You in the blessings.*

Day 250

SING AND MAKE MUSIC

Robert Ingersol was a politician, orator, and Civil War veteran for the Union Army known for his agnosticism. When he died, the funeral notice read: "There will be no singing at the funeral." No praise in the valley of the shadow of death. No faith in God. No hope of eternal life. There was nothing to sing about.

Psychology, science, and medicine confirm the power of singing on the human soul and the body. Singing is used in treatment with dementia patients to improve brain functioning. Singing is central to our faith. Job said God "gives songs in the night" (Job 35:10). The psalmist said, "Sing to [the Lord] a new song; play skillfully, and shout for joy" (Psalm 33:3). We are taught to "sing and make music from [our] heart to the Lord" (Ephesians 5:19).

When we sing to God, we join the symphony of creation: "Let the rivers clap their hands, let the mountains sing together for joy" (Psalm 98:8). The prophet declared, "The mountains and hills will burst into song before you, and all the trees of the field will clap their hands" (Isaiah 55:12). John the Revelator heard "every creature in heaven and on earth and under the earth and on the sea, and all that is in them, saying: 'To him who sits on the throne and to the Lamb be praise and honor and glory and power, for ever and ever!'" (Revelation 5:13).

If the rivers and trees clap their hands, and if the mountains and the hills sing together, how much more should we who have been saved by His grace sing to our Lord? We who have been given eternal life, tasted the goodness of God, and been called out of darkness into His wonderful light must sing God's praise!

Prayer for the Day: *Lord, I may not have the best voice, but I will always sing Your praises, for You are a good God who loves His children. I will bless Your holy name at all times and in all circumstances.*

Day 251

SERVE GOD'S PURPOSE

Everyone wants to live with purpose. Our greatest reason for living is when we live for God's purpose, not just ours. King David "served God's purpose in his own generation" (Acts 13:36). That is one of my favorite statements in the Bible and one that guides my personal life.

Some people are historians, focused on what generations before them did. They love to watch the *History Channel*. Other people are futurists, concerned about their legacy after them and projecting what will happen in the future. They love to watch sci-fi movies.

I want to be like King David, who served God's purpose in his own generation. The time is now. This generation is our generation, so let's focus on making an impact for the glory of God in our day. If we will take care of the present, the future will take care of itself. The future is the fruit of the seeds sown in the present. God's purpose is for us to be in a close relationship to Him and bring Him glory in everything we do.

Use all your talents and abilities to serve God in all the plans you pursue. The Lord says, "You are my witnesses" (Isaiah 44:8). Be a living witness of God's love, grace, and truth in all you do and say. Go out and face today with purpose, praying as Jesus taught us to pray: "Your kingdom come. Your will be done on earth as it is in heaven" (Matthew 6:10 NKJV).

Prayer for the Day: *Lord, I am so guilty of making my own plans and then asking You to bless them. I am reminded today that I should seek Your plans first so I may see Your purpose fulfilled.*

Day 252

GOT VISION?

The human eye is an amazing organ. It can distinguish over 8 million colors. Light enters the cornea and continues to the retina, where 130 million light-sensitive rods cause photochemical reactions that transform the light into electrical impulses. The optic nerve, consisting of 12 million nerves, sends the data to the brain at the rate of 10 million bits per second. The eye gives us natural vision, but our mind gives us spiritual vision.

Do you have a vision—a master plan and a divine purpose for your life? When God gives you a vision, follow His advice: "Write down the [vision] and make it plain on tablets so that a herald may run with it. For the [vision] awaits an appointed time; it speaks of the end and will not prove false. Though it linger, wait for it; it will certainly come and will not delay" (Habakkuk 2:2-3).

Write down your vision. Make specific goals and plans for your life. Spell it out in detail, instead of having a vague idea of what you want to do. Then go to work to make your vision a reality. God will do His part to fulfill His plan for your life, but you must do your part as well. "Do your best to present yourself to God as one approved" (2 Timothy 2:15).

Wait for the vision, because it will surely come. When your vision is based on God's promises for your life, it will come to pass. If you have a vision, you won't be in a hurry but will naturally pace yourself.

I am one of the most impatient people who has ever lived. But when it comes to the things that matter, I am patient and methodical to see it come to pass. I have learned to walk by faith and wait on the Lord. I may not wait on anything else, but I have learned to wait on the Lord. "Wait on the Lord . . . and He shall strengthen your heart" (Psalm 27:14 NKJV). When you have a vision, you will be able to endure the difficult times to see the vision come to pass.

Prayer for the Day: *Lord, I pray that You place Your vision into my heart and mind. Lead me in every way that will bring this vision to fruition for Your glory.*

Day 253

THE GREATEST COMPLIMENT

What is the greatest compliment you have ever received? Hopefully, you have had so many compliments you cannot say which is the greatest one! Compliments boost our confidence and lift our spirits. "A word fitly spoken is like apples of gold in settings of silver" (Proverbs 25:11 NKJV). A compliment is very valuable.

While getting compliments from people is great, how much greater to get a compliment from God! The greatest compliment the Lord can give us is the same one He gave to young David, the shepherd who became a king. God said of him: "I have found David son of Jesse, a man after my own heart; he will do everything I want him to do" (Acts 13:22). Wow! What an amazing compliment. If you are like me, you want God to say the same thing about you.

What does it mean to be a person after God's own heart? I have heard people say it means to worship God with great enthusiasm and passion. I love music as much as anyone, and it is important to worship the Lord with passion. But that is not what it means to be a person after God's own heart.

God clarifies what it means to be after His heart: "He will do everything I want him to do." So, to be a person after God's own heart means to be submissive and obedient to His will. The emphasis of this age is for us to do everything we want to do. What a challenge for us to surrender to God's perfect will and to do everything He wants us to do! When you surrender to God's perfect will, you will also be a person after God's own heart.

Prayer for the Day: *Lord,* surrender *is a word that most are uncomfortable with. We often see it as a form of weakness. But, when it comes to serving You,* surrender *means obedience to Your will. I will surrender to You, Lord, because I know You love me and always have my back.*

Day 254

INSIDE OUT

Learning to live from the inside out is one of the most important lessons for effective living. What do I mean by "inside out"? We put so much emphasis on our outer life—physical appearance, finances, possessions, relationships, and careers. We are constantly trying to improve or better the outer life. But the fact is that the outer life is often a result of the inner life.

What goes on within us has a direct impact on what goes on around us. In many ways, the inner life creates and controls the outer life. The Bible says, "As [a person] thinks in his heart, so is he" (Proverbs 23:7 NKJV). What we think and how we think affects everything about us, including the condition of circumstances. Paul said he could handle his problems because "inwardly we are being renewed day by day" (2 Corinthians 4:16).

Who you are will be reflected in the world around you. Your circumstances will conform to your character. If you are negative, you will create a negative world. If your thoughts are chaotic, your life will be in chaos. If your mind is cluttered, your house will be cluttered. If you are a good person, your life will be good. As a person thinks, so is he.

The more you cultivate your inner life through your relationship to the Lord by prayer, reflection, and worship, the more your outer life will improve. When you don't like something in your life, don't start by changing it; start by changing yourself. If you do, your circumstances and situation will naturally start reflecting your inner life. Do it from the inside out!

Prayer for the Day: *Lord, I always try to make a good impression with people so they will like me. This year I am going to focus on making a good impression with You from the inside out. As You pour into my inner life, may it overflow to my outer life so they see You, Jesus, not just me!*

Day 255

HEAVEN ON MY MIND

It has been said that some people are so heavenly minded, they are no earthly good. The fact is, the most heavenly minded person who ever lived was Jesus, and He did the most earthly good! Jesus' ministry is summed up this way: "How God anointed Jesus of Nazareth with the Holy Spirit and power, and how he went around doing good and healing all who were under the power of the devil" (Acts 10:38).

When our mind is on Heaven and the promise of eternal life, we will have a positive attitude toward life and live in victory. We, too, will go about doing good to others. If our mind is too divided and distracted by all the worries and hassles of life, then "set your minds on things above, not on earthly things" (Colossians 3:2).

Jesus spoke of Heaven over one hundred times in the Gospels, and He brought the good news of the kingdom of Heaven. He showed us the way to live in the kingdom of Heaven while we still live on the earth. He taught us to pray, "Thy kingdom come, thy will be done." He assured us Heaven is real: "My Father's house has many rooms; if that were not so, would I have told you that I am going there to prepare a place for you?" (John 14:2).

I don't know if all dogs go to Heaven (although I believe mine are going!), but I do know all believers are promised Heaven. Take your mind off the pressures you are facing and think about Heaven, and you will experience God's peace even in the midst of trouble.

In John Bunyan's classic, *Pilgrim's Progress*, Mr. Feeble-mind said: "But this I am resolved on: to run when I can, to go on when I cannot run, and to creep when I cannot go. . . . My mind is beyond the river that has no bridge."

Prayer for the Day: *Lord, it's difficult to focus on Heaven when I'm distracted by the world I live in now. Today I'm making a choice to read about Heaven in Your Word on a regular basis so I'm reminded that all my worries are temporary and will cease when I see You face-to-face.*

Day 256

AFTER AN UPROAR

In Acts 20:1-2, we read: "When the uproar had ended, Paul sent for the disciples and, after encouraging them, said goodbye and set out for Macedonia. He traveled through that area, speaking many words of encouragement to the people."

We all go through times of uproar. An *uproar* is a "state of violent and noisy disturbance or turmoil." Synonyms like *disturbance, commotion, turbulence, clamor, furor, chaos,* and *pandemonium* describe an uproar. Are you going through any of that today? Do you have friends and family going through an uproar today?

If your life is one big noisy disturbance that has you in a state of turmoil, be encouraged today. Let God encourage you as you go to Him in prayer and give your frustrations to Him. Surrender your frustrations instead of venting them. The psalmist said, "Cast your cares on the Lord and he will sustain you; he will never let the righteous [fall]" (Psalm 55:22).

Take some time to talk with friends who will remind you that you will get through the uproar to a new season of peace. Also, remember to follow the example of the Apostle Paul and call others to encourage them. He took the initiative to go to as many people as he could to speak words of encouragement. Don't ever participate in spreading discouragement, criticism, or complaint, but rather speak words of encouragement. That is how we win even when life is in an uproar.

Prayer for the Day: *Lord, there are people in my life who would like to destroy my peace and involve me in their chaos. Please give me the ability to encourage them with words of wisdom, and help me step back when I need to avoid an uproar.*

Day 257

UP TO MY NECK

Do you ever feel like you are up to your neck with problems? It seems like when one problem arises, suddenly more problems come with it until we are up to our neck.

The psalmist felt that way one time. He wrote, "Save me, O God, for the waters have come up to my neck. I sink in the miry depths, where there is no foothold. I have come into the deep waters; the floods engulf me. I am worn out calling for help; my throat is parched. My eyes fail, looking for my God" (Psalm 69:1-3).

We can get up to our neck with so many problems, we feel like God doesn't care about us and we are going to drown. God is with you in the deep waters, so keep swimming. He won't let you drown. He will bring you out if you trust Him.

The psalmist kept his faith strong when he was up to his neck and declared, "But I pray to you, O Lord, in the time of your favor. . . . I will praise God's name in song and glorify him with thanksgiving" (Psalm 69:13, 30). When you pray, remember God has a time of favor for you. Don't focus on the time of frustration you're in right now, but on the time of favor on the horizon.

The time of trouble you are in right now will pass. When you believe that truth, you can face today by praising God's name in song. He will lift you out of deep waters and place your feet on a solid rock! Then you will be up to your neck in blessings!

Prayer for the Day: *Lord, when I get to that place where I can't take it anymore and I'm up to my neck in trouble, help me to focus on You. I trust You to part the waters for me and save me from drowning in my sorrows. I receive Your supernatural peace in the midst of all that the enemy throws at me.*

Day 258

FEAT NO EVIL

What are you afraid of? *Fear* is a feeling of dread, alarm, panic, and anxiety. It ranges from mild anxiety to panic attacks to crippling phobias. Fear comes in all shapes and sizes: the fear of success, the fear of failure, the fear of rejection, the fear of disease, the fear of the past, the fear of the future, and the fear of death. Fear paralyzes decision-making, immobilizes action, hinders prayer, limits faith, restricts relationships, lowers productivity, jeopardizes health, and steals our happiness.

The psalmist David shows us the way to defeat our fears: "Yea, though I walk through the valley of the shadow of death, I will fear no evil; for You are with me" (Psalm 23:4 NKJV). Three words stand out to me: *shadow*, *valley*, and *through*. We all go through valleys in life. We wish we could stay on the mountain peak, but all mountains have valleys. But we can be blessed in the valley just as we are on the mountain. Keep your eyes on the mountain ahead of you, and you will get through the valley.

Barbie and I have been to the actual Valley of the Shadow of Death in Israel, which goes from Jerusalem to the Dead Sea. The phrase can be translated, "the glen of gloom." Life is filled with shadows. Valleys bring times of darkness, discouragement, and depression. God's presence is the light in the darkness of the valley. "The Lord is my light and my salvation; whom shall I fear?" (Psalm 27:1 NKJV).

David says we pass "through" the valley. God won't leave us in the valley! The shepherd leads the sheep to the mountain peaks by way of the valleys for three reasons: (1) the valley is the easiest grade, (2) it is well-watered, and (3) it has the best forage along the route. The valley is a dangerous place for the sheep, subject to the attacks of predators, mudslides, thunderstorms, heavy rains, and falling rocks. Yet, the abiding presence of the shepherd keeps the sheep calm and assured, fearing no evil, danger, or harm.

The key to overcoming fear is to practice the presence of the Lord: "For You are with me." Whatever you are afraid of today, face it with faith and declare, "Lord, I will fear no evil, danger, or harm because You are with me and You will never leave me nor forsake me!"

Prayer for the Day: *Lord, You know the fears I face. You also know that sometimes they get the best of me. When that fear begins to overwhelm me, may I see You as my great Shepherd leading me through the situation, covered with Your power and filled with Your peace.*

Day 259

WHAT IF?

Mark Twain described *anxiety* this way: "I've suffered through a great many catastrophes in my life, most of which have never happened." One of the greatest emotional battles we fight is anxiety. Some psychologists believe anxiety lies at the root of all our psychological struggles. Anxiety is a feeling of blind, apprehensive fear. We fear what might happen in the future. We imagine the worst possible thing that might happen to us.

Anxiety is a battle of the mind. We worry about things that haven't actually happened but what we imagine might happen. Mentally, we don't focus on living in the present and suffer from a "racing mind." Physically, our heart races, our blood pressure goes up, and we have difficulty sleeping. Socially, we are on edge and snap at others. Emotionally, we feel depressed and have a negative outlook. Spiritually, we feel detached from God and wonder if He cares about us.

Anxiety haunts us with "What if?" What if my health fails? What if I don't get the job? What if I fail the exam? What if I miss the opportunity? What if my finances fail? What if my marriage gets in trouble? The only answer to anxiety is assurance in God that says, "I know." Answer every "what if" with "I know." The Apostle Paul said, "I know whom I have believed and am persuaded that He [God] is able to keep what I have committed to Him until that Day" (2 Timothy 1:12 NKJV).

It is when we focus on what we know, not on what we don't know, that we conquer anxiety. I read about a psychiatrist who treated a pastor for anxiety. He asked the pastor, "Do you have faith in God?"

"Certainly," he said, "I'm a minister."

The psychiatrist replied, "Well, use your faith."

I saw a sign that read: "Fear knocked at the door. Faith answered. There was no one there!"

Prayer for the Day: *Lord, every time I feel like I have a handle on my anxiety, it seems to creep in, undermining my faith in You. Give me the strength to stand up to it and say, "I know God and believe He is bigger than my fears. He loves me and will care for me."*

Day 260

CONVENIENT

I believe in doing things *now*! Especially when it's something important. The most important thing in your life is your relationship with God. The quality of your spiritual life will determine the quality of everything else in your life.

When the Lord speaks to you about something or directs you in some way, respond by taking action now. We learn this lesson from an experience of the Apostle Paul. He had to testify before a Roman governor, Felix, about the message of Christ he was proclaiming. "As Paul talked about righteousness, self-control and the judgment to come, Felix was afraid and said, 'That's enough for now! You may leave. When I find it convenient, I will send for you'" (Acts 24:25).

Felix had a golden opportunity to listen to the message of God and deal with spiritual matters. Paul spoke about how he could become righteous through faith in Christ, how we could live an overcoming life, and how we could face death with confidence and not face judgment because of the grace of God. That was the most important message Felix had ever heard or would ever hear. But he trivialized the urgency of the moment. He needed to make a commitment to Jesus right then, but he chose the convenient over the important.

God doesn't work in our time frame when things are convenient. When He speaks and moves and reveals Himself to us, let's listen, believe, and act. "Today, if you hear [God's] voice, do not harden your hearts" (Hebrews 3:7-8). Don't settle for what is convenient or put off important things by procrastinating; do it now!

Prayer for the Day: *Lord, please forgive me for procrastinating when You have given me a task to do, for putting it off until it is convenient for me. Help me to listen and look for Your opportunities, that I may open the door and walk in as You direct.*

Day 261

GO ON!

A group of tourists were visiting an old town. They asked a local resident, "Were any great people born in this town?"

"No," the man replied. "Only babies."

There are no instant heroes, champions, or leaders. Growing up takes time and experience. So, we are challenged in our faith to "[leave] the elementary teachings about Christ and [go on] to maturity, not laying again the foundation" (Hebrews 6:1).

I like the punch of that phrase "go on." I'm always on the go. I don't like sitting around doing nothing. That is a good place to be in your life—on the go.

It is important spiritually to be on the go. When we stop moving, we get stagnant. If we are going to continue to grow and reach our potential, we have to move beyond elementary teachings. Our spiritual foundation of the basic teachings of Christ are vital, but we have to build on that foundation.

If we go on and build on the right foundation of our faith in Jesus, we reach "maturity"—our full potential. The only way to avoid mediocrity, living beneath our privileges, and falling short of our potential is to "go on."

If you are stuck today in your personal life, your family, your career, or your spiritual life, make a decision now to leave the place where you are stuck and go on!

Prayer for the Day: *Lord, I've been stuck in this one place for a while now. I guess I've become too comfortable here. I feel the nudging of Your Spirit moving me to go on time! Help me to leave my place of comfort, allowing You to grow me in Your grace and knowledge.*

Day 262

LET NOTHING MOVE YOU

We get knocked off course so easily. The least problem, stress, or conflict can make us want to give up on our dreams, commitments, and relationships. We give in to discouragement and give up fighting for the things that matter most.

What happened to staying power? The ability to hang in there, fight through the conflict, rise above the stress, overlook the injustice, push through the pain, forgive the grievances, and press on until we achieve victory.

When the winds of opposition, disappointment, and frustration threaten to blow you over and uproot you, remember the Lord's challenge: "Let nothing move you" (1 Corinthians 15:58). Lean on God's power and make up your mind to let nothing move you.

Don't let your emotions move you. Your faith is more important than your feelings. Feelings come and go, but true faith is rooted in the facts of God's Word, and His Word never changes.

Don't let other people move you. Be strong in your convictions, principles, and values in spite of what the world around you says. Before you became a child of God, you were lost, but now you're found. The world is lost, so don't listen to its foolish, misguided advice. Jesus said, "If the blind lead the blind, both will fall into a pit" (Matthew 15:14). You have the light of the Lord in your heart, so don't let the darkness of the world move you away from the light within you.

Don't let circumstances move you. Life is hard for all of us at times. God is good to us even when life hurts. Don't lash out at God; lean on Him. Whatever you face today, let nothing move you.

Prayer for the Day: *Lord, You are my rock. I'm holding on to You so I can't be moved. Life is hard and it's easy to give up, but I won't be moved!*

Day 263

RAINY DAYS

One morning we woke up to a torrential downpour of rain. The pounding of the rain on the roof must have sounded the same when it rained on Noah's ark. We were even surrounded by animals like Noah's family—by two miniature dachshunds!

While we usually dread a rainy day, if the weather has been hot and dry, rain brings much-needed refreshment. It cools things down, washes away pollen, and causes the grass and flowers to grow. So, I say, welcome the rain.

Just as God sends physical rain, He also sends spiritual rain. If you are going through a dry time spiritually, ask God to fulfill His promise in your life today: "I will pour water on the thirsty land, and streams on the dry ground; I will pour out my Spirit on your offspring, and my blessing on your descendants" (Isaiah 44:3).

The key to receiving the outpouring of the rain of the Holy Spirit on your heart and home is to be thirsty. God says, "I will pour water on the thirsty land." Spiritual complacency is what turns our souls into a spiritual desert. But the rain of the Holy Spirit can end the spiritual drought you have been experiencing so you can start growing and flourishing again.

Jesus said, "Blessed are those who hunger and thirst for righteousness, for they will be filled" (Matthew 5:6). Open your heart today and ask the Lord to pour the rain of His Spirit on your heart and your home, and be refreshed in your faith and renewed in your joy.

Prayer for the Day: *Lord, at times I feel like I'm walking in a desert. I am thirsty for You to pour out Your Spirit on me so I can continue to grow and be refreshed with the joy of our relationship. End this drought and water my soul. I praise and thank You!*

Day 264

DON'T GRAB A DOG BY ITS EARS!

I love my two miniature dachshunds, Mikey and Beau. They are incredible pets. They are playful, but aggressive. In fact, they are the most aggressive of all breeds. They can't stand for you to grab them by their big, fluffy ears. You can't control or direct a dog by pulling on its ears. If you try it, you may get bit.

Proverbs 26:17 tells us to learn a valuable lesson from our dogs: "Like one who grabs a stray dog by the ears is someone who rushes into a quarrel not their own." Social media tempts us all to get involved in disputes and arguments that are not ours. We are tempted to get drawn in and offer our advice to everybody about everything.

We overhear friends, family, or coworkers in a disagreement and feel the need to get in the middle of it and straighten things out. If you play the role of a peacemaker in a quarrel that is not yours, you may get bit in the process. People have a way of turning on you if you get involved when they didn't ask for your help.

It is very difficult to learn to mind our own business, and let other people have their space and work out their own issues. But that is the best thing we can do for healthy relationships. If people ask us for our help, then it's OK to try to help them resolve their issues. If they don't ask, don't get involved.

So, the next time you feel like playing the mediator, fixer, or peacemaker and get involved in other people's business, remember the wisdom of God's Word—don't grab a dog by its ears!

Prayer for the Day: Lord, I have gotten in the middle of disputes that were never resolved because I tried to help when they didn't want my help. Thank You for this proverb. It has given me a timely reminder.

Day 265

KEEP DOWN THE DRAMA

Nothing ruins the day faster than a lot of drama at home, at work, or with friends. Our lives often resemble the immature behavior of the people on a TV reality show. Drama keeps us stirred up internally, and it makes us avoid the people who cause it (and sometimes we're the ones causing it).

So, here is some sound advice to "whoever would love life and see good days. . . . They must seek peace and pursue it" (1 Peter 3:10-11). What a great goal for all of us to adopt! When the drama starts, we need to say to ourselves, "Seek peace and pursue it."

Peace doesn't happen automatically. We must be intentional, and work at creating it and maintaining it. We must "pursue it," which means to go after it aggressively and passionately.

Do you want to live a life you love and see good days? If so, make every effort to seek peace and pursue it in all your relationships and endeavors. If you sow seeds of peace, you will reap the harvest of a happy and healthy life.

Prayer for the Day: *Lord, I need less drama in my life. I'm going to make it my goal to seek peace so I have a life filled with love and good days.*

Day 266

ARM YOURSELF

We live in a day of heightened security. Our nation is on high alert to an enemy of attack from terrorists and anarchists. Nuclear proliferation of weapons threatens global security.

We also face spiritual enemies. There is a spiritual war going on for our faith, our families, and our souls. We need to arm ourselves for spiritual battle by putting on a Christlike attitude: "Since Christ suffered in his body, arm yourselves also with the same attitude" (1 Peter 4:1).

Living with the attitude of Christ is a spiritual weapon to defeat temptation, fear, and doubt. Jesus had a victorious attitude, even when He faced suffering on the cross: "For the joy set before him he endured the cross" (Hebrews 12:2).

Our attitude determines whether we win or lose life's battles. That means we win our battles first internally before we win them externally. In fact, life around us is never better than the attitude within us.

A bad attitude equals a bad life. A defeated attitude equals a defeated life. But a godly, joyful, and hopeful attitude equals a victorious life! Viktor Frankl, survivor of the Nazi holocaust and death camps, said, "The last of all human freedoms is the freedom to choose one's attitude in any given set of circumstances."

You can't choose your circumstances, but you can choose your attitude, and that will make all the difference. So today arm yourself with the attitude of Christ Jesus!

Prayer for the Day: *Lord, I realize my attitude has been bad lately. Your Word has made me really think about how my bad attitude affects the rest of my life. Today I am myself with Your power to defeat this harmful attitude and choose to be more positive.*

Day 267

MORNING HAS BROKEN

One morning I was greeted by the sun breaking over the horizon during an early walk. I thought of this hymn about God's creation:

Morning has broken like the first morning
Blackbird has spoken like the first bird.
Praise for the singing, praise for the morning,
God's re-creation of the new day.

The prophet Zephaniah brought a word of encouragement to the people of Jerusalem in troubled times: "The Lord within her is righteous; he does no wrong. Morning by morning he dispenses his justice, and every new day he does not fail, yet the unrighteous know no shame" (Zephaniah 3:5).

We see injustice every day in our world, but we can trust our God to act justly on our behalf. If we are serving Him, He will defend our cause. Instead of letting the negative things in our world get us down today, we should let the morning remind us of God's constant faithfulness.

God never fails to shine the light of His blessing, grace, and favor on us. A new day means new opportunities, challenges, and promises. Things don't have to stay the way they were yesterday. Yesterday is over; let's put it behind us. It's a new day!

Just as the morning is constant every day to rise and bring us a new day, the Lord is constant to rise and shine His light upon us, giving us a new day. Let's live it with joy!

Prayer for the Day: *Lord, I praise You for this new day of blessing and opportunity. Thank You that yesterday is in the past and I can move forward in Your grace today!*

Day 268

BLINDED BY THE LIGHT

Jesus said of Himself, "I am the light of the world" (John 8:12). When His light shines in our heart, it dispels the darkness of deception, fear, and guilt. Everything is visible in the light.

Light not only gives us spiritual vision, it also blinds us to things that used to gain and hold our attention. That is the paradox of light. It makes us see and blinds us at the same time! Have you ever walked out of your house on a bright, sunny day and the light blinded you until your eyes adjusted to the light or put your sunglasses on? Well, the same is true spiritually.

One hymn writer said:
Turn your eyes upon Jesus
Look full in His wonderful face
And the things of earth will grow strangely dim
In the light of His glory and grace.

That is what happened to Paul when the risen Lord appeared to him in a vision on the Damascus road. Paul was going there to persecute

Christians until Jesus appeared to him. Paul later recounted: "Suddenly a bright light from heaven flashed around me. . . . My companions saw the light, but they did not understand the voice of him who was speaking to me. 'What shall I do, Lord?' I asked. . . . My companions led me by the hand into Damascus, because the brilliance of the light had blinded me" (Acts 22:6, 9-11).

The light of Christ will blind us to the things of this world that used to attract us. His light will blind us toward others so we hold no malice, prejudice, or bigotry, and we see all people as equal. His light blinds us to self-centeredness and gets our eyes on the needs of others.

May we be blinded by His light today so we can focus on the things God wants us to see.

Prayer for the Day: *Lord, I always thought of light as a way You reveal truth to us. Yes, it does that, but it also blinds us to what can hurt us. May I walk in Your blinding light protected from harm and led down the right path of grace and knowledge.*

Day 269
THE POSSIBILITY OF CHANGE

Is there anything about yourself or your life that seems impossible to solve? You must believe change is possible before it actually comes. Faith comes before action. Jesus said, "Everything is possible for one who believes" (Mark 9:23).

Change can be hard for us because the fear of the unknown is greater than the discomfort of the known. We get used to the way we are and the way things are going in our lives. We settle for our sorrow. We manage our misery. We get through the grind. We don't like it, but we are used to it. The uncertainty of doing something new and making changes keeps us from taking the risk and stepping out in faith.

Jesus spoke the words "Everything is possible" to a man whose son's situation seemed hopelessly controlled by an evil spirit. The man responded to Jesus' words by saying, "I do believe; help me overcome my unbelief!" (Mark 9:24).

That was enough. The father's confession of faith, as little as it was, resulted in Jesus immediately delivering the boy into a new life.

Push back the fear of the unknown and take a step of faith today. Confess to the Lord, "I do believe; help me overcome my unbelief."

Prayer for the Day: *Lord, there is something in my life that needs to change, but it is impossible without Your help. Increase my faith, and bring about change, I pray.*

Day 270

IF YOU KNEW

We live in the knowledge explosion with new technology and scientific advancements occurring at a rapid pace. We emphasize education and learning new skills as the key to success and promotion.

The quality of our lives is often dictated by our level of knowledge. The Bible says, "Get wisdom. Though it cost all you have, get understanding" (Proverbs 4:7). The greatest knowledge is of God and, in particular, knowing who Jesus is. Once you discover who Jesus really is, you will believe in Him as your Savior and commit your life to Him as your Lord.

Jesus met a woman by a public well in Samaria and asked her for a drink of water. She was shocked that He was asking her. He replied, "If you knew the gift of God and who it is that asks you for a drink, you would have asked him and he would have given you living water" (John 4:10). Look at His words—"If you knew."

Once you know who Jesus really is—the Son of God and the Savior of the world—you will ask Him for "living water," which means eternal life, and He will give it to you freely. Ask Him today for what you need, and you will be amazed at the blessings He pours out on your life!

Prayer for the Day: *Lord, I have heard it said that I don't have because I don't ask. I know You, Lord—My Savior, Teacher, and Healer. I know You to be loving, generous, and forgiving. Today, I ask You to look into my heart and grant me its desires so I can serve You better.*

Day 271

SECRET STRENGTH

In April 1963, the nuclear submarine *Thresher* vanished about two hundred miles off the coast of New England. It had been undergoing deep submergence tests when radio contact was lost. Frantic attempts to contact the crew failed. The submarine had gone deeper than it was pressurized to go. In one terrifying moment, the pressure on the outside became greater than the pressure on the inside, and 129 American sailors were lost.

How can we handle the pressures of life—the pressures of marriage stress, family problems, job loss, financial difficulty, illness, divorce, and emotional issues? The only way to survive is when our inner strength is greater than our outer stress. When the power inside you is greater than the pressure around you, you can be victorious!

When the psalmist David was on the run as a fugitive, he hit an emotional low point. The men who had pledged their support turned on him. The town of Ziklag had been attacked, and the women and children had been kidnapped. When David's men returned from battle and found the town empty, they were bitter toward David and even talked about killing him. David himself became *distressed*—that means stress had turned to complete hopelessness. But then something extraordinary happened to David—he "found strength in the Lord his God" (1 Samuel 30:6).

Get alone with the Lord today, regardless of the pressure you are going through, and you too will find strength in the Lord your God. Strength to get up and go on—strength to get through your problems to victory!

Prayer for the Day: *Lord, You know the pressure and stress I'm under. Like King David, I need to find my inner strength in You so my outer strength is capable of withstanding whatever the world sends my way. Please strengthen me with Your supernatural power for every situation of life.*

Day 272

ABOVE ALL

When John the Baptist started to promote Jesus to others, he said, "The one who comes from above is above all" (John 3:31). John clearly told people he was not the Messiah, but "the voice of one calling in the wilderness, 'Make straight the way for the Lord'" (1:23). John's ministry was to introduce Jesus to the world!

Since Jesus is from Heaven, He is above all. He is above all religions, all great world leaders, and all spiritual leaders. Jesus is greater than all of them who have ever lived and ever will live because He is from above.

Everyone else is from the earth. John explained this: "The one who is from the earth [all of us] belongs to the earth, and speaks as one from the earth" (John 3:31). All religious leaders, prophets, and teachers are just like you and me—they are from the earth. They are mere humans, and we speak only as human beings. I have read the writings and sayings of countless historical religious figures, and all their words lack something of eternal value. They speak as one from the earth.

But, when I read the words of Jesus, His words are spirit and life because He is from above—He is the divine Son of God who speaks the very words of God. He is "above all." I am not saying all spiritual and philosophical teachings have no value. God has given men and women great truths throughout history that have made a positive impact on our lives. But the words of Jesus are above all other words ever spoken or written. He is from above; therefore, He is above all.

Measure everything you hear or read by the absolute standard of the truth of the words of Jesus, for they are the words of God; and you will "know the truth, and the truth will set you free" (John 8:32). Live by His words, and you can live above all fear, stress, and discouragement.

Prayer for the Day: *Lord, there are some really good Christian authors out there, producing good material for Your people. But I want to thank You for the Holy Scriptures. The Bible brings truth and balance to man's words because You are above all writers. Jesus, You are God, the author, and finisher of my faith!*

Day 273

MENTAL FLOSS

I saw a phrase that caught my attention the other day: *mental floss*. My dentist says flossing my teeth and gums is even more important to dental health than brushing my teeth! Brushing is easy; flossing is a hassle.

Mental health requires flossing. The Word of God tells us: "Be clear-minded and self-controlled so that you can pray" (see 1 Peter 4:7). Psychotic illnesses are physical diseases and ailments that are caused by mental and emotional distress. Mental health determines physical health.

So, when God says "be clear-minded," He means we need to mental-floss *spiritually*. King David prayed, "When I kept silent [not admitting sins], my bones wasted away through my groaning all day long. . . . Then I acknowledged my sin to you and did not cover up my iniquity. . . . And you forgave the guilt of my sin" (Psalm 32:3, 5). Forgiveness is God's mental floss for our souls.

We need to mental-floss *emotionally*. "Get rid of all bitterness, rage and anger, brawling and slander, along with every form of malice" (Ephesians 4:31). That's some serious stuff we need to release. Toxic emotions can destroy us if we don't mental-floss, so let's get rid of that stuff.

We need to mental-floss *personally*. Stop thinking and speaking negatively about yourself. You only weaken yourself and create a spirit of fear and timidity that keeps you from reaching your potential. Remember, "God has not given us a spirit of fear but of power and of love and of [self-discipline]" (2 Timothy 1:7 NKJV).

Remember to mental-floss every morning; then you can face the day with confidence and joy!

Prayer for the Day: *Lord, every morning when I look into the mirror, may I be reminded to confess my faults to You so nothing hinders my prayers or my relationship with You. Remind me to mentally floss, ridding myself of any sin that I am unaware of.*

Day 274

STILL CONFIDENT

When we face difficulties in life, we often lose our confidence. We give way to fear, worry, and depression. Instead of expecting the best in life, we imagine the worst. How do we keep our confidence when life comes crashing in on us?

The psalmist David shares how he kept his confidence in the face of difficult times. David's son Absalom was rebellious and wanted to overthrow his father's kingdom. He organized his own army and attacked the city of Jerusalem. While David himself did not fight in the battle, Joab led Israel's army to a crushing defeat of Absalom's rebel forces with 20,000 soldiers killed in battle. Worst of all, Absalom was killed.

When the news of Absalom's death reached David, he fell into deep depression. Finally, he found his way out when he worshiped the Lord. He wrote "I remain confident of this: I will see the goodness of the Lord in the land of the living" (Psalm 27:13).

The phrase "the land of the living" shows we should focus on the gift of life and of living life to its fullest, regardless of what difficulties we may face. Life may have brought you hardship, but you can still be confident that you will see the goodness of the Lord. God is good, even though the circumstances of life may be bad. Bad times pass, but God's goodness remains. So, put aside your fears and depression today. Go out and face the day and say, "I am still confident!"

Prayer for the Day: *Lord, life has been difficult lately. This has definitely brought me sadness, depression, and even fear. But I am reminded in Your Word that this will pass because life as we know it is temporary. I have confidence in Your love and goodness for me and those I love.*

Day 275

GO TO THE DESERT

Soren Kierkegaard said: "If I were a physician and I were allowed to prescribe one remedy for all the ills of the world, I would prescribe silence. For even if the Word of God were proclaimed in the modern world, how could one hear it with so much noise? Therefore, create silence!"

There is no place in the world more silent than a desert. Barbie and I enjoyed our first visit to the Sinai Desert, where God led Israel in preparation for the Promised Land. Early in the morning our group headed out to climb Mount Sinai. I will always remember the sacred solitude of the early morning air and watching the sun rise on the place where Moses received the law of God and saw the glory of God.

Think of this powerful truth: "Jesus was led by the Spirit into the wilderness [desert]" (Matthew 4:1). Two things happen in the desert: We see God and we see ourselves. It is a place of God-awareness and self-awareness, of revelation and introspection. The desert represents the spiritual place we can go in our hearts and minds called "solitude." The place where we silence the noise and demands of everyday life and experience God. Richard Foster teaches solitude as one of the great principles of spiritual life in his classic book, *The Celebration of Discipline*.

We don't naturally prefer the desert. We prefer the workplace, the shopping mall, or social media where we can keep busy, but we desperately need the desert.

The only way to balance the demands, noise, and stress of every day is to follow Jesus into the desert. "Jesus often withdrew to solitary places where He prayed" (see Mark 1:35). You have to withdraw in order to be renewed. Get alone with God today in the desert and "renew your strength like the eagle's" (see Psalm 103:5).

Prayer for the Day: *Lord, silence can be a difficult thing for those of us who are used to noise. However, You don't yell but silently nudge us by Your Spirit when the world closes in and I need to hear You speak. I will find a place of solitude, read Your Word, pray, and listen in the silence for You to speak.*

Day 276

KING BY FORCE

The only miracle of Jesus recorded in all four Gospels (Matthew, Mark, Luke, and John) is the day He fed five thousand people with only five loaves and two fish! When the miracle was over, the people began to say, "This is the Prophet who is to come into the world" (John 6:14).

The people were right in their observation. Jesus is the Prophet of whom Moses predicted, the Messiah of God: "The Lord your God will raise up for you a prophet like me from among [your brothers]. You must listen to him" (Deuteronomy 18:15).

However, their enthusiasm got the best of them. "Jesus, knowing that they intended to come and make him king by force, withdrew again to a mountain by himself" (John 6:15). Jesus always lived with a clear sense of His divine purpose. He wouldn't let anyone get Him off track by either tempting Him to sin or by exalting Him as an earthly king.

You will meet people in life who try to pull you down to the lowest level. You will also meet people who will try to lift you up to a place that is contrary to God's will for you. They will try to make you what they want you to be by force.

Resist the pressure of others by withdrawing to a place of prayer to get direction from the Lord. Success and promotion don't come by force, but by the favor of God in His perfect time so we can do His perfect will. It is not by force that we get ahead in life, it is by faith! Trust Him more and you won't have to try so hard.

Prayer for the Day: *Lord, there are so many voices in my life. Well-meaning Christians think they know what is best for me. I have decided to resist their advice and trust in You to lead me and open the doors You want me to enter . . . when You want me enter them.*

Day 277

CURE FOR SKEPTICS

One day a Roman official approached Jesus in desperation. His son was at home, sick to the point of death. So, he begged Jesus to come and heal his son.

Jesus then addressed the crowd that was around Him because they were very skeptical of Him. He said of them, "Unless you people see signs and wonders . . . you will never believe" (John 4:48).

That sounds like a lot of people today. Skeptical and always demanding some miraculous evidence of God, even though we live in a world surrounded by astounding miracles.

The man again pleaded with Jesus, "Sir, come down before my child dies" (John 4:49). Once a person reaches the end of themselves, they call on God to help them just like this man did. His need of God was now greater than his skepticism of Jesus.

Jesus is so merciful to us. He told the desperate father, "Go . . . your son will live." What a relief those words must have been to him. "The man took Jesus at his word and departed" (John 4:50).

That is the cure for skepticism—take Jesus at His word. Don't question or disagree with Him. Believe Him, obey Him, and take Him at His word!

Prayer for the Day: Lord, I have seen so many skeptics and even Christians who constantly dissect Your Word. They want to believe, but they want proof. I always tell them the same thing—read the New Testament first, then the Old Testament, and open Your heart and ask God to reveal Himself to You. You know, Lord, it works!

Day 278

SNATCHED

Barbie and I watched the thriller movie *Kidnap*, in which Hallie Berry plays the part of a single mother whose only son is snatched in a public park when she is on the phone and he is out of sight. She panics, running through the park looking for him and screaming his name. Other people join in with her. As desperation takes over and the stark realization that her son is gone, she catches a glimpse of a rough-looking woman forcing her son into a car.

She runs to the car screaming, "Give me my son," grabbing hold of the car as it speeds off. She finally has to let go, and takes a hard fall. Getting up, she jumps in her minivan and pursues the car. The long, terrifying chase results in one accident after another, finally ending with her finding the house of a kidnap ring. She saves her son and several other kids who had been snatched.

As a parent, I share her fighting spirit to save her son no matter the cost. She reminded me of God's love for us and Jesus' promise and power to keep us: "My sheep listen to my voice; I know them, and they follow me. I give them eternal life, and . . . no one will snatch them out of my hand" (John 10:27-28).

What a secure place to be when you know that no matter what happens in the course of your life, no one or nothing can snatch you out of the Lord's hand!

Prayer for the Day: *Lord, thank You for reminding me that I am Yours and You are mine. I will always hold on to You and You to me. No one can take away my security in You!*

Day 279

DON'T LEAVE HOME WITHOUT IT

We all lose things we value from time to time. Have you ever stood at the checkout in a store, looked in your wallet, and couldn't find your debit card and wondered where you left it? Or, you're running late for work one morning and can't find your car keys? Or, you can't find your smartphone that contains your whole life?

When you leave the house every day to go to work, school, church, or even shopping, don't forget your faith. American Express used to advertise their credit card with the slogan, "Don't leave home without it." The gift of faith God has given you is the greatest power you have to face the challenges and opportunities of life. "This is the victory that has overcome the world, even our faith" (1 John 5:4).

Psalm 106 chronicles the ups and downs of Israel's spiritual journey. After God brought them out of slavery in Egypt and parted the Red Sea, "they believed his promises and sang his praise. But they soon forgot what he had done and did not wait for his [counsel]. . . . They forgot the God who saved them" (Psalm 106:12-13, 21).

Take time every day to remember what God has done for you and, most of all, for what Jesus did for all of us on the cross and the Resurrection, when He delivered us from sin and death and gave us eternal life!

Prayer for the Day: *Lord, as I look back over my life, I can see You everywhere and in every situation, bad or good. Thank You for the cross, my salvation, and eternal life! You have always led me, even when I didn't realize it. I have faith in You to complete my journey.*

Day 280

SOME SAID IT THUNDERED

Everybody wants to know how to recognize God's voice when He speaks to us. God speaks to us to reassure us of His presence, reveal His will to us, and give us direction. God's voice will always build you up, not tear you down.

Even those times when God speaks to convict and correct us, He never condemns. "There is now no condemnation for those who are in Christ Jesus" (Romans 8:1). When God speaks to us to discipline us, it is always to restore us, not to ruin us; to develop us, not to destroy us.

We have to expect God to speak and anticipate His voice if we want to hear Him. We also have to get quiet and slow down. God speaks in the secret place of our souls. We are often too busy and rushing around in a house and a world filled with loud noise. Tune in through prayer, reading Scripture, and meditation to listen to God. Pray, "Speak, [Lord], for your servant is listening" (1 Samuel 3:10).

It takes faith to hear God's voice. People who doubt don't hear from God because they don't believe He speaks. Jesus was very troubled as He faced the cross. The last week of His life, He was in Jerusalem for Passover. He would die for our sins before the week was over. God spoke to Him to reassure Him!

Jesus said to the crowd around Him, "'Now my soul is troubled. . . . Father, glorify your name!' Then a voice came from heaven, 'I have glorified it, and will glorify it again.' The crowd that was there and heard it said it had thundered" (John 12:27-29).

There is more going on in this noisy world than just thunder. God wants to speak to you. Listen carefully and you will hear His voice.

Prayer for the Day: *Lord, I believe in You. I am expecting You to speak into my life through Your Word and in my heart through the Holy Spirit. Speak, Lord; I am listening.*

Day 281
THE 10% MYTH

How many times have you heard that we only use 10 percent of our brains? We have all grown up hearing that story. It's a myth! The truth is, we use 100 percent of the brain all the time!

"The brain is always working at full capacity," said Marcus Raichle, M.D., "whether you are engaged in a challenging task or simply daydreaming the afternoon away." No one knows who started the myth. Some think it dates back to a statement by William James (1842-1910), the father of American psychology, in an essay about people only using a small part of their abilities ("The 10% Myth," *Brain Power*, 2017).

Now that we know the truth, we are confronted with a greater challenge—how are we using our brains? Since they are working all the time, we need to use our brains in ways that are positive, powerful, and productive. Think thoughts that are positive and based on the promises of God to overcome negative feelings.

Think thoughts that are empowering—helping you reach your God-given potential and boosting your self-worth as a child of God. Think thoughts that help you maximize your abilities so you produce, create, and accomplish great things with your life.

Your brain is the key to living a life of fulfillment, purpose, and joy. "Since, then, you have been raised with Christ, set your hearts on things above, where Christ is, seated at the right hand of God. Set your minds on things above, not on earthly things" (Colossians 3:1-2).

Prayer for the Day: *Lord, You are amazing! My brain, which You created, is incredible, not to mention the rest of my body. Because my brain is the key to life, I will care for it as I care for the rest of my body. I will read Your Word, think and pray with a positive attitude, and use my brain to reason well and create things that honor You.*

Day 282
SIGNS AND SYMBOLS

Our lives are filled with signs and symbols—from road signs, to designer clothing, to fine jewelry. Many people ask to see a sign from God so they will believe in Him.

One of the signs of God is His people. Every one of us who believes in God and who follows Jesus as Lord is a sign and a symbol of His presence and power in the world. Isaiah the prophet said, "Here I am, and the children the Lord has given me. We are signs and symbols in Israel from the Lord Almighty" (Isaiah 8:18).

God has placed you as a sign and a symbol in your family, friends, and community. You are a sign from God where you work, play, and worship. A *sign* is an object, quality, or event whose presence or occurrence indicates the probable presence or occurrence of something else. A kiss, for example, is a sign of affection. A gift is a sign of friendship. A compliment is a sign of affirmation. In the same way, we are signs to others that God is real!

A *symbol* is a mark or character that represents something else. A lion is a symbol of courage. An eagle is a symbol of power. A crucifix is a symbol of love. You, too, are a symbol to others of God's love and grace.

You are not invisible to others. You are God's sign and symbol to others that He is real. So, let's live today in a way that represents Him well.

Prayer for the Day: *Lord, I never really thought about me being a sign and symbol to others, but it's so true. May I always be a sign for others to follow and a symbol of Your great love for all people. May I wear it on my forehead for all to see so that they look to You as Lord and Savior.*

Day 283
JILTING JEALOUSY

Joseph's brothers sold him into captivity because they were jealous of him (Genesis 37:4). King Saul tried to kill David because he was consumed with jealousy (1 Samuel 18:8-11). The older brother of the Prodigal Son was so jealous of his younger brother that he refused to share in his restoration (Luke 15:28).

You can defeat jealousy by being content with your lot in life. God has placed you where you are. Paul wrote, "I have learned to be content whatever the circumstances.... I have learned the secret of being content in any and every situation.... I can do all things through him who gives me strength" (Philippians 4:11-13).

You defeat jealousy by rejoicing over the success of others. "Rejoice with those who rejoice" (Romans 12:15).

William Law said, "If someone is leaving you behind and you are becoming jealous and embittered, keep praying that he may have success in the very matter where he is awakening your envy; and whether he is helped or not, one thing is sure, that your own soul will be cleansed and enabled."

Prayer for the Day: *Lord, please forgive me when I have allowed jealousy to entrap me. Teach me to rejoice with others in their successes and to find personal contentment as I follow You.*

Day 284

HIDDEN

One day Jesus healed a young boy of convulsions, and the people were amazed at the greatness of God. "While everyone was marveling at all that Jesus did, he said to his disciples: 'Listen carefully to what I am about to tell you: The Son of Man is going to be delivered into the hands of men.' But they did not understand what this meant. It was hidden from them, so that they did not grasp it, and they were afraid to ask him about it" (Luke 9:43-45).

Jesus' disciples didn't understand how He could go from being the most popular person alive to being rejected and then dying on a cross. They didn't understand how the seasons of life can change. They certainly didn't understand how God could redeem the world from sin by the cross.

We also struggle with the mysteries of life. Living by faith accepts that some things are hidden from us like they were hidden from Jesus' disciples. We discover the answers to life's mysteries as we live by faith and continue on in our journey with God.

When you struggle with unanswered questions, remember: "The secret things belong to the Lord our God, but the things revealed belong to us and to our children forever, that we may follow the words of this law" (Deuteronomy 29:29).

Don't be like the disciples, who were afraid to ask Jesus what He meant by His words. Ask God in prayer to reveal things to you and ask others who are seasoned in the Christian faith. God sent the Holy Spirit to "teach you all things" and to "guide you into all the truth" (John 14:26; 16:13).

The Lord hides things from us for two reasons: We cannot receive the truth, or it isn't the right season for us to know. Trust God and seek Him through prayer and reading the Scriptures, and the Holy Spirit will reveal to you what you need to know in every situation you face.

Prayer for the Day: Lord, I am aware that You are omniscient—You know all things. Sometimes I struggle not knowing the answers to my questions. But I trust You to reveal to me these answers when I'm ready to hear them in just the right season of my life. Until then, I will keep my eyes focused on You, the finisher of my faith!

Day 285

DAILY LIFE

We often fret over the past and worry about the future. We regret what has happened and fear what might happen. But life is lived daily—one day at a time. If we live today well and do that every day, our daily life will take care of the past and the future. The future is nothing more than a collection of todays.

So, how should we live daily so we lead the best life possible? Listen to the counsel of the Word of God: "Make it your ambition to lead a quiet life: You should mind your own business and work with your hands . . . so that your daily life may win the respect of outsiders and so that you will not be dependent on anybody" (1 Thessalonians 4:11-12).

These two verses give three simple goals for a powerful life. *First, lead a quiet life.* That means to be at peace with God, with others, and with yourself. Jesus said, "Blessed are the peacemakers, for they will be called children of God" (Matthew 5:9). Don't stir up trouble, create drama, or complain about things. Lead a quiet life so others will follow your lead.

Second, mind your own business. That is so difficult to do in our day of social media and constant communication. We are using more words today than at any other time in history. We talk all the time in one form or another, and we have an opinion about everything. People share their business on social media to the point that nothing is private anymore. But God teaches us to mind our own business—to show discretion with what we talk about and who we talk to.

Third, work with your hands. Don't be dependent on other people, but make your own way in life and make a living for yourself so "you will not be dependent on anybody" (1 Thessalonians 4:12). Work hard and prosper. "All hard work brings a profit, but mere talk leads only to poverty" (Proverbs 14:23).

Don't fret over the past or worry about the future. Instead, focus on your daily life and you will lead your best life.

Prayer for the Day: *Lord, please help me to remember that I don't have to have an opinion about everything. Teach me to be more discreet so I may be at peace with myself and You.*

Day 286

#HATE IT

Perhaps you have seen this bumper sticker: "Hate is not a family value." Hatred—in the sense of anger, rage, and spite—is always wrong. However, there is another way the word *hate* is used when it is a value. Ecclesiastes 3:8 says there is "a time to love and a time to hate" (3:8).

Jesus made a controversial statement about a time when hate is a faith value: "If anyone comes to me and does not hate father and mother, wife and children, brothers and sisters—yes, even their own life—such a person cannot be my disciple" (Luke 14:26). Jesus made this statement to a crowd who were following Him while He was on His way to Jerusalem to die for the sins of the world.

The cost of the cross was on His mind. Jesus knew following Him as Lord would require the cost of commitment, perseverance, and sacrifice for His disciples. The word *hate* is not a "feeling" word in Aramaic, the language which Jesus spoke. It actually means to abandon or leave behind, the way a sailor abandons a sinking ship.

Jesus challenges us to leave behind the things that hinder us from following Him completely as Lord, and to put Him first in our lives. If we count the cost and pay the price of discipleship, we will reap incredible blessings. Jesus said whatever we give and give up for Him will be returned to us as a blessing that is "a good measure, pressed down, shaken together and running over" (Luke 6:38), which will be poured into our lives.

Prayer for the Day: *Lord, I know there will always be something going on in my life to try and hinder me from following You. May I always see it for what it is and leave it behind.*

Day 287

DRINK IN THE RAIN

When I was a little boy, I liked to walk on our street after a summer rain. The hot summer sun was tempered by the aftermath of the rain. The street I grew up on had curbs made of big pieces of granite. It formed a canal on the edge of the street where the rainwater flowed like a gentle stream. We would walk in that small canal barefoot in the flowing water and the drizzling rain. Every now and then we would look up and try to drink some of the rain.

That is what we need to do spiritually—drink in the rain. The rain is a symbol of the Holy Spirit in the Bible. God says, "For I will pour water on the thirsty land, and streams on the dry ground; I will pour out my Spirit on your offspring, and my blessing on your descendants" (Isaiah 44:3).

We need to ask God to send the rain of the Holy Spirit on us. When the Spirit of God moves in our life, we need to drink in the rain. That means we need to be receptive to what God is saying and desiring to do in our life. The Holy Spirit is a gift to us from God, and a gift must always be received. If we resist the work of the Holy Spirit, we will fail to receive the blessings God has for us.

Don't resist the Word of God and the work of the Holy Spirit by unbelief, stubbornness, or insensitivity. Stephen, the first martyr of the Christian faith, challenged his generation: "You always resist the Holy Spirit" (Acts 7:51).

When God sends the rain of the Holy Spirit, drink deeply. "Land that drinks in the rain often falling on it and that produces a crop useful to those for whom it is farmed receives the blessing of God" (Hebrews 6:7). The key to God's blessings is to drink in the rain of the Holy Spirit.

Prayer for the Day: *Lord, may I always look up and allow the Holy Spirit to rain down on every area of my life. May I always keep my arms lifted up with open hands to receive Your many blessings and to be thankful for Your mercy and grace!*

Day 288

GET SOME REST

The word *sabbath* is associated with rest. Research shows that many people do not get enough rest. Sleeplessness and restlessness are major contributors to high stress and poor health. Just as we need physical rest, we also need spiritual rest if we want to be healthy.

We need to learn to rest in the finished work of salvation. I think the highest level of faith a person can achieve is when they rest in God. "My soul finds rest in God [alone]; my salvation comes from him" (Psalm 62:1-2).

When Jesus died on the cross for our sins, He declared, "It is finished!" The plan of salvation and the promise of eternal life was finished. We don't work for God's love, forgiveness, or eternal life. It is finished! We need to receive the free gift of eternal life in Jesus by faith and rest in the finished work.

The Sabbath rest of *creation* pointed to the Sabbath rest of *salvation*: "There remains, then, a Sabbath-rest for the people of God; for anyone who enters God's rest also rests from their works, just as God did from his" (Hebrews 4:9-10).

Get some rest today, spiritually speaking, as you rejoice in the finished work of Jesus for your salvation.

Prayer for the Day: *Lord, sometimes it is difficult to rest. I always feel that I should be doing something. It is good to know that You encourage us to rest so we are strengthened to take on the world, but not all the time.*

Day 289

MORE GRACE

Grace is the most magnificent word in our Christian vocabulary; it means God's unconditional love and His unearned favor. *Grace* also means to give freely. It is the same word as *gift* in the Greek language.

"By grace you have been saved, through faith—and this is not from yourselves, it is the gift of God" (Ephesians 2:8). Let those words sink in—*the gift of God*. But there is more to the word *grace*. It also means the power of the Holy Spirit at work in us. God says, "My grace is sufficient for you, for my power is made perfect in [your] weakness" (2 Corinthians 12:9).

Grace and *power* are synonymous. That is why the *gifts* of the Holy Spirit are actually the *graces* of the Holy Spirit. *Grace* also teaches us: "For the grace of God has appeared that offers salvation to all people. It teaches us to say 'No' to ungodliness and worldly passions, and to live self-controlled, upright and godly lives in this present age" (Titus 2:11-12).

While we cannot get more saving grace once we receive the gift of eternal life, we can get more grace to empower us, equip us, and educate us. This is what James 4:6 means: "He gives us more grace." How can we get more grace at work in our lives? Verse 6 continues, "God opposes the proud, but [gives grace] to the humble."

Today, if you need more grace (like I do), then let's humble ourselves before the Lord in prayer, faith, and dependency, and we will receive a fresh measure of grace to live today for God's glory.

Prayer for the Day: *Lord, Your grace is so amazing in our life. Your power that enables us to help ourselves and others is awesome. Today I humble myself and say "all grace for Your glory."*

Day 290

VERBAL ARSON

Recently, a Tennessee fire captain was arrested for torching his home and then filing a bogus insurance claim. He tried to benefit from starting a fire in his own house!

The story reminds me of verbal arsonists who also burn down their homes. "The tongue also is a fire, a world of evil among the parts of the body. It corrupts the whole body, sets the whole course of one's life on fire, and is itself set on fire by hell" (James 3:6). The Apostle James tells it like it is! What a caution to verbal arsonists who naively believe they can reach their goals in life by burning down their own house and relationships with destructive speech!

We need to remember words are like fire—very powerful and destructive. When we use words of anger, manipulation, threats, abuse, name-calling, and profanity, we are corrupting ourselves and setting the whole course of our lives on fire. We will end up burning everyone and everything around us down to the ground if we don't stop setting fires in our marriages, our families, the workplace, the church, and the nation.

Words are a wonderful gift from God, and the power of speech is a great privilege. Let us use our words like Jesus did: "All spoke well of him and were amazed at the gracious words that came from his lips" (Luke 4:22).

Prayer for the Day: *Lord, may I always remember to think before I speak. "May these words of my mouth and this meditation of my heart be pleasing in your sight, Lord, my Rock and my Redeemer" (Psalm 19:14).*

Day 291

STRIKE THE ROCK

As a counselor, I understand the value of what we call *catharsis*—the cleansing of the mind and soul. When we go to see a counselor, we are able to bear our souls and express our deepest hurts, fears, and feelings. We feel better when we do. More importantly, we can go to God and confess our sins and be cleansed!

In the Old Testament, God told Moses: "Go out in front of the people. Take with you some of the elders of Israel and take in your hand the staff with which you struck the Nile, and go. I will stand there before you by the rock at Horeb. Strike the rock, and water will come out of it for the people to drink" (Exodus 17:5-6). This event pointed to Jesus' death on the cross: "They all ate the same spiritual food and drank the same spiritual drink; for they drank from the spiritual rock that accompanied them, and that rock was Christ" (1 Corinthians 10:3-4).

Two thousand years ago, Jesus carried the cross to Calvary. God was present as He was on the day Moses struck the rock. The soldiers had beaten Christ—they struck "the spiritual rock." Jesus then died for the sins of the world. He prayed from the cross, "Father, forgive them; for they know not what they do" (Luke 23:34 KJV). He shouted in victory, "It is finished!" (John 19:30). He prayed His final prayer, "Father, into your hands I commit my spirit" (Luke 23:46). Then He gave up His spirit and died.

After six hours of Jesus hanging on the cross, a Roman soldier thrust a spear into His side, "bringing a sudden flow of blood and water" (John 19:34). Blood and water cleanse the body internally but, symbolically, represent the life of Jesus being given for the cleansing of our sins. The soldier struck "the rock" at Calvary for the final time.

"On that day a fountain will be opened . . . to cleanse them from sin and impurity" (Zechariah 13:1).

So, "If we confess our sins, he [God] is faithful and just and will forgive us our sins and purify us from all unrighteousness" (1 John 1:9).

Prayer for the Day: *Lord, I praise You every day for the sacrifice of Yourself on Calvary's cross for me and for all who will believe in You. I thank You for the cleansing power of Your grace and for the salvation of my soul.*

Day 292
TAKE POSSESSION OF IT

One of the greatest people in Biblical history is Abraham. He is called the friend of God in the Bible because of his great faith and close relationship with the Lord. When God gave him a promise that he would be the father of a great nation (which seemed preposterous and impossible), he "believed the Lord, and he credited it to him as righteousness" (Genesis 15:6). Today, the nation of Israel still thrives as a reminder that God keeps His promise.

Abraham, who lived about 2000 BC, left his home and family and traveled to Canaan, an undeveloped and unsettled territory. He, his family, and his workers traveled from place to place as shepherds. God told him not only would his children become a great nation, but God would give him and his descendants that land—which is exactly where the nation of Israel exists today! So, the land of Israel and the Jewish people are a living testimony to all of us that God keeps His word.

Now, to my point. When God told him all of this in a vision that the land would be his permanent home, He gave him a charge: "I am the Lord, who brought you out of Ur of the Chaldeans to give you this land to take possession of it" (Genesis 15:7). What a word for us today—God gives us the land, but we must take possession of it.

Regardless of what promise God gives you, it will only be fulfilled if you take possession of it. Don't be passive; take possession of it! There are a lot of unpossessed promises. So, go out and live today with confidence. Whatever you desire in life that God has promised you in His Word, take possession of it.

Prayer for the Day: *Lord, I am a child of God, the seed of Abraham, and an engrafted Jew. Because of my heritage and relationship with You, I take possession of all You have given me in Christ according to Your Word and personal promises.*

Day 293

USE IT OR LOSE IT

It is more than a cliché; it is a fact of life. We need to use what God has given us or we will lose it. Listen to this challenge: "Each of you should use whatever gift you have received to serve others, as faithful stewards of God's grace in its various forms" (1 Peter 4:10). Let's break it down.

"Each of you" reminds us every person who knows the Lord has been given a spiritual gift. You need to see yourself as gifted, not as average. The gift is something you have "received" from God, and that fact alone should make you humble. Everything you have is something you received from God, so give Him the praise.

The goal of God's gifts is "to serve others." Our gifts and talents are not given to make us rich and famous but to bless others. We need the attitude of a servant if we want to get ahead in life and lead a life that matters. We need to be "faithfully administering" the gifts God has given to us to serve. We need to be steady, dependable, and trustworthy with our gifts and our calling from God. The people in our lives need to be able to count on us.

Finally, let us remember we are administering "God's grace," not our judgments or opinions, but God's unmerited favor and unconditional love to others. If we are not ministering grace, then we are not ministering at all! Grace comes in "various forms" as each one of us plays a unique role in God's kingdom. Let us celebrate each other's special gift God has given us, and never pressure others to be like us or for us to try to be someone else.

Prayer for the Day: *Lord, I thank You for the spiritual gifts You have given me through the power of the Holy Spirit. May I always seek to develop them and use them to minister to Your people by the grace of God.*

Day 294

IF YOU SUFFER

We all deal with tough times. The Apostle Peter, who experienced persecution, wrote, "If you suffer as a Christian, do not be ashamed, but praise God that you bear that name" (1 Peter 4:16). I think we could change the phrase "if you suffer" to "when you suffer." It is not a matter of *if*, but *when*.

Suffering can bring embarrassment—"do not be ashamed." We often withdraw from others when we are going through difficulty, but that is when we really need each other. We need to surround ourselves with people who love us and know how to pray in faith, so we gain victory over suffering.

So, how can we handle suffering? "So then, those who suffer according to God's will should commit themselves to their faithful Creator and continue to do good" (v. 19). We need to do two things to handle suffering—*commit* and *continue*.

Commit yourself and your situation to God in total faith, believing that, in the end, He will work out everything for your good. Turn everything over to God in a prayer of release, and let go of your fears. Put everything in God's hands today.

After you commit, you need to *continue*. Suffering makes you want to quit and give up. So, you need to continue in your work, going to church, enjoying hobbies, hanging out with friends, and spending time with family. If suffering has made you stop, get up today, commit it all to God, and make up your mind to continue.

Prayer for the Day: *Lord, suffering is a word no one likes. When it happens to us, it is easy to fall apart. But we need to remember we live in an imperfect world that has been scarred with sin, and You will never forsake us while we're here. I will trust You, Lord, in and through everything!*

Day 295
WIN WITHOUT WORDS

We often dig ourselves into a hole by our words. We wish we could take back some of our words because they caused harm, not good.

We want to win the struggles of life at home, at work and in all our relationships. But we cannot win all our battles, reach all our goals, or solve all our problems by our words.

Consider this powerful Scripture verse: "They may be won over without words" (1 Peter 3:1a). The Apostle Peter writes to Christian women to be supportive of their unbelieving husbands so they may be won over to Jesus without words.

While people must hear the good news of Jesus to be saved, after we share the message of salvation with them, we don't need to keep preaching. Instead, we need to start living right before them. The apostle added, "They may be won over without words by the behavior of their wives, when they see the purity and reverence of your lives" (1 Peter 3:1-2a).

Winning without words applies to all of us. Words are important, but they aren't enough. When others see the sincerity of our faith, values, and love, we win them over.

Prayer for the Day: *Lord, may I win my unbelieving family and neighbors by living out Your Word. I can love them, pray for them, share Your Word with them, and be there for them when they need me most. As Jesus said, "By this everyone will know that you are my disciples, if you love one another"* (John 13:35).

Day 296

IF YOU OBEY

In the Book of Zechariah, the prophet was charged to make a crown and place it on the head of Joshua the high priest—a priest crowned king! This was a symbolic act pointing to the coming of Jesus the Messiah, who is both our High Priest and King of kings (Zechariah 6:11-12).

God told Zechariah that Israel would be restored, the Temple would be rebuilt, and prosperity and blessing would come to Israel after the devastating effects of the Babylonian Captivity. Babylon was now defeated by Persia, and King Cyrus of Persia had returned the exiles back to their home in Israel.

What does this mean to us? At the end of this message of promised prosperity and peace, God told the people, "This will happen if you diligently obey the Lord your God" (Zechariah 6:15).

God has the power to restore us when we are defeated, exiled, and have suffered great loss. No matter how hard your life is today or what you have lost, God can and will restore it for you and give you a new season of peace and blessing. But, it is up to you. The condition for all of us to experience restoration is, "If you diligently obey the Lord your God."

The promise of restoration comes with the prerequisite of obedience. Let us diligently, passionately, and wholeheartedly obey the Lord our God, and we will see His power, promise, and provision in our life.

Prayer for the Day: *Lord, I need Your restoration in my life. I have suffered loss, but I know Your Word says if I obey You in all I do, You will care for me and turn things around for my good. I need a new season of peace and prosperity.*

Day 297

IMMOVABLE

The Lord told Zechariah: "On that day, when all the nations of the earth are gathered against her, I will make Jerusalem an immovable rock.... Then the [leaders] of Judah will say in their hearts, 'The people of Jerusalem are strong, because the Lord Almighty is their God'" (Zechariah 12:3, 5).

Just as Jerusalem was under attack from her enemies, we too are under attack. Yet, in the day of battle God will make us an immovable rock so our enemies cannot defeat or destroy us. We are strong because the Lord is with us. When our enemies come against us, they will strike themselves against the "rock" and be defeated. God's strength in us is greater than the stress around us.

The word *Judah* means "people of praise." Did you know the Hebrew word for *praise* also means "strength"? You keep yourself spiritually strong when you live a life of praise instead of panic. The nation of Judah was under attack, but they praised God. They lived up to their name. Praise is an act of faith that declares, "I am depending on God's presence and power to deliver me!"

As you depend on the Lord in praise, prayer, and faith, He will make you an immovable rock.

Prayer for the Day: *Lord, I am under attack. Although I am tired and weary, I will continue to be strong because You are with me. I sometimes get fearful and panic, so I'm depending on You to deliver me.*

Day 298

ASK FOR RAIN

While reading the tenth chapter of Zechariah, I was challenged by verse 1: "Ask the Lord for rain in the springtime; it is the Lord who [makes] the [storm clouds]." If you are like me, you need the fresh rain of God's refreshing in your life.

Rain is a symbol of God's blessing and restoration after a time of drought. We all go through seasons of spiritual drought for many reasons; it brings a drought in every area of our life. Things dry up and no longer bear fruit. But, we can ask the Lord for rain! God showers us with the rain of His grace to break the drought so we begin to blossom with abundant prosperity. "You heavens above, rain down my righteousness; let the clouds shower it down . . . let righteousness flourish with it" (Isaiah 45:8).

The Lord "makes the storm clouds." The reason the term *storm clouds* is used is to assure us there is a storm of a heavy rain of divine blessings on its way when we ask Him. God does more than we ask or think. When He sends the rain of His blessings, it is not a light, sporadic drizzle. He opens the windows of heaven: "The Lord will open the heavens, the storehouse of his bounty, to send rain on your land in season and to bless all the work of your hands" (Deuteronomy 28:12).

In Isaiah 44:3, the Lord says, "For I will pour water on the thirsty land, and streams on the dry ground; I will pour out my Spirit on your [children] and my blessing on your [family]."

Stop now and ask the Lord for rain, and get ready for a new season of blessing, prosperity, and refreshing on your life and your family!

Prayer for the Day: *Lord, I praise You for the rain on the earth and for the spiritual rain of blessings in my life. Just as the earth goes through seasons of drought, so does my soul. Thank You for Your refreshing rain of blessings.*

Day 299

LEAVE IT

When Jesus invited Peter, Andrew, James, and John to follow Him for a lifetime of adventure, "they [immediately] left their nets and followed him" (Matthew 4:20). What a picture of what it means to follow Jesus and to experience His purpose for our life!

They were career fishermen, just as their fathers were, in the town of Capernaum, which was located on the northern shore of the Sea of Galilee. It was a fishing town. The town of Nazareth, where Jesus grew up, was near Capernaum. Jesus' ministry was launched in this area.

These men had already met Jesus and spent some time with Him, having been introduced to them by John the Baptist. Once they had a relationship with Jesus, He took it a step further and invited them to give up everything they knew and to go on an adventure with Him. They would go from catching fish to catching people for the kingdom of God. They went from a career to a calling! Jesus would take the skills they had for fishing and show them how to use those skills to serve the purpose of God. Remember, all the education, training, and skills you have can be put at Jesus' disposal and be used for His glory.

Jesus is calling you today to go beyond a relationship with Him and answer His calling on your life. He has a purpose for you, but you must follow Him. In order to follow Jesus, you must leave some things behind. As you follow Jesus, He will reveal His purpose for you one step at a time with every step you take. Just go where Jesus goes, and you will find your destiny!

"They [immediately] left their nets." They stopped what they were doing and started pursuing His purpose. We too must leave things behind and leave them *now*, if we want to go on a lifetime of adventure with Jesus. His purpose is waiting for us. He is calling us to a closer relationship, and we must not procrastinate.

Prayer for the Day: *Lord, when You first called me, I thought about some of the things I would have to give up to become a fully devoted disciple. You know what? I haven't had to give up anything that I miss. You have given me a life of love and fulfillment. Each day with You is greater than anything the world has to offer!*

Day 300

RADIANT

When I was a youth pastor during the summer break of my last year in college, I was living with the pastor's family. One day I came out of my room from a time of reading the Bible and praying, and the pastor's wife, who is a spiritual mother to me, said, "David, I can always tell when you've been with the Lord. I can see it on your face."

Our countenance reflects our thoughts, feelings, and attitudes. What we feel on the inside radiates on the outside. Just as our faces show our age, they also show our attitude.

Just as faith, happiness, and joy show on your face, so does your anxiety, anger, and depression. So, here is the way to change your countenance: "I sought the Lord, and he answered me; he delivered me from all my fears. Those who look to him are radiant; their faces are never covered with shame" (Psalm 34:4-5).

When we look to the Lord in prayer, worship, and faith, our faces radiate with the joy of the Lord! Release your fears to the Lord, and your face will radiate with faith. Release your sadness to the Lord, and your face will radiate with joy. Release your anger to the Lord, and your face will radiate with love. Spend time with the Lord and your light will shine to others.

Prayer for the Day: *Lord, when people look at me, I want them to see You. I want to radiate Your glory so it becomes an open door to share my faith. I want to let my light shine so it leads people to You!*

Day 301

FORGOTTEN FAITH

Forgetting is an amazing gift to help us move on from disappointment, failure, and hurt. However, when we forget what God has done for us, we get into trouble. Many people are raised in a Christian home and taught the Word of God, but then they forget their faith and go the way of the world.

That is what happened to Israel after God delivered them from Egypt. During the forty years of wandering through the wilderness and then when they inherited the Promised Land, they often forgot God and went the way of the world. The consequences were dire for them, just as they are for us.

The psalmist recounted how they got off track spiritually, as a caution to us not to forget the Lord: "They believed his promises and sang his praise. But they soon forgot what he had done and did not wait for his [counsel].... They gave in to their craving ... [and] put God to the test. ... Many times he delivered them, but they were bent on rebellion and they wasted away in their sin" (Psalm 106:12-14, 43).

The people went from believing God's promises and singing His praise to forgetting what God had done! Like our generation of "whatever feels good, do it," they also gave in to their cravings. As a result, they wasted away in their sin.

God created you to thrive, not to waste way. So, treasure your faith in God and don't forget what He has done for you. Today, believe His promises and sing His praise!

Prayer for the Day: *Lord, may I never forget all You have done in my life—salvation, healing, restoration, the power of the Holy Spirit. I treasure my faith in You!*

Day 302
MUTUAL INTEREST

Our lives revolve on the axis of our relationships. Our greatest happiness and sadness come from our relationships. Our greatest worries are about the important people in our lives. We pray more for our family and friends than we do anything else.

Relationships can make us or break us, depending on whether or not they are healthy or unhealthy, So, let's keep it mutual. We need relationships that benefit everyone in them. That means everyone has a responsibility to help create healthy relationships and not do anything that hurts or hinders someone else.

Our personal health and happiness often depend on whether or not we are in healthy relationships. People get sick, depressed, and defeated when they are in unhealthy relationships. However, we grow and flourish when we have healthy relationships.

In his letter to the believers in Rome, Paul expressed this great principle for relationships: "I long to see you so that I may impart to you some spiritual gift to make you strong—that is, that you and I may be mutually encouraged by each other's faith" (Romans 1:11-12).

You need to impart spiritual gifts—the grace of God—to others when you see them. You are a minister of grace to everyone! Get close to people where you mutually encourage each other, and avoid toxic relationships and interactions that tear you down. The sign of a good relationship is that it is a mutual giving of grace and encouragement—not one-sided, where you have to do all the work. Keep it mutual!

Prayer for the Day: *Lord, relationships are so important but can be so difficult. Please give me wisdom to be able to handle each one the way You would. If I should have any unhealthy relationships, make me aware so I treat them with special care.*

Day 303

KEEP IT REAL

We have reality TV and talk shows where we are encouraged to "keep it real." But the thing that's never real is reality TV!

The truth is, we don't want to keep it real. No one wants to hear the truth. That is why we emphasize political correctness. That is why the mob shouts us down when we speak the truth. When Stephen (the first martyr for Christ) told the court about Jesus Christ and confronted them with their hardness of heart toward God, "they were furious and gnashed their teeth at him. . . . They covered their ears and, yelling at the top of their voices, they all rushed at him, dragged him out of the city and began to stone him" (Acts 7:54, 57-58).

Truth brought tragedy! As Stephen died that day, he saw Heaven open, "fell on his knees and cried out, 'Lord, do not hold this sin against them.' When he had said this, he fell asleep" (Acts 7:60). God keeps us in a safe place if we are faithful to the truth.

So, here is our challenge: "To the lady chosen by God and to her children [that's first-century code for the Church], whom I love in the truth—and not I only, but also all who know the truth—because of the truth, which lives in us and will be with us forever" (2 John 1-2). Here we find three steps to keep it real in a day when the world covers their ears and yells at the top of their voices so they cannot hear the truth of Jesus Christ: (1) Love the truth; (2) Know the truth; (3) Live the truth.

Let's keep it real. The plastic, synthetic, and fantasy world we live in can be free only if we keep it real and remain faithful to the truth that Jesus Christ is Savior and Lord.

Prayer for the Day: *Lord, we are living in strange times. So many people are content to live a lie as long as that lie keeps them happy. Not so for me! "But as for me and my household, we will serve the Lord" (Joshua 24:15).*

Day 304

IT IS WELL

The Great Chicago Fire occurred in 1871. Over three hundred people perished, and another 100,000 were left homeless. One of the heroes of the fire was an attorney named Horatio Spafford, who lost a lot of real estate in the inferno. His son also died about the same time. Yet, he helped others who were homeless and in need as a result of the fire. Because of his generosity and service, he was well known throughout Chicago as a genuine Christian.

A couple of years later, in November 1873, Spafford and his family decided to take a vacation. Spafford was a good friend of D. L. Moody, the powerful evangelist, and his family decided to meet Moody on one of his evangelistic campaigns in England. From there, the family would travel around Europe. But, before they were to leave, Horatio was unexpectedly detained by business concerns in Chicago. His wife, Anna, and their daughters went on ahead to England, where he would later join them.

Just off Newfoundland, the ship collided with an English sailing vessel and sunk within 20 minutes. Anna Spafford was one of the 47 passengers who survived. Tragically, all four of their daughters were part of the 226 who died. Anna Spafford's heartbreaking telegram to her husband simply read, "Saved alone." Horatio immediately set sail for England to join her.

As the ship he was traveling on passed by the location where his daughters had drowned, Horatio Spafford penned the words: "When peace, like a river, attendeth my way, / When sorrows like sea billows roll; / Whatever my lot, Thou hast taught me to say, / It is well, it is well with my soul."

When the pain and pressure of life weighs great on you, find a place of peace in the presence of God. Draw near to Him, and you will find His "peace . . . [that] transcends all understanding" (Philippians 4:7). Only by God's grace can we say, "It is well with my soul!"

Prayer for the Day: *Lord, when the world around me is going crazy, there is a peace that surpasses human understanding. Because I am Yours and You are in control, I trust You to care for me and those I love. "It is well with my soul."*

Day 305
SOW THE WORD

Do you ever ask yourself, *What can I do to make a difference in the world?* There are over 7 billion people alive today. That is an overwhelming number that can make you feel you can't make a difference, but you can.

You are not called to impact the whole world—you are called by God to make a difference in your world with your family and friends. Focus on your world and you will make a difference for God's glory. Jesus said, "Go into all the world and preach the gospel" of His saving grace (Mark 16:15). "The world" starts with *your world.*

Jesus summed up His mission and ours in the parable of the sower. He said, "A farmer went out to sow his seed," and He clarified the meaning— "the farmer sows the word" (Mark 4:2, 14). You are the farmer. The field is your world. The seed is the Word of God.

So, today in your conversations, social media, and texts, sow the Word! If you plant the seed of God's Word in people's hearts, you will make a difference in their life.

Prayer for the Day: *Lord, please provide me with open doors of opportunity as I seek to share Your Word in my world. Give me a heart of compassion as I sow the Word into people's hearts. May it result in many accepting You as Savior and Lord.*

Day 306

DONE AND TAUGHT

Leo Tolstoy, the famous Russian author, said, "The only significance in life is to help establish the kingdom of God on earth." Living with purpose is the only way to really live an abundant life.

Jesus gives us the greatest purpose as He sends us into our world as ministers of His grace to our family, friends, and community. After Jesus sent His *apostles* ("those sent with a purpose") out to preach the good news of the kingdom of God, they came and reported to Him—they "gathered around Jesus and reported to him all they had done and taught" (Mark 6:30).

Living a life of purpose boils down to what we do and what we teach. We read this phrase again in Acts 1:1: "I wrote about all that Jesus began to do and to teach until the day he was taken up to heaven." It is what we do and what we teach that makes a difference.

One day, we too will gather around Jesus in Heaven and report to Him all we have done and taught. So, live today with spiritual purpose by doing and teaching something that enriches the lives of others for the glory of God.

Prayer for the Day: *Lord, may I always be aware of what I'm doing and teaching and how it affects others around me. May I live my life with purpose and, by doing so, teach others to do the same.*

Day 307

GROW BIGGER

In 1924, two climbers were part of an expedition that set out to conquer Mount Everest. As far as we know, they never reached the summit and they never returned. Somewhere on that gigantic mountain they were overpowered by the elements and perished. After the failure of the expedition, the rest of the party returned home.

Addressing a meeting in London, one of those who returned described the adventure. He turned to a large photograph of Mount Everest, mounted on the wall behind him. "Everest," he declared, "we tried to conquer you once, but you overpowered us. We tried to conquer you a second time, but again you were too much for us. But, Everest, I want you to know that we are going to conquer you, for you can't grow any bigger, but we can!"

The key to winning in life's struggles and difficulties is to grow bigger. "Grow up in your salvation, now that you have tasted that the Lord is good" (1 Peter 2:2-3). Grow up in your faith to believe God for great and mighty things. Grow up in your attitude to give thanks in all circumstances. Grow up in your love for others so you never give in to resentment. Grow up in your forgiveness so you can travel light. Grow up in your understanding of God's Word so you live by truth and not error. Grow up in power so that you can stand firm in every storm. Grow up in joy so that you can conquer depression and discouragement.

When life seems overwhelming, grow bigger!

Prayer for the Day: *Lord, I am growing bigger because I am maturing in "grace and knowledge" (2 Peter 3:18). It is one thing to be sure of my salvation; it is much more to know Your Word and to keep growing so my life on earth has purpose!*

Day 308
SPIRITUAL INSIGHT

God created us with five natural senses—sight, sound, smell, taste, and touch. While all five are vital for life, perhaps vision is the most important. While we need natural vision, we also need spiritual vision. Vision is a picture of who you want to be and what you want to accomplish. The word *vision* in Hebrew means "revelation or spiritual insight" into God's Word. It is used thirty-five times in the Old Testament.

God created us to be visionaries—people who can envision the future. A visionary has original ideas about what the future will or could be like. Are you stuck where you are, blinded by the present circumstances, or can you envision a new future? A new vision will get you unstuck and get you moving forward.

In the Old Testament, God gave the prophet Joel a vision (revelation) about future revelations. God told him, "I will pour out my Spirit on all people. Your sons and daughters will prophesy, your old men will dream dreams, your young men will see visions" (Joel 2:28).

We are living in the days Joel prophesied about. God speaks to people through the Scriptures, and sometimes He speaks through prophecies, dreams, and visions. When God speaks in those ways, they are always in agreement with His written Word.

Prayer for the Day: *Lord, give me ears to hear Your voice and eyes to see where I should go. As I study your Word, reveal its truths to me, and give me a new vision.*

Day 309

RESTORATION PROJECT

One of the great mysteries of the Old Testament was this prophecy about Elijah: "See, I will send the prophet Elijah to you before that great and dreadful day of the Lord comes" (Malachi 4:5). Since the Bible does not teach reincarnation, how could Elijah appear again? Actually, the prophecy meant the forerunner to announce the Messiah would be a person coming "in the spirit and power of Elijah," not Elijah himself (Luke 1:17).

Jesus told His disciples that John the Baptist was the fulfillment of the Elijah prophecy. "They asked him, 'Why do the teachers of the law say that Elijah must come first?' Jesus replied, 'To be sure, Elijah does come first, and restores all things. . . . Elijah has come . . . just as it is written about him'" (Mark 9:11-13).

What did John the Baptist restore? To *restore* something means to "bring it back to its original condition." John restored Judaism to a religion of eternal salvation through faith and repentance for all people. The teachers of the Law made Judaism a religion of customs and traditions and a national identity. They excluded people, but John included everyone.

John announced, "Look, the Lamb of God, who takes away the sin of the world!" (John 1:29).

John the Baptist called every person, Jew and Gentile—regardless of religious, political, economic, or personal characteristics—to repent of their sins and put their faith in Jesus. "So John came, baptizing in the desert region and preaching a baptism of repentance for the forgiveness of sins" (see Mark 1:4).

When you and I repent of our sins, we receive the forgiving grace of God that alone has the power to restore all things in our lives. Repentance and faith in Jesus bring restoration.

Prayer for the Day: Lord, before I came to know You, I had made a mess of my life, being seduced by the ways of the world. Now that You have become my Lord, I am grateful for all that You are restoring in my life. It is true, "You make all things new" (see Revelation 21:5).

Day 310

PICK UP THE PACE

I like to run both physically and practically. It takes a lot more energy to run than it does to walk, plus I get to my destination faster. I have been running all my life. As a boy, I would run around the church after services and was always playing kickball, kick the can, and chase. But I would invariably fall and tear a hole in the knees of my pants. Instead of buying me new pants, because a lot of them had holes in the knees, my mom would sew patches on the knees. In the summer heat, the patches got sticky, which was really uncomfortable. I had pants with three layers of patches. I can still hear Mom saying, "David, stop running!"

But, when I didn't run, I couldn't get as much done. I know there is a time to walk and a time to wait, but run toward your goals in life. Don't walk or, as Barbie says, "Don't lollygag." Don't procrastinate because it will cause you to lose your desire to reach the goal. "Pick up the pace" is my challenge to you today. Whatever goals you have set for your life, family, finances, education, career, or ministry, pick up the pace! If you are moving too slow and it is taking you too long to finish, start doing it faster and you will see better and quicker results. Some people say good things come to those who wait. But I say great things come to those who run!

Run to win: "Run in such a way as to [win] the prize" (1 Corinthians 9:24). *Run with discipline:* "Everyone who competes in the games goes into strict training" (1 Corinthians 9:25). *Run with the right people:* "You were running a good race. Who cut in on you to keep you from obeying the truth?" (Galatians 5:7). *Keep running:* "Let us run with perseverance the race marked out for us" (Hebrews 12:1). Pick up the pace, and you will get there faster!

Prayer for the Day: *Lord, it is so easy to become inactive in our world with smartphones, the internet, TV, and even good books. I pray that You will give me the desire and strength to get moving so I may accomplish my goals and the race You have marked out for me.*

Day 311
GO WHERE YOU LOOK

I have a close friend who recently took the BMW driving course at the BMW Performance Driving School in South Carolina. It was both a performance and defensive driving course over two days. In learning to drive on a racetrack, they have a maneuver called the "lane throw" to teach how to avoid a collision. While it is a difficult maneuver, the principle is that if you look at the leading cone, your car will hit it every time. However, if you look at the open space between the cones, you will succeed. So, look where you want the car to go!

The principle is true for life as well. Look where you want your life to go. Look where you want your family to go. Look where you want your finances to go. Look where you want your career to go. We need to focus on our vision—not on our problems or obstacles. We go to the thing we are focused on. Proverbs 29:18 says, "Where there is no vision, the people perish" (KJV).

If you focus on your problems, you will stay stuck in your problems. If you focus on your fears, you will be too afraid to try anything new. If you focus on your obstacles, you will never make the changes you need to make. But, if you focus on your goals, you will move forward toward them. As you move forward, you will naturally get your life unstuck from where you are and begin to experience a new, dynamic life.

So, just as skilled race-car drivers look where they want to go, we need to focus on where we want our lives to go. We, too, can miss the cone, avoid a collision, and cross the finish line with victory!

Prayer for the Day: *Lord, sometimes I get distracted by things around me—people, temptations, and what looks like opportunity but usually isn't. Please help me to stay focused on the important and on what You have called me to do so that I avoid all obstacles and eventually cross the finish line in victory.*

Day 312

SHARE IT

One of the greatest underlying causes of illness is repressed thoughts and feelings. We often take our painful and anxious feelings and suppress them rather than share them. When we share our feelings, thoughts, fears, and failures with others, we experience healing.

God teaches us, "Confess your sins [faults] to each other and pray for each other so that you may be healed. The prayer of a righteous person is powerful and effective" (James 5:16). Share your faults with someone you trust who loves you with nonjudgmental love. Remember, when someone shares their deepest feelings, simply listen to them and pray for them. Don't offer them your opinion or your advice. Always pray for them in faith that they will be healed, because "the prayer offered in faith will make the sick person well" (James 5:15).

The article "Confession May Be Good for the Soul," published in the *Lexington Herald-Leader*, read: "Confession, whatever it may do for the soul, appears to be good for the body. New studies show persuasively that people who are able to confide in others about their troubled feelings or some traumatic event, rather than bear the turmoil in silence, are less vulnerable to disease." The article included several experiments that confirm the "long-term health benefits" of sharing our pain with others.

Dr. James Pennebaker of Johns Hopkins School of Medicine conducted research that showed "the act of confiding in someone else protects the body against damaging internal stresses that are the penalty for carrying around an onerous emotional burden such as unspoken remorse." Similar research conducted at Harvard University showed those who do not share have "less effective immune systems."

Don't store your hurts, fears, and anger—share it, and you will be healed!

Prayer for the Day: *Lord, I pray that You would choose a confidante for me, someone who is wise that I can share with and pray with. Someone I can trust with my secrets and sins. I thank You and praise You!*

Day 313

FIGHTING SPIRIT

In *The Maverick War*, author Duane Schultz tells the story of Art Chen, a fighter pilot for the Chinese in the 1930s when Japan was determined to conquer China. During one battle, Chen took on three Japanese fighters. He shot one down before running out of ammunition. He deliberately rammed the second Japanese plane, then bailed out. He landed close to the wreckage of his plane and salvaged one of the machine guns. He carried it eight miles back to the base. Presenting the heavy gun to his commanding officer, Chen asked, "Sir, can I have another plane for my machine gun?"

Sometimes we give up in life's battles. We too need a fighting spirit to achieve victory in the battles we face. I once heard that the gift of faith is free, but the life of faith is a fight. The Bible says, "Fight the good fight of the faith" (1 Timothy 6:12). Fight for your health. Fight for your family. Fight for your ministry. Fight for your principles. Fight for your aspirations.

We face enemies in life. We fight against "the powers of this dark world and against the spiritual forces of evil in the heavenly realms" (Ephesians 6:12). We fight against personal attacks of others who are jealous, envious, and critical. "If you are insulted because of the name of Christ, you are blessed" (1 Peter 4:14). We fight against our own sin nature. "The flesh wars against the spirit" (see Galatians 5:17).

Don't give up; keep on fighting! By faith, you can win every battle!

Prayer for the Day: *Lord, sometimes I feel like giving up. It would be easier than this constant fight for my soul. But then I remember what You did for me on the cross at Calvary, and I, once again, put on my spiritual armor and get back into the fight of faith.*

Day 314

DON'T LEAVE YET

Have you ever left a party, a meeting, or a gathering early, and later someone told you, "You really missed it!"? Or, you missed church one Sunday and everyone tells you it was the greatest worship service ever? Or, you left a baseball game in the ninth inning because you were convinced your team would lose, only to find out a player hit a grand slam and they won on the last play of the game!

More importantly, when God is speaking to you or ministering to you, don't leave until God is finished speaking. When God appeared to Abraham and gave him a vision for his life that would create the nation of Israel, Abraham stayed at that place of prayer until God was finished speaking to him. In Genesis 18:33, we read, "When the Lord had finished speaking with Abraham, he left, and Abraham returned home."

Don't be in a hurry when you pray and worship the Lord, or when you are reading His Word. Don't leave that special place of communion with the Lord and "go home," which means to go back to the daily routines of life, until God is finished speaking. God not only speaks *to* us, He speaks *with* us, just like He did with Abraham.

The Lord wants to speak *with* you. He desires a relationship with us as a father does with his children. He wants to hear from you as you share your deepest thoughts, fears, and dreams. Whenever you truly commune with God, you will leave that place strengthened, encouraged, and refreshed by His presence.

Prayer for the Day: *Lord, help me to wait on You during my times of prayer and Scripture reading. Quiet my soul that I may listen to Your voice as You teach and direct me!*

Day 315

LAST CHANCE

We all miss some opportunities that come our way. We all look back at life and wish we had not let some things slip away.

One day Jesus visited the town of Jericho with His disciples. We don't know how long Jesus stayed there, but it probably was not for long because He was on His way to Jerusalem for the Passover festival.

As Jesus was leaving the city, never to return there, a blind man named Bartimaeus was sitting by the roadside begging. When he heard that Jesus was passing by, he began to shout, "Jesus, Son of David, have mercy on me!" (Mark 10:47). (I pray that prayer a lot!) He made such a disturbance that people told him to be quiet. In fact, they rebuked him. Maybe they laughed at him or tried to shut him up. But it is hard to shut up a person desperate for a miracle! He was blind and destitute. Society had not helped him. He needed redemption, but all he got from the crowd was a rebuke.

The blind beggar kept shouting, "Have mercy on me!" This is the greatest prayer any person can pray. God responds immediately to the person who prays for mercy. In fact, God "delight[s] to show mercy" (Micah 7:18). Jesus stopped dead in His tracks at the cry for mercy. He called for Bartimaeus and asked him, "'What do you want me to do for you?' . . . The blind man said, 'Rabbi, I want to see'" (Mark 10:51).

Jesus said, "'Go . . . your faith has healed you.' Immediately he received his sight and followed Jesus along the road" (v. 52).

Why was the blind man so desperate? Because it was his last chance to meet Jesus personally and to be made whole. Jesus is passing by you today. Have you received Him as your Savior? One day it will be your last chance to experience His saving grace. Today, believe on the Lord Jesus Christ and you will be saved. Don't miss your chance.

Prayer for the Day: *Lord, lead me to witness to people who don't know You, giving them the opportunity I had to meet You.*

Day 316

RANSOMED

Thousands and even millions of dollars have sometimes been paid as ransom money for kidnap victims. The highest reward fund (or ransom) ever paid, however, came in the form of blood—when Jesus paid for our salvation. Just as a ransom is paid to kidnappers to free a captive, Jesus paid the highest ransom for our salvation, freedom, and safe return.

Jesus said, "For even the Son of Man did not come to be served, but to serve, and to give his life as a ransom for many" (Mark 10:45). The Son of God came to this world to serve us by paying the ransom for our salvation. He came to save us from the penalty and power of sin so we can live a new life for God's glory.

What was the ransom He paid? Himself! He sacrificed His life as a "ransom for many." No religious or political authorities took Jesus' life when He died on the cross. He *gave* His life for us! That's how valuable you and I are to God!

Jesus gave His life for everyone, so receive Him as your ransom payment and you will be set free to live an abundant life!

Prayer for the Day: *Lord, I thank You and praise You for giving Your life so I may be saved, live an abundant life here, and see You soon in Heaven.*

Day 317

FOR-*GIVE*-NESS

Did you realize the root of the word *forgiveness* is GIVE? Forgiveness is something we give others. It basically means to cancel a debt, give up a grudge, and release a resentment. Forgiveness is being generous with our love.

We tend to think of forgiveness as something we must earn. People often make forgiveness rare because they don't want to release us from the grip of their anger, resentment, and displeasure. They want to make us earn forgiveness so we will appreciate it more. People can be stingy with love the same way they are with money.

However, God gives us His forgiveness as a gift. He gives forgiveness freely and consistently. He always forgives us when we ask Him and admit our wrongdoing. "Who is a God like you, who pardons sin and forgives the transgression of the remnant of his inheritance? You do not stay angry forever but delight to show mercy" (Micah 7:18).

We need to be like God! Don't make people beg or work for your forgiveness. Give them forgiveness as a gift. Bless them the way God blesses you. Make it easy on people in your relationships the way God makes it easy for you. Don't stay angry, but delight to show mercy to others. Be merciful, not mean, and you will experience God's blessings and favor.

Prayer for the Day: *Lord, forgiveness seems to be too hard when we have been hurt by someone we love. But then I think about Your forgiveness to us as sinners, and it enables me to forgive, allowing You to heal and restore.*

Day 318

TAKE ADVICE

A farmer was approaching a pond on his way back from picking blackberries. Two women were skinny-dipping, and they immediately dropped below the water when they saw him. "We're not coming out until you leave!" they shouted.

"I didn't come to watch you swim naked," replied the farmer, holding up his fruit bucket. "I'm just here to feed the alligators." And, then, ...

We often overreact to people's words. We get defensive and question their motives instead of listening to them. We sometimes assume people are attacking us when actually they are advising us.

One of the marks of maturity is the ability to take advice. Wise people do more than take advice; they seek wisdom from others. God teaches us to take advice: "The way of fools seems right to them, but the wise listen to advice" (Proverbs 12:15 NKJV).

Prayer for the Day: *Lord, give me discernment when receiving advice from another. Don't allow me to be defensive, but to listen and weigh the counsel according to Your Word so I can grow in grace and knowledge.*

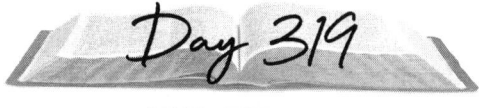

Day 319
NO FEAR

What if you could live your life with no fear? You can! There is a secret to living with no fear: "They will have no fear of bad news; their hearts are steadfast, trusting in the Lord" (Psalm 112:7).

Ours is a day of bad news. Even when there is good news, the media is bent on manufacturing bad news or looking for stories of bad news. The media markets fear, turning the news into a thriller movie.

We also experience bad news personally—marriage trouble, family stress, financial concerns, health issues, and emotional battles. When bad news comes, fear rises in our heart. It can destroy our happiness and our health.

Thankfully, we can live with no fear when we put our heart steadfastly on God's presence with us, His promises to us, and His power in us! When we focus on Him, we trust Him. Trusting God means to control what you can control, and leave the rest to Him. If you do, you will see the Lord work everything together for your good and for His glory!

Prayer for the Day: *Lord, remove the fear from my heart and give me Your peace as I wait on You and trust in You to care for me.*

Day 320
DO WHAT YOU CAN

One of the most moving stories in Jesus' life occurred toward the end of His ministry when He was in Jerusalem for the Passover. He went to a party at the home of Simon, a leper who lived in Bethany, just outside Jerusalem.

While the dinner party was going on, a woman came over to Jesus, opened a very expensive jar of perfume, and poured it on His head. Some people criticized her harshly, saying she had wasted the perfume. It could have been sold for a lot of money and given to the poor, they objected.

Their criticism was countered by Jesus' compliment! What the world criticizes as wasteful, God commends as worship! Jesus said, "She has done a beautiful thing to me. The poor you will always have with you.... But you will not always have me. She did what she could" (Mark 14:6-8).

I know you want to make a difference with your life, so here's the key—do what you can. God does not expect you to be like anyone else or to try to accomplish what they accomplish. Do what you can with what God has given you and always seek to honor the Lord Jesus, just like this woman who anointed Jesus.

Jesus said her story of love would always "be told, in memory of her" (Mark 14:9). So, do what you can with what you have, and you too will be remembered.

Prayer for the Day: *Lord, You have blessed me so much in this life. Please lead me to always do what I can with what You have given me. I praise You!*

Day 321

BEND TOWARD JUSTICE

Theodore Parker, a nineteenth-century American reformer, made the following statement as he championed the cause for the abolition of slavery: "I do not pretend to understand the moral universe; the arc is a long one, my eye reaches but little ways. I cannot calculate the curve and complete the figure by the experience of sight; I can divine it by conscience. But, from what I see, I am sure it bends towards justice."

In his famous "Where Do We Go From Here?" speech in 1967, Martin Luther King Jr. paraphrased Theodore Parker as he looked forward to a nation of unity: "The arc of the moral universe is long," he said, "but it bends toward justice."

God's people are called to promote justice for everyone. In fact, the gospel of Jesus Christ, when it is believed and lived, brings justice! Jesus said, "The Spirit of the Lord is on me . . . to proclaim good news to the poor. He has sent me to proclaim freedom for the prisoners and recovery of sight for the blind, to set the oppressed free, to proclaim the year of the Lord's favor" (Luke 4:18-19).

True social justice can only begin with a change of people's hearts as we love God and love our neighbor as ourselves. Let us follow Jesus' example and bring God's justice and righteousness, in word and deed, to those in need of His saving grace.

Prayer for the Day: *Lord, may I be an example of Your justice and righteousness in all I do and say.*

Day 322

FREEDOM FIGHTERS

The Bible predicts a coming Antichrist who seeks to establish a one-world government that opposes everything God ordains for life. "The man of lawlessness is revealed, the man doomed to destruction. He will oppose and will exalt himself over everything that is called God or is worshiped, so that he sets himself up in God's temple, proclaiming himself to be God" (2 Thessalonians 2:3-4).

What will the Antichrist do? "The lawless one will be revealed, whom the Lord Jesus will overthrow with the breath of his mouth and destroy by the splendor of his coming. The coming of the lawless one will be in accordance with how Satan works. He will use all sorts of displays of power through signs and wonders that serve the lie, and all the ways that wickedness deceives those who are perishing" (2 Thessalonians 2:8-10).

The stage is already being set by politicians, leaders, and economists who suppress individual and national freedom, and champion global government and control of our lives. For example, Brock Chisholm, the first director of the World Health Organization, said, "To achieve One-World Government, it is necessary to remove from the minds of men their individualism, their loyalty to their traditions and national identification."

God is a God of freedom. "Where the Spirit of the Lord is, there is freedom" (2 Corinthians 3:17). God created us to be free. Jesus gave His life on the cross so we can be free. May we enjoy the freedom God has given us.

Prayer for the Day: *Lord, may I never take the freedom I have as a U.S. citizen and a child of God for granted. Remind me to pray for all Christians around the world to be free to live life like You created us to live it—free and holy.*

Day 323

OVERFLOWING

Israel has two main bodies of water—the Sea of Galilee in the north and the Dead Sea in the south. Three streams of water flow from the mountains in the north to form the fountainhead of the Jordan River. The Jordan flows into the Sea of Galilee and exits on the south, where it flows through the land of Israel until finally pouring out into the Dead Sea.

For centuries, rabbis have used the example of these two bodies of water to illustrate two types of people. Some are like the *Sea of Galilee*. Its fresh waters are filled with fish and its banks are surrounded by lush, fertile land. The continual inflow and outflow of its waters keep it fresh.

Others, however, are like the *Dead Sea*, which has an inlet from the Jordan River but no outlet. Consequently, it has a 33 percent salt and mineral content, making its waters thick and oily. Every year more and more of the Dead Sea disappears through evaporation. The land around the Dead Sea is a desert. Its salty waters prohibit life and growth.

What kind of Christian are you? Are you a Sea of Galilee Christian who receives the abundance of God's blessings and then joyfully shares what God has given you with others? Or are you a Dead Sea Christian, always receiving but never giving?

Joy comes when we experience the cycle of grace. Jesus said, "Freely you have received, freely give" (Matthew 10:8). Paul says we should be "overflowing with thankfulness" (Colossians 2:7). Pour out to others as

God pours into you, and your life will always overflow with joy. Keep the cycle of grace moving in your life.

Prayer for the Day: *Lord, thank You for the grace and favor You pour into my life. I commit to letting Your blessings flow from me to others.*

Day 324

I AM NOT INFERIOR

It is hard to believe that a nation which prides itself on freedom now has groups infringing on our right to free speech—especially if you hold views based on God's absolute truth found in Scripture. They pressure us to surrender our right to think for ourselves and speak our mind. They seek to mold us in the image of their groupthink. They hypocritically teach "tolerance" for everything but the truth of God's Word. In a secular culture, there is no tolerance for Biblical truth.

When the Old Testament's Job went through a season of great suffering, his friends judged and blamed him for his difficulties. Yet, he courageously stood up against their views and for his own views. He replied to their pressure by saying, "Doubtless you are the only people who matter, and wisdom will die with you! But I have a mind as well as you; I am not inferior to you" (Job 12:1-3).

Where did his views on life come from? "I have treasured the words of [God's] mouth more than my daily bread" (Job 23:12).

You have a mind as well! Use your mind, think for yourself, and speak your mind regardless of the groupthink that suppresses freedom of thought and speech. More importantly, "we have the mind of Christ!" (1 Corinthians 2:16). The mind of Christ in us is a mind filled with the truths of the Word of God that we treasure more than our daily bread.

When the group tries to force you to shut up, sit down, and get in line, remember you are not inferior to anyone!

Prayer for the Day: *Lord, in a world that constantly puts people down and pressures them to go with the crowd, may I always stand up with confidence and faith, not allowing others to put me in their box. I am free and I am not interior!*

Day 325

UNCHANGING

We live in a world of rapid change, but God's purpose is unchanging. "Because God wanted to make the unchanging nature of his purpose very clear to the heirs of what was promised, he confirmed it with an oath" (Hebrews 6:17). God's purpose for creation, for history, and for our personal lives is unchanging in its nature. The fundamental nature, quality, and substance of God's purpose never changes.

The *purpose* of God is the *why* behind what He does. His purpose is His will and the final goal of everything He decides and decrees. So, the plan of God for your life is unchanging, no matter what changes happen to you and around you. Even when you and I get off track from doing God's will, His purpose for us is unchanging.

"I the Lord do not change" is His promise to us (Malachi 3:6). We also know, "Every good and perfect gift is from above, coming down from the Father of the heavenly lights, who does not change like shifting shadows" (James 1:17). Problems come and go, but God's purpose is unchanging.

So, face the challenges of a changing world with the confidence that God has made the unchanging nature of His purpose very clear!

Prayer for the Day: *Lord, the world is always changing. It is good to know that You never change. You are the same yesterday, today, and forever. You save, fill with the Holy Spirit, and direct the lives of all who serve You as Lord, now and always.*

Day 326

POWERLESS

Lord Acton's observation about power stills hold true: "Power corrupts, and absolute power corrupts absolutely." We often strive for personal power, political power, and economic power. We like to be in charge and in control.

But we are not as powerful as we think we are. In fact, spiritually we are not powerful at all. We are too weak to save ourselves! The good news of Jesus is that He came to save us because we are too weak to save ourselves.

Religion appeals to our pride and power, falsely telling us that by our good works and religious rites we can be right with God and atone for own sins, so we don't need divine assistance. Karl Marx, the founder of communism, said religion is a crutch for weak people, and offered a social solution based on atheism. Humanism believes man is the measure of all things, and we are self-sufficient to solve all our problems and reach our potential.

However, the downward spiral of humankind into sin and suffering, seen in the negative statistics of our day, is overwhelming evidence that we are too weak to save ourselves. But there is hope! The Bible says, "At just the right time, when we were still powerless, Christ died for the ungodly. . . . God demonstrates his own love for us in this: While we were still sinners, Christ died for us" (Romans 5:6, 8).

We are utterly powerless to save ourselves from sin and its destructive effects, but in our powerlessness His power is made perfect. All we need to do is to admit our powerlessness and call on the name of the Lord, and He will save us, deliver us, and heal us. "Everyone who calls on the name of the Lord will be saved" (Romans 10:13).

Prayer for the Day: *Lord, I am powerless to save myself and those I love, so I am depending on You to open doors for me to tell people of Your great power to change lives. I praise You, Almighty Lord!*

Day 327
STRANGE ADVICE

Have you ever been given some strange advice? Well, here's some: "We [rejoice] in our sufferings" (Romans 5:3). How can we rejoice in our sufferings? Why should we rejoice in our sufferings? What happens when we rejoice in our sufferings?

The power of our faith in God enables us to look at sufferings and to handle sufferings differently from people who have no faith. When you have no faith, you also have no joy and no hope in life.

The Apostle Paul explains why we rejoice: "We know that suffering produces perseverance . . . character . . . hope. And hope does not put us to shame, because God's love has been poured out into our hearts through the Holy Spirit" (Romans 5:3-5).

We don't rejoice because we're suffering; that would be illogical. But we rejoice *in* our sufferings. In the middle of our sufferings, we rejoice in the blessings of God. We focus our faith on the promises of God, not the problems of life. The problems are temporary; the promises, eternal!

When we rejoice, we become larger than life. Circumstances don't shape our attitude and feelings. We choose to be victors rather than victims; worshipers, not worriers; and faithful, not fearful. Life is tough, but God is good!

When you are going through sufferings, don't let them get the best of you. Get the best of them and win the battle over suffering by rejoicing in the Lord.

Prayer for the Day: *Lord, rejoicing in suffering seems illogical, but I trust You to use my circumstances of suffering to teach me. I choose to be victorious.*

Day 328

JUSTIFIED

We live in a time of rampant accusations. People often accuse one another with no evidence of any wrong being done. Accusation alone can seem powerful enough to destroy us.

We even accuse ourselves. We blame ourselves and live in shame, even when we're not in the wrong. Psychologists call that an "over-exaggerated conscience." A guy once told me he grew up in a church where he left feeling so guilty that he called his church "Our Lady of Perpetual Guilt."

Then the good news of Jesus breaks into our world of accusation and offers us freedom from accusation! "There is now no condemnation for those who are in Christ Jesus" (Romans 8:1). Your faith in Jesus and His saving grace frees you from accusation.

When we trust Christ as our Savior, we are justified by faith. *Justified* means to be "pardoned and acquitted of guilt." One of my favorite Bible passages is Romans 5:1: "Since we have been justified through faith, we have peace with God through our Lord Jesus Christ." We can live in peace today, knowing we are justified in Christ.

Prayer for the Day: *Lord, I praise and thank You for freedom of accusation and the peace that comes from knowing and trusting You.*

Day 329

BURIED TREASURE

Do you ever stop to realize how incredible you are? You are created by God. And when you accept Christ as your Savior, the Holy Spirit comes to live within you, giving you power to handle everything you will face in life.

The Apostle Paul wrote, "We have this treasure in jars of clay to show that this all-surpassing power is from God and not from us" (2 Corinthians 4:7). The power within us is greater than the pressure we feel on the outside with the problems of life.

While we are like fragile "jars of clay" made from the dust of the earth, we should not focus on our frailty, faults, and flaws, so that we see ourselves as weak, inadequate, and powerless. We should not think we are not beautiful enough, talented enough, gifted enough, smart enough—just jars of clay.

We need to look deeper. Buried treasure lies within us. We are jars of clay, but inside the jar there resides a treasure—the all-surpassing power of God. The power of God in us is real, giving us the ability to handle anything in life. The power within us surpasses the power of positive thinking, positive imaging, or positive confessing. This power comes from God through the Holy Spirit, who lives in us.

Live today with confidence, knowing that buried treasure lies within you. You are not weak; you are strong. You are not inadequate; you are capable. You are not a failure; you are a success. Because you possess the all-surpassing power of God, you can say with Paul, "I can do all [things] through him [Christ] who gives me strength" (Philippians 4:13).

Prayer for the Day: *Lord, it is good to know that You are inside of me, empowering me to do all things through Your strength and power. You are my buried treasure.*

Day 330

FRUSTRATED

We all get frustrated at times. We take a risk, but we fail. We set goals, but we don't reach them. We expect something, but we don't achieve it. We get frustrated with our job, our marriage, our family, our health, our friends and, most of all, ourselves. Life's frustrations make us want to quit. Frustration drains our energy, making us like zombies. Frustration steals our joy.

The world we live in is in a state of frustration: "I consider that our present sufferings are not worth comparing with the glory that will be revealed in us. . . . For the creation was subjected to frustration. . . . We know that the whole creation has been groaning as in the pains of childbirth right up to the present time" (Romans 8:18, 20, 22).

Faith is the answer to frustration. "The Spirit helps us in our weakness. We do not know what we ought to pray for, but the Spirit himself intercedes for us. . . . The Spirit intercedes for us [in] accordance with the will of God" (Romans 8:26-27).

Turn your frustrations over to God in prayer. When you do, the Holy Spirit will help you with the weakness you feel and give you renewed power to get back in the game of life.

Prayer for the Day: *Lord, I am so glad that in my frustrations of life, You are there to help me and renew me with Your power to live life well.*

Day 331

OUT OF PLACE

Are you in a place of discouragement or depression so that you feel like giving up on life? The prophet Elijah felt that way at one point. Queen Jezebel threatened to kill him because he had defeated the prophets of Baal. He "was afraid and ran for his life" into the desert (1 Kings 19:3).

Exhausted and alone, Elijah came to a broom tree where he prayed that he might die: "I have had enough, Lord" (1 Kings 19:4a). He was frustrated with the stress of ministry, the rejection of God's word, and the threats of King Ahab and Queen Jezebel. He told the Lord, "Take my life" (1 Kings 19:4b), and then he fell asleep. "All at once an angel touched him and said, 'Get up and eat'" (1 Kings 19:5).

Strengthened by the rest and the food, he traveled for forty days to Mount Horeb, the mountain of God. There God asked him, "What are you doing here, Elijah?" (1 Kings 19:9). Elijah was out of place.

Elijah said, "I have been very zealous for the Lord God Almighty. . . . I am the only [prophet] left, and now they are trying to kill me too" (1 Kings 19:10). The Lord told him to stand on the mountain, for He was about to pass by.

God sent a powerful wind, then an earthquake, and then fire, but the Lord was not in any of those signs. Then came "a gentle whisper" (1 Kings 19:12). The Lord told Elijah to go and anoint Jehu as the next king of Israel and Elisha as the next prophet.

If you, like Elijah, are in the wrong place, listen to the gentle whisper of God's voice reminding you that He is always with you and He still has a plan for your life.

Prayer for the Day: *Lord, if I ever get off track with Your plan for my life, please guide me back to where You want me. I pray that I will hear You say, "This is the way, walk in it!"*

Day 332

GOOD TIMES

Everyone loves good times. We have got plenty of money. Marriage is great. The house is peaceful. Work is fun. We are healthy. Friendships abound. No drama! Everything is clicking on all cylinders.

Then, with no warning, the bottom falls out. I talked with close friends recently who told me, "We feel like we're living out the story of Job! Everything was great, but now we are facing one problem after the other."

The Bible speaks to us in difficult times: "Consider what God has done: Who can straighten what he has made crooked? When times are good, be happy; but when times are bad, consider this: God has made the one as well as the other. Therefore, no one can discover anything about their future" (Ecclesiastes 7:13-14).

The fact is, life is a mixture of good times and bad times. The same faith in God you have in good times can carry you through the bad times. Practice your faith in tough times by reading the Scripture and communing with the Lord in prayer. Get together with God's people for worship. Don't get isolated in suffering. Think about your blessings, not your burdens. Surround yourself with encouragers and continue to be involved in ministry to others. Serving outside of ourselves helps to keep our minds off the bad times we're going through!

Remember, above all, the Lord promises, "Never will I leave you; Never will I forsake you" (Hebrews 13:5). So, whether times are good or bad, God holds you in the palm of His hand.

Prayer for the Day: *Lord, when times are bad, remind me that it won't always be that way. Help me to grow during hard times and remember You are always there caring for me.*

Day 333

THINK OF YOURSELF

How should we think of ourselves? The Apostle Paul warns, "If anyone thinks they are something when they are not, they deceive themselves" (Galatians 6:3). We must not fool ourselves about ourselves.

So, how should we think of ourselves? Paul says, "For by the grace given me I say to every one of you: Do not think of yourself more highly than you ought, but rather think of yourself with sober judgment, in accordance with the [measure of] faith God has [given] you" (Romans 12:3).

First, remember you are what you are by "the grace" and goodness of God. That will keep you from sinful pride. Second, avoid an exaggerated view of yourself—"more highly than you ought." You need a positive self-image, but you also need to respect others as much as you do yourself.

Third, "think of yourself with sober judgment." *Sober* means to have a realistic and honest view of our strengths and weaknesses instead of being intoxicated with pride and self-centeredness. Fourth, think of yourself "in accordance with the [measure of] faith God has [given] you." This refers to the gifts, talents, and abilities God has given you.

You and I are what we are, have what we have, and accomplish what we accomplish because God has given us a measure of faith; so let's give Him praise for all things. That will keep us from the pitfall of pride.

Prayer for the Day: *Lord, help me to keep all thoughts of myself based on how You see me. I have strengths and weaknesses, but I'm still growing in grace and knowledge. Keep me humble and faithful.*

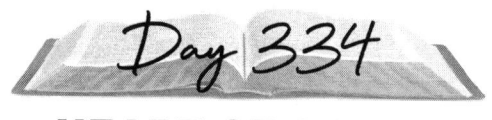

Day 334

HEART OF A KING

A king sensed something special about his servant Omar. So, he made Omar his personal attendant and gave him fine clothes. But a courtier became jealous. He spied on Omar until he found a flaw in his character. Every day Omar took a large bag into the treasure chamber and left with the same bag. The adviser told the king that Omar was stealing.

The next morning the king hid outside the treasury to see for himself. As usual, Omar entered, opened the bag, and pulled out his old servant's robe. He held the old robe in front of him as he said to his reflection in a mirror, "Omar, once you were a servant. Never forget who you are and how blessed you are."

The king stepped into the treasure chamber and said to Omar, "I knew there was something special about you, and I was right. Although I may be the king, you have the heart of a king."

As God blesses us, favors us, and grants us success, let's remember who we are and live with humility and gratitude. May our affirmation be, "By the grace of God I am what I am" (1 Corinthians 15:10).

Prayer for the Day: *Lord, thank You for all Your many blessings in my life. May I never forget where I came from and what You have done for me, Your servant!*

Day 335

AUTHORITY

The word *authority* means "the power or right to give orders, make decisions, and enforce obedience." God has established authority in the world for our peace and well-being. Ours is a day of independence, and even disobedience to authority in the home and in society.

As Christians, we are taught to respect those in authority. "Everyone [must] be subject to the governing authorities, for there is no authority except that which God has established. The authorities that exist have been established by God" (Romans 13:1).

The only exception to us obeying authority is when it is abused and we are instructed to compromise our faith and values. When that happens, as when the early believers were persecuted and told not to preach the gospel of Christ, "we must obey God rather than human beings!" (Acts 5:29).

Whom has God placed in authority in your life? Do you respect and honor them? Respect for those in authority brings the blessing of God. "Have confidence in your leaders and submit to their authority, because they keep watch over you as those who must give an account. Do this so that their work will be a joy, not a burden, for that would be of no benefit to you" (Hebrews 13:17).

Prayer for the Day: *Lord, as You use me and place me in places of authority, may I always be a good representative of that power and remember You have authority over all.*

Day 336
OVERCOMERS

God's people are called "overcomers" in Scripture. The Apostle John wrote, "Everyone born of God overcomes the world" (1 John 5:4). Face the challenges of every day by declaring, "I am an overcomer!"

What does that mean? The word *overcome* means to defeat an opponent in battle. Every day we face a spiritual battle for our beliefs, attitudes, and values. The secular world influences us to go our own way, while the Spirit of God compels us to go God's way.

Here is how we overcome the spiritual conflicts we face: "Do not be overcome by evil, but overcome evil with good" (Romans 12:21). Evil is real. The word *evil* means "that which is sinful and harmful." We are often the victims of evil in our relationships. We face gossip, jealousy, anger, and manipulation.

When you are treated wrong in your relationships, don't strike back with evil, but overcome the evil you experience with good. *Goodness* is kindness, gentleness, and forgiveness. Even when Jesus was being crucified by evil men, He prayed for God to forgive them.

Don't allow the evil influences of this world to defeat you. Live out your faith and values in Christ, as you overcome evil with good!

Prayer for the Day: *Lord, relationships can be difficult. There have been times when I was treated unfairly and felt as if I was in a battle against evil. Thankfully, even though I may face challenges, because of my faith in You, I know I am an overcomer.*

Day 337

DIFFERENCE-MAKERS

One of the greatest marks of a mature and healthy person is what psychologists call "the extension of the self." That means we live outside of ourselves to help others. Immature people are self-absorbed and self-centered. Mature people are God-centered and people-centered. While we all need to take care of ourselves, we also need to balance self-care with taking care of others.

There are three qualities of difference-makers. The Apostle Paul said, "I myself am convinced . . . that you yourself are full of goodness, [complete in] knowledge and competent to instruct one another" (Romans 15:14).

1. We need to be "full of goodness." Egotistical people want to become great, and often suffer from a delusion of grandeur. But the world needs good people. The fruit of the Holy Spirit is *goodness*, not greatness. We make a difference when we are good to others and don't try to be great.

2. We need to be "complete in knowledge." The word *complete* means "mature" and "finished." Students go through a series of graduations—elementary school, high school, and college. The goal of education is to finish. As disciples of Jesus, we need to finish our training and graduate with a deep knowledge of the Word of God so we can teach others.

3. We need to be "competent to instruct." If you are like me, you have sat in a classroom and listened to teachers who were knowledgeable about the subject but not effective at teaching. We need to know our faith, but we also need to be able to share with others to help them. Be a difference-maker for someone today!

Prayer for the Day: *Lord, today I want to make a difference in someone's life. Lead me to see the need in another person and to fill that need as You direct. Help me to be Christ today in someone's life.*

Day 338

HAPPY NEW YOU!

When our son David Paul was a boy, I went into his room to tell him goodnight. I noticed a folded paper towel on his night stand, so I picked it up. As I started to unwrap it, I asked, "What's this?" He replied, "It's a snakeskin!"

For a person with a snake phobia like me, I was scared to open it! I hate snakes, and I'm proud of it. A snakeskin was the last thing I wanted to see before I went to bed, giving me nightmares about snakes! But my son was proud of it, so I had to act interested as I hid my fear.

He and his friend had found a dried snakeskin that day, and he thought it was so cool he was going to keep it. When I saw the snakeskin, I was reminded of an important life principle. Just like a snake can shed its skin and grow a new one, we too can shed the old and put on the new. "Put off your old self . . . put on the new self" (Ephesians 4:22, 24).

Ask God for a new work of grace in your life, giving you the power to put off the old self and to put on the new self. Happy new you!

Prayer for the Day: *Lord, just like a snake that sheds its skin, so I need to rid myself of some things that affect my relationships and may hinder my prayers. I am asking for a new work of grace as I shed the old self and put on the new self in You.*

Day 339

BEHIND THE SCENES

Do you ever feel like one of those people who is never in the limelight but always behind the scenes? The early church leader Epaphroditus was a man like that. He was a behind-the-scenes leader. Paul called him "my brother, co-worker and fellow soldier, who is also your messenger, whom you sent to take care of my needs" in his letter to the church in Philippi (Philippians 2:25).

Through the supplies Epaphroditus brought to Paul, the apostle was "amply supplied." He called those supplies "a fragrant offering, an acceptable sacrifice, pleasing to God" (Philippians 4:18).

The believers in Philippi were the behind-the-scenes people who provided the supplies Paul needed, and Epaphroditus was the willing delivery person. They all faithfully did their part.

Jesus asked the thought-provoking question, "When the Son of Man [returns], will he find faith on the earth?" (Luke 18:8). God is looking for faithful followers who will work without any fanfare to do what is needed. Will you be one of the faithful ones?

Prayer for the Day: *Lord, allow me to be a faithful servant like Epaphroditus. Open the doors for me to inspire others to serve You, love You, and remain true to You.*

Day 340
KINDLE THE FIRE

One of the most important spiritual questions we can answer is, Why did Jesus come into the world? Why did He teach and work miracles? Why did He die on the cross? Why did He rise from the dead and return to Heaven? And why will He come again at the end of the age?

Here is why—Jesus came to "destroy the devil's work" (1 John 3:8). Jesus said, "The thief comes only to steal and kill and destroy; I have come that [you] may have life, and have it [more abundantly]" (John 10:10). We, too, need to destroy the things that destroy us. We all struggle with destructive words, habits, and relationships. We need to fight the spiritual battle within us, and destroy the things that destroy the work of God in us and keep us from the abundant life.

In 1665, the Great Plague broke out in London, England. Tens of thousands of people died. Every morning, bodies were picked up off the streets and loaded on carts taking them outside the city for burial. Nothing could stop the plague. A few months passed, and a fire broke out in one part of the city. It started with one house, spread to another, and then got out of control. It devastated a large section of the city. History calls it the great fire of London. Yet, its flames swept through the hidden places, destroying the rats and fleas that carried the Great Plague, bringing it to an end.

Jesus said, "I have come to bring fire on the earth, and how I wish it were already kindled" (Luke 12:49). In the Bible, *fire* often represents the Holy Spirit. Ask the fire of the Holy Spirit to sweep through every area of your life, leaving you pure and refined and reflecting the image of Christ.

Prayer for the Day: *Lord, rekindle the fire of the Holy Spirit in me to burn up the dross, purifying and refining me so I reflect You in all I say and do.*

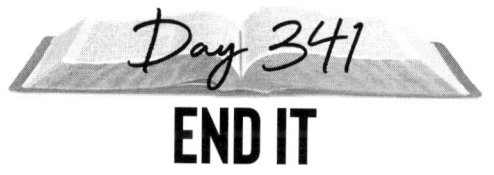

Day 341
END IT

Endings can be very difficult. It is tough to end a project, a relationship, a job, or a habit. We get used to the way things are. But an end is just a beginning in disguise. Life is series of beginnings and endings.

The Crucifixion ended Jesus' ministry, but the new covenant began. History will end when Christ returns, but it begins a new heaven and new earth. Jesus says, "I am . . . the Beginning and the End" (Revelation 22:13). The two—beginnings and endings—go hand in hand. They are two sides of the same coin.

The Book of Ecclesiastes says, "The end of a matter is better than its beginning. . . . Do not say, 'Why were the old days better than these?'" (7:8, 10)

You have to end the old before you can begin the new. It is the ending that makes way for the new. While we are used to the old things, the old blocks make way for the new things we want and need to begin. So, don't be sad or frightened when things end; the end is only a beginning.

Yesterday's solutions will not solve today's problems. The ways and means of the past are insufficient for the present. So, get yourself ready for the new things God has for you and the new things that you want to do with your life by ending the old. Make a list today of what needs to end in your life. Decide you are going to stop doing those things.

By faith, end it! Then you will step into a new and exciting season for your life.

Prayer for the Day: *Lord, I have been afraid to let go of those things in my life that just are not working anymore. Today, help me to end the old and look forward to all the new opportunities that lie ahead.*

Day 342

EXPIRATION DATE

Everything we purchase has an expiration date. Nothing lasts forever, except eternal life in Christ. Your troubles also have an expiration date. "Weeping may endure for a night, but joy comes in the morning" (Psalm 30:5 NKJV). You may be going through the darkest night of stress, financial pressure, marriage problems, health issues, or a family crisis.

The nighttime you are facing will end. The sunrise of God's power will dispel the darkness of the night you are living through right now. Joy is coming in the morning!

Draw near to God in prayer, stand on His promises, and trust Him with all your heart. When people can't help, turn to God, who has the power to deliver us. "People cry out under a load of oppression; they plead for relief from the arm of the powerful. But no one says, 'Where is God my Maker, who gives songs in the night, who teaches us more than he teaches the beasts of the earth and makes us wiser than the birds in the sky?'" (Job 35:9-11).

Worship Him during the darkest night of your troubles. He will give you a supernatural song of faith in the night. He will teach you and even make you wise through the tough times. Trouble has an expiration date. Joy comes in the morning!

Prayer for the Day: *Lord, it has been a troubling time for me. I know this cannot continue, so I'm crying out for Your help! Give me my joy back that I may worship You!*

Day 343

REGENERATE

Every year the human body completely regenerates itself. All the cells in your body are regenerated. The food you eat determines the quality of cell growth. You are a new person every year.

The same is true spiritually. The Word of God is the spiritual food that regenerates the heart, mind, and soul. "For you have been born again [regenerated], not of perishable seed, but of imperishable, through the living and enduring word of God" (1 Peter 1:23).

The word *regenerate* means "new birth, new beginning, new genesis." That is why the first book in the Bible is called *Genesis*, meaning "beginning." You can change, and your life can change as your thinking and living comes in line with the Word of God.

The person who "looks intently into the perfect law that gives freedom, and continues [to do this]—not forgetting what [he has] heard, but doing it—[he] will be blessed in [everything he does]" (James 1:25).

Take time to read the Bible and listen to God speak to you through its sacred writings, and you will experience miraculous regeneration!

Prayer for the Day: *Lord, I thank You that just as my body regenerates, Your Word regenerates my soul. It saves me, heals me, and makes me whole.*

Day 344

SPEAK

Words can shape the nature of relationships, business, politics, and world events. The media is often more obsessed with what people say rather than what they do.

As God's people, we have the power of the Holy Spirit in our life. One of the great qualities of the Holy Spirit is the way He communicates with us. When we are filled with the Holy Spirit and under His influence, He speaks to us and through us.

Jesus said, "He who has an ear, let him hear what the Spirit says to the churches" (Revelation 2:7 NKJV). Paul wrote, "What no eye has seen, what no ear has heard, and what no human mind has conceived . . . these are the things God has revealed to us by his Spirit. The Spirit searches all things, even the deep things of God" (1 Corinthians 2:9-11). So, when you read the Bible, ask the Holy Spirit to speak to you, showing you the deep things of God so you will grow spiritually as you discover incredible truths.

The Spirit of God also speaks *through* us. Jesus said when we have to defend our faith in Him, "Do not worry about what to say or how to say it. At that time, you will be given what to say, for it will not be you speaking, but the Spirit of your Father speaking through you" (Matthew 10:19-20). That is incredible! So, when you share your faith in Jesus with others, the Holy Spirit will also be at work giving you the right words in the right way!

Will you let the Holy Spirit speak to you and through you today?

Prayer for the Day: *Lord, may I put a guard over my mouth and always be cautious with my words. I pray that when I speak You will put Your words in my mouth, and that I may bring encouragement, healing, and hope to others.*

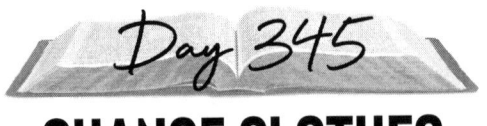

Day 345

CHANGE CLOTHES

*D*epression is the "common cold" of emotional issues. Depression makes us the victim of our feelings. When we're depressed, we lose motivation. We don't feel like doing anything—going to work or school, playing sports or exercising, going to church or praising God. We also feel bad about ourselves and hopeless about our situation.

There is a way out! The psalmist said, "Why, my soul, are you downcast? Why so disturbed within me? Put your hope in God, for I will yet praise him, my Savior and my God" (Psalm 42:11).

Here is the secret: "For I will yet praise him, my Savior and my God." When you praise God, you are looking to Him in faith to deliver you. *Praise is faith in action!* It is unconditional praise! In spite of your depression, say, "I will yet praise Him." The key word is *yet*. Worship is not an act of emotions but an act of our will. Praise brings joy, and joy gives you strength! "They that wait upon the Lord shall renew their strength" (Isaiah 40:31 KJV).

Depression exhausts us, but praise refreshes us. Listen to Isaiah 61:1-3: "The Spirit of the Sovereign Lord is on me . . . [to give me] a garment of praise instead of a spirit of despair." When you put on a garment of praise, you will defeat the spirit of despair and depression.

Have you ever gotten dressed, then looked at yourself in the mirror and didn't like the way your clothes made you feel? You just cannot face the day looking like that. So, you change into some clothes that make you feel positive and confident. Well, put on the spiritual garment of praise to drive out depression. When you worship, you put on the garment of praise and face life with hope and confidence.

Stop putting on the old garments that make you feel depressed. Stop putting on the worn-out shirt of depression. Stop wearing the old sweater of anxiety. Stop wearing that paisley shirt of negativism. Put on the garment of praise, and you will drive out the spirit of despair!

Prayer for the Day: *Lord, it is time to change my clothes. It is time to take off this fear and sadness and, in its place, put on a garment of praise for a spirit of heaviness. I praise You for Your healing and peace.*

Day 346

WAIT YOUR TURN

If you are like me, you grew up hearing your parents tell you often, "Wait your turn." As a kid, I never liked to wait for things (and I'm still like that). Yet, when it comes to us experiencing God's plan for our life, we must wait on Him. God has a perfect time for everything He desires to do in our lives.

Learning to wait on God's perfect time is so important in our success. God "[makes] everything beautiful in its time" (Ecclesiastes 3:11). I am not talking about being patient sitting in traffic, or waiting for meal in a restaurant after sitting there for thirty minutes with no service, or standing in a long line for a Coke and popcorn. No one is patient at those times.

I am talking about being patient for God's plan to unfold in your life in His time. Take God's promises to heart: "Blessed are all who wait for him!" (Isaiah 30:18). "Let us not become weary in doing good, for at the proper time we will reap a harvest if we do not give up" (Galatians 6:9). "Humble yourselves, therefore, under God's mighty hand, that he may lift you up in due time" (1 Peter 5:6). Wait your turn!

Prayer for the Day: *Lord, I know my turn is coming. I know Your blessings are at the door. I will be patient and wait for Your perfect timing.*

Day 347
GET YOUR OWN DIRT

One day a group of scientists got together and decided that humankind had come a long way and no longer needed God. They selected one scientist to go and give God the news. So, the scientist went to God and said, "We've decided we no longer need You. We can get along well by ourselves. We're so advanced in knowledge, science, and technology that we can do anything You can do."

God listened patiently. After the scientist was finished talking, God said, "Why don't we have a man-making contest?"

The scientist replied, "OK, great!" God added, "Now, we're going to do this just like I did back in the beginning with Adam."

"Sure, no problem," said the scientist as he bent down and grabbed himself a handful of dirt.

God looked at him and said, "No; you go and get your own dirt!"

God has given us the ability to dream, to imagine, and to create. Humans are not part of the animal kingdom. We are created in God's image, and we have His divine spark within us. As Christians, we have an eternal soul that will live on in Heaven after our body wears out. What also separates us from animals are choice and creativity.

Animals function by instinct, but we function by intelligence, inspiration, and ingenuity. So, tap into your creative self. Use the "dirt"—the natural talents God has given you—for His glory. "Whatever you do, do it all for the glory of God!" (1 Corinthians 10:31).

Prayer for the Day: *Lord, never let me forget the "earth is the Lord's and everything in it" (Psalm 24:1). I'm just a temporary occupant.*

Day 348

BLUEPRINT

My father was a mechanical contractor. I have seen many blueprints of designs of corporate buildings he developed. Your life is a blueprint in the making, and you play a part in drawing the blueprint of your life.

God's will is a combination of His call and your choices. God does not have a specific will for every decision we face. Most of the decisions we make can be made on the basis of common sense, counsel from others, and guidance from Scripture. God's will unfolds one day at a time. You help determine your destiny by the decisions you make.

Destiny is not predetermined; it is always in process. We have the power and privilege to make decisions. God created us to use our freedom to make choices that honor Him and benefit others. If our decisions meet those criteria, we will shape our destiny positively. The great news is, we can receive forgiveness for poor choices we have made and turn our life around with God's help.

God promises to give us wisdom to make good decisions. "If any of you lacks wisdom, you should ask God, who gives generously to all without finding fault, and it will be given to you" (James 1:5). While the will of God is about His larger purpose for us, wisdom is given for daily decisions. We need to make plans and pursue our goals with an attitude of desiring to do His will in all things. "Instead, you ought to say, 'If it is the Lord's will, we will live and do this or that'" (4:15). When you ask God to give you wisdom for your decisions and submit to His will, you will discover your destiny.

Prayer for the Day: *Lord, thank You for giving me wisdom to make good decisions based on Your Word. I have peace knowing that if I trust You, You will show me which path to take at every crossroad.*

Day 349

NEVER DIE

Shakespeare said death is the "undiscovered country." In the book *Life After Death*, D'Souza says there is scientific and philosophical evidence of life after death. Socrates made the argument for life after death, teaching that although the physical body dies, the mind (the immaterial part of us) lives on.

Jesus came into this world to defeat death and to give us eternal life. "Since the children [that's you and me] have flesh and blood, he too shared in their humanity so that by his death he might break the power of him who holds the power of death—that is, the devil—and free those who all their lives were held in slavery by their fear of death" (Hebrews 2:14-15).

What incredible news! In fact, Jesus promised, "Whoever lives by believing in me will never die" (John 11:26). Let those words sink in—*never die*! Our faith in Jesus means we will live forever.

The body is temporary, but the soul is eternal. One day we will take off our body the same way we take off our clothes so we can put on a new outfit. We dress for the occasion. The physical body is simply clothing we wear for this world. But when it's time to relocate to Heaven, we will put on our eternal clothes. "It is sown a natural body, it is raised a spiritual body" (1 Corinthians 15:44). Keep your faith in Jesus, and live forever with God!

Prayer for the Day: *Lord, I am so excited to know that one day when my time on earth is over, I will rise to meet You in Heaven. I will take off the clothes of mortality and put on the clothes of immortality, which are the garments of praise, and be with You forever.*

Day 350

TRUTH HURTS

We don't always like to hear the truth because truth can hurt. Truth demands that we face reality and responsibility. It also leads to liberty and maturity.

The Apostle Paul confronted believers in the church at Corinth about their immoral behavior. It was immoral because it was disobedient to God's standards set forth in Scripture. So, he told them the truth about their sin, and they got upset with him. At first, they rejected God's truth and their own way. The term used today is "my truth." Quite often, that term means we are going to do what we want even though it is contrary to God's will. Remember, "Sin is transgression of God's law" (1 John 3:4).

Finally, the Corinthians changed their mind and their behavior and obeyed God (the Bible calls it "repentance"). So, Paul encouraged them by writing: "If I caused you sorrow . . . I do not regret it . . . because your sorrow led you to repentance. . . . Godly sorrow brings repentance that leads to salvation and leaves no regret" (2 Corinthians 7:8-10).

When it comes to spiritual, moral, and social issues of your life, your truth and my truth don't matter. It is only God's truth that is really true and leads to a great life. Jesus said, "You will know the truth, and the truth will set you free" (John 8:32).

Prayer for the Day: *Lord, I know Your truth sets us free and, although it may hurt, it is a good hurt that brings healing and wholeness to my soul. I praise You for the truth of Your Word.*

Day 351

PRIORITIES

Over the three doorways of the Cathedral of Milan are three inscriptions spanning the beautiful arches. Over one is carved a beautiful wreath of roses with the words, "All that which pleases is but for a moment." Over another arch is the cross of Christ with the words, "All that which troubles us is but for a moment." Beneath the main entrance and center arch is the inscription, "That only is important which is eternal."

When we have the right priorities, the rest of life falls into place. This is what Jesus meant by saying, "Seek first [God's] kingdom and his righteousness, and all these things will be given to you" (Matthew 6:33). What is the *kingdom of God*? It is the will of God in your life. *Righteousness* means that which is right according to God's Word. Everything will be given to us when we put first things first.

When we have the wrong priorities, we build the kingdom of self instead of the kingdom of God. You cannot do everything. You cannot have everything. You cannot experience everything. What is really important in your life? What is essential? Cut away the nonessentials and focus on your priorities.

I read about a guy won $300 million in the lottery. Seven years later, he had spent it all; he had no sense of priorities. When we have no priorities, life slips through our fingers and leaves us with nothing. When we have God's priorities and put first things first, all these other things will be given to us as well.

Prayer for the Day: *Lord, my priority will always be to spend time with You so that I will know Your will for my life. You are first, my ultimate priority—yesterday, today, and forever!*

Day 352

IT'S OK TO BRAG

I am sure you were taught as a child not to brag. But, it's OK to brag at times. The word *brag* means "to say something in a boastful manner, to show off, or to congratulate yourself."

Paul talked about when to brag and when not to brag: "We, however, will not boast beyond proper limits, but will confine our boasting to the sphere of service God has assigned to us" (2 Corinthians 10:13). To say thanks to someone who says you did a good job is healthy. We all need encouragement, so when people are kind enough to notice our hard work and good performance, let's say thanks. We don't need to knock ourselves down when someone lifts us up.

You can also celebrate your success! Paul said, "Neither do we go beyond our limits by boasting of work done by others" (2 Corinthians 10:15). Lately, I have seen politicians who no longer hold office take credit for economic success of the policies passed by current politicians. Their time in office is over, but they are trying to take credit for what new leaders are doing. Celebrate your success as the blessing of God, but don't steal someone else's thunder.

Finally, always brag about the Lord! The word *praise* means to boast, to brag, and to celebrate the goodness of God! "Let the one who boasts boast in the Lord! For it is not the one who commends himself who is approved, but the one whom the Lord commends" (2 Corinthians 10:17-18).

Make it your goal in life to win the approval and commendation of the Lord, and brag to everyone about the goodness of our God!

Prayer for the Day: *Lord, I praise You alone for giving me the ability to accomplish great things for Your purpose. I will always use my bragging rights to glorify You alone.*

Day 353

STAY IN ORBIT

Our solar system is a gravitationally bound system of the sun and the nine planets that orbit it. All the planets move in a circular path around the sun by its gravitational force. It is the sun that keeps the solar system in one harmonious dance.

In the same way, your life is in orbit, with individual "planets" making up your life. Just like Mercury, Venus, Earth, Mars, Jupiter, Saturn, Uranus, Neptune, and Pluto, you have your personal life, family, finances, career, relationships, hobbies, and spiritual life. Just as the sun is the center of the universe, the sun of your life is your highest purpose around which everything revolves.

What do you orbit around? The "sun" you were made to orbit around is the glory of God. "Whatever you do, do it all for the glory of God" (1 Corinthians 10:31).

This one principle—to glorify God—will keep all the parts of your life in perfect orbit so you don't fly off into space. Always ask yourself, Does this glorify God? When you make decisions. When you set moral convictions. When you deal with people. When you set goals. When you spend money. When you manage time. Your life will orbit in perfect peace when you glorify God in everything you do.

Prayer for the Day: *Lord, thank You for holding me together and keeping me in peace in my orbit, so I never drift away from You. You have my life in Your hands just as You have the universe in its proper orbit accomplishing Your purpose.*

Day 354

GIVE THE GLORY

A man was always boasting to his next-door neighbor about how he had the best of everything. Every time he bought something new, he would brag about how it was the best and the greatest. One Saturday they spoke to each other in their front yards. The man said, "I got this new hearing aid to improve my hearing. It's the latest and greatest technology. It's the best on the market. It cost me $5,000. I can hear the wind blowing in the trees, the birds singing, and a gentle whisper 1,000 yards away."

His neighbor was so tired of hearing him brag about everything, he said, "Good for you. What *kind* is it?"

The arrogant man looked at his watch and said, "It's about one o'clock."

Take a compliment when someone acknowledges your work and faithfulness. Say, "Thank you," but give the glory to God. This means to love, honor, praise, respect, and reverence God. Enjoy the compliment; then give God the glory.

God tells us, "Whoever offers praise glorifies Me" (Psalm 50:23 NKJV). Jesus said, "Let your light shine before others, that they may see your good deeds and glorify your Father in heaven" (Matthew 5:16). When we get along with others and are loving and kind, we glorify God: "So that with one mind and one voice you may glorify the God and Father of our Lord Jesus Christ" (Romans 15:6). Give Him the glory.

Prayer for the Day: *Lord, it is my desire to allow Your light in me to shine brightly so others see You and receive You as Lord and Savior. I give the glory to You always.*

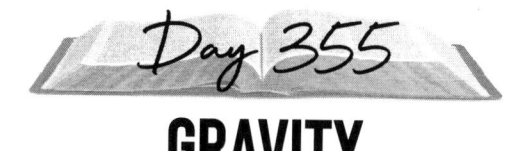

Day 355

GRAVITY

Gravity is a natural, God-created phenomenon by which all things with mass or energy (planets, stars, galaxies, and even light) are brought toward each other. On Earth, gravity gives weight to physical objects, and the moon's gravity causes the ocean tides. Gravity in the universe caused the formation of stars and grouped them into galaxies. The gravity of the sun keeps the nine planets of our solar system in their rotation, providing separation and boundaries so they don't collide or drift away into space.

God's Word is the spiritual gravity that gives us boundaries. We live in a day without boundaries. How do we live a godly life in an ungodly world? How do we live holy in an unholy world? How do we live a spiritual life in a secular world? How do we live by absolute truth in a world of moral relativism?

We have the authority of Scripture as the gravity of our life. While the Bible does not specifically address every issue, it does give us absolute truth we can apply to every issue we face. "All Scripture is [inspired by God] and is useful" (2 Timothy 3:16).

Following are four questions you can ask to help decide right from wrong and stay in the safe place of the gravitational force of God's Word, so you don't fly off into space:

1. Would I need to keep it a secret?
2. Where would it lead me?

3. Would it help me to be my best self?
4. What would the person I most admire do if he or she were in my situation? (As Christians, that person is Jesus.)

Prayer for the Day: *Lord, Your Word gives me stability and keeps me grounded in a world gone mad. Your Spirit is the gravity that keeps me safe and secure. Your love helps me make sense out of it all as I hold onto You in faith.*

Day 356

WHAT'S GOING ON?

Every day we face troubling news of world events. It seems like there are crises on every hand—economic uncertainty, political unrest, natural disasters, humanitarian needs, and ecological changes.

On top of that, we face personal problems and challenges to our happiness, our health, and our homes. Many of the troubling things happening in our world today were foretold by Jesus when He gave prophetic signs of His second coming.

When religious teachers asked Jesus to give them "a sign from heaven" to prove He was the Messiah, He said, "You know how to interpret the appearance of the sky [weather] but you cannot interpret the signs of the times" (Matthew 16:3). *CNN*, *Fox News*, and social media cannot interpret world events, but we as Christians can.

The signs of the times remind us Jesus is coming again. Although we do not know the day nor the hour of His return, we must remember that while this world is being shaken, we are a part of the unshakable kingdom of God!

Jesus told us how to interpret troubling world events. He said, "When [you see] these things begin to take place, stand up and lift up your heads, because your redemption is drawing near" (Luke 21:28). Don't get caught up in fake news or fear news; instead, listen to faith-building news from the Bible. God's Word assures us that our world is not headed for ruin but for redemption when Christ returns in power and great glory.

Prayer for the Day: *Lord, the unbelievers look at the craziness of our world and ask, "What's going on?" We, Your children, look up and say, "Maranatha!" Come, Lord Jesus! We are anxiously awaiting Your return to remove the chaos and bring sanity to our world.*

Day 357

CONTRADICTIONS

I walked up to the counter of a store to purchase a denim shirt. The woman checking me out asked, "Do you want a bag?"

Confused by the question, I replied, "Sure. Why do you ask?"

She said, "You'll have to pay for a paper bag. We don't use plastic bags anymore. We're a green company."

Really confused, I asked, "A green company? What does that mean?"

She asserted (as though I shouldn't ask such a logical question), "We're a green company—we don't use plastic!"

I could not resist my next remark, since she was taking the shirt off a plastic hanger. "You're not a green company. Nearly everything in the store is made of plastic. Like the hanger you're taking my shirt off of, and the credit card machine, and the scanner in your hand."

She didn't appreciate me pointing out the glaring contradiction. She snapped back, "We *are* a green company. We don't use plastic."

I gave her a big smile as I paid and said, "You're not a green company. You just sell paper bags when you used to give away plastic ones."

Personally, I like the "green" cause, and I think we should be environmentally safe, taking care of the amazing world God entrusted to us. However, I do not like contradictions. Why did she say they don't use plastic while she held a plastic hanger in her hand? Because the corporate office taught her to say it.

Our world is conditioning us to repeat the party line like parrots and not use our minds to think for ourselves. We all need to face contradictions between our words, thoughts, and actions. God's Word teaches us, "Do not merely listen to the word [of God], an so deceive yourselves. Do what it says" (James 1:22); "Rid yourselves of all malice and all deceiet, hipocracy" (1 Peter 2:1).

Prayer for the Day: *Lord, open my eyes to see the contradictions of our world. May I always look to You for answers to keep my feet on the ground and my head out of the clouds.*

Day 358

EXCEL

Isaac D'Israeli said, "It is an awful taste to be gratified with mediocrity when the excellent lies before us." Excellence is the master key to success. Excellence speaks of that which is the very best quality, superiority, and exceptionally good.

Edwin Bliss said, "The pursuit of excellence is gratifying and healthy. The pursuit of perfection is frustrating, neurotic, and a terrible waste of time." Booker T. Washington said, "Excellence is to do a common thing in an uncommon way."

There is no room for status quo and mediocrity in the kingdom of God. God created us for excellence. Jesus deserves our excellence. The Holy Spirit empowers us for excellence. This requires us to "make every effort to add to [our] faith" (2 Peter 1:5). Success doesn't come from making *an* effort but by making *every* effort. Let these three words be your standard for life—*Make every effort!*

Success doesn't come easy for anyone. When we see successful people, we think it came easy for them because we don't know the journey they had to take to be successful. We only see the end product of their hard work and tireless effort.

Making every effort means to bounce back from failure and try again and again and again! Keep up the effort and pursue your goals with passion and persistence. When you have made every effort, then and only then, will success be yours.

Prayer for the Day: *Lord, show me the better way, the more excellent way, that I may excel in what You have called me to do and that it may bring You glory.*

Day 359

CHURCH MATTERS

Active church members have a 60 percent less chance of a heart attack and they live an average of 5.7 years longer. Active church members who see God as their life partner have fewer colds, headaches, and ulcers.

The National Institute of Health once showed five ways to help fight heart disease. The leading one is weekly church attendance. I once read a report by a life insurance company that showed the single most important variable in health-promoting lifestyles was religious affiliation.

When Jesus used the word *church*, He meant the gathering of His followers. Every Christian helps to make up the Church. The Church is people, but the people gather in a place. "When the day of Pentecost came, they were all together in one place" (Acts 2:1).

Smartphones and computers give us the ability to be "present" for times of worship when we are traveling out of town or unavailable to physically go to church. While technology is a great tool, it can never replace the power of personal relationships when we get together to worship the Lord. A computer screen is one-dimensional, but life is 3-D.

So, go to church and you will receive both incredible personal benefits and be equipped to help change the world for Christ. The Church needs you, and you need the Church!

Prayer for the Day: *Lord, I always knew attending church services was good for my soul, but knowing it is also good for me physically and mentally is an extra plus. Church matters, so thank You for making me part of Your Church.*

Day 360

SILENCE

Science shows the personal benefits of times of silence. Some people think being silent means being bored or having nothing to do. But taking time to be silent is healthy.

Silence has physical benefits. Silence lowers blood pressure, boosts the immune system, promotes growth of new brain cells, supports hormone regulation, lessens stressors, and prevents plaque in arteries. In addition, silence has emotional benefits—boosting our creativity, aiding self-reflection, and renewing energy.

The Apostle John has visions of the world in chaos in the Book of Revelation. In one scene, he sees Jesus open a scroll with seven seals that show the images of war, famine, ecological disasters, and persecution. John is overwhelmed by the images of the last days shortly before Jesus' return.

However, when the seventh seal is opened, "there was silence in heaven" (Revelation 8:1). He then sees a golden bowl in Heaven before the altar of God "filled with the prayers of God's people" (Revelation 8:5). Finally, he hears the victorious worship of Heaven reminding him that God is in control: "The kingdom of the world has become the kingdom of our [God] and of his [Christ], and he will reign forever and ever" (Revelation 11:15).

Take time for silence today, and God will give you new strength to face life's challenges.

Prayer for the Day: *Lord, the world is such a noisy place. It drowns out Your voice and keeps people on edge. I appreciate my quiet moments and the silence of my home where I am at peace and my heart can hear You speak. Speak, Lord; Your servant is listening.*

Day 361

SEE THE BEAUTY

A couple purchased an expensive landscape painting from a local artist for their house. When they displayed it, the captivating beauty of the painting made them realize how worn the furniture was, how faded the paint on the walls had become, and how messy the shelves were. The beautiful painting motivated them to paint the house, replace the flooring, and clean up the entire house.

When Jesus enters our heart, we begin to make changes we need to make to live up to His beauty in us. Growing spiritually in our relationship to the Lord means to make changes that adjust all of life to the beauty of Christ in us. "Christ in you, the hope of glory" (Colossians 1:27). The presence of Christ in us and with us motivates us to change the way we think, speak, and act to be like Him.

We are not motivated to change by religious laws, but by Christ's love for us. Worship enables us to "gaze on the beauty of the Lord" (Psalm 27:4). The beauty of His love makes us more loving. The beauty of His grace makes us more graceful. The beauty of His humility makes us humbler.

Real, lasting change does not come from outside pressure, but from the inner presence of Christ as He "dwells in your hearts through faith" (Ephesians 3:17). Let us practice Jesus' presence today so that we will reflect His beauty to others.

Prayer for the Day: *Lord, may Your face shine upon me, and be gracious to me.*

Day 362

PURSUE GOD

Someone said you will become as great as your most dominant aspiration or as small as your most controlling desire. So, what is your most dominant aspiration? What goal eclipses all other goals? What pursuit transcends all other pursuits?

The psalmist David teaches us that our dominant aspiration should be the pursuit of God. He wrote, "O God, You are my God; with deepest longing I will seek You. . . . My soul clings to You" (Psalm 63:1, 8 Amp.).

When Barbie and I were on our honeymoon, I read a book by A. W. Tozer titled *The Pursuit of God*. It taught me that I had to pursue a close relation to the Lord, just like I pursued Barbie when I fell in love with her. I didn't get Barbie by being passive. I was aggressive in going after her because I was in love with her.

God loves us and calls us into a close relationship of love. We need to pursue God as our most dominant aspiration in life. We cannot be passive or careless about our relationship to the Lord. Just as He seeks us, we need to seek after Him with all our heart. When we seek the Lord first, we will be richly blessed.

Prayer for the Day: *Lord, I often pursue my own desires, putting You second. Forgive me and teach me how to pursue You first, so I will know Your ways and stay focused on Your will for my life.*

Day 363

FIRE AND RAIN

One of my favorite songs by James Taylor is "Fire and Rain." We all go through times of fire and rain in our lives. The psalmist writes, "We went through fire and water, but you [God] brought us to a place of abundance" (Psalm 66:12).

When we go through the fires of adversity, God will use those experiences to refine our faith. Adversities come "so that . . . your faith—of greater worth than gold, which perishes even though refined by fire—[may be proved genuine and] may result in praise, glory and honor when Jesus Christ is revealed" (1 Peter 1:7). Even though you go through the fire, remember God's promise: "When you walk through the fire, you will not be burned" (Isaiah 43:2b).

When we are overwhelmed by the waters of life, God will keep us safe. He kept Noah safe in the ark in raging waters of the Great Flood. He opened the waters of the Red Sea for the Israelites to cross safely. He will keep you through the waters that overwhelm you. God promises, "When you pass through the waters, I will be with you . . . they will not sweep over you" (Isaiah 43:2a).

Trust God in the tough times. Surrender your worries to Him and know He is with you. He will bring you through the fire and rain to a place of abundance!

Prayer for the Day: *Lord, I am trusting You through this situation that has come into my life. I know You have my back and will bring me through this fire and rain.*

Day 364

OVERLOAD

People are under stress overload these days. Fear is the prevailing mood of the day in light of world events. Jesus foretold world events, and He calls us to faith in God:

"There will be signs in the sun, moon and stars. On the earth, nations will be in anguish and perplexity at the roaring and tossing of the sea. People will faint from terror, apprehensive of what is coming on the world, for the heavenly bodies will be shaken. At that time, they will see the Son of Man coming in a cloud with power and great glory. When these things begin to take place, stand up and lift up your heads, because your redemption is drawing near" (Luke 21:25-28).

We can either faint from terror or stand in faith. When the signs of the times are being fulfilled, look up! When false prophets appear, look up! When nations rise against nation, look up! When there are wars and rumors of war, look up! When there are famines and earthquakes, look up! When persecution comes, look up! When the heavenly bodies are shaken, look up! We are looking for the blessed hope and glorious appearing of our Savior!

If we can trust God with the prophetic, we can trust Him with the personal issues we face. "[Don't worry] about anything, but in every situation, by prayer and petition present your requests to God. And the peace of God, which transcends all understanding will guard your hearts and your minds in Christ Jesus" (Philippians 4:6-7).

Prayer for the Day: *Lord, sometimes I get weighed down, overloaded, and feel anxious. But knowing You will be returning soon causes me to rejoice. You are on the throne and watch over every detail of my life. I am blessed.*

Day 365

RUN THE RACE

The first Olympic race took place in 776 BC in Greece. History has been marked with amazing runners who have set world records with their ability, dedication, and discipline. Jesse Owens won four gold medals in the 1936 Berlin Olympics, dispelling the Nazi myth of a superior Arian race. Roger Bannister broke the four-minute mile barrier in the 1954 British Empire games—then believed to be impossible.

Kathrine Switzer was the first woman to compete in the Boston Marathon with a numbered entry, when women weren't allowed to wear numbers (a man tried to trip her, but her boyfriend shoved him out of the way). Florence Griffith-Joyner is considered the fastest woman ever. (Unless you count Eve, who came first in the female race!)

We are all runners in the race of life. We need to "run in such a way as to [win] the prize" (1 Corinthians 9:24). Don't just run; run to win.

You need to avoid people who will trip you up. "You were running a good race. Who cut in on you to keep you from obeying the truth?" (Galatians 5:7). Did you get tripped up in your Christian life? Get up today and get back to running for Christ.

Run with, "Let us run with perseverance the race marked out for us" (Hebrews 12:1). Whatever you do in life, at some point, you will feel like quitting. You may be tempted to quit school, or your marriage, or your exercise program, or even your ministry. Push back the thought of quitting. Run until you cross the finish line!

Prayer for the Day: *Lord, give me the strength and stamina to run the race You have marked out for me. May I not look to the right nor to the left, but keep my eyes focused on the finish line.*